Beat Drama

Methuen Drama Engage offers original reflections about key practitioners, movements and genres in the fields of modern theatre and performance. Each volume in the series seeks to challenge mainstream critical thought through original and interdisciplinary perspectives on the body of work under examination. By questioning existing critical paradigms, it is hoped that each volume will open up fresh approaches and suggest avenues for further exploration.

Series Editors

Mark Taylor-Batty
Senior Lecturer in Theatre Studies, Workshop Theatre,
University of Leeds, UK

Enoch Brater
Kenneth T. Rowe Collegiate Professor of Dramatic Literature &
Professor of English and Theater, University of Michigan, USA

Titles

Brecht in Practice: Theatre, Theory and Performance
by David Barnett
ISBN 978-1-4081-8503-2

Postdramatic Theatre and the Political
edited by Karen Jürs-Munby, Jerome Carroll and Steve Giles
ISBN 978-1-4081-8486-8

Theatre in the Expanded Field: Seven Approaches to Performance
by Alan Read
ISBN 978-1-4081-8495-0

*Ibsen in Practice: Relational Readings of Performance,
Cultural Encounters and Power*
by Frode Helland
ISBN 978-1-4725-1369-4

*Rethinking the Theatre of the Absurd: Ecology, the Environment
and the Greening of the Modern Stage*
edited by Carl Lavery and Clare Finburgh
ISBN 978-1-4725-0667-2

Howard Barker's Theatre: Wrestling with Catastrophe
edited by James Reynolds and Andy W. Smith
ISBN 978-1-4081-8439-4

The Contemporary American Monologue: Performance and Politics
by Eddie Paterson
ISBN 978-1-472-58501-1

*Theatre of Real People: Diverse Encounters from Berlin's Hebbel
am Ufer and Beyond*
by Ulrike Garde and Meg Mumford
ISBN 978-1-4725-8021-4

Beat Drama

Playwrights and Performances of the 'Howl' Generation

Edited by Deborah R. Geis

Series Editors
Enoch Brater and Mark Taylor-Batty

Bloomsbury Methuen Drama
An imprint of Bloomsbury Publishing Plc

B L O O M S B U R Y
LONDON • OXFORD • NEW YORK • NEW DELHI • SYDNEY

Bloomsbury Methuen Drama

An imprint of Bloomsbury Publishing Plc

Imprint previously known as Methuen Drama

50 Bedford Square	1385 Broadway
London	New York
WC1B 3DP	NY 10018
UK	USA

www.bloomsbury.com

BLOOMSBURY, METHUEN DRAMA and the Diana logo are trademarks of Bloomsbury Publishing Plc

First published 2016

© Deborah R. Geis, 2016

British Library Cataloguing-in-Publication Data
A catalogue record for this book is available from the British Library.

ISBN:	HB:	978-1-4725-6788-8
	PB:	978-1-4725-6787-1
	ePDF:	978-1-4725-6790-1
		^78-1-4725-6789-5

ng-in-Publication Data
ɔle from the Library of Congress.

ɔited, Bungay, Suffolk
ɔd in India

Contents

Acknowledgements   viii
Notes on Contributors   ix

Introduction   1

Part 1   The 'Canonical' Beats

1   Mediation and Immediacy: The I and You of Jack Kerouac's
Theatre of Voice   13
Tim Hunt

2   *Howl* and the Performance of Communion   25
John Whalen-Bridge

3   Gregory Corso's Dada-Surrealist-Absurd Beat Plays   33
Ronna C. Johnson

4   Unfair Arguments with Existence: Lawrence Ferlinghetti's
One-Acts and the Modes of Beat Drama   55
Deborah R. Geis

5   William S. Burroughs and the Shooting of Joan Vollmer
Burroughs as Performance   63
William Nesbitt

6   *The Stoop*: Anne Waldman's Early Drama   71
Lisa Chinn

Part 2   The 'Afro-Beats'

7   Amiri Baraka's Revolutionary Theatre: Black Power Politics,
Avant-Garde Poetics   83
Jimmy Fazzino

8   Sounding Across the City: Ted Joans's *Bird Lives!* As Jazz
Performance   97
Amor Kohli

9   Radical Ritual Performance in the Early Prophetic Poetry
    of Bob Kaufman   109
    Thomas Pynn
10 Adrienne Kennedy: A Kindred Spirit to the Beats   125
    Nita N. Kumar

Part 3   Poets Theatre and the Beats

11 Bunny Lang and the Cambridge Poets' Theatre in the 1950s   139
    Heidi R. Bean
12 Diane di Prima as Playwright: The Early Years 1959–1964   155
    Nancy M. Grace
13 Homely Persons, Rude Speeches: Camp Personalities, Cold
    War Sensibilities and Dystopian Impulses in Frank O'Hara's
    Loves Labor, an Eclogue   177
    Jason Lagapa
14 Outlaw Tongues: The Stimuli for Michael McClure's *The Beard*   189
    Kurt Hemmer
15 Poetry Takes Centre Stage: John Wieners' *Still Life* at the New
    York Poets Theatre   205
    Erik Mortenson

Part 4   Early Off-Off Broadway Theatre

16 Evenings of Bohemian Cruelty: The Living Theatre in the 1950s   221
    Tim Good
17 Eas[ing] the Possible Past the Expected: A Restaging of
    Hettie Jones   233
    Tatum Petrich
18 Cowboy in the Rock Garden: Beat Influences in Sam Shepard's
    Early Plays   245
    Deborah R. Geis
19 Rochelle Owens: Off Beat, Off-Off Broadway   257
    Amy Friedman
20 Rosalyn Drexler: Savvy, Savage, Sassy Polymath   269
    Dorothy Chansky

Part 5   Film and Beat Performance

21 Kerouac's *The Subterraneans*: When Film Adaptation Becomes
    Cultural Betrayal   281
    Sara Villa
22 'This Was My Hollywood Career': Jack Kerouac's *On the Road*
    and 1950s Hollywood   293
    Matt Theado
23 The Many Movies of Kerouac's *Big Sur*   309
    Terence Diggory
24 Angel Tendencies and Gratuitous Acts: *Kill Your Darlings* and
    the Legacy of Lucien Carr   327
    Fiona Paton

Notes   345
Index   355

Acknowledgements

My profound gratitude goes to Enoch Brater for his mentorship and for his enthusiasm about this project. At Bloomsbury Methuen Drama, I thank Mark Dudgeon and Emily Hockley for their insight and guidance. For the graphic that accompanies her chapter, Amy Friedman wishes to thank Steve Finger, publisher of the *LA Free Press*, and Jesse Friedman. At DePauw University, I thank the staff members (Annie Weltz and Terry Bruner) who have helped to make every aspect of this project easier. I am also grateful to Brian Casey, Tim and Caroline Good, Anne Harris, Tiffany Hebb, Amy and Andrew Hayes, Keith Nightenhelser, and Jonathan Nichols-Pethick for their continued support. On a daily basis, what sustains me is the good will and fierce intelligence of my English Department colleagues, especially Meryl Altman, David Alvarez, Samuel Autman, Harry Brown, Tom Chiarella, Istvan Csicsery–Ronay, Vanessa Dickerson, Emily Doak, Ron Dye, Angela Flury, Wayne Glausser, Eugene Gloria, Peter Graham, Susan Hahn, Joe Heithaus, Lynn Ishikawa, Marnie McInnes, Greg Schwipps, Mike Sinowitz, Andrea Sununu, Chris White, and Lili Wright.

My mother (Dorothy Geis) and sisters (Nancy Geis Bardgett and Sarah Geis Williams) are owed more thanks than I can possibly give them here. I'm also deeply indebted to my far-flung college and New York City friends, particularly Anthony Barone, Glenn Burger, Ava Chin, Tracy Cornelius, Billy Finnegan, Hillary Kelleher, Steven F. Kruger, Ed Ku, James Magruder, Wayne Moreland, Kathleen Moore, Lee Papa, Janet Pennisi, Richard Pisciotta, Ron Scapp, Peter Schamel, Meryl Siegman, Chari Smith, Don Summa, Robert Vorlicky, Karen J. Vrotsos, John Weir, David J. Weiss, and Regina Rousso Wilmes. Finally, I want to extend my strongest gratitude to my spiritual twin Carlos A. Marsh, whose daily conversations and whose unparalleled wit and compassion have meant the world to me throughout the time that I was working on this project; like the Beats themselves, he is a true original.

Notes on Contributors

Heidi R. Bean is Assistant Professor of English at Bridgewater State University. She is editor (with Mike Chasar) of *Poetry after Cultural Studies* and she is the author of multiple journal articles, reviews, and interviews on the intersection of theatre and poetry.

Dorothy Chansky is Director of the Humanities Centre at Texas Tech University, where she teaches theatre history, theory, and criticism. Her publications include *Composing Ourselves: The Little Theatre Movement and the American Audience* and *Kitchen Sink Realisms: Domestic Labor, Dining, and Drama in American Theatre.*

Lisa Chinn is a doctoral candidate in the department of English at Emory University and an Andrew W. Mellon Graduate Teaching Fellow at Dillard University in New Orleans. She's currently researching mid-century print counter-culture journals and print culture's relationship to sound studies.

Terence Diggory is Emeritus Professor of English at Skidmore College. His books include *Encyclopedia of the New York School Poets*, *The Scene of My Selves: New Work on New York School Poets* (co-edited with Stephen Paul Miller), *William Carlos Williams and the Ethics of Painting* and *Yeats & American Poetry: The Tradition of the Self.*

Jimmy Fazzino is a lecturer in the Literature Department and Writing Program at the University of California, Santa Cruz. He is the author of *World Beats: Beat Generation Writing and the Worlding of US Literature.*

Amy Friedman holds a PhD in Post-colonial Satire from Goldsmiths College, University of London. Currently she is Assistant Professor of English at Temple University in Philadelphia, teaching courses on Beat Writers, Satire, and Anglo-American Women Modernists, and writing about satire and mimesis.

Deborah R. Geis is the Raymond W. Pence Professor of English at DePauw University. Her previous books include *Postmodern Theatric(k)s* and *Suzan-Lori Parks*; she is also co-editor (with Steven F. Kruger) of *Approaching the Millennium: Essays on Angels in America* and editor of *Considering MAUS: Approaches to Art Spiegelman's 'Survivor's Tale' of the Holocaust.*

Tim Good is Professor of Communication and Theatre and Director of Theatre at DePauw University. He has written about The Living Theatre for *Theater Journal*; *Theatre/Practice*; The Association for Theater in Higher

Education; The National Communication Association; The Popular Culture Association; The Mid America Theatre Conference; and The Lessac Training and Research Institute.

Nancy M. Grace is the Virginia Myers Professor of English at The College of Wooster. Her books include *The Feminized Male Character in Twentieth-century Literature*, *Girls Who Wore Black: Women Writing the Beat Generation* (with Ronna C. Johnson), *Breaking the Rule of Cool: Interviewing and Writing Women Beat Writers* (with Ronna C. Johnson), *Jack Kerouac and the Literary Imagination*, and *The Transnational Beat Generation*.

Kurt Hemmer is Professor of English at Harper College in Palatine, Illinois and the editor of the *Encyclopedia of Beat Literature*. With filmmaker Tom Knoff he has produced several award-winning films: *Janine Pommy Vega: As We Cover the Streets*, *Rebel Roar: The Sound of Michael McClure*, *Wow! Ted Joans Lives!*, *Keenan*, and *Love Janine Pommy Vega*.

Tim Hunt is University Professor of English at Illinois State University. His publications include *Kerouac's Crooked Road: Development of a Fiction*, *The Textuality of Soulwork: Kerouac's Quest for Spontaneous Prose*, and *The Collected Poetry of Robinson Jeffers*. His poetry collections include *Fault Lines* and *The Tao of Twang*.

Ronna C. Johnson is a Lecturer in English and American Studies at Tufts University. She is co-editor and co-author (with Nancy M. Grace) of *Girls Who Wore Black* and of *Breaking the Rule of Cool*. She is a founder of the Beat Studies Association, and co-editor (with Nancy M. Grace) of the *Journal of Beat Studies*.

Amor Kohli is Associate Professor and Director of the African and Black Diaspora Studies Program at DePaul University. His essays have appeared in *Callaloo*, *MELUS*, *African Identities*, and *Journal of Commonwealth Literature*, among other places. Most recently, he co-edited the book *Uprooting Urban America: Multidisciplinary Perspectives on Race, Class, and Gentrification*.

Nita N. Kumar is Associate Professor of English at S. P. Mukherji College, University of Delhi. Her articles have appeared in *African American Review*, *Black Arts Quarterly*, *Journal of American Drama and Theatre*, and *Theatre India: National School of Drama's Theatre Journal*.

Jason Lagapa is Associate Professor of English at the University of Texas – Permian Basin. He has previously published work on contemporary poetry in *Contemporary Literature*, *Journal of Modern Literature*, *College Literature*, and *The Salt Companion to Charles Bernstein*.

Erik Mortenson is Assistant Professor in the Department of English and Comparative Literature at Koç University in Istanbul, Turkey. He is the author of *Capturing the Beat Moment: Cultural Politics and the Poetics of Presence* as well as *Ambiguous Borderlands: Shadow Imagery in Cold War American Culture.*

William Nesbitt is Associate Professor of English and Chair of Interdisciplinary Studies at Beacon College. His work has appeared in *Kudzu House Quarterly, Route 7 Review, The Southeast Review,* and *The Journal of Evolutionary Psychology.*

Fiona Paton is Associate Professor of English at the State University of New York at New Paltz. She has published essays on Jack Kerouac, William S. Burroughs, and Alexander Trocchi.

Tatum Petrich teaches in the First-Year Writing Programme at Montclair State University and has published for *Women Writers: A Zine* and *The Literary Encyclopedia.*

Tom Pynn is Senior Lecturer of Interdisciplinary Studies at Kennesaw State University. His previous articles include 'The Dao De Jing on Cultivating Peace' (*Peace Review*), '"I am Not an I": Performative (Self) Identity in the Poetry of Bob Kaufman' (*The Philosophy of the Beats*), and 'Down the Trail, Back to this World: Kerouac's The Dharma Bums and the Diamond Sutra' (*East-West Connections*).

Matt Theado teaches American Culture at Kobe City University of Foreign Studies in Kobe, Japan. His books include *Understanding Jack Kerouac* and *The Beats: A Literary Reference.*

Sara Villa is Professor of English at John Abbott College and a visiting scholar at the International Institute for Critical Studies in Improvisation (IICSI), McGill University. She is also the translator of Jack Kerouac's journals into Italian and the author of a monograph on the film adaptation of Virginia Woolf's *Orlando.*

John Whalen-Bridge is Associate Professor of English at the National University of Singapore. Author of *Political Fiction and the American Self* and of *Tibet on Fire: Buddhism, Rhetoric, and Self-Immolation,* he is co-editor (with Gary Storhoff) of the SUNY series 'Buddhism and American Culture'.

Introduction

There are many stories about the origins of the 'Beat Generation' and the term 'Beat'. In a 1959 piece for *Playboy* magazine, Jack Kerouac says, 'When I first saw the hipsters creeping around Times Square in 1944 I didn't like them either.' But he adds that when Herbert Huncke approached him 'with radiant light shining out of his despairing eyes' and said, 'Man, I'm beat,' he knew what he meant. Kerouac goes on to describe the 'raving mad,' continuously talking hipsters and the jazz and bop playing constantly, adding, 'By 1948 it began to take shape' (Theado 2003: 24–25). In a now-famous 1952 essay for the *New York Times Magazine* called 'This is the Beat Generation', John Clellon Holmes credits Kerouac for more-or-less inventing the term by first putting 'Beat' and 'generation' together in a conversation they had. Holmes writes, 'It involves a sort of nakedness of mind, and ultimately, of soul; a feeling of being reduced to the bedrock of consciousness' (Theado 2003: 22). 'Beat' also took on the sense of 'beatific' – that these characters were demonic-seeming angels who bared their souls and suffered for their art. The term 'beatnik' evolved as a play on 'Sputnik', but also had clear origins in the Yiddish-influenced talk of the New York City streets. Some credit *San Francisco Chronicle* writer Herb Coen for popularizing the word via an April 1958 article. Sputnik was launched in October 1957, and it and the Beats were 'equally far out' (McIntosh 2003: 2).

We now think of the Beat Generation as encompassing a specific period, beginning just after World War II, reaching its peak in the mid-1950s, and ending in the second half of the 1960s as many of its key figures joined the Hippie generation (Allen Ginsberg), died far too young (Kerouac in 1969, whose politics had also shifted away from the counterculture at the end of his life), or pursued other political goals (LeRoi Jones/Amiri Baraka). The term 'Beat' or 'Beat Generation' was not just a period in time; obviously, not all writers of this era were 'Beats'. It also reflected a mindset, an ethos, and an undercurrent of rebellion. There was a parallel with the 'Angry Young Men' (a term most closely associated with the playwright John Osborne) in England at the same time, but the Beats were uniquely American, coming directly out of a pushback against the apparent normative values – those of the white middle-class capitalist patriotic nuclear family which seemed to pervade

American culture just after the war, reflected in 'Dick and Jane' readers, 'Ozzie and Harriet' television programmes, and in so many other public forms.

By the mid-1950s, news of the Beats had reached middle America, with articles about them in magazines like *Time* and *Life*, parodies in *Mad* magazine, TV characters on shows like *Dobie Gillis*, a proliferation of record albums teaching listeners to play the bongos. Rent-a-Beatniks were even available for fashionable parties. Like other counter-cultural movements (hip-hop comes to mind), what was once a form of rebellion was gradually becoming a product, at least in bastardized form, for mass consumption. However, in the period leading up to these moments of cultural appropriation, and even continuing through that time, significant works of literature emerged: Kerouac's *On the Road*, William Burroughs' *Naked Lunch*, Allen Ginsberg's *Howl*, to name but a few.

Drama is a vital but somehow neglected genre of study within Beat Generation literature. Virtually all of the significant Beat writers (including Kerouac, Ferlinghetti, Gregory Corso, Diane diPrima, Michael McClure, and LeRoi Jones [Amiri Baraka]) have experimented with writing plays. Much of what we would now call 'performance art' or 'performance poetry' owes a huge debt to the work of Allen Ginsberg, William Burroughs, Ted Joans, and Bob Kaufman. Some of the less canonical Beat writers (such as Bunny Lang and John Wieners) were known as playwrights; other Beat writers (such as Hettie Jones) have worked in the theatre. Playwrights of the early off-off Broadway theatre (such as Maria Irene Fornes, Sam Shepard, Rosalyn Drexler, Rochelle Owens, and others) who went on to become major voices of the 1970s and 1980s started out as young members of the Beat scene in the early 1960s. There is also an overlap between the work of the avant-garde filmmakers of the period (such as Robert Frank) and the emergence of a Beat dramatic aesthetic. Scholarship on the Beats has proliferated for many years: despite the frequent relegation of Beat writers (and, at least in earlier years, those who wrote about them) to the very margins, and has continued to explore everything from underrepresented women and African American Beats to the Beats and Buddhism to – most recently – how critical trends such as object-orientated ontological criticism might apply to writers like Kerouac. Yet attention to Beat drama – both in terms of unearthing some of these writers' primary dramatic texts and in writing *about* this work – has been surprisingly sparse.

Performance was central to the Beat aesthetic. It marked not only the kind of spontaneity and improvisational skills – responding to the moment – that had been part of jazz music for a decade or so already (and which Kerouac writes about so skilfully in *On the Road*), but also became the platform on which a loosely defined community of Beat artists began to form and to share their works. Possibly the most famous moment in Beat performance – honoured in the title of this book – took place when Allen Ginsberg declaimed his epic poem *Howl* at the Six Gallery on 7 October 1955. (Kenneth Rexroth was the master of ceremonies. Other readers included Philip Lamantia, Michael McClure, Philip Whalen, and Gary Snyder.) When he and Gregory Corso wrote about the event later, they described the audience members, including Kerouac (who later wrote a fictionalized account of the event in *Dharma Bums*), passing around a bottle of wine. 'This was no ordinary poetry reading', Ginsberg and Corso remarked (Ginsberg 2006: 165). The delivery of *Howl* was the pivotal event – 'driving forward', as they put it, 'with a strange ecstatic intensity' (Ginsberg 2006: 165). Their characterization of the evening's impact takes on further spiritual/religious overtones as they end by saying that 'a new forceful stir of young poets … [had] taken it upon themselves, with angelic clarions in hand, to announce their discontent, their demands, their hope, their final wondrous unimaginable dream' (Ginsberg 2006: 166).

While the reading at the Six Gallery was one of many pivotal moments in West Coast Beat performance, what was happening in New York City during this same era was also key to the eventual flourishing of Beat theatre. The central phenomenon was that the idea of theatre was no longer confined to Broadway or even off-Broadway; what eventually became known as off-off Broadway started to expand as Beat writers and artists gathered and created play performances in cafes, storefronts, churches, basements, and apartments. 'Theatre' was now something that could happen almost anywhere, and the audiences began to grow. The freedom inherent in forming these new and overlapping performance groups and spaces – to name only a few, the New York Poets Theatre, the Judson Poets Theatre, Theatre Genesis, Caffe Cino – also meant a new kind of artistic freedom, as Stephen J. Bottoms has discussed in his important study of this era (2004). From the communal work of The Living Theatre to the poetic creations of Michael McClure and Frank O'Hara; from the many artists who experimented with incorporating dance, painting, and music into their work to the wild (slightly later) narrative experiments of Sam Shepard's early plays, the very definition of theatre was transformed during this period and would never be the same again. Diane di Prima, a significant Beat poet who co-founded the New York Poets Theatre, writes of this period: 'It was through the theatre and the music that we caught a glimpse of the power of what we were doing. That it existed beyond the studio, the typewriter, the apartment. Cast a new light on these streets. That it – even briefly – changed the world' (2001: 147).

Early reviewers of Beat drama included *Village Voice* writers Jerry Tallmer (who coined the term Off-Off Broadway) and Michael Smith (who also ended up directing some of Sam Shepard's early plays); pieces by these and other like-minded journalists, even when mixed in their appraisals, brought audiences downtown. Sometimes, small presses run by some of the Beats themselves (like Hettie Jones and LeRoi Jones, or Diane di Prima) published these plays and play/poem hybrids. Generally, though, the improvisational and collaborative, intentionally ephemeral nature of many of these works meant that Beat drama texts were not often published, or were only printed in very limited editions. At the time, publishers thought that plays tended to be more marketable if directors and actors wanted to use the texts for their own productions. Such demand seemed unlikely due to the unconventional, moment-based nature of these works. Smith's and Nick Orzel's collection *Eight Plays from Off-Off Broadway*, published by Bobbs-Merrill in 1966, was the first major anthology of these plays. It included pieces by O'Hara, Lanford Wilson, Joel Oppenheimer, Maria Irene Fornes, and others – as well as brief accounts of some of the aforementioned theatres. But it was only later understood that just as readers enjoy the avant-garde play texts of modernist writers like Gertrude Stein (and indeed continue to this day to attempt productions of their works), works by Beat dramatists deserved to be available and to be read (and produced) by later generations. A fair number of Beat drama works were eventually published many decades later – but many now exist only in archives. They deserve further attention from scholars, as several of the writers in this collection attest.

Part 1 of this volume considers the drama of the so-called 'canonical' Beat writers. In this category, we could certainly include Jack Kerouac's play *The Beat Generation* and his own sometimes difficult role as a performer of his work. After *On The Road* was published, an off-Broadway producer named Leo Garin asked Kerouac if he would write a play. He started composing *The Beat Generation Or the New Amaraean Church* (Sargeant 1997: 13) in October of 1957 while staying with his mother in Florida; the text draws on material from *Visions of Cody* and *Desolation Angels* (Charters 1973: 302) but it was based on a visit that Kerouac made to Neal and Carolyn Cassady in California in the fall of 1955. As Jack Sargeant summarizes it, 'The first act was set in the apartment of a seaman, Al Sublette, with Neal, Al Hinkle, and Charlie Mew, the second act followed Neal to the race track, and the third act focused on the events which transpired when the Bishop [Swiss Bishop Romano] visited the Cassady house' (1997: 14). Playwright Lillian Hellman thought that it needed extensive revisions before it could ever be produced (Charters 1973: 305). Kerouac was able to use the third act, with improvised voiceover narration, as the basis for the film that he, Robert Frank, and Alfred Leslie had co-created. The title *The Beat Generation* had already been copyrighted by MGM for a 'B' movie they were making, so the new title was *Pull My Daisy*, the term for removing a stripper's G-string (Sargeant 1997: 14). Tim

Hunt's chapter takes us further inside the original play text of *The Beat Generation* and locates its connections to Kerouac's better-known fiction. From his legendary debut reading of *Howl* in 1955 (mentioned earlier) to his later, post-Beat activist moments, we can locate Allen Ginsberg not just as a forerunner of the slam poetry scene that took off in this country in the late 1980s, but also as a precursor to the solo performance artists of the 1990s such as Eric Bogosian and Karen Finley, who used their bodies and voices to merge the autobiographical and the political. John Whalen-Bridge invokes the moment of Ginsberg's reading of *Howl* to discuss its larger implications not only for how it came to change the meaning of 'performance,' but also how it informed the later trajectory of Ginsberg's career. Another significant 'canonical' Beat poet who delved into playwriting was Gregory Corso, whose dramatic works evolved during the time he spent at Harvard between 1954 and 1956 (though he was never actually a student there himself). In one of these, *In this Hung-Up Age* (which, in the print version, has the subtitle 'A One-Act Farce Written 1954'), he creates a parodic encounter between a 'hipster' and a Radcliffe student (Theado 2003: 11; Corso 1964: 149-161). Ronna C. Johnson's chapter explores this piece as well as several other rarely-discussed Corso plays in terms of what the emerging idea of 'Beat' meant within the context of Cold War anxieties. The prolific poet, publisher, and artist Lawrence Ferlinghetti published two books of one-act plays that owe a great deal to the French surrealists, with elements of the Japanese Noh Theatre thrown in as well. As I argue in my chapter on these plays, many of them contain elements that less imaginative co-creators would consider unproduceable, from a six-foot alligator to a piece that ends with crashing light bulbs. Yet most of these plays were indeed performed, particularly in the newly developing off-off Broadway theatre scene in New York (as well as in San Francisco), again showing the Beats' willingness to take artistic and theatrical risks.

William Burroughs, best known for books like *Naked Lunch*, collaborated with Brion Gysin to create avant-garde works, part drama and part film, which were known as 'cut-ups'; 'all writing is in fact cut-ups,' he wrote (1999: 182). In certain ways, Burroughs and Gysin ventured into the multimedia dramatic experiments we would see again in artists who followed shortly after him, such as Richard Foreman and Robert Wilson, as well as later avant-garde theatrical innovators such as Charles Mee and Moises Kaufman. In 1990 in Germany and in 1993 at the Brooklyn Academy of Music, a play version of Burroughs' *The Black Rider: The Casting of the Magic Bullets*, with music by Tom Waits, was produced (Theado 2003: 10). Burroughs was also someone who lived his entire life as a performance of sorts. In his chapter, William Nesbitt takes us back to one of the most famous moments in

Burroughs' life, one that would haunt him: the 'William Tell' episode in which he accidentally killed his wife, Joan Vollmer Burroughs. Performance poet Anne Waldman began to find her voice during the later years of the Beat period, and emerged as a powerful artist in the decades that followed. Many of her later poems such as *Fast Speaking Woman* can be viewed as dramatic works, but her earliest experiments in playwriting have largely been underexplored. Lisa Chinn's piece on Waldman's 1964 play *The Stoop* gives us a sense of how she was already challenging boundaries in her work – in terms not only of genre, but also of gender categories.

In Part 2, the focus turns to the dramatic work of African-American Beat writers, or 'Afro-Beats'. LeRoi Jones (later Amiri Baraka), whose play *Dutchman* (1964) received major public attention, later became a significant figure in the Black Arts/Black Power movement. Jimmy Fazzino looks at Baraka's drama in terms of its strong connections to French surrealism and Antonin Artaud's 'Theatre of Cruelty', showing how Artaud's insistence upon waking up audiences profoundly influenced Baraka's emerging political voice. Also in this group are Ted Joans and Bob Kaufman, both of whom were political poets whose public acts can be seen as precursors to contemporary performance art. Amor Kohli takes us back to the moment of Joans' 'Bird Lives!' graffiti and shows how this radical act of improvisation connects to the importance of the jazz aesthetic and the embodiment of Blackness. Kaufman, an outspoken street performer in the Beat Generation, later took a vow of silence for ten years in protest of the Vietnam War. Tom Pynn's chapter discusses Kaufman's early public performances in the context of his 'prophet' status. Situated in the later part of the Beat period, we also find the surrealist work of playwright Adrienne Kennedy (whose *Funnyhouse of a Negro* initially appeared off-Broadway on a double bill with Jones' *Dutchman*). Nita Kumar shows how, even though Kennedy's work was intensely personal and autobiographical and she did not consider herself part of the Beat clique, our understanding of her plays is now deeply enhanced by appreciating their thematic and historical connections to Beat writing.

Part 3 concerns the significance of what came to be known, in different contexts both in Cambridge (Massachusetts) and New York, as Poets Theatre (see Killian and Brazil 2010). Heidi Bean's chapter traces the dramatic writing of V.R. 'Bunny' Lang, a founding member of the Cambridge Poets' Theatre. The New York Poets Theatre was created by Diane di Prima and several artist/writer friends (including Fred Herko, Alan Marlowe, John Herbert MacDowell, and Jimmy Waring) during the golden era of the Beat Generation. Together for four seasons, they produced primarily one-act plays written by poets with sets painted by artist friends 'from both coasts' (Knight 1996: 126). Di Prima, most well-known as a poet and memoirist, was deeply involved in all aspects of creation – from producing to scene design to playwriting – during her years with the New York Poets Theatre, as she documents in her autobiography *Recollections of My Life as a Woman* (2001). Her better-known theatrical work, including such plays as *Murder Cake* and *Whale Honey* (about the death of Percy Bysshe Shelley), sheds light on the history of newly evolving collaborative, multi-disciplinary creations of this period that bridge the gap between the Federal Theatre Project's political experiments of the 1930s, and the emerging off-off Broadway theatre of the 1960s. Nancy Grace, whose chapter looks at some of di Prima's early rarely discussed drama, focuses on the modernist aesthetics that inform di Prima's plays and shows the connection between these works and the thematic preoccupations evident in her poetry.

Other important figures associated with the New York Poets Theatre all collaborated many times. The most famous of these is Frank O'Hara, who overlapped between the Beats and what came to be known as the Language poets. O'Hara's *Awake in Spain*, for instance, ran as part of Jimmy Waring's 'dark night' series at The Living Theatre along with di Prima's *Murder Cake* (di Prima 2001: 187). Jason Lagapa's chapter discusses O'Hara's *Loves Labor, an eclogue*, which the Poets Theatre produced at the New Bowery Theatre in 1964. Michael McClure, whose pieces such as *The Pillow* and *The Feast* (the latter of which was written in 'beast language' (di Prima 2001: 276–77), were part of the Poets Theatre, later won Obie awards for his plays *The Beard* and *Josephine: The Mouse Singer*. He comments about this period, which included *The Blossom, or Billy the Kid*: 'We were outlaws – still today, people of deep or myriad feeling are outlaws ...' (1999: 166). Each night, before *The Blossom* began, the theatre blasted a radio piece by Antonin Artaud out of giant speakers from the front windows; di Prima recalls how '[i]t sounded above the traffic, above the rest of the city racket, and in the long dusk Artaud's work, like he always meant it to be, was a magickal [*sic*] act' (2001: 388). In his chapter, Kurt Hemmer pays special attention to *The Beard* and to McClure's fascination with outlaw Billy the Kid and the actress Jean Harlow, both of whom haunted him throughout his affiliation with the New York Poets Theatre and afterwards. John Wieners, who was initially associated with the Black Mountain poets (Charles Olson and others) and who became an important Beat writer, also collaborated with the New York Poets Theatre; Erik Mortenson looks closely at Wieners's 1961 play *Still Life* in terms of its experimental dialogue and its production history.

Part 4 concentrates on the writers closely affiliated with the Beats whose revolutionary creations marked the emergence of Off-Off Broadway theatre in the late 1950s and early 1960s. This includes the early days of The Living Theatre, founded by Julian Beck and Judith Malina. Its original productions such as Jack Gelber's *The Connection* were hugely influential, as Tim Good discusses in his chapter. Hettie Jones, who was married during the Beat era to LeRoi Jones (Amiri Baraka) – and whose book *How I Became Hettie Jones* is a significant memoir of the period – had an early passion for the theatre and worked with many of the other major Beat artists. Yet, as Tatum Petrich argues in her chapter, she was largely overshadowed by the figure of her more famous husband. Most of us are familiar with Sam Shepard not only as an actor, but also as a Pulitzer-winning playwright of the 1980s whose 'family trilogy', including *Buried Child*, is now part of the contemporary dramatic canon. Less well-known, though, is that Shepard began his career as a playwright in the later days of the Beat Generation. I consider his earliest plays such as *The Rock Garden*, *Chicago*, and *Icarus's Mother*. Off-off Broadway was also shaped by the early work of such playwrights as Maria Irene Fornes, Rochelle Owens, and Rosalyn Drexler, all of whom became important dramatic writers in the subsequent decades. Amy Friedman's chapter on Owens looks at the path that her work took, featuring a discussion of Owens's controversial play *Futz* and its critical reception. Dorothy Chansky gives us new insight into the importance of Rosalyn Drexler as a playwright whose rebel status, attention to visual artistry, and fearlessness about gender dynamics made her a force to be reckoned with in the off-off Broadway scene.

The final section of this collection expands the notion of performance into cinematic creations and re-creations, with a special emphasis on Jack Kerouac's work. Sara Villa's chapter considers why the Hollywood-era film of Kerouac's novel *The Subterraneans* was an abysmal failure, albeit an interesting one. Given the cinematic quality of Kerouac's narration in *On the Road*, as well as the way he was initially courted by Hollywood producers after the book's success, it is striking that it was never made into a film in Kerouac's lifetime; in his chapter, Matt Theado uncovers the reasons for this. The last two chapters focus on very recent attempts to capture the Beats on film. Terence Diggory discusses the 2013 adaptation of Kerouac's *Big Sur* and sets it into context with his fiction, while Fiona Paton looks at the visual and narrative choices that the creators of the recent film *Kill Your Darlings*, about a murder committed by Lucien Carr (a legendary Beat figure who was a close friend of Ginsberg and Kerouac), made in their cinematic portrait of the real-life Carr.

Many of the plays of the Beat Generation have been largely forgotten – some for good reason. As with so much of the literature of this period, we are only now beginning to catalogue and describe its merits and its place in literary and cultural history. This collection is, I hope, a step in that direction.

Works cited

Bottoms, S. (2004), *Playing Underground: A Critical History of the 1960s Off-Off Broadway Movement*, Ann Arbor: University of Michigan.

Burroughs, W. (1999), 'The Cut-Up Method of Brion Gysin' in A. Waldman (ed.), *The Beat Book: Writings from the Beat Generation*, Boston: Shambhala, 182–85.

Charters, A. (1973), *Kerouac: A Biography*, New York: St. Martin's.

Corso, G. (1964), *In This Hung-Up Age* in J. Laughlin (ed.), *New Directions in Prose and Poetry* 18, New York: New Directions, 149–161.

Diggory, T. (2004), 'What Abstract Art Means in *Pull My Daisy*' in J. Skerl (ed.), *Reconstructing the Beats*, New York: Palgrave Macmillan.

di Prima, D. (2001), *Recollections of My Life as a Woman*, New York: Penguin.

Ferlinghetti, L. (1962), *Unfair Arguments with Existence* [one act plays], New York: New Directions.

Ferlinghetti, L. (1964), *Routines*, New York: New Directions.

Ginsberg, A. (2006), *Howl: Fiftieth Anniversary Edition*, New York: Harper Perennial.

Jones, H. (1990), *How I Became Hettie Jones*, New York: Grove.

Killian, K. and D. Brazil (2010), *The Kenning Anthology of Poets Theater 1945–1985*, Chicago: Kenning.

Knight, B. (1996), *Women of the Beat Generation*, Berkeley, CA: Conari.

McClure, M. (1999), *Huge Dreams*, New York: Penguin.

McIntosh, M. (ed.) and D. Priore (2003), *Beatsville*, Melbourne, Australia: Outré Gallery.

Orzel, N. and M. Smith (eds), (1966), *Eight Plays from Off-Off Broadway*, Indianapolis: Bobbs-Merrill.

Sargeant, J. (1997), *The Naked Lens: An Illustrated History of Beat Cinema*, London: Creation.

Theado, M. (2003), *The Beats: A Literary Reference*, New York: Carroll & Graf.

Waldman, A. (1989), *Helping the Dreamer*, Minneapolis: Coffee House.

Part One

The 'Canonical' Beats

Mediation and Immediacy: The I and You of Jack Kerouac's Theatre of Voice

Tim Hunt

Jack Kerouac is best known for *On the Road* (1957) and *The Dharma Bums* (1958), two novels that draw on personal material but are perhaps less autobiographical than readers, then and still, anxious to cast him as the King of the Beats, have assumed. Kerouac's work includes, however, not only these relatively traditional novels but also experimental fiction (such as *Dr. Sax* and his posthumously published masterwork *Visions of Cody*), poetry collections (most notably *Mexico City Blues*), and an array of less categorisable, experimental works (*The Book of Dreams*, *Some of the Dharma* and others) that document his restless search for ways to release and record what he termed, in an early journal entry, the 'big rushing tremendousness in me and in all poets' (2004: 94–95).[1] In 2005, the posthumous publication of *Beat Generation* further complicated our picture of Kerouac's generic restlessness by adding a '3-Act Play' to the mix (Kerouac 2005: iii).

Beat Generation, as Gerald Nicosia has explained, was written shortly after *On the Road* was published in September 1957, as Kerouac confronted the sudden demand for his work that his status as a celebrity had created. Nicosia writes (1983: 559):

> Meanwhile, off-Broadway producer Leo Garin wanted a play from him, and as soon as he got back to Florida Jack wrote it in one night. "The Beat Generation" comprised three acts: the first set in Al Sublette's apartment with Neal [Cassady], Al Hinkle, and Charley Mew; the second a day at the races with Neal; and the third the night the Bishop came to Neal's house.

In spite of the interest in all things Kerouac at the time, the play was not produced, and it has remained very much on the margin of his canon in the decade since its 2005 publication (a staged reading in 2012 seems to be its only public performance to date).[2]

Kerouac would not be the first novelist to discover that his strengths as a writer of fiction failed to translate to the stage (neither Henry James nor Mark Twain, for instance, flourished as playwrights), and it would be easy to dismiss *Beat Generation* as a curiosity. Yet, its portrayal of Beat experience can help us understand something of the dilemma that *On the Road's* notoriety created for Kerouac as a writer when it was first published and perhaps as well why Garin and (presumably) others declined to produce it in spite of Kerouac's popularity at the time. Moreover, the play's mode and style can add to our understanding of the dynamics of Kerouac's experimental aesthetic, and this in turn points to the challenges inherent in creating dramatic works that would be Beat in both manner and matter.

Both *On the Road* and *Beat Generation* portray Beat non-conformity, and in both works Neal Cassady is the basis of a central character (Dean Moriarty in the novel, Milo in the play). These parallels are noteworthy, but so too are the differences between the novel and play. Where *On the Road* presents characters rejecting conventional domesticity and social norms in order to risk the possibilities of Beat discovery on the road, *Beat Generation* presents characters who are trying to maintain the possibility of visionary experience within the alternative modes of domesticity that they have fashioned and are attempting to maintain. That *Beat Generation* offers a quieter, more reflective, take on being Beat – one more aware of the cost of living moment-by-moment in and for the moment – is perhaps in large part because the characters in the play are older than those in *On the Road*. A desire for some degree of stability has tempered the desire to break free of social conventions. While the characters still reject middle-class norms and goals (they are Beat, not square), the ratio between the desire for kicks and the desire for belief has shifted.

This shift is evident in the differences in how Kerouac projects his relationship to Cassady (as Dean) in *On the Road* and his relationship to Cassady (as Milo) in *Beat Generation*. Dean as the Holy Goof exemplifies the possibilities of being fully, both hedonistically and spiritually, in the moment. Dean as Beat avatar and Sal (the character Kerouac based on himself) as acolyte are the central pair in the novel. Their relationship drives the narrative and is its focus. For all their differences, Sal and Dean are fully aligned in their commitment to the quest for 'IT'. In *Beat Generation*, Milo and Buck (the character based on Kerouac) remain buddies and remain committed to each other, but their relationship is now complicated by Milo's attempt to sustain a marriage and family and by the competing versions of the spiritual and of success they have come to hold. For Milo, the ecstatic immediacy of 'IT', of knowing Time and entering it so fully that one transcends it, has been replaced with Edgar Cayce's Theosophy: the spiritual is something to be achieved and is to be realized beyond life, not in it. For Buck, operating more from a Buddhist perspective, the spiritual already *is*, and the challenge is simply to accept this and put aside the anxious spiritual striving that is driving Milo. 'IT', for Buck, is no longer a matter of transcending the ordinary; it is a matter of accepting the ordinary as already infused with transcendence. The visionary, rather than being opposed to the ordinary, is within the ordinary, and one achieves it by embracing the ordinary rather than striving to escape it. That Milo and Buck, in their ad hoc and arbitrary terms for these positions, can argue about them, underscores their friendship but also means that they are now each travelling different, even diverging, Beat paths rather than blazing the same Beat trail. (Milo's hostility to Manuel, a character based on Gregory Corso, at the race track in Act Two, also underscores this shift: Manuel is younger, more naïve and more idealistic than either Milo or Buck, which charms Buck but irritates Milo; that Manuel is reminiscent of Sal Paradise in *On the Road* suggests the distance in age, attitude and experience between Dean and Milo and Sal and Buck.)

Similarly, Milo and Buck have radically different senses of success. Milo's gambling misadventures at the race track reflect, as Buck seems to recognize, a desire for material success coupled with a fantasy of being free of the need to work. Buck, conversely, seems to have rejected material success; by reducing his needs to a place to roll out his sleeping bag and enough coin to buy beer or wine, he has minimised the need to work. In *Beat Generation*, Milo and Buck remain buddies because of their shared past and shared rejection of what we now term 'containment culture', but not through their shared views or positions in the present.

The contrast between the Beat ethos of *On the Road* and that of *Beat Generation* is perhaps most evident in Act Three. The bulk of the act presents Buck, Irwin and Paul (the character based on Peter Orlovsky, Ginsberg's long-time partner) challenging a 'Bishop', whose services Milo and his wife Cora attend, with questions about God, sex and what is holy. This burlesque of straight or square culture and playful rejection of religious dogma is the one segment of the play that recaptures something of the behavioural spontaneity found in *On the Road*, and it's quite understandable that this is the segment of the play that Alfred Leslie and Robert Frank drew on in developing their 1959 short film *Pull My Daisy* (Nicosia 1983: 582–585).

However, the opening and closing scenes of Act Three emphasise loss, uncertainty and change – not playful spontaneity – darkening Kerouac's evocation of the Beat as if to emphasise (or confess) that the hopefulness of the Beat impulse of the late 1940s and the Beat reality of the late 1950s are different things. Act Three opens with Buck and Irwin at Milo's house awaiting the Bishop's arrival. Irwin poses an implicitly critical question: 'What does Milo see in the Bishop?' Buck, in a kind of defence, offers that Milo's 'just an old Jesuit, you know, actually' and that he 'gets down on his knees with the kids and says the Lord's Prayer' (Kerouac 2005: 87). Irwin isn't satisfied with this, in part because the Bishop is 'a pretty dull sort of ugh bore'. But his next comment is even more telling: 'All this mediocrity that's come later in our lives, when Milo was young and I was young and we kneeled on the dark Texas Plain at night and vowed eternal holy friendship like – you know ...' (2005: 88). Neither Irwin nor Milo is now 'young', and the 'friendship' they have in the present is something different than, and seemingly diminished from, the all-encompassing intensity of 'eternal holy friendship' they once shared. In his comment Irwin both recognizes this change and implies it has to do with growing older, and Buck and Irwin, in the exchange, bond through their reflection on the past rather than their participation in the present. If *On the Road* offers a celebration of possibility and immediacy, evoking a vision of the Beat – its mythos – *Beat Generation* offers a continued hope for this immediacy but mixed with the recognition of its lack. As a result, the headlong and heedless search for IT has given way to a more reflective search for belief – whether Milo's idiosyncratic reading of Cayce's Theosophy or Buck's home-grown Buddhism.

The play's final scene further underscores this shift in Kerouac's sense of the Beat. After the Bishop and his two aunts extricate themselves and leave, Irwin, Paul, Buck and Mezz (described as 'A BOPCAP, A REAL HEPCAT' and who, it seems, may be involved with Cora, Milo's wife)[3] improvise cowboy 'routines', as if continuing the improvisational play of the exchanges with the Bishop. Milo then steps in, as if to continue the collective improvisation, but actually rejecting and ending it (perhaps because Mezz, his seeming rival, has initiated the game) (Kerouac 2005: 115):

Mezz (*responding to* **Buck**)   What'd you do then?

Buck   I turn into a ball of electricity and they all drop dead.

Milo   (*suddenly*) I'll tell you mine ... Preacher ridin into town, I'm standin there at the bar with the preacher as he makes his sermon on the Lord quotin chapter 26 verse 18 in the New Testament 'Not a jot and tittle verily shall ye know that was left' ... So there's a drunk in the corner drinkin from his glass sittin crosslegged on the floor drinkin while the preacher makes his speech, I pull out my gun and aim it right at his head and say 'Don't you believe in G a w d?' ... and let him have it, right through the head.

Milo then exits to go to bed, and Buck, who understands Milo's speech as a dismissive rejection, asks Irwin and Paul, 'Why do you think that Milo shot me through the head after this long day that I spent with him?' (2005: 116), then adds (2005: 117):

> But ah, *hell*, I'm goin back to the coast, I'm goin back to Frisco. I'm goin out with this sleeping bag, and you know why? When I wake up at 3 A.M. and I don't know where I am and I see all the stars above my sleep I realize what a vast bright room I'm in, the real room . . . I really sleep out there.

As the play ends, Buck is alone in the yard playing Milo's flute, while Milo, off stage, is presumably paired off with his wife Cora, and Irwin and Paul, also paired off, are settling down to sleep on the couch. When Paul wonders why Buck is 'playing the flute under the stars', Irwin offers, 'Must be because . . . he's trying to figure out what all this is all about . . . whatever it's all about, you know . . . the world is what form is, and that's all you can about it, huh?' (2005: 120). As the curtain falls, 'THE FLUTE PLAYS', functioning as the play's final line and emphasizing Buck's solitariness in the 'vast bright room' that is 'the real room'.

Whether this final moment – Buck playing to the stars, as he drifts beyond Milo and Cora and Irwin and Paul in their respective domesticities – is a moment of Beat affirmation, a matter of Beat doubt, or a kind of regretful acceptance as Buck muses on his changed relationship with Milo is, I'd suggest, left open and unresolved, and this ambiguity, and the reflectiveness it suggests, gives *Beat Generation* a distinctly different tone from *On the Road* (where affirmation mixes with, but overrides, the recognition of change implicit in Dean and Sal separating at the end of the novel each to pursue his own road and the reality of loss implicit in their failure to find, as the closing line puts it, 'Old Dean Moriarty the father we never found, I think of Dean Moriarty' [Kerouac 1957: 307]). In *On the Road*, one acknowledges the reality of loss to be on the road, but the road itself leads beyond loss. In *Beat Generation*, loss is the road, or rather all roads lead to loss. What then matters is whether one recognizes this and accepts it and whether one, then, searches for the vision within loss as opposed to the vision beyond loss.

That Kerouac should write *Beat Generation* in the months immediately following *On the Road's* publication and in the midst of his ascension to celebrity status underscores the extent to which he found his sudden fame, as his friends have recalled, deeply unsettling. The world of *On the Road* was a decade in the past.[4] It's possible that the play functioned, for Kerouac, as a kind of reflection on the gap between his Beat past and his Beat present. If so, the play stands in an interesting relation to his two most widely read novels: as a kind of coda to *On the Road* (a documentary updating its central characters and where their Beat journey has led them) and as a kind of prequel to *Dharma Bums*, where Kerouac remythologizes (reinterprets, reimagines) the Beat vision with Ray Smith (the narrator and character based on himself) and Japhy Ryder (a character based on Gary Snyder) as a pair of Beat/Buddhist seekers at the centre. Instead of the Beat journey being a matter of Dean and Sal driving the road from coast to coast in search of kicks, it becomes, in *Dharma Bums*, a matter of Japhy and Ray climbing a mountain trail.

Adding *Beat Generation* into the Kerouac canon brings into relief the difference in perspective between *On the Road* and *Dharma Bums*. This suggests that the popularity of the two books when first published and their continued popularity as paradigmatic evocations of the Beat has less to do with their thematic similarities than it does with the way they each offer and celebrate alternatives to middle class conformity. Moreover, both present the Beat (albeit each a different sense of the Beat) as if it is fully in the present. *Beat Generation*, though, in spite of the celebratory play of Paul, in his innocent enthusiasm asking the Bishop, 'Do you know about teenagers and how they wanta go to the moon, do you know about masturbation, did you ever walk down the street in the morning and rejoice in the little round asses of girls?' (Kerouac 2005: 107), portrays the characters as moving farther and farther away from the enthusiasm of 'teenagers' and documents how they are increasingly caught in time and entangled in the complexities of their lives (the implied triangular relationship of Milo, Cora and Mezz; Milo's money problems; the strains in the friendship of Buck and Milo). Buck's comment, 'Well as you say it all goes down the same hole', in response to Irwin's lament that 'All this mediocrity [has] come later in our lives' (2005: 88) is more the play's emotional and thematic centre than Paul's innocently speaking whatever comes to mind. In the play, the Beat vision is less a matter of what the characters experience in their present and more a matter of, on the one hand, a remembered intensity (Irwin recognizing that his 'eternal holy friendship' with Milo is only 'eternal' in memory) and, on the other, what they now search for spiritually, each finally in isolation from the other. At the end of the play, as Buck exits to play the flute, alone, under the stars, he says to Paul, 'Good night brother Paul … goodnight Saint Paul' (2005: 117). Buck, here, seems to cast Paul as a gentler, more innocent, version of 'brother' Dean in *On the Road*, as if recognizing Paul as the one figure who has managed to continue to be young in spirit – and thereby Beat in the earlier sense. Paul's Beat saintliness in part both depends on and requires Irwin, who protects and directs him. By participating in the 'mediocrity' of things so that Paul can be shielded from them, Irwin has seemingly compromised, even lost or sacrificed, the unselfconsciousness of Beat immediacy. In the play, Paul is the exception to the rule, the one character who is allowed to fully retain the innocence the others have lost. As such, *Beat Generation* functions not simply as a coda to *On the Road* but as a kind of elegy for it; this is, plausibly, one reason why Garin did not produce the play. For Garin and *On the Road's* initial readership in late 1957, Dean and Sal represented the Beat present, not its past. Playgoers would have also wanted this Beat present to be present, not past, and they would have expected affirmation, not elegiac reflection. If *Beat Generation* was out of synch with the public's expectations for Beat product in the late 1950s, this seems, at least in part, ironically, to be because it was so in synch with Kerouac's changing relationship to his own Beat experience – and his willingness to document doubts and loss.

Garin and the others who presumably passed on staging *Beat Generation* when Kerouac first wrote it probably did so not simply because of its themes and meandering action, but also because of the play's style. The writing lacks the momentum and richness of play, tone and implication found in Kerouac's fiction. This is plausibly, in part, a matter of Kerouac wanting to leave room for the actors to shape the characters in performance. But his attempt to construct, 'wright', a 'play' seems to have moved him back to a more conservative aesthetic than he'd developed in his fiction (just as his biographical situation had moved him to a more conservative version/vision of the Beat scene and a more complex, even problematic, relationship to it).

In Kerouac's fiction (especially as he developed Spontaneous Prose while writing *Visions of Cody* and explored it in the novels that followed) the desire for an immediate (and as if unmediated) connection to the reader as 'you' drives both his rejection of conventional approaches to point of view and fictional rhetoric (as exemplified in Henry James's *The Art of Fiction*, which Kerouac read and, not surprisingly, rejected) and the experiments that evolved into Spontaneous Prose. In order to write for 'you' (the reader as if a participating auditor) rather than what he once termed (in a 28 December 1950 letter to Cassady, four months before composing *On the Road*) as 'the mysterious outside reader' (Kerouac 1995: 247) of conventional fiction, the writer must imagine speaking as if to 'you' in actual time (rather than composing a representation of the narrator addressing the reader as if in actual time). This casts the writer as a performer – a figure performing in writing to produce writing, which the reader as 'you' (rather than the abstract, conventionalized position of 'mysterious outside reader') reads/listens to as if participating in the same elapsing time of the writer's writing/telling.

For *Beat Generation* to be Beat aesthetically in the same way that *Visions of Cody* (and parts of *On the Road*) are Beat, the play would need to allow (actually require) the cast members to function as improvisational co-creators with the playwright (through the script) and with each other in the process of the performance, simultaneously actualizing the script and recasting it in and through each unique performance. The actors would, that is, function in a manner akin to jazz musicians for whom the piece of music to be performed is less a text that dictates their actions and more a set of elements and possible operations functioning as an occasion for collaborative elaboration.

In *Beat Generation*, in spite of the conversational off-handedness of the dialogue, the play is a fully composed (in effect completed and closed) text that the cast would necessarily interpret in production but not alter. With *Beat Generation*, that is, the script marks and enforces a divorce between the originating and authentically performative action (Kerouac writing the script) and what the actors would 'stage' (a representation of a representation) for an observing audience. The script seems neither to invite nor support the more (aesthetically) radical option of the play as a collaborative invention between the writer, the cast as act(ion)ors, and the audience as co-participants.

Ironically, Kerouac's relatively conventional understanding of theatre seemingly did not allow him to move toward the more experimental praxis (the incorporation of ensemble improvisation, the violation of the audience's passivity by projecting actors into the audience and drawing audience members onto the stage, and the guerilla street theatre and the happenings of the mid- and later 1960s) that companies like The Living Theatre and San Francisco Mime Troupe would soon be exploring. In *Beat Generation*, Kerouac seems to have imagined the actors as agents who would deliver the improvisationally generated script, not as improvisational, and existentially authentic, co-creators. As a result, *Beat Generation* stands as a 'Beat' play because of its material, what it represents and presents, but it neither exemplifies nor embodies a Beat aesthetic, which raises the question of why Kerouac was either unable to adapt his experimental approach to fiction to drama or chose not to. Oddly enough, his handling of stage directions offers a clue.

In Act Two, Scene Two, as Milo, Buck, and Manuel consider betting strategies, the race begins, stopping Buck mid-phrase. The stage directions then read, 'AND THE RACE IS RUN, "THEY'RE OFF! AND IT'S BURNING BUSH TAKING THE LEAD," AND ... ALL THAT STUFF, AND YOU KNOW THE WAY A RACE' (Kerouac 2005: 64). The stage directions can be read two ways. They can be taken as calling for sound effects (the noise of the race beginning and the announcer's race call). Read this way, 'ALL THAT STUFF, AND YOU KNOW' signals that the details of the announcer's call are to be worked out in production (presumably in taping the sound cue). But the off-handedness of the comment also shows, I'd suggest, Kerouac straining against the script form – and its rhetoric. Stage directions function as glosses on the action to be presented. As such, they are a kind of aside to guide the director and others. In reading (as opposed to staging) a play, one uses stage directions to contextualize the characters' scripted lines. In either case, the stage direction is a secondary, supporting discourse that provides data. In this stage direction, though, the 'YOU' seems to be directed to the actual audience as well (or instead), as if the playwright is speaking to the playgoer in a kind of performative, quasi-improvisational voiceover. At this moment in drafting the play, Kerouac seems, that is, to be spinning both the characters' lines and the stage directions as if he is improvising fictional narrative in which the various voices remain embedded in his own narrating voice rather than fashioning a script that becomes fully independent of the writer's presence. The stage directions, I'd suggest, reflect a desire, an impulse, to generate the play improvisationally and cast it as the writer's voice recalling, projecting, and then riffing from the imagined voices of the characters as the narrating/performing writer engages the material as if in the presence of the audience (the audience as 'YOU' rather than abstracted, belated 'mysterious outside reader').

This stage direction and others that less overtly reflect the same impulse function as narrative action, even though the conventions of the dramatic script mean that the gesture of the writer interacting directly with his material as if performing (and thus, as well, this additional narrative overtone) would not be available to the audience. As such, the stage direction reflects the basic incompatibility of Kerouac's experimental fictional rhetoric with the rhetoric of the play script – at least as he seems to have understood, and practised it. In his experimental fiction, Kerouac performatively (improvisationally) dramatizes his experiences into, and as, narrative. It is a quite different matter, though, to compose one's experiences into dramatic representations for others to subsequently craft into performances. In Kerouac's experimental fiction, the text records and transmits performance. To write is to perform; to read is to engage performance. In his relatively conventional drama, performance is an element in composing the text, but the text is not, itself, performance. It is, instead, a set of fixed elements to be played (as a musician would play the notes from a score) in order to actualize the fixed elements and relationships of the 'text' as script. In the experimental fiction, performance and text interpenetrate and function dialectically. In the play, the initiating performance (the writing) and the subsequent performance of an actual production, while necessarily related causally, are decoupled, and the relationship(s) between these two discrete and different orders of performance and the text that links, yet separates them, is, finally, more dichotomous than dialectical.

The problematic nature of improvisational performativity in *Beat Generation* hinted at in various stage directions is most evident in the scene in Act Three after the Bishop and his aunts leave. Milo turns on the radio, tuning to Symphony Sid's program of bop, and Mezz, who has observed the exchanges with the Bishop without participating, suddenly jumps in: 'Turn that up, man, give me some of that wine. Did I ever tell you show you my cowboy routine?' (Kerouac 2005: 112). As Milo, Buck and Irwin talk on about being hungry, Mezz, despite their seeming inattention, launches into his 'routine' (2005: 113):

> see, my cowboy routine, I come into this dusty old town in Arizona on my piebald pony and get off and go stompin – turn on that radio louder man, that's great, Dizzy Gillespie man! – from the long ride from Flagstaff down to the desert, shake the dust off my hat, walk in the Four Star to slake my thirst, a bittermaker boiling maker maybe two three and there's Blackjack Slim at the end of the bar, "Wal Blackjack it's been a long time" I say.

As Mezz continues to invent from the occasion of the routine, Buck assumes the role of Blackjack Slim, the two square off, and Mezz narrates the shooting of Blackjack, as both Mezz and Buck play out their parts. The routine ends with Mezz reporting that Blackjack Slim, now designated 'Black Bart', 'lies with his gun still stuck in his holster and beer drooling out of his lips' (2005: 114). After which Buck, Irwin and Paul all propose doing their own cowboy routines.

For Mezz, the 'routine' is neither a text nor a composition to be enacted. It is, instead, a kind of riff to be performed; he does so by interacting with his immediate audience (Buck and the others) and by drawing them into to the play(ing), and he does so by responding, as well, to his immediate circumstances ('turn on that radio louder man'), so that there is no distinction between the imaginative space and time of the routine (as a set of elements and moves) and the actual space and time of performing (the immediate physical and social circumstances). But for Mezz, the audience that joins him in his performance and enables it is not the audience that might attend a performance of *Beat Generation*. It is, instead, Buck, Irwin, Paul and Milo, and Mezz's routine is not actually the play (interplay) of the characters; it is, instead, a composed representation of that play/interplay, for actors to mime from the script for an audience that will observe the representation as outsiders to it. This is the central dilemma for Kerouac in *Beat Generation*: his understanding of the genre forces him to compose a representation of spontaneous interplay and thereby to reify and falsify it. The need to locate authority in the composed script means that *Beat Generation* can record Beat characters interacting in Beat scenes musing upon Beat themes, but without actually achieving (or creating an alternative to) the Beat aesthetic of

Kerouac's fictional practice with its textually mediated relationship of the performing writer (I) to the participating reader (you).

Beat Generation, while not a major addition to the Kerouac canon, is revealing and valuable. By offering what seems a relatively documentary portrait of Kerouac on the cusp of writing *Dharma Bums*, it helps us better understand both why that novel has struck readers as so similar to *On the Road*, yet also underscores the need to attend to how much Kerouac's sense of the Beat had changed between writing *On the Road* in 1951 and its publication in 1957. Kerouac's seeming difficulty in fashioning a fully experimental textual rhetoric in *Beat Generation* helps clarify the experimental nature of his fiction in the years between *On the Road* and *Beat Generation*.

But perhaps most intriguingly, the relatively conventional form of voice and rhetoric in *Beat Generation* points to the significance of Kerouac's improvised narration to *Pull My Daisy*, in which he not only engages and reacts to the film's action as he narrates it, but also voices each of the characters in the process. The final version of the narration came from (according to David Amram, who played Mezz in the film and composed the music used for the soundtrack) two improvised performances as Kerouac watched the edited film. As Amram's account makes clear, Kerouac was not working from scratch.[5] Most of the filmed scenes have material from Act Three as a source, and the 'actors' in the film – the painter Larry Rivers as Milo, Allen Ginsberg and Peter Orlovsky as themselves, and Gregory Corso filling in for Kerouac – were all friends. But it is also clear from comparing the narration and the play that Kerouac, as he ad libbed the two versions of the narration, was not trying to reattach the lines of the play to the action of the film but was instead treating the filmed scenes as occasions to re-imagine and reinvent the situations. The script, or rather the cast's filmed improvisations from it, functions, that is, as a series of routines to be elaborated through riffs and play, and what we hear is Kerouac in the process of inventing from the material (the script of the play, the film as it is being screened, and his awareness of Amram, Frank and Leslie in the studio with him).

As we watch the film or listen to the soundtrack, what we hear is not Kerouac representing his text (the *Beat Generation* material), but instead, Kerouac generating a new text performatively – or even more, Kerouac erasing the need for a text through the improvisational immediacy (and multi-dimensional play) of his performing (which analogue tape recording is able to capture directly as the performance is happening and transmit as if directly). The verbal energy and artistry of the soundtrack is completely unlike anything in *Beat Generation*, in part and perhaps precisely because Kerouac, in the taped narration for *Pull My Daisy* as in his best experimental fiction, risks making his own ability to engage the moment and riff from it the centre of his art and the centre of his textual practice – a practice, an aesthetic, in which art is created through performance, not composition and whereby art gains its integrity and power in part by the 'writer's' ability to make the textual medium seem transparent.[6]

Where *Beat Generation* presents a representation of Mezz improvising from a routine, *Pull My Daisy* presents Kerouac performing a routine. This difference between them helps explain why *Pull My Daisy* seems so much more fully 'Beat' and fully 'Kerouac' than *Beat Generation*. It also suggests that for drama not only to be Beat in what is represented but also Beat in how it is 'represented' would require making actual improvisational performance (not representations of it) the play. As such, the play would be play – actual play and not a re-creation of the play from a textual representation of the play. Kerouac was, it seems, unable to make this move in *Beat Generation*, perhaps because he was unwilling or unable to empower those who would perform the script and those who would attend performances as co-creators. He was, however, able to make this move in *Pull My Daisy*. This was, in part, because the medium of tape recording allowed his performative process and the record of it (the resulting 'text') to be, in effect, the same thing. It was also, in part, because he erased the need for either actors or audience as he 'became' all of the actors through his narration, replacing the abstraction of an eventual audience by performing to and for those in the studio with him, so that they were an immediate and actual 'you' to his performing 'I'.

Works cited

Amram, D. (2002), *Offbeat: Collaborating with Kerouac*, New York: Thunder's Mouth.

Holmes, J.C. (1967), *Nothing More to Declare*, New York: E.P. Dutton.

Hunt, T. (2014), *The Textuality of Soulwork: Jack Kerouac's Quest for Spontaneous Prose*, Ann Arbor, MI: University of Michigan.

Kerouac, J. (1957), *On the Road*, New York: Viking.

Kerouac, J. (1958), *The Dharma Bums*, New York: Viking.

Kerouac, J. (1972), *Visions of Cody*, New York: McGraw-Hill.

Kerouac, J. (1995), *Selected Letters, 1940–1956*, A. Charters (ed.), New York: Penguin.

Kerouac, J. (2004), *Windblown World: The Journals of Jack Kerouac, 1947–1954*, D. Brinkley (ed.), New York: Viking.

Kerouac, J. (2005), *Beat Generation: An Original Play*, New York: Thunder's Mouth.

Nicosia, G. (1983), *Memory Babe: A Critical Biography of Jack Kerouac*. New York: Grove.

Howl and the Performance of Communion

John Whalen-Bridge

All the instruments agree that Allen Ginsberg was a fine performer, one who showed genuine respect, even love, for his audience. I have been at more than one reading where listeners who came too late were denied entrance into the auditorium. Ginsberg's response in both cases was to show up late for his own reading – because he first went outside to give a mini-performance to those who would have been excluded. He was a deeply inclusive writer. His performances made available a poetry that could soar, joke, and grieve; they always imply a human touch that reaches towards the audience to demonstrate that no fourth wall, or any other wall, necessarily has to obstruct communication. If you saw a Ginsberg performance, you felt like you were part of a conversation; the written texts, if you read them the way they want to be read, also cajole you into conversation.

In a voice that offered commonality and community (rather than the implicit division, say, of T.S. Eliot's Greek and Latin footnotes or the mandarin tonalities we enjoy in Eliot's recorded works), Ginsberg read in galleries, community centres, libraries, concerts, and university auditoriums. He used the stage to advantage, sometimes performing behind a simple table set with a glass of water and a simple-but-elegant ikebana flower arrangement, in the manner of his guru Chögyam Trungpa, an admirer of Japanese, Zen-influenced aesthetics. The influence of even subtle stage-setting is not to be ignored – one or two ikebana flowers contextualize the performance of a surrealistic rant about the destruction of the best minds of one's generation.

Undoubtedly, the most important performance in the history of Beat literature took place at the Six Gallery in San Francisco on 7 October 1955. Before the October reading, in January 1954, Ginsberg attended a performance of Robert Duncan's play *Faust Foutu* at the end of which 'Duncan stripped off all his clothes to explain the principle of nakedness to his audience' (Morgan 2007: 197) – a highly influential moment, as Ginsberg would later literalize the act of poetic self-disclosure in exactly the same way. Morgan makes this point in *I Celebrate Myself: The Somewhat Private Life of Allen Ginsberg* (2007: 197):

> Years later, when Allen copied Duncan doing by doing the same thing at a reading, people thought it was so outrageously daring and original that it became one of the most often repeated stories about Ginsberg, but Duncan's example is virtually forgotten.

This was the sort of thing that could happen in North Beach, not New York. It does not detract from Ginsberg's own originality – something that almost always disappears when we look at contexts and influences in a finely-grained way – to see how his performance style and poetic style were each influenced by his West Coast experience. Morgan rightly notes that Ginsberg's literary nakedness was a matter of influence and lineage, not an *ab ovo* birth of a previously non-existent kind of writing.

How about the exuberant rant of 'Howl'? Kenneth Rexroth (1905–1982), who was a literary father to Beat writers and master of ceremonies at the Six Gallery reading, wrote a four-part rant against the commercialization and various other corruptions of American life entitled 'Thou Shalt Not Kill'. While Tony Trigilio (2000) places Ginsberg in a prophetic lineage that includes Blake and H.D., Rexroth was perhaps the most immediate literary predecessor in the art of expressing social outrage through jazz-inflected, highly rhythmic free verse. Linda Hamalian describes this poem as an 'indictment of society at large' that 'stands out as undisguised and rhetorical social protest, its message so important that William Carlos Williams believed copies of the poem should be deposited on college campuses across the country' (Hamalian 1992: 231). This poem was an influence in terms of form, content, and also performance style. Hamalian also notes that it was 'not necessarily an example of [Rexroth's] finest work' (1992: 231) and the differences between Rexroth and Ginsberg's prophetic rants can be explained this way: Ginsberg's is the funny one, Rexroth's the more earnest and (therefore more hectoring). Dramatically speaking, 'Howl', in its explosive juxtapositions and self-mocking confession of not-yet-ready-for-mainstream sentiments animates the audience but also allows for role distance. Recall the non-existent fourth wall – Ginsberg's comic role distance creates the space for poetry at once hysterically funny and earnestly engaged; it opens the door for full-throated self-expression, but in a way that precludes narcissism or preciosity.

Ginsberg's 'Howl' was first read at the 7 October Six Gallery reading, but the event was not merely the first hearing of a great poem or a great poet: it was the eruption of a movement. As the title of Michael Davidson's 1991 study *The San Francisco Renaissance: Poetics and Community at Mid-Century* underscores, this movement must be understood as the intersection of poetics and community. In addition to Ginsberg, the line-up included Philip Lamantia, Michael McClure (who organized the programme along with Ginsberg), Gary Snyder, and Philip Whalen. Lew Welch, contrary to what one careless critic wrote, was away in Chicago recovering from a nervous breakdown, and so missed this event (Whalen-Bridge 2006–2007: 93). Ginsberg tried to get Jack Kerouac to agree to read, 'but Jack refused adamantly, saying that he was too shy to perform like a court jester' (Morgan 2007: 207). Shy Kerouac was less shy after pulling on a jug of red wine, and so Ginsberg was urged on 'by shouts of "Go, man" and "Yeah" from Kerouac who kept rhythm by tapping on a wine jug' as Ginsberg, in the second public reading of his life, read 'Howl' (Morgan 2007: 209). Not all great performances translate so quickly into great books, but Lawrence Ferlinghetti reports that on the following day he sent Ginsberg a telegram, echoing Emerson to Whitman, that read, 'I greet you at the beginning of a great career—When do I get manuscript of *Howl?*' (Morgan 2007: 209). (Ginsberg did not remember receiving said telegram, and Morgan doubts it was sent because telegrams were expensive, but it is nonetheless one of those stories that, even if it were not true, should have been.)

Although he continued after this ecstatic career-launch to experience some doubts about his poetic ability, his sexual orientation, and about 'Howl' in particular (Morgan 2007: 209), the rest of the world believes that Ginsberg became Ginsberg on or about 7 October 1955. Morgan reports that Ginsberg's confidence really began to soar in the months after, during which he read everything by Walt Whitman and identified the following as his primary poetic commitments: '(1) a spontaneous method of composition, (2) a long imaginative line, (3) using the immediate consciousness of the transcriber (or writer) as the subject of the poem' (Morgan 2007: 210). The third item is of primary interest, here: Ginsberg hesitated, interestingly, between himself as transcriber and writer. To these two possibilities, we add a third role: performer. 'Howl' can be seen as a torrent of language that seized the transcriber, and that notion adds to the shamanistic appeal of the ranting prophet. Of course, it was a poem, written by a poet, reflecting the poet's growth and the conditioning factors of local and national history. But the text of this particular poem also became the basis of a series of performances. Would self-doubting Ginsberg have gone on to become the key figure in the Beat Movement if he had not performed the poem publicly when he did? It is possible that he would not have. Ginsberg's writing insistently calls to our attention the ways in which our stream of consciousness is a performance that we would seem to put on for ourselves, inwardly, and the spunkily rhythmic word streams also cry out to be read aloud, to others.

We think of poetic performance as a singular event, but let us consider the multiplicity of performance: a poem that is performed or a song that is sung is at once a single thing and a stream of events. The poet standing before the audience verbally enunciating poems *is* a performance: but, afterwards, the poet speaking to audience members – naïve, hip-jaded, in love – is another performance. Performance is never purely a matter of written words or notes that already are fully meaningful, which contain and then transmit the full meaning to the audience through the medium of speech or instrument. Whatever the ratio of prior text to improvisation, performance involves an element of both, and Ginsberg excelled at creating poems that make his audience participate in the improvisation of the present moment. Philip Whalen's 'picture or graph of the mind moving' is not a representation of just the poet's mind: when the experience represented by the poem – or the shared experience of the poem – can be said to refer equally to shifts and swerves in the minds of poet writer and audience/reader, then alienation has been defeated in some small way (Whalen 2007: 153).

The Six Gallery Poets (and later, the spokespersons gathered in the groundbreaking anthology *The New American Poetry*) practiced and theorized a poetics of community informed by Buddhist scepticism about language and concepts, twentieth-century returns to orality as a tribal treasure, and jazz improvisation. This communion is the bridging of subject and object, of speaker and audience, of percept and awareness. The aesthetic experience for writers like Ginsberg, Gary Snyder, Philip Whalen and Joanne Kyger is the momentary escape from identity-bondage. We could say that much art – perhaps even all great art astonishes us – Latin ex- 'out' + tonare "to thunder". The whack of art has more than a little in common with the *keisaku*, the long paddle that is used in Zen Buddhist lengthy meditation practices to help the meditator snap out of distracted mind. Poets like Snyder, Whalen, Kyger and Ginsberg all had long careers that searched for similarities between artistic and contemplative practices, and the theoretical explorations are performed in the poems.

In their relative way, and against the Modernist and New Critical hegemony of the Word-made-book, the Beats put more emphasis on the possibility that the reading was just a bit more important than the book. The poet talking to the audience and living in a community, queer or straight, mad or sane, in love or enraged, becomes an extension of the performance. Some performances are better than others, but the commitment to performing an awareness of awareness that is meant to heal and make joyful is a completely consistent characteristic of Ginsberg's artistic activity, and this characteristic is sharpened and perhaps perfected as he ages. Countercultural heroes are remembered, most precisely, for their earlier work, for youthful exuberance and, sometimes, trite rebellion. Harder to commodify is the kind of performance that survives the energies and willful ignorance of youth, which may be why some surviving 'Beats' scowl at the word.

Immediacy, spontaneity, honesty, and friendliness are the chief characteristics of Ginsberg's style. A quick flip through his *Collected Poems* shows his work to be stylistically unified. Poems written across a half-century in dozens of countries and in response to every kind of social and historical stimulation bring the Ginsberg voice back to us; we can reconnect with that mind when we perform the poem on the mind's stage, so long as mind and art are both shapely. 'First thought, best thought' is worst thought when it blocks revision and refinement (Ginsberg 1994: 13). Early on, Ginsberg's academic critics accused him of being the byproduct of readers enamoured with the famous poet whose random rambling was not unlike their own. Be-ins, performance art, and poetics of the breath were genuinely risky activities. Less dramatically, we can say not every experiment succeeds. Sixty years ago there was a 'Howl'. It was not until about twenty-five years ago – sometime before the mid-1980s – that a treaty was signed in heaven in which it was declared Ginsberg had won and that tribute would be paid to him for the rest of his life.

Ginsberg outperformed his critics by producing a steady stream of poems that were ways of being-in-the-world, performance on the page that the reader could practice like a musical score. We can experiment, following William Carlos Williams' triplet lines, in different ways: the red wheelbarrow is not always the same. Blake's 'Tyger' can be sung in various ways. We become musicians of the phrases ourselves as we learn to perform the pointing-out-instructions in befitting ways, meaning ways that allow us to see that the mind is the cup holding everything else, so hold it carefully. The poems point to an awareness that contains the world. As Emily Dickinson said in her transcendentalist manifesto 'The Brain Is Wider than the Sky' (1924: n.p.):

> The brain is just the weight of God,
> For, lift them, pound for pound,
> And they will differ, if they do,
> As syllable from sound.

Brain, here, is synecdoche for phenomenological experience: it differs from the totality of God – all that is – primarily in that it is slightly more organized. (All syllables are sound, but not all sounds are syllables.) She did not perform her transcendental declarations for a physical audience, but the music survives her, was discovered by a later audience, has been performed continuously ever since. We have to consider the ways in which the performance is between the artist and the audience, transmitted through sound waves in the air, through books, or through pixels. This transmission saves lives and shatters the seven underworlds of homophobia, imperialism, greed, snobbery, competitive individualism, despair, and humourlessness. Sometimes Ginsberg could get all seven in one poem, with a wrathful smile and a sinking, deathward eye that saw and accepted consequences.

Prosaically, and perhaps inaccurately, I have been separating awareness and world, but we become aware of what the art points to because, as Stephen Daedalus would have it, we bump our sconce into it. The materiality of the world is not apart from symbols, since things are symbols of themselves, but we mistake things for things that have a pure thingness, apart from any performance of the thingly world in which awareness somehow finds itself. There is a little risk involved, and it is really the same risk: we might fetishize our own awareness. Without having properly found the certificates and charts or tendons or neurons that link 'I' and awareness, we might get sold a bill of goods that rewards narcissism or leaves us thinking, nihilistically, that there is no reason for kindness, love, joy, or equanimity. Ginsberg worked out sentences that avoided foundationalist arrogance on one side and coldness on the other.

Part of Ginsberg's mission was to point out how we relate to our own stream of consciousness, but the outer dimension of this same effort involved connecting this awareness to how beings in the world treat one another, too often as a result of ignorance. Poems about sexuality, destructive habits, and political economy become another kind of performance: Ginsberg happily took on the role of culture warrior. The verbal performances in courtrooms and on talk shows were extensions of these poems; Ginsberg's performances consistently followed from his estimation about how primordial awareness works, whether or not he ever experienced this directly. How would we know? At the end of his life he said he did not know what was going on, but he always said this with a knowing laugh that made us confident in our own knowledge. That is to say: fundamentally, 'self' is a mistake we make, so it would be a mistake, for example, to hate Jesse Helms. Successfully or not, Ginsberg tried to make senators and right-wing interlocutors laugh with him.[1]

Philosophical nondualism is a tool, the spiritual/philosophical equivalent of a pair of vice-grip pliers, for loosening or removing the conscious notion of self when it is an obstructive exaggeration in the mind. That said, it is still an attention-getting bit of weirdness to even mention such notions – which Ginsberg most frequently did. His Buddhist influences risked dismissal or disparagement from the cultural mainstream. To traffic in such ideas is to get on the wrong side of the Judeo-Christian God, at least as He was constructed by T. S. Eliot in *After Strange Gods*. If performance implies a separation of speaker and audience in a subject/object manner, then it would be absurd to say that Ginsberg's poetry was in many instances a performance of non-duality, though Ginsberg would not have conceded the premise that performance depends upon a strict separation of artist and audience. The tendency, however, is to lionize the rebellious aspect of the Beat writer (just as I have, dualistically and even moralistically, set Ginsberg against Eliot). Our sense of what 'Beat performance' must be risks being caught in an increasingly distant past. If we celebrate the writers' youth, we privilege immaturity over wisdom and rebellion over affiliation and cooperation.

Works cited

Davidson, M. (1991), *The San Francisco Renaissance: Poetics and Community at Mid-Century*, Cambridge and New York: Cambridge University.

Dickinson, E. (1924), 'The Brain Is Wider than the Sky', in *Complete Poems* [1924] Available at: www.bartleby.com/113/1126.html (last accessed 5 August 2015).

Ginsberg, A. (1963), *Reality Sandwiches: Pocket Poets Series, 18*, San Francisco: City Lights.

Ginsberg, A. (1984), *Collected Poems, 1947–1980*, New York: Harper and Row.

Ginsberg, A. (1994), *Cosmopolitan Greetings: Poems, 1986–1992*, New York: Harper Perennial.

Ginsberg, A (1996), *Selected Poems, 1947–1995*, New York: Harper Perennial.

Ginsberg, A. (1999), *Death & Fame: Poems 1993–1997*, New York: Harper Flamingo.

Hamalian, L. (1992), *A Life of Kenneth Rexroth*, New York: W.W. Norton.

Ide, T. (2006), 'Party Line: Allen Ginsberg and Political Expression in Death & Fame', *The Hilltop Review: A Journal of Western Michigan Graduate Research* 2.1–2, Available at: http://scholarworks.wmich.edu/hilltopreview/vol2/iss1/2 (last accessed 5 August 2015).

Morgan, B. (2007), *I Celebrate Myself: The Somewhat Private Life of Allen Ginsberg*, New York: Penguin.

Trigilio, T. (2000), *'Strange Prophecies Anew': Rereading Apocalypse in Blake, HD, and Ginsberg*, Madison: Farleigh Dickinson University.

Whalen, P. (2007), *The Collected Poems of Philip Whalen*, Middleton, CT: Wesleyan University.

Whalen-Bridge, J. (2006/2007), '"For/From Lew": The Ghost Visitations of Lew Welch and the Art of Zen Failure (A Dialogue for Two Voices)', *Connotations: a Journal of Critical Debate*, 16.1–3: 92–115. Available at: www.connotations. uni-tuebingen.de/whalen-bridge01613.htm (last accessed 5 August 2015).

Gregory Corso's Dada-Surrealist-Absurd Beat Plays

Ronna C. Johnson

Gregory Corso may be the least-heralded major Beat poet – he was younger, with fewer publications and a long hiatus after his advent – but he is no less a Beat literary founding father. He was in on the first cut-ups with William S. Burroughs (see Corso 1968) and, interleaving a further graphic element in Beat writing, often provided original illustrations; he composed poetry, plays, and literary myth; he proposed composition techniques and elaborated his Beat poetics: to use one of his favorite tropes, he was part of the whole 'ball game'. Allen Ginsberg confirmed Corso's 'crucial position in world cultural revolution mid-XX century as originator of the "Beat Generation" literary movement, along with Kerouac, Burroughs, Orlovsky and others' (Corso 1968: xiv). Burroughs certified Corso 'one of the Daddies' of Beat poetry; a "gambler" who 'suffers reverses, like every man who takes challenges' and whose 'resilience always shine[s] through, with . . . the immortal light of his Muse' (Corso 1968: xix). Kerouac described Corso in 1958 as 'a tough young kid from the Lower East Side who rose like an angel over rooftops and sang Italian songs as sweet as Caruso and Sinatra, but in *words*'; '. . . the two best poets in America', he declared, are Corso and Ginsberg (Corso 1976: back matter). Grand and sincere testimonials like these by the famous intimates of Beat literature inevitably accompany introductions to or assessments of each other, and suggest coterie aspects of Beat movement writing. Unlike typical literary coterie production,[1] Beat writers and writing indisputably charged outward at the world beyond the scenes that fostered them. Indeed, these self-referential self-promoting male Beat writers could be termed anti-coterie coterie writers: they first met and wrote for each other's ears in the parochial hipster milieu of New York, but also, refusing those boundaries, aimed their literary utterances at the universe, demanding audience and validation far beyond coterie or scene of inception.

Corso specifically rejected 'schools, groups, coteries'. '[T]he only poetry worth anything is inspired poetry', unanticipated poetry written 'carelessly and spontaneously, with much inspiration' (Morgan 2003: 133–34): poetry that is free of the conformities imposed by school or manifesto. This purified poetics is difficult to sustain, for it, too, becomes a conformity or 'school'. In his 1953 *Essentials of Spontaneous Prose* Kerouac recommended writing 'without consciousness' in semi-trance (like Yeats' later 'trance writing'), 'following free deviation (association) of mind into limitless blow-on-subject seas of thought' (1992: 57–58). In 1957, Ginsberg quoted Corso on his advocacy of 'automaticism … an entranced moment in which the mind accelerates "a compositional thought flow … that is intentionally distracted diversed into my own sound"' (in Corso 1968: 9). These claims fit with the influential and relevant first Surrealist manifesto of 1924, in which Andre Breton advocated 'a pure psychic automatism', an unguided surrealism 'by which it is proposed to express, verbally, in writing, or in any other way, the real functioning of thought', itself a linguistic model for the random and freely deviating text (in Esslin 1961: 378). For Corso, thought's distraction is a bulwark against literary conformities responsible for what he deemed 'bad poetry': 'poetry that sounds like poetry' (Morgan 2003: 133–34). Corso did concede a liability of his methods: 'of course many will say a poem written on that [inspired]order is unpolished, etc. – but that's what I want them to be – because I made them truly my own– which is inevitably something NEW – like all good spontaneous jazz' (in Corso 1958b: 10). In 1966, he added: 'I write from the top of my head and to write so means to write honestly, but it also means to write clumsily. No poet likes to be clumsy. But … it allows me to speak the truth. If the poet's mind is shapely, then his poem will come out shapely' (Corso 1966: 173).

Corso's resistance to literary determinacy and his insistence on spontaneity and unhindered composition suggest the legacy of surrealism (Skau 1999: 8), but also indicate energies of the American sublime that interpellated both Kerouac and Corso, even while in the post-war literary world of its Beat generation occurrence, detractors such as Norman Podhoretz found its expressions to be disruptive and hostile.[2] This 'new' unfettered creative expression would be, Corso hoped, 'accepted and expected – by hip people who listen' (in Corso 1958b: 10), indicating a coterie audience. In this Moebius of literary creation, Corso's poetry of inspired, spontaneous art resistant to school or coterie dicta, yet aimed at a certain elite reception ('hip people who listen'), cites him both outside and within Beat literature. Further complicating such distinctions is Corso's conviction that 'There's no such thing as the Beat Generation' or that it is a paradox of nihilism: the 'BG [Beat Generation]', Corso wrote to Ginsberg in 1959, 'was the happy birthday of death' (Morgan 2003: 214), a line he used to title a later book. Refusing category, insisting that he is not a Beat poet but 'an individual, [a] nothing' (Corso 1961: 88) and that

Beat is existential consciousness, Corso the Beat originator can be seen as an anti-Beat Beat poet, an advantage of professed non-allegiance that enhances 'new' utterance and form.

The plays of Gregory Corso complicate these perplexed poetics. Plays are dependent on performance of a text, and do not lend themselves to spontaneous composition or automaticism, unless, like those of The Living Theater, they subsist on improvisation. Martin Esslin notes that: 'The stage is far too deliberate an art form to allow complete automatism in the composition of plays. It is most unlikely that any of the plays we can class today as Surrealist were written in the way Breton ideally wanted them composed' (Esslin 1961: 379); even in surrealist or avant-garde dramatic compositions, deliberation is implicated. The plays of Gregory Corso – surrealist-beat poets theatre of the Absurd – are hybrid forms of multiple influences whose global directives manifest energies distinguishing Beat generation writing from that of its contemporaries in mid-twentieth century US literature. Corso's plays, often short, pithy, and augmented by graphics, challenge social conventions of both Beat in-group and mainstream culture: they are beat and surreal, absurd and catholic theatre of the individual sublime. In this chapter I touch on four: two from 1954, *Sarpedon* and *In This Hung-Up Age*; the illustrated *Standing on a Streetcorner: A Little Play*, written in 1953 and published in 1962; and the descriptive dramatic narrative *That Little Black Door on the Left [a play]* published in 1968. Because Corso often changed his accounts of composition and completion, this bibliographic genealogy is unstable, except for dates that can be confirmed by a work's publication and/or, as in the case of *In This Hung-Up Age*, its date of performance.[3] Vagaries of documentation enhance Corso's appeal as 'black poet' literary enigma, but also thwart his study.

Corso is not known as a playwright, and his dramas are esoteric or obscure, and often hard to locate – seven are acknowledged, referred to and/ or accounted for in archives; not all are published. The published plays appeared in small press or eclectic journals, such as the online chapbook *Bardo Matrix*, or in incidental anthologies such as the collection of screenplays, *Pardon Me Sir, but Is My Eye Hurting Your Elbow?* (1968).[4] *In This Hung-Up Age* has come to recent attention because it is collected in the excellent and comprehensive 2010 *Kenning Anthology of Poets Theater 1945–1985*. Corso's 1954 play was included because it exemplifies a specialized genre, plays written by poets, not because it is the poet Gregory Corso's composition.[5] Given its hipster vernacular and the eponymous character who speaks it, and its saxophone-wielding avatar 'Beauty', *In This Hung-Up Age* signals writing of a Beat poet, but in 1954, Beat poets were not yet recognized as such. Corso noted in a 1958 letter to poet Isabella Gardner that his 1954 play is 'all about hipsters and beat people, long before any of this Beat nonsense came to light' (Morgan 2003: 131). *In This Hung-Up Age* is Beat Generation literature *avant la lettre*, a harbinger of the actual hipsters who will become the infamous Beats after Ginsberg reads 'Howl' in 1955 at the Six Gallery in San Francisco; the book prevails in a sensational obscenity trial in 1957; and Kerouac publishes *On the Road* that same year. In a 1962 'Note On My Play', 'a funny note sure to bug everybody as setting myself up as originator of Hip', Corso wrote to Ginsberg and Orlovsky in 1961 (Morgan 2003: 301), Corso is nevertheless emphatic about the hipster/beat antecedence of *In This Hung-Up Age*, as he says in his 'Note on My Play' (Corso 1962b: 90):

> I can safely claim that this play, indeed document, predates anything ever written about the Hipster and hip-talk, the Square, and the advent of San Francisco's 'poesy rebirth' – all of which came to light in 1956 [Ginsberg, 'Howl'], Mailer 1957 ['The White Negro'] . . . What is important is this: the late seers of Hip (not Beat) recorded their see *seriously*, whereas I termed this play a farce. I saw the advent and deemed it farce . . . [the] entire American social-revolution to come, was very real before my eyes . . . but being that I was truly a hipster, the only hip thing to do was laugh that silly vision straight in the face, and I did.

And, he contends, 'I still hold it a farce' (Corso 1962b: 90) – yet the play is more complex than mere buffoonery and horseplay, its characterizations more poetic, and weighty Cold War era anxieties and prejudices are mixed with the ludicrously improbable situations of farce. Typical of ruling tensions in Corso's work, *In This Hung-Up Age* runs on contending discourses of flippancy and critique: as a hipster, Corso 'laughs at the silly vision' of the 'real' 'American social-revolution to come' that he also takes seriously (Corso 1962b: 90).

Cambridge, Massachusetts, 1954

The notorious Beat generation nascence initiated by 'Howl' and its trial, and the publication of *On the Road,* was unanticipated and certainly unimagined in the experimental Cambridge dramatic arts scene of 1954, where Corso wrote *In This Hung-Up Age* and had it produced, he claims, 'in April 1955 at the Harvard Dramatic Workshop by both Harvard and Radcliffe students' (Corso 1962b: 90; Morgan 2003: 301–302) at the Cambridge Poets' Theatre. The oracular play is coterie-born but coterie-defying, written for, yet a critique of a closed elite audience of academic Cambridge aesthetes and would-be bohemians. When Corso came to Cambridge from New York in 1954 he served the coterie-exploding function of the Beat movement of the mid-1950s, a duty he was especially fitted to discharge. The oft-repeated and undeviating narrative of his early life[6] recounts a hardscrabble youth of abandonment and poverty, and frequent detention, where he 'encounter[ed] Hipster and hip talk way back in 1943 in Tombs with spades . . . [a] good indoctrination' (Morgan 2003: 301), a youth that culminated at age 17 in a three-year sentence for robbery in Clinton State Prison, in Dannemora, New York. There, in the prison library, he discovered his life-long model and poetry master, Percy Bysshe Shelley, and learned real life existentialism: 'I had to deal with men, all kinds of men, caught in a single fate . . . In that time I read many great books and spoke to many amazing minds – men who had spent years on Death Row and had been reprieved – one can never forget talking to such souls' (Corso 1966: 172). His 1968 play *That Little Black Door on the Left* memorializes such soul teachers. Released from Clinton in1950 at age 20, adrift on the Lower East Side, Corso began stealing again to survive (Morgan 2003: 130). In 1951, he serendipitously met Allen Ginsberg in the Pony Stable Inn, a lesbian hangout in Greenwich Village (Morgan 2003: 429, n. 97). Ginsberg appreciated Corso's poetry and introduced him to Burroughs, Kerouac, and John Clellon Holmes, initiating his trajectory in Beat literature.

Momentous though meeting Ginsberg was, the crucial intervention that transformed Corso from street urchin and convicted thief into dramatist, published Beat poet, and Harvard man was the result of the whimsy of V.R. 'Bunny' Lang (Violet Ranney Lang, 1924–1956), a Boston socialite and dramatist, poet, actor, and founding member of the Cambridge Poets' Theatre (in 1951) who met the 24-year-old Corso in New York (Gooch 1993: 280, 279; Sayre 1995: 200) and sent him to friends in Cambridge for a two-year sojourn at Harvard College from 1954 to 1956, which Nora Sayre, then a Radcliffe student, noted was 'probably a deliberate act of sedition' (1995: 202). Lang presciently heard in Corso 'what would soon be the voice of the immediate future', a poet headed to a 'far larger stage than the little stretch of uneven boards' that was the Cambridge Poets' Theatre (Sayre 1995: 201–202). While Beat 'Daddy' Burroughs attended Harvard in the usual way, Corso crashed it; he was unofficially enrolled, auditing classes and using the libraries, installed at Lang's behest in the Eliot House dorm room of Peter Sourian, a young Harvard novelist.[7] Harvard would-be bohemians appreciated Corso's Ur-Beat looks and uncouth, slightly menacing charm, his Brandoesque allure; Sayre reports that he was called '"the black poet" – due to the blackness of his hair, his periodic scowl, and his disdain for detergents; also [for] his black garments . . . [an] epithet hardly intended as a compliment' but one the poet eagerly embraced ('he was delighted: "Yes! I am! I am . . . the black poet"')

(Sayre 1995: 201); Corso's line-drawing of the black clad young man/ protagonist of *Streetcorner* comically accords with this delighted affirmation. Like Kerouac with his movie-star, football-hero dark good looks, Corso had glamour. But real hip, he insisted, was a state of mind: 'the actual meaning of "hip", at the time before the general public got hold of the word, had nothing to do with juvenile delinquency ... nothing to do with creeps who have switch-blade knives or abuse of marijuana' – nothing to do with rebels without causes. Hip meant 'awareness; that almost Nirvana state of KNOWING' (Morgan 2003: 132). Notwithstanding that to Corso a hipster was 'a person in the know' (Morgan 2003: 132), to Harvard he embodied a more literal antiestablishment – which is to say anti-coterie – radical *difference*. Sayre recalls that Lang took Corso 'to starchy [Harvard] gatherings and urged him to be insolent'; and that 'to most of the New Critical section men, he appeared as a symbolic threat to Harvard's traditions, an explosive device that might fragment custom and usage' (Sayre 1995: 203). Thus if, as Peter Sourian speculated, 'Bunny [Lang] had plucked Corso from Greenwich Village to flout the Cantabridgian principles that she herself was eager to derail' (Sayre 1995: 203), she had found her proper avatar.

Cambridge, as much as the Beat Daddies, played a definitive role in Corso's launch into literary history. Corso's extensive readings in the Western canon while he was in prison served him well in Cambridge when, in 1954, he wrote a '12 page' Homeric play 'in verse' (Morgan 2003: 405), one of his first dramas, the still unpublished and never performed *Sarpedon* (Corso 1978). *Sarpedon* might be called a closet drama (Killian and Brazil 2010: vi), one meant to be read, not played on a stage.[8] Indeed, one version of its origins has it as a play Corso wrote as a test of his bona fides, on a dare likely from one of those 'New Critical section men' (Sayre 1995: 203). Corso recounts that 'Mr. Finley, a great Greek scholar, was running Eliot House and I was told by one of his TAs [that] if I could write a Greek play I could stay at Eliot House. I did it overnight. Now the way you do it, you take the Homeric hit, like Aeschylus, Sophocles, Eurpides, they all played on it ...' So the convict-street poet took the 'Homeric hit' like the great Greek dramatists, and wrote a play about Zeus's son Sarpedon killed on the fields of Troy.[9] In one way, *Sarpedon* is the essence of a poets theatre coterie play, albeit a hipster-academic one: it's a slangy portrayal of Hades, Charon, Zeus and others bickering at the River Styx during the Trojan War, written in Homeric-inspired verse for classical Greek scholars at Harvard's Eliot House; Corso called it 'a great funny *Prometheus Unbound* ... [written] all in meter and rhyme' (Morgan 2003: 200). *Sarpedon* is best known as a text based on Corso's 1978 recorded reading of it at the Naropa Institute, on which my commentary is based; it is also a manuscript held in an archive.[10] In one sense, it typifies closet drama's persistence through textuality, but in another, Corso's solo reading of it provides the play a history of (one) documented performance. Thus, as genre or type, it is a hybrid work.

The closet play, Killian and Brazil suggest, is 'like poets theater ... a subdivision of "textuality", bourgeois textuality, and therefore opposed to the avant-garde, director and performance-dominated theater of the '60s' (2010: vi). In this view, as merely words on a page – '"ambivalent" and "ambiguous" [in its] relation to the stage' (Killian and Brazil 2010: vi) – *Sarpedon* could not rival avant-garde 1960s guerilla theatre on the ad hoc proscenium of the streets. However, *Sarpedon* is more subversive than this assessment of closet drama suggests; it is anti-establishment Beat writing. In *Sarpedon*, Corso, an autodidact of 'inspired' literary utterance over 'bourgeois' forms, writes Greek myth in Homeric verse out of the Lower East Side sounds of his poetic imagination. He vowed in a 1958 letter to Isabella Gardner to 'defy the system of academic poetry that has been the death to American poetry' (Morgan 2003: 132). In that same letter, however, Corso also wrote, 'I don't think I'll ever forget the beauty of Harvard, and all the great lovely youth I met up there; all so very different from my youth, and the youth I've known' (Morgan 2003: 131). Like these conflicting simultaneous claims about Harvard, *Sarpedon* is a divided house. Its Homeric verses are peppered with hipster vernacular, ejaculations and formulations that mock and confute the sonorous rhymes: Charon is a 'stool-pigeon'; Hermes is 'this fucker': other mythological figures tell 'sob stories' and are 'bugged'; Hades is advised 'Easy, man'; Aphrodite is 'the immortal end' (Transcription, n.p.).

Passing the Eliot House test with *Sarpedon*, Corso was sent by Lang to the Cambridge Poets' Theatre; she 'made the group shelter' him, insisting that Corso be 'hired to sweep the theater' (Sayre 1995: 200). He also wrote another subversive play there that played to and mocked the arts coterie's idea of its own 'exciting aura of counterculture ... [of] intentional delinquency' (Sayre 1995: 199). '[I]f I were dictator', Corso once declared, 'I'd have poets throwing bombs!' (Morgan 2003: 5). Corso's new Cambridge play, *In This Hung-Up Age*, embodied a linguistic IED, for which an indigenous establishment culture and counterculture – those 'aesthetes who exulted in irreverence' (Sayre 1995: 199) – was needed to explode. If, as Killian and Brazil contend, in the arts 'major efflorescences happen in both a place and a time', Cambridge and Harvard in the mid-1950s, surely an *ancien regime* of assailable tradition, provided 'scenes' of inception that act, they posit, as 'vortices, almost in the Poundian sense ... lightning rods ... to receive the influxes of new energy from whatever direction' (2010: i) such as Corso's anti-academic dramatic compositions.

Written in 1954, *In This Hung-Up Age* was performed either that year or in 1955 at Cambridge Poets' Theatre (Skau 1999: 200; Corso 1962b: 90; Morgan

2003: 301–302). It dramatizes and narrativizes poetics of the contemporaneous *The Vestal Lady of Brattle*, Corso's first poetry book, also published in Cambridge in 1955 via his Harvard connections.[11] Corso reports that 'the [Harvard] *Crimson* … said [*In This Hung-Up Age*] was the best play of the year there; and Roger Shattuck' – an instructor at Harvard who was an editor and the author of *The Banquet Years* – 'told me he liked it very much' (Morgan 2003: 131, 178, 430 n.129). Corso valued, though he did not exactly court, such academic or establishment praise on the one hand, but, on the other hand, he lampooned and critiqued it. In *In This Hung-Up Age*, literary invention and linguistic brio are harnessed in insults disparaging elitism and socio-political toxicity, pitched perfectly, paradoxically, to earn respect from the very objects of their ridicule sitting in the audience – Cambridge/Harvard and the Cambridge Poets' Theatre, its student poets and actors, and its local audience of academics and bohemian sophisticates. The poet mocking the very scene and coterie from which he derives status and occasion thus plays the Beat rebel, but also assists in and resists his own co-optation. Eliot House, after all, dared him to poeticize Greek mythology, and the Cambridge Poets' Theatre glamorized his bohemian 'blackness', each using elements Corso himself put on offer, but for the consolidation of their own coteries and scenes, rather than for the poet's aggrandizement.

In This Hung-Up Age is about a group of Americans on a bus headed for San Francisco that breaks down midway across the continent, leaving them to stew and argue while the driver carries out repairs; in the comic-apocalyptic ending, the repairs come too late and bus and passengers are trampled in a stampede of rampaging buffalo. The play is helplessly funny. Its eight 'farcical' (Corso 1962b: 90) archetypal characters – Hipster, Tourist, Mrs Kindhead, Poetman, Apache, College Girl, Bus Driver, Beauty, as in 'Truth and Beauty' – are set in conflict about matters their types are devised to espouse, driving serious Cold War themes of American exceptionalism and decline, nuclear tension and social anxiety, distress at censorship and stupefying Eisenhower conservatism. The play was first published in January 1954, in the 100th anniversary issue of *Encounter* and includes, unlike in its subsequent publications, Corso's whimsical and oddly literal line-drawings of the cast of characters. Starting with the bus driver in uniformed cap holding his steering wheel, the characters are seated horizontally one in front of the other, all looking or orientated ahead, identified by name below the image in childish printed script. Hipster has a smile and dark eyes under a mop of dark hair – all dreamy and approachable – while Poetman, in evident distress or depression, is collapsed on the floor. Beauty, in the last seat on the bus, suggests a transcendent beyond, with an ethereal nimbus above her head as she plays the saxophone. This nimbus also appears in Corso's drawings for

Standing on a Streetcorner, in which the 'innocent' hero, a 'dreamer', is drawn with messy hair wreathed in a buzzing cloud of 'little stars and angels' except when he is unhappy (Corso 1962c: 457, 462). But Beauty, serene in her poetic remove, is pictured with musical notes teeming about her head as she wails on her saxophone. In Corso's illustrations the nimbus is an attribute of divinity – immortal, mythic, ethereal; the sign of the artist. The line drawings in the 1954 publication of *In this Hung-Up Age* also follow a block of text titled 'Note On My Play', from which I have quoted above. The 'Note' concludes: 'Thank you, Gregorio Nunzio Corso – my full name, which means: The Watchful One, The Announcer, The Way.' 'Nunzio' has variable permutations: to Kerouac it signifies 'Herald' (Corso 1958b: backmatter). Translating all three names into nominatives as Corso does here transmutes the qua-Beat poet to a linguistic fiction, an author function of his own Theatre of the Absurd.

What Camus termed in the 1940s 'our disillusioned age' (Esslin 1961: 24), Corso names a 'hung-up age', the titular trope frequently repeated in the play's exegesis that also evokes W.H. Auden's 1947 poem *The Age of Anxiety: A Baroque Ecologue*, set in a wartime New York City bar with four characters, as well as the global post-war Atomic Age. Martin Esslin identified this resonant trope as 'the attitude most genuinely representative of our own time'; the attitude of the Absurd that reckons the 'senselessness of the human condition' (Esslin 1961: 24, 22–23). These tropes for an age in distress complement the shorthand hipster vernacular of the Corso play. '[M]y Hipster', Corso wrote, 'is a Lower East Side delinquent who talks in "dese dem dose – goil", intermingled with "man, crazy, cool, square, flip etc."' (Morgan 2003: 301); his is a mixed vernacular and dialect. In 'The Origins of the Beat Generation' Kerouac handily recognized this vernacular as a 'new language, actually spade (Negro) jargon', admirable in its compression and complexity, '. . . like "hung up" couldn't be a more economical term to mean so many things' (Kerouac 1979: 362). For Norman Mailer in 'The White Negro', hip is a 'pictorial language . . . like non-objective art', in which man 'is seen more as a vector in a network of forces' (1992: 594–595). Killian and Brazil call this 'vector' a Poundian 'vortex' for 'new energy' to gather and explode (2010: i). As in Mailer's analysis of Hip, Esslin sees Theater of the Absurd as non-objective art, 'part of an "anti-literary" movement of our time, which has found its expression in abstract painting, with its rejection of "literary" elements in picture' (1961: 26). Corso takes both paths. The line drawings for *Streetcorner*, like those for *In This Hung-Up Age*, do figure 'literary' attributes, while *Black Door* is abstract, profoundly anti-pictorial, blacked out in anti-dialogue narration. Mailer's 'vector', Killian and Brazil's Poundian 'vortices', and Kerouac's notion of Hip as vernacular container all find quarter in Corso in Cambridge in 1954, where, as Sayre recalls, his kind of poetry 'was anathema to much of Harvard', and the 'New Critical section men' were appalled by 'the hipster language he imported', so 'utterly new to Harvard Square' (Sayre 1995: 203) – so resistant, perhaps, to the literal abstractions of the then-current fashion in academic rhetoric.

With this play, Corso averred, 'my Hipster is the first Hipster', a Beat Generation American Adam (Morgan 2003: 303). The bus of the play's setting acts as a vortex of conflict, riddled with hipster lingua franca and characters of literalized identities (Corso 2010: 101–102):

College Girl (*to* **Hipster**)   You sound New York.

Hipster   Right on the button, baby. Where you from?

College Girl   From Cambridge, Mass.

Hipster   What's happening there?

College Girl   Did you ever hear of Harvard?

Hipster   You mean the school? I thought it wuz only for cats.

College Girl   Cats?

Hipster (*annoyed*)   Men, boys, guys. God, wotta square.

College Girl   I'm sorry if you seem slightly obtuse to me.

Hipster (*pushing back his duck-assed hair*):   I seen worser lookin' cats.

College Girl   I did not mean your appearance. No. I don't go to Harvard. I go to Radcliffe. I guess you've never heard of Radcliffe?

Hipster   I heard of some things.

College Girl   Yes. Well, Radcliffe is a girls' college; it's juxtaposed with Harvard.

Hipster   You don't say? . . . What's your name?

College Girl   Guess.

Hipster (*perplexed, and bugged*)   Guess? And you say you go to college? ... Baby, you're too much. (*He turns from her mockingly.*) Bon swah!

Hipster shock is lobbed in this passage that twits Harvard's tribal, hermetic culture and its pretensions to humanist values and ethics. In a sophisticated recognition of inequality written the same year as the 1954 *Brown* v. *Board of Education* ruling, the play indirectly – unintentionally – denounces Harvard's 'obtuse' segregation of women from men at the separate-but-unequal institution, Radcliffe College, that, underscoring the point with comedic exaggeration, Hipster has never even heard of. Corso amplifies the insufferable pretension of College Girl in a 1956 letter from his second year in Cambridge: 'I just met the most obnoxious Radcliffe girl. Good God where do they come from? I knew her slightly last year so I went up to her and said "Hello". She said, "Hello, you [are] back. Ah, still wearing P.Y.'s jacket from last year – and R.S's shoes? What [did] you do, come back here for a new wardrobe?"' (Morgan 2003: 5). In real life, insulted by snooty Cantabridgians, Corso in his play avenges his dismissal for poverty, for being the 'black poet' playwright of rags and insufficient personal hygiene, for here the 'Cliffie, not the hipster, is depicted as the clueless, declassee fashionista.[12] But Corso is not facile. The play's themes range widely over literary and political topics, defending Beauty and Poetry, but also decrying the history of Euro America's Native American genocide. Hipster tosses racial slurs at Apache: 'Hey, Tonto, wot's up wid dat chick in the corner, do you think she's really flipped?' (Corso 2010: 99); 'Hey, chief, tell me, did the Apaches really fight like dey show in the movies?' (Corso 2010: 100). These slurs are witlessly addressed by Mrs. Kindhead, who rues to Apache 'How shameful it is that we took this country away from you. If anyone's a true it is you, sir' while also wondering 'Do you live on a reservation?' (Corso 2010: 100). Cambridge fatuousness is a residue on the dramatic discourse of its comeuppance.

The Cold War moment of nuclear threat and the social discomfiture of diverse Americans forced together on a stranded bus index a critical domestic and international moment, the burgeoning Civil Rights Movement, which had a strong hearing in Cambridge. Corso's formative Cambridge sabbatical fostered a prophetic 'inspired poetry' in a loopy prequel drama of 1954 in which the American 'bus' functions as a synechdoche of Cold War conflicts; simultaneously, the 'bus', filled with quarrelling American passengers stranded on the continental plains, farcically under attack by indigenous buffalo, is a vortex of the social and civic domestic unrest that catalyzed the explosive remedies of civil rights activism adumbrated in *In This Hung-Up Age*.

New York 1953: The Cold War Fifties

In *Standing on a Streetcorner: A Little Play*, first published in 1962 and set in New York, the fall-out shelter, the domestic commodity and iconic product of the Cold War era, is a Poundian vortex (or Mailerian vector) of Surrealism, Dada, and the Absurd, contained in a network of Cold War paranoia and bids for nuclear disarmament. The fall-out shelter that pervades this Ban-the-Bomb play obsesses the 'hero ... a happy doltish chubby young man who spends most of his time observing people and things' while standing at '12th Street & 6th Ave.', the play's setting; its 'time is today' (Corso 1962c: 456), the early 1950s of the Cold War. Michael Skau reports that a manuscript for this work held in the Department of Special Collections of the Kenneth Spencer Research Library, University of Kansas, at Lawrence, indicates that the play was once called 'Power' and was written in 1953 (Skau 1999: 214), the year before Corso came to Cambridge from New York: the year of the Rosenbergs' execution. Corso evidently renamed the play and reused the title 'Power' for 'my first free poem' written 'right after *Vestal Lady*' in 1955 (Morgan 2003: 143, 330), a long poem that is tangibly related to *Streetcorner*. Lawrence Ferlinghetti refused to publish the poem 'celebrating "Power" ... because he saw it as "fascistic"' (Skau 1999: 92); Corso's 1958 protest of this accusation to the editor Don Allen also describes aims of the play *Streetcorner*: '... my feeling of *Power*; it's not fascistic as Ferlinghetti puts it; I used the word *Power* to give it new meaning, and to destroy its old' (Morgan 2003: 143).[13] The poem broaches this intention; but *Standing on a Streetcorner* is distinguished by the re-birth of meaning – a redefinition of the signifier 'power' – pitched to invalidate the Bomb.

The play dramatizes the hero's confrontations with people on the street, the offhand succession of these encounters resembling the random happenings of free association. As Corso described the play in 1961, 'a great young man does nothing but stand on street corner.' '"Standing on a street corner waiting for no one is power"', he adds, quoting his poem *Power*;[14] the play's hero embodies this concept of 'power', a self-sufficiency of 'waiting for no one'. The challenge of the play's donnée, Corso notes, is 'to keep people interested in a guy standing on a street corner ... but God what possibilities, all the mad occurrences on that corner' (Morgan 2003: 303). These 'occurrences' or encounters structure the play on a series of revisions in the image of the fall-out shelter that link the story's disparate parts to themes of Cold War disarmament.[15] These revisions, both in *Streetcorner* and those that Corso claims for the 'new meaning' of power in the later poem, defy 1950s Cold War logic, since they work to disarm the arms race and nullify war. Such impulses are vintage Beat generation anti-establishmentarianism, and also evoke the Dada and Surrealist movements with which Corso's early plays are engaged. This play challenges accepted, simplistic accounts of the temporal sequence of those movements. While Andrei Codrescu is sceptical of 'the chronological fixation on Dada as a precursor to Surrealism' (2015: 31), Martin Esslin refines the purported sequence: 'Dada was reborn in a changed form in the Surrealist Movement. Where Dada was purely negative, Surrealism believed in the great positive, healing force of the subconscious mind' (1961: 378). In Esslin's view, Dada and Surrealism are enmeshed, not successive, movements. Their nexus is apparent in Corso's play as the mutually embedded elements of Dada and Surrealism freely mingle in the mini-narratives of the hero's street corner encounters, ultimately succumbing to Dada nothingness in the play's ambiguous open ending: a stark stage direction that postulates a dark limbo of deferred choices.

Corso has little on record about *Streetcorner*, but his comments about 'Power' amplify the play. Foreshadowing a Sixties era hippie-inflected theme also expressed in the play, in 1958, Corso contends that 'in [the poem] *Power* as in [the poem] *Bomb* I am professing love; and I find that my love stems from humor and originality . . . I can condone no harm to man, but I can see with opened eyes the harm there be' (Morgan 2003: 137); '*Power*. . . is a poem of love, of self-discovery, a poem that rose me from East Side Italian truck driver gloom to self, not political self, but ethereal self' (Morgan 2003: 159). Corso's defence of the poem as a force for self-love, spirituality, and existential ascension from the real ('political') to the sublime ('ethereal') resonates with the play's unnamed protagonist, an innocent of ecstatic belief – 'I got little stars and angels in my hair, that's why I don't get it cut' (Corso 1962c: 462) – taken for an indigent even though he has 'six twenty-dollar bills' in his wallet (Corso 1962c: 459); he's a guileless urban observer who 'talk[s] to people about bombs and things, it's what's happening to us in this day and age, isn't it? . . . So it's good to talk about it. Good, all of it good. Everything is good' even when and if it is not (Corso 1962c: 462). Dialogues about the Bomb are thwarted, however, by history and precedent: if the 'question today, [is] to build or not to build' fall-out shelters, a 'PRETTY NEGRO' girl logically notes that the bomb 'fell before so I don't see why it can't fall again' (Corso 1962c: 461), confirming Cold War paranoia and refuting denials of a nuclear standoff. More than a Cold War artifact, the fall-out shelter as civil defence unit materially exposes life's *de facto* enmeshment in death: 'What with everybody so bomb conscious . . . all the babies to come will have to ask what the shelters are, and the parents will have to explain to them, and not many parents can explain death, so the poor kids will have to consult their deaths when everything about them is life' (Corso 1962c: 460). This carefully tuned insight resonates with Corso's unusual recognition in 1959 that 'the BG [Beat

Generation] was the happy birthday of death . . . surely not a death that stinks a body; just an acceptance and an awareness to myself that Death is me' (Morgan 2003: 214–15). The Beat poet finds in nuclear era life eternal mortal certainties. But the unspoken mission of the play's hero – a 'dreamer' (Corso 1962c: 456), street corner observer, naive interventionist – is to palliate that mortal certainty, mitigating the Cold War and its fall-out shelters with seductive visions of a post-Bomb world, the hippie-peacenik pleasure dome of the post-modern Sixties.

In a succession of surreal fantasies of the fall-out shelter as ark or library or love nest, the Bomb is refigured from death agent to love instrument; the 'negative' Dada is 'reborn in changed form' in the Surrealist 'great positive' (Esslin 1961: 378). In these mini-narrative fantasies, the fall-out shelter is discursively reformed from instrument of self-defence to leisure zone, from modern technological anxiety about preserving human existence to an ancient mythic mode of survival: I 'discovered that America was the new promised land like ancient Israel . . . because when the flood came they had Noah's ark and today when the bomb falls they'll have fallout shelters' (Corso 1962c: 459). The absurdity of the fall-out shelter as survivalist haven, its Absurd 'senselessness' as a modern-day ark, challenges its metamorphoses in the hero's visions into 'meditation rooms, love nests and the such' (Corso 1962c: 457). In one such vision he construes the Cold War as innocuous; the poetic imagination of the Absurd negates its martial danger (Corso 1962c: 456):

> Hey, . . . I think fallout shelters ain't so bad, I mean what they stand for is awful but consider this: a nice family owns one and one day that father, all tired from work, wants some privacy, peace, solitude – so he gets up from the dinner table and says to his wife and sons and daughters 'I'm gonna go fall out in the fallout shelter.' You see? It can be put to good use! For privacy! . . . Just leave the dinner table and take a nice book along and close the shelter door, turn on the air conditioner, and lie down comfortably and read!

These are the first lines of the play and they announce resistance to US propaganda about the imminent threat of nuclear attack by Russia, which is interposed by a random passer by, 'LADY', who in a meaningful non *sequitur* cries: 'Everybody today crazy! It's the bomb, it's Khrushchev, he do this to us, make us nuts!' (Corso 1962c: 459). Depicting the fallout shelter as a library to which the American patriarch may retire for respite from his family is comically Surrealist, with its preference for 'expressing essences rather than appearances' (Esslin 1961: 362). Though it appears to be a civil defence contrivance, the fall-out shelter is, in essence, a room for retreat, even if a father taking refuge from his family there is not the self-preservation envisioned by architects of the military-industrial complex. In a similar surreal vein, the punning deconstruction of the nominative 'fallout' – 'fall out in the fallout shelter' – comically interpolates hipster jargon in Cold War directives; Corso's use of Hip beyond literary vernacular and reader litmus test makes linguistic play embrace political reform.

In another vision of the fallout shelter that immediately follows the opening gambit, it is figured as a domestic space for the private sexual enjoyment of females in their pursuit of males. The protagonist imagines (Corso 1962c: 457):

> a young daughter ... maybe she'd like the shelter because what if she wanted to kiss her boyfriend, what a wonderful place for a love nest! See? I mean what harm can an extra room do? ... I don't think the bomb's gonna fall so watch and see: all them fallout shelters are going to end up being meditation rooms, love nests, and the such – you watch!

In surreal understatement, this metamorphosis of the fall-out shelter merges the 1950's lovers' sanctuary with the 1960s Buddhist retreat; it's a stolen kiss in a bonus 'meditation' room. This anticipates, in another stroke of Corso's prescience, the ubiquitous 1960s slogan 'Make Love Not War'. In a fourth evocation of the fall-out shelter, the hero asks the 'PRETTY NEGRO' girl if her parents have one: 'They're talking about it. But we live in an apartment, so where we gonna put it? ... my father said he wasn't prepared to dig a hole in the cellar nohow' (Corso 1962c: 461). The absurd redundancy of digging a shelter in the cellar – itself already a shelter – suggests obstacles to transcending the Cold War. Urban apartment dwellers cannot contrive the detached fall-out shelter as private retreat or love nest and so cannot advance efforts to turn swords into ploughshares that this 'streetcorner' play implicitly endorses. In this instance, the surreal is neutralized by the real. Yet, even in the face of evidence to the contrary (the bomb '*did* fall before!' [Corso 1962c: 461]) *Streetcorner* nevertheless vacillates from the 'big no' of Dada (Codrescu 2015: 31) and the 'senselessness of the human condition' of the Absurd (Esslin 1961: 24), to optimistic engagement and disarmament, a Surrealist 'art more real than reality', making fallout shelters into arks, libraries, and love nests. The fallout shelter cum 'love nest' is materially, essentially, more real than the delusional Cold War fantasy that the shelter is a space adequate to preserve human life against the Bomb's radioactive poison.

As the play's oscillating logics intimate, Dada overtakes Surrealism in the discursive failure to neutralize the Cold War bomb into peacetime love. The wincing cynicism of the play's denouement, in which a cruel interlocutor – 'a tall impressive looking man' whom Corso draws as a dominating dark figure (1962c: 461–62) – accusing the hero of disingenuousness, reinstates the 'negative' of Dada. The 'TALL MAN' to the hero: 'You pretended innocence – that is the only way you could speak about the bomb; say the things you say about it, by feigning ignorance' (Corso 1962c: 462). This blow has impact: 'terribly brought down', the hero 'sags against the street light determined never to stand on a street corner again, determined never to be unaware of himself, of anything, ever again' (Corso 1962c: 462). The trailing repetitions of negatives in this sentence shorten and overlap with each iteration of despair and surrender, evoking, in Codrescu's words, Dada's 'radical negation of art and reason' (2015: 31). The outcome of *Streetcorner* complicates its terms through the inscription of chance and contingency by means of two equally plausible alternative endings. The two paratactic endings, undecided alternatives, introduce elements of the post-modern indeterminacy that characterizes the next phase in Cold War culture and the arts. In a final iteration of a comic repeating encounter, the hero accedes to a child's request: 'He takes her hand, and begins to cross the street.' The last words of the play follow: 'The play might end with a car running them both down or it could end with him taking her across safely, it very well could end that way' (Corso 1962c: 463). These words indicate an open ending, if not by bomb, then by life. The play's denouement of deferred choices exceeds the Dada-Surrealist-Absurd sequence for the anti-metanarrative post-modernism of instability of meanings.

This play first conceived in 1953 anticipates the indeterminacy of the emerging postmodern, for neither of the either-or endings of the play – death or safe passage, also the choices suggested by the fall-out shelter – prevails. The endings are parataxes. On the same horizontal plane of perpetual undecided outcome, they remain in simultaneous play, evoking the limbo of 'Standing on a street corner waiting for no one' from the play's namesake poem *Power*. By gesturing to the emergence of post-modernism and thus surpassing the Dada-Surrealist-Absurd vortex by which the play has skirted admission of fear and threat, *Standing on a Streetcorner* finally registers, albeit indirectly, at its ambiguous, ominous ending, terrors of the 1953 Cold War: the Bomb is 'so real and sad and horrible' (Corso 1962c: 461). In a similar penetration of the real, on 19 June 1953, Julius and Ethel Rosenberg were executed by electrocution, having been found guilty in 1951 of treason related to the passing of information about the atomic bomb to the Soviet Union. A decade later, in 1963, Andy Warhol made silk screen images of electric chairs, but by the post-modern standards of the pop art Warhol invented, the politics of simulated representation voids the real, a post-modern move that *Streetcorner* cannot complete. However, Corso's 1968 piece *That Little Black Door on the Left*, did succeed in the Warholian evacuation of meaning from execution by electrocution. In *Standing on a Streetcorner*, the existential self-sufficiency of 'waiting for no one' in the limbo of undecided conclusions forestalls death's *de facto* place in life implied by fall-out shelters and the Rosenbergs' execution in the year of its first composition.

Postscript: *That Little Black Door on the Left [a play]*

Corso's *That Little Black Door on the Left [a play]* was published in 1968 in a book of screenplays titled *Pardon Me Sir, But Is My Eye Hurting Your Elbow?* (see note 4). There is no record of its performance or filming. It is unclear when Corso wrote *Black Door*, which is likely his fourth play. If it was written near the date of its 1968 publication, it could fairly be called a late Beat movement work, but an earlier vintage is suggested by its marked affinity to Corso's previous plays, hence its salience here. *Black Door* indirectly references experiences of Corso's three-year incarceration in Clinton State Prison in the late 1940s; it is an artifact of Cold War-era violence and the notorious 1953 Rosenberg electrocution at Sing Sing Prison in Ossining, New York; it specifically identifies its circumstances and, accordingly, its style, as surrealist and absurd; it has a 'reprieve' revenge that resounds with the Cambridge comeuppance of *In This Hung-Up Age*, a trademark effect in some early Corso plays in which targets of ire and retribution are identified in objects of affirmative dramatic attention.

That Little Black Door on the Left [a play] is a comic-macabre bombshell set in a prison's Death Row where a condemned man eats his last meal. There is no eleventh-hour reprieve. He is escorted to the death chamber by eight prison functionaries who, because the prisoner's obesity prevents him from fitting in the electric chair, haplessly botch the execution, all of them dying instead of the condemned man. At this denouement, the true climax is met: the play ends with the condemned man walking out the Little Black Door, graced with survival and freedom via a facetious sabotage. This outcome is not a reprieve per se but, two generations after Sartre's *No Exit* (1944), it comically provides an actual – and titular – exit that subverts the stern existential verdict of its predecessor. It may also stand as poignant critique of the controversial electrocution of Julius and Ethel Rosenberg, enacting the remission for which their supporters fought in vain.

The play is a short dramatic narrative of a cliche – the last hour in the life of a prisoner condemned to death. The comic reversal that spares his life while his executioners die in his stead suggests a convict's fantasy, recalling Corso's report of Clinton Prison, where he met 'men who had spent years on Death Row and had been reprieved' (Corso 1966: 172). *Black Door* imagines its reprieve as an absurd mishap, refining the play's gallows humour by an economical implementation of tropes of the twentieth century art and culture movements that Corso worked to great effect in his earlier plays. Surrealism and Theater of the Absurd are invoked as modifiers in metaphorical constructions: the condemned man is 'surrealistically being stuffed' (Corso 1968: 161) into the electric chair, his pinched and pummelled flesh incongruously imaged as rubber and steel, rendering the human form an unconscious thought 'surrealistically' brought into awareness. Theatre of the Absurd is also deployed here in everyday usage of existential misery made literal: the derailed execution of a person too fat to be killed by the state and the 'sad absurd mess', the terrible senselessness, made of this situation (Corso 1968: 161).

The play uncannily reverberates with an unusual event in the history of the Theatre of the Absurd. Martin Esslin reports that on 19 November 1957, members of the San Francisco Actors' Workshop performed Samuel Beckett's *Waiting for Godot* for an audience of 1,400 convicts at San Quentin penitentiary. 'No live play had been performed at San Quentin since Sarah Bernhardt had appeared there in 1913. Now, forty-four years later the play that had been chosen, largely because no woman appeared in it' was *Waiting for Godot* (Esslin 1961: 19). The penitentiary setting of this performance bears on the drear existential crisis of the eternally unfulfilled Beckett characters as well as on Corso's *That Little Black Door on the Left [a play]*. As with the Cambridge audience for *In This Hung-Up Age*, the San Quentin audience provided a real-life correlative of the dramatic themes and events of *Godot* (Esslin 1961: 20–1). By all accounts, the prisoners 'immediately grasped' the play (Esslin 1961: 19); they knew they were the existentially imprisoned Vladimir and Estragon, themselves both the satirists and the subjects of their own satire, just as *Hung-Up* palliated the bohemian-academic patrons of its Cambridge performance who were also the objects of its ridicule. While Corso did not view the San Quentin *Godot*, it is of a piece with the reprieved condemned men, those godfather 'souls' of his coming of age in Clinton Prison, where he learned existential equanimity: 'I left there a young man, educated in the ways of men at their worst and at their best. For this reason I am unable to say anything really bad about prison' (Corso 1966: 173). This evenness fits with the condemned man's calm, untroubled exit through the Black Door at play's end. *Black Door* summarizes Corso's range and progression as a poet-playwright negotiating diverse inspirations and movements – Dada-Surrealism-Absurd, Beat, and incipient post-modernism – that inform his early works.

Conclusion

The plays of Gregory Corso, considered here with their inbuilt, but often unrealized, expectation of a live audience, illustrate the fluidity of skills and artistic vision that characterize more than one writer of the Beat movement. Cross-genre, hybrid genre, mixed media, movement influences – all interact freely in these Corso plays. On one hand, they are Beat generation and hipster antecedents as Corso insists, especially *In This Hung-Up Age*; but they are also, on the other, departures from some Beat writing as they veer from the coterie into Corso's hallmark concerns with the Cold War and Atomic bomb threats, and his history of poverty and prison that no Harvard sojourn could mitigate. His graphic metaphysical concerns and grinding carceral experiences made for literature that exceeded coterie devotions to wield instead protests against mass death, cruelties of crime and punishment, and the rush of modern life observed on street corners. Killian and Brazil note the 'social function' of theatre as 'a public, indeed civic, event [an] . . . instrument by which the body of the citizens could see and experience itself, and most particularly its deepest conflicts and crises' (2010: xiii). This is surely the work of Corso's plays, to critique through a mirror, providing images for civic self-examination of antagonisms and exigencies both. Corso's plays reflect larger social, political and philosophical concerns while giving vent to his own. Warring gods, warring Americans, warring impulses, warring conclusions are mitigated by an edge of comic sweetness in Corso's dramatic writing. That comedy, there in spite of all, is the muttering impatience of the hipster calling for all 'squares' to consider how hung-up conscience can be.

Works cited

Allen, D.M. (ed.), (1960), 'Corso, Gregory: Biographical Note' in *The New American Poetry*, New York: Grove, 429–430.

Andre, M. (1981), Gregory Corso Interview (1973), *Unmuzzled Ox* 6.2: 123–158.

Artaud, A. (1958), *The Theater and Its Double*, M.C. Richards (trans.), New York: Grove.

Auden, W.H. (1947/2011), *The Age of Anxiety: A Baroque Ecologue*, Princeton, NJ: Princeton University.

Breton, A. (1972), *Manifestoes of Surrealism*, R. Seaver and H.R. Lane (trans.), Ann Arbor: University of Michigan.

Brukenfeld, R. (2015), 'Foreword' in R. Schober (ed.), *The Whole Shot: Collected Interviews with Gregory Corso*, Arlington, MA, Tough Poets, Proof Copy 11–14.

Codrescu, A. (2015), 'Against Manifestoes', rev. of J. Rasula, *Destruction Was My Beatrice: Dada and the Unmaking of the Twentieth Century, New York Times Book Review*, 28 June 2015, 31.

Corso, G. (1955), *The Vestal Lady on Brattle and Other Poems*, Cambridge, MA: Richard Brukenfeld.

Corso, G. (1958a), 'Bomb', Broadside, San Francisco: City Lights.

Corso G. (1958b), *Gasoline* (Pocket Poets Series 8), San Francisco: City Lights.

Corso, G. (1960/1968), *Minutes to Go*, with S. Bieles, W. Burroughs, and B. Gysin, San Francisco: Beach.

Corso, G. (1961), 'Variations on a Generation' in T. Parkinson (ed.), *A Casebook on the Beats*, New York: Crowell, 88–97.

Corso, G. (1962a), 'From an Interview: On the "Beat Movement"' *Nomad New York* 10–11: 49.

Corso, G. (1962b), 'Note On My Play', *In This Hung-Up Age: A One-Act Farce (1954)* and Corso drawings of characters, *Encounter* 18.1: 83–90.

Corso, G. (1962c/1968), *Standing on a Streetcorner: A Little Play*, in *Evergreen Review*, 6.23: 63–78, rpt. *Evergreen Review Reader: A Ten-Year Anthology*, 456–463.

Corso, G. (1966), 'Some of My Beginning . . . And What I Feel Right Now' in H. Nemerov (ed.), *Poets on Poetry*, New York: Basic, 172–181.

Corso, G. (1968), *That Little Black Door on the Left [a play]* in B. Booker and G. Foster, *Pardon Me Sir, But Is My Eye Hurting Your Elbow?*, New York: Geis, 159–163.

Corso, G. (1976), *Gasoline/The Vestal Lady on Brattle*, San Francisco: City Lights.

Corso, G. (1978), Reading of 'Sarpedon', Socratic Poetry Rap at Naropa Institute, Allen Ginsberg Library and Naropa University Archives, File name 78PO33. mp3. 7/20/1978 (last accessed 20 May, 2015).

Corso, G. (2010), *In This Hung-Up Age: A One-Act Farce (1954)*, in K. Killian and D. Brazil (eds), *The Kenning Anthology of Poets Theater 1945–1985*, Chicago: Kenning, 95–106.

Esslin, M. (1961/2001), *The Theatre of the Absurd*, New York: Vintage.

Gaiser, C. (1961), 'Gregory Corso: A Poet, the Beat Way' in T. Parkinson (ed.), *A Casebook on the Beats*, New York: Crowell, 266–275.

Gooch, B. (1993), *City Poet: The Life and Times of Frank O'Hara*. New York: Harper Perennial.

Jones, L. (A. Baraka) (1964/1971), *Dutchman and The Slave*, New York: Harper Perennial.

Kerouac, J. (1959/1979), 'The Origins of the Beat Generation' in S. Donaldson (ed.), *On the Road: Text and Criticism*, New York: Viking, 363.

Kerouac, J. (1992), 'Essentials of Spontaneous Prose' in A. Charters (ed.), *The Viking Portable Beat Reader*, New York: Viking, 57–58.

Killian, K. and D. Brazil (eds), (2010), 'Introduction: Why Poets Theater?' and 'Gregory Corso (1930–2001)' in *The Kenning Anthology of Poets Theater 1945–1985*, Chicago: Kenning, i–xiv and 544–545.

Mailer, N. (1992), 'The White Negro' in A. Charters (ed.), *The Viking Portable Beat Reader*, New York: Viking, 582–605.

Morgan, B. (ed.), (2003), *An Accidental Autobiography: Selected Letters of Gregory Corso*. New York: New Directions.

Podhoretz, N. (1958/2001), 'The No-Nothing Bohemians' in A. Charters (ed.), *Beat Down to Your Soul*, New York: Viking, 481–493.

Sayre, N. (1995), 'The Poets' Theatre: A Memoir of the Fifties' in *Previous Convictions: A Journey Through the 1950s*', New Brunswick, NJ: Rutgers University, 195–210.

Schober, R. (ed.), (2015), *The Whole Shot: Collected Interviews with Gregory Corso*. Arlington, MA: Tough Poets.

Schwartz, M. (1983), 'Gregory Corso' in A. Charters (ed.), *The Beats: Literary Bohemians in Postwar America, Dictionary of Literary Biography*, 16.1: 117–140, Detroit: Gale.

Selerie, G. (ed.), (1985), Introduction, *The Riverside Interviews: 3–Gregory Corso*, London: Binnacle, 5–20.

Shaw, L. (2006), *Frank O'Hara: The Poetics of Coterie*. Iowa City: University of Iowa.

Skau, M. (1999), '*A Clown in a Grave*': Complexities and Tensions in the Works of Gregory Corso*. Carbondale, IL: Southern Illinois University.

Stephenson, G. (1989), *Exiled Angel, A Study of the Work of Gregory Corso*. London: Hearing Eye.

Wilson, R. (1965), *A Bibliography of Works by Gregory Corso*. New York: Phoenix.

Unfair Arguments with Existence: Lawrence Ferlinghetti's One-Acts and the Modes of Beat Drama

Deborah R. Geis

Best known for his own poetry and his support of other Beat writers as the co-founder, with Peter D. Martin, of City Lights Books in San Francisco in 1953 – as well as for his early 'jazz poetry' performances (Kenneth Rexroth said that he and Ferlinghetti started this trend [Theado 2003: 87]) – Lawrence Ferlinghetti also ventured at times into playwriting. Yet his theatre work has largely been neglected by scholars and producers. This brief discussion hopes to begin to remedy that by exploring a few of his most challenging – and most beautiful – short plays, accompanied by a sense of how we might read them not only as significant performance works in their own right, but also as texts that go side-by-side with his poems in their style and their themes. Ferlinghetti's avant-garde one-acts have been published in two collections, *Unfair Arguments with Existence* (New Directions, 1963) and in *Routines* (also New Directions, 1964); my discussion here will refer to the plays in the former and better-known collection.

It would be tempting to assume on the surface that these works are 'closet dramas' – plays meant to be read but not performed – and in a different time and place, this may have been true. Ferlinghetti comments in his 'Notes on the Plays' that they were written 'nowhere near a stage', but he then adds: 'Yet they seem to me very theatrical, in the best & worst sense' (1963: vii). On the one hand, the pieces, like many of those by Ferlinghetti's earlier Dadaist and Surrealist European brethren, often seem to be unstageable: it requires a leap of imagination to embody Shooky, the six-foot alligator character in *The Alligation*, or the crashing light bulbs at the end of *The Victims of Amnesia*, and the monologue of *The Customs Collector in Baggy Pants* makes no effort to embrace or seduce its audience. Reflective of the Beats' willingness to take artistic risks, then, is the fact that most of Ferlinghetti's short dramas were, indeed, staged: *The Alligation*, for example, at the San Francisco Poetry

Festival in June, 1962 (directed by Lee Breuer of later Mabou Mines fame) and again in November and December of that year at The Hamlet in Houston; *The Customs Collector in Baggy Pants* by the R.G. Davis Mime Troupe in San Francisco and later by Warren Finnerty in New York 'circa 1965', as Ferlinghetti puts it (1963: ix).

In fact, as Stephen Bottoms explains, the latter production of *Customs Collector* was in April 1965 at Theatre Genesis, where the play appeared on a double bill with Sam Shepard's one-act play *Chicago* (which is discussed in Chapter 18 in this volume). Bottoms points out that the two pieces work together because both 'are essentially rhythmically driven monologues … and in both, the trajectory is one of gradual intensification in the monologuist's mood, from playfully ludicrous beginnings toward an eruption of near-hysterical anxiety by the end' (2004: 117). Finnerty (an actor previously affiliated with The Living Theatre), who performed the play (and who also had a small role in the Shepard piece), delivered such a powerful performance that, according to Bottoms, his 'pulsating delivery of the text' inspired the work of other poet-playwrights such as Murray Mednick (2004: 118).

In his plays, Ferlinghetti is clearly indebted to the French avant-garde and surrealist dramatists whose own theatrical experiments were so critical a few decades earlier. In Tristan Tzara's 1920 play *The Gas Heart*, the characters are 'Eye, Mouth, Nose, Ear, Neck, and Eyebrow' (Benedikt 1966: 132). These figures intersperse a running commentary about how 'The conversation is lagging, isn't it?' (Benedikt 1966: 133) with chorally configured lists and arguments, along with images that celebrate their own disembodiedness; at one point, Ear says, for example, 'I'm running toward happiness/I'm burning in the eyes of passing days/I swallow jewels/I sing in courtyards/love has not court nor hunting horn to fish up/hard-boiled egg hearts with' (Benedikt 1966: 134). In the first of Andre Breton's *Manifestoes of Surrealism*, he emphasizes the importance of spontaneous speech as the literary equivalent of the psychoanalytic unveiling of the unconscious (Benedikt 1966: xxiii). Perhaps most significantly, Antonin Artaud's manifestoes for a 'Theatre of Cruelty' as well as his 1927 play *Jet of Blood* called for theatre to be pure emotion, an uninhibited and unabashedly violent form of expression: 'It is upon this idea of extreme action, pushed to its limits, that the theatre must be built' (in Benedikt 1966: xxviii).

In some instances, Ferlinghetti's acknowledgement of his Dadaist and surrealist predecessors is an explicit one. In particular, he mentions an indebtedness to Artaud's 'Theatre of Cruelty' manifestoes though, he adds, 'I don't love his madness' (1963: ix). Furthermore, he explains that his play *The Victims of Amnesia* came about after reading two passages in Andre Breton's *Najda*. The first one was, 'She enjoyed imagining herself a butterfly whose body consisted of a Mazda (Najda) bulb toward which rose a charmed snake (and now I am invariably disturbed when I pass the luminous Mazda sign on the main boulevards)' (1963: viii). The second one was, 'a man comes into a hotel one day and asks to rent a room. He is shown up to number 35. As he comes down a few minutes later and leaves the key at the desk, he says: "Excuse me, I have no memory at all. If you please, each time I come in, I'll tell you my name: Monsieur Delouit. And each time you'll tell me the number of my room ..." Soon afterwards, he returns, and as he passes the desk says: "Monsieur Delouit." – "Number 35, Monsieur." – "Thank you." A minute later, a man extraordinarily upset, his clothes covered with mud, bleeding, his face almost not a face at all, appears at the desk: "Monsieur Delouit." — "What do you mean, Monsieur Delouit? ... Monsieur Delouit has just gone upstairs!" — "I'm sorry, it's me ... I've just fallen out of the window ..."' (1963: viii).

After Ferlinghetti delivers this lengthy quotation from Breton, he claims that the resemblance to his own *Victims of Amnesia* ends there, but this is a bit disingenuous. In his play, a night clerk at a transient hotel checks in a woman named Marie, who is wearing an 'elegant maternity dress' (Ferlinghetti 1963: 39); they haggle over the language on the registry form. As in Breton's story, she tells him she has no memory, and comes back downstairs to ask for her room number a second time. In the second scene, alone in her room, Marie gives birth – not to a baby, but to a giant light bulb, which she lowers out the window, followed by the same action with a medium and then a small light bulb; Ferlinghetti notes that this scene 'must be played with intensity, in a classic tragic manner, absolutely straight, not in any way to suggest comic overtones' (1963: 45). And in the final scene, a Young Woman (who may or may not be played by the same actress) comes into the hotel and claims that she is Marie and has just fallen out the window; this is followed by a 12-year-old girl (again, possibly played by the same actress) who comes in and asks for the room number, then finally a Baby whose syllables of 'Dada' and 'Nada' obviously have other resonances. The clerk at this point is at his wit's end. He shakes his fist at the audience, saying, 'All of you! With your blind feet! Taking you who knows where! Like as if any of you even knew what brung you in here! Incomprehensible transients! Inscrutable wanderers! Victims of amnesia!' (1963: 53). With this, he starts up the stairs with the baby and a rifle, telling everyone to drop dead. The play ends with a haunting and surreal closing image (1963: 55):

A medium-size light bulb is thrown down the stairwell and breaks on stage. Then a large bulb. Then an enormous bulb. As each bulb crashes, louder than the preceding one, the light on the stage is diminished, the last crash leaving all in darkness; no more feet pass at the windows.

Clock tolls endlessly in the darkness. Train whistles far off. In the darkness a very small light bulb is lowered very slowly and hesitantly down the stairwell. It grows brighter and brighter as the houselights come up.

The light bulbs are grotesque births, but they are also ideas, brought forth or birthed into a world that is merely a way station, a home for transients – and mothered by someone in a state of repressed consciousness or forgetting. Like Breton, Ferlinghetti uses both cyclicity and transformation, both of which clearly have mythological and archetypal resonances, to show the anger and alienation in the artist's struggle; it's not too much of a stretch of the imagination to consider how this would be an attractive theme for a Beat writer. More than that, Ferlinghetti recognizes, along with Artaud, that the violence of an unspeakable or unstageable moment, as well as an assault upon the senses, shakes audience members out of their complacency and forces them to interact with what they have seen. In this play, we have the loud crashing of the light bulbs, the 'endless' tolling of the clock, the train whistling, and the probably maddening image of the light bulb being lowered ever so slowly and brightening as the house lights come up. His other plays often end in such Artaudian moments. In the conclusion of *Three Thousand Red Ants*, we hear an alarm ringing that grows from a 'whisper' to a 'shout' (1963: 18). And *Alligation* ends with '[g]reat vines and leaves' that have 'completely filled the doorway' (1963: 35), then a strobe light in which we see the alligator raping Ladybird; the Blind Indian cries out to the audience for help while the 'TV flickers on in the darkness' (1963: 36). Even the relentlessness of the monologue that comprises *The Customs Collector in Baggy Pants* might be said to be an Artaudian act of theatrical aggression. While a poet like Bob Kaufman, who is also clearly interested in surrealism, uses it for the juxtaposition of incongruous visual images, Ferlinghetti's plays draw more forcefully upon the Dadaists' and Surrealists' notion of a serious play, in which flagrantly absurd and even untheatrical stagings speak to an increasingly alienating and disturbing universe. This is a universe that calls for 'no more masterpieces', to use Artaud's famous cry (Artaud 1958: 74), for a destruction of the commonplaces and banalities of conventional culture.

Since Ferlinghetti – along with Rexroth, Ginsberg, and others – was one of the initiators of what we would now call performance poetry, it is also worthwhile looking at the connections between his short plays and his contemporaneous body of poetical work. Famously, for example, when Ferlinghetti's dog Homer urinated on a cop, the poem 'Dog' was the result; Ann Charters remarks that it was 'conceived for jazz accompaniment as a spontaneously spoken "oral message" rather than as a poem written for the printed page' (1992: 245). The word that resonates throughout 'Dog' is 'reality': 'the things he sees/are bigger than himself [later, this becomes "smaller than himself"]/and the things he sees/are his reality' (Ferlinghetti 1994: 113); also, the dog is 'a real realist/with a real tale to tell/and a real tail to tell it with/a real live/barking/democratic dog' (1994: 114). It's not necessary to belabour the obvious and wonderful image of the dog as the ultimate roving beatnik creature and artist, one who wanders freely through the world and creates his own reality in defiance of conventions: 'he will not be muzzled' (Ferlinghetti 1994: 114). For our purposes here, though, it's even more interesting to see a similar vein running through Ferlinghetti's plays.

In *The Alligation*, a play whose punning title riffs off both the title character of the alligator and the idea of what Ferlingetti calls 'any connexion, situation, relationship obsession, habit, or other hang-up which is almost impossible to break' (1963: 20), Shooky the alligator is kept, figuratively, on a short leash by his owner, Ladybird. Visits from the Blind Indian, a very Pinterian character, warn her to let him go free: 'You say How, you mean How keep alligator pet, How keep alligator baby, How not let grow, How not let free – How keep everything same! How not change, how not see, how not hear small voice –' (1963: 33). In both 'Dog' and *The Alligation*, to confine a creature is to silence the 'small' voice that protests dominant discourse, that urges us to reperceive 'reality' and create it anew. 'Dog' ends with its subject as a kind of oracular speaker, imaged as the Victor Records dog 'looking/like a living questionmark/into the/great gramophone/of puzzling existence/which always seems/just about to spout forth/some Victorious answer to everything' (1963: 115). But the end of *The Alligation*, as mentioned earlier, goes terribly wrong, with the alligator raping Ladybird and the Blind Indian crying out for help; here, the attempt to suppress the wild ends up in a kind of apocalyptic counter-violence.

Another poem from Ferlinghetti's *Coney Island of the Mind*, 'Constantly Risking Absurdity . . ', is a sort of *ars poetica* that imagines the poet or creator as a high-wire circus act: 'Constantly risking absurdity/and death/whenever he performs/above the heads/of his audience/the poet like an acrobat/climbs on rime/to a high wire of his own making' (Ferlinghetti 1994: 96); later, 'For he's the super realist/who must perforce perceive/taut truth [with an obvious pun here of "taut" and "taught"]/before the taking of each stance or step' (1994: 96). Again, the Beat artist is a risk-taker, but one who consciously takes those risks as part of the performance before an audience; his version of reality is a 'super' reality that is somehow larger than life, or more real than what is conventionally seen as real.

We might look at the play *Three Thousand Red Ants*, with its Daliesque title, as a parallel piece in many ways. Ferlinghetti calls it 'a little parable of the crack in anybody's egg or universe, through the looking glass – ontology at its most simple-minded' (1963: vii). The piece is a very simple one: two characters, Fat and Moth (whose names are meant to be shortened versions of Father and Mother, but these shortened appellations call up direct visual images as well), are lying naked in a 'great big bed almost anyplace by the sea' (1963: 3). When Fat finds an ant from their cupboard within the pages of Moth's book, it leads to an existential argument about the relationship between the great and the small; Fat accuses Moth of caring more about her dropped egg-cup than about the 'three thousand troops in Red China that just got drowned in the floods' (1963: 7). At the end of the play, they use binoculars to watch (or pretend to watch; the difference is immaterial here) parachutes descend from a plane towards the survivors of a shipwreck; they feel the emptiness of the universe yet also imagine that through the binoculars, they can see '[k]ind of a – crack in the ice, sort of – Through which to see – into eternity maybe' (1963: 18).

Perception, as in 'Constantly Risking Absurdity,' means stretching the truth and making it 'taut'. It means taking leaps through space and time (the high-wire acrobat, the parachutist); it means achieving a breathtaking act of balance – between the high and the low, the great and the small, and understanding their relationships. And perhaps the most telling passage in *Three Thousand Red Ants* comes when Fat says that they 'Make up [their] identities as we go along, on demand, as needed. Improvised names and faces! Improvised characters!' Moth responds, 'Behold the improvised philosopher!' as she turns away from him and closes her eyes. Fat remarks, 'Improvisational Philosophy ... We're all in a gutter ... Improvising each step, to balance, counterbalance, to keep our balance – before we drop off, and disappear!' (Ferlinghetti 1963: 5–6). Whether in the gutter or on a high-wire trapeze, the balancing act described here requires a certain kind of daredevildom, a certain performative élan – yet it also entails a willingness to negotiate with whatever appears before one in space at any given moment – and here we see the 'taut truth' of the Beat poet or, in this case, the Beat playwright.

Works cited

Artaud, A. (1958), *The Theater and its Double*, M. C. Richards (trans.), New York: Grove.

Bottoms, S. (2004), *Playing Underground: A Critical History of the 1960s Off-Off Broadway Movement*, Ann Arbor: University of Michigan.

Benedikt, M. and G. E. Wellwarth (eds and trans.), *Modern French Theatre*, New York: Dutton.

Charters, A. (1992), *The Portable Beat Reader*, New York: Penguin.
Ferlinghetti, L. (1963), *Unfair Arguments with Existence*, New York: New Directions.
Ferlinghetti, L. (1964), *Routines*, New York: New Directions.
Ferlinghetti, L. (1994), *These Are My Rivers: New and Selected Poems 1955–1993*, New York: New Directions.
Theado, M. (2003), *The Beats: A Literary Reference*, New York: Carroll and Graf.

William S. Burroughs and the Shooting of Joan Vollmer Burroughs as Performance

William Nesbitt

Throughout his career, William S. Burroughs blurred textual and visual parts and media. Similarly, grey areas arise when distinguishing between his (semi-)private performances for friends and other strangers and his (semi-) public performances for strangers and other friends. Records indicate that he did not give his first public performance/reading until 1963 in London (via a recorded message); his first American reading was in 1965, and his first solo exhibit did not take place until 1987. He was neither a reader nor an audience member at the 1955 Six Gallery reading, which many consider the most essential Beat performance ever. In fact, he was actually in Tangier and would not even arrive in San Francisco until November 1974. Other major events such as the Nova Convention (1978) and the Beat Generation conference and its associated Town Hall Beat Generation reading (1994) would come later.

However, it is Burroughs's early work and performance, much of it neither well-publicized nor particularly well-attended – or even designated as public reading/performance events – that provide the foundation for his later work. His pre-professional activities/performances such as 'the routines' were, however, influential to his development and progression. Steven Watson (1995: 248) points out that the sources for *Naked Lunch* included letters to Allen Ginsberg and pieces of narratives and routines gathered from Burroughs's floor and notebooks. Davis Schneiderman (2014) believes that 'the text's best feature proves that what makes *Naked Lunch* so effective is that *it's not a novel at all* ... but a collection of routines and juxtapositions calculated to turn the modern novel into an exploded diagram'. In a letter to Ginsberg in June 1954, Burroughs even goes so far as to speculate that 'maybe the real novel is letters to you' (1954b: 217). Jed Birmingham (2007) believes that Burroughs was more interested in his work on the page: 'The performative aspects of the writer, embraced by Ginsberg, held little interest for him.'

The term 'performative' has special meaning in both the Beat and Burroughsian contexts. Michael Davidson (1989: 20–22) explains that 'public performance is matched by a form of operational rhetoric in which the poet attempts to engage the reader in a more interactive role'. Davidson specifies that he uses 'performative' in the context of speech act theory: an utterance that 'performs' what it describes and which 'uses language to go beyond language' resulting in 'a crucial component of the performative – as opposed to the constative or denotative – utterance is its function as an act'. The performative utterance, then, is both representation and action.

This theorization of the performative is helpful when it comes to defining Burroughs' 'routines', which are often slippery and multivalent. In a letter to Ginsberg in December 1954, Burroughs writes: 'Routines are completely spontaneous and proceed from whatever fragmentary knowledge you have. In fact, a routine is by nature fragmentary, inaccurate.' He finishes the explanation by saying, 'there is no such thing as an exhaustive routine, nor does the scholarly mind run to routines' (1954c: 244).

We might locate the origin of the routine genre during the years of Burroughs's post-secondary education. While attending Harvard, Burroughs and Kells Elvins began to develop skits, creating dialogue and incorporating disturbing images. Essentially, they were developing routines. 'Twilight's Last Gleamings' in 1938 was one of the earliest, if not *the* earliest, of Burroughs's routines (Watson 1995: 14). In *Shift Linguals: Cut-up Narratives from William S. Burroughs to the Present*, Edward S. Robinson (2011: 36) notes that the first time Burroughs used the term *routine* was in a May 1953 letter to Ginsberg introducing 'Roosevelt after Inauguration'. Thus, Ginsberg, who presumably had not heard the term prior to the letter, incorrectly, but understandably, identified this as the first routine in a footnote contained within *The Yage Letters*. Robinson (2011: 36) states, however, that this 'is not the case, as some of the routines contained in *Naked Lunch* actually date from as far back as 1938, but they had gone unclassified until this point'.

In any event, this routine concerns the sinking of the Titanic and the infamous, crazed surgeon Dr Benway, a recurring character in Burroughs's work. Ginsberg (1966: 36) thought this particular routine so important that in an interview published in 1956, he said it 'is really the whole key of all his work'. Later routines would emerge such as 'Talking Asshole', which Burroughs (1955: 259–62) fleshed out in a letter to Ginsberg in February 1955. Barry Miles (2013: 276) identifies it as 'one of his most celebrated – at least by academics – routines', perhaps because academics identify it as a major key to understanding Burroughs's work.

Featuring sinking ships, deranged doctors and humans overcome by their anuses, the routine, then, is anything but. One might summarize a routine as a performance possibly involving composed material with room for spontaneous improvisation involving physical and spoken delivery of material that may be funny and/or serious and/or even horrific but always containing (a) significant point(s). Beyond the literary, the routines served a more personal purpose for Burroughs. As he explains in an April 1954 letter, 'routines [are] like habit[s]. Without routines my life is chronic nightmare, gray horror of Midwest suburb' (Burroughs 1954a: 201).

Despite developing fictional characters; distorting historical events and figures; and creating scenes, scenarios and characters that qualify as outright science fiction, the routines were deeply personal for Burroughs. We might consider another possible source for the routines that pre-dates Burroughs's collaborations with Elvins. Watson (1995: 51) recounts Burroughs renting an open room in Joan Vollmer's apartment in early 1946 and quickly becoming 'the apartment's resident teacher and analyst'. For several months, Kerouac and Ginsberg made a daily practice of lying on a couch and free associating. Eventually, 'the afternoon free association evolved into evening skits that mixed vaudeville routine and psychodrama' (Watson 1995: 53). In effect, what Burroughs, Ginsberg and Kerouac did was create deeply resonating routines derived from the deep recesses of their unconsciousness. Perhaps this is why the routine permeated Burroughs's work and also why 'placed before a camera forty years later, [Ginsberg] and Burroughs launched into those routines as if they had been rehearsed the night before' (Watson 1995: 53). The routines, however, would have implications and begin to manifest themselves in ways for which even Burroughs was not prepared.

In his June 1954 letter to Ginsberg, Burroughs (1954b: 216) says 'I've been thinking about routine as art form, and what distinguishes it from other forms. One thing, it is not completely symbolic. That is, it is subject to shlup over into "real action" at any time'. He proceeds to give the example of Adolf Hitler. He writes that 'in a sense the whole Nazi movement was a great, humorless, evil *routine* on Hitler's part'. The routine, then, has the potential to be an act with real world implications; an act that becomes more than an act, not just an act but an *action*, blurring and crossing the demarcation between make believe and reality – sometimes with devastating and irrevocable consequences. Burroughs would experience this most profoundly on Thursday 6 September 1951, while living in Mexico with his wife Joan Burroughs, formerly Joan Vollmer, from whom he had previously rented a vacant bedroom in her apartment.

There is conjecture and speculation on why, how and whether the act was completely an accident. Various sources contain diverse accounts and/or attempts to review and even synthesize the competing narratives.[1] However, one thing remains certain: Joan Burroughs died from a gunshot wound resulting from a shot fired at her head by William S. Burroughs. All perspectives agree on the following points with minimal narrative divergence:

Burroughs had a. 380 automatic to sell and went to middleman John Healey's apartment with Joan to await the buyer. At Burroughs's prompting, Joan put a glass on her head, Burroughs fired the shot, the bullet struck her head, and that was that. Four people were present at the shooting: William Burroughs, Joan Burroughs, Lewis Marker and Eddie Woods: the accounts of three men presumably both surprised and scared out of their wits. The accounts of Burroughs and Marker both refer to the phrase 'William Tell act' as the means by which Burroughs initiated the sequence of events that led to the shooting, although Burroughs would say, 'she dared me to shoot a glass off her head'. In Burroughs's version, he said to Joan, 'I guess it's about time for our William Tell act' (Miles 2013: 274 and Morgan 2012: 208).

To return to the idea of applying speech act theory to this event, JL Austin uses the term *performative utterance* to refer to acts of communication that not only *describe* but also *do* something. Comprising this concept are three levels: locution (the actual words spoken, written, or otherwise expressed), illocutionary force (what the speaker intends to have happen by making the utterance) and perlocutionary force (the actual effect the speaker, by agency of the locution, has on the audience or those otherwise taking part in the communicative act). At the first two levels of this model, we see contradictions, revisions, breaks and disruptions in the shooting narrative. In short, we do not know for sure what Burroughs said (locution), why he said it or even if he even knew for sure what he said or why he said it (illocutionary force). We only know that the final result, the perlocutionary force, was Joan's death. This particular performative utterance is largely one of non-closure. We find closure only at the last and most tragic level.

Burroughs's recounting of the shooting even constitutes a performance, one that changes and with each narrative retelling constituting a performative act in itself. In a 1965 interview, Burroughs refers to the shooting as 'that terrible accident with Joan Vollmer, my wife'. He explains that 'I had a revolver that I was planning to sell to a friend. I was checking it over and it went off— killed her'. This is, more or less, the official statement his attorney advised him to give to the authorities and in court. However, he fails to mention the William Tell portion and says, 'A rumor started that I was trying to shoot a glass of champagne from her head William Tell-style'. Thus, the act becomes just an utterance, a rumour that Burroughs declares 'absurd and false' (Burroughs 1965: 76).

In a letter to Ginsberg in March 1952, Burroughs (1952a:103) discusses the finer points of securing legal representation in Mexico and comments that after paying a flat fee for his lawyer, 'The only extra has been $300.00 (US) to influence 4 ballistic experts appointed by the court.' We see another attempt to create a different version of events, this time played out on the stage of the courtroom as the court attempts to settle on a unified and definitive performance of the shooting. Correspondence dated 13 July 1952 demonstrates the complication of the shooting in Burroughs's narrative. He discusses the possible inclusion of an additional chapter in *Junkie* (or JUNK as he refers to it) and writes: 'I have inserted references to my wife here and there. She does not disappear.' Since she 'has no bearing on the story', he explains, she is 'only mentioned casually and occasionally'. 'The last reference', as he identifies it, is the nebulous statement, 'my wife and I were separated at this time'. 'If they insist', Burroughs offers to 'insert a drunken car accident and some jail scenes', although he does say that it 'would be an artistic error and does not belong in this book'. Nonetheless, he reaffirms that he can manipulate the narrative account and that 'if they want it I will write it'. There is another option: 'Alternatively they could simply cross out all references to her' and eliminate her entirely from the book. He reiterates, 'she has no bearing on the story whatever' (Burroughs 1952b: 135). He seems quite intent on circumventing or even erasing her and any mention of the shooting.

The death of Joan Vollmer Burroughs had numerous reverberations. Burroughs felt forever haunted by the event. As Miles states: 'Her death was always with him ... Burroughs believed he was both possessed by an Ugly Spirit and that the shooting was a life-defining event.' According to Miles, 'Burroughs believed the Ugly Spirit was responsible for the key act that had determined his life since September 6, 1951 ... Her death also became the single most important motivation for him to write' (Miles 2013: 3, 613; Burroughs 1952b: 135). Burroughs (2010: 134–35) expounds upon this in the introduction to the 1985 edition of *Queer*:

> I am forced to the appalling conclusion that I would never have become a writer but for Joan's death, and to a realization of the extent to which this event has motivated and formulated my writing. I live with the constant threat of possession, ... and a constant need to escape from possession, from Control. So the death of Joan ... brought me in contact with the invader, the Ugly Spirit, and maneuvered me into a lifelong struggle, in which I have had no choice except to write my way out.

'No choice' is an interesting phrase since Burroughs describes his routines as a kind of compulsion. In a letter to Ginsberg in April 1954 he (Burroughs 1954a: 201) explains, 'I have to have receiver for routine. If there is no one there to receive it, routine turns back on me like homeless curse and tears me apart, grows more and more insane.'

In a February 1955 letter to Ginsberg, Burroughs speculates that he 'may yet attempt a story or some account of Joan's death'. He writes that his hesitation in so doing is not a result of thinking 'It would be in bad taste to write about it'. Instead, he claims that he is '*afraid*'. However, this fear is 'not exactly to discover unconscious intent', presumably on his part or Joan's. He says that 'it's more complex, more basic and more horrible, as if the brain drew the *bullet* toward it' (Burroughs 1955: 263). Perhaps this situation is more complicated than victim blaming. Perhaps what Burroughs theorizes is an alternative, sinister performance in which the brain, Joan's brain, covertly orchestrates the entire act. Joan and William are reduced to extras, not even actors but acted on in the same way Joan is. The ultimate agent.

Thus, we must consider the possibility of the shooting as a real-life routine, a one night only opening and closing performance. In *William Burroughs and the William Tell Legend*, Jed Birmingham opines that 'this may have been a real-life routine for them, which eventually had disastrous consequences. What does this routine mean? ... Why not approach the incident like a Burroughsian routine stage-played as a crime?' (2009: 1). Thus, we can consider the shooting of Joan Vollmer Burroughs as a routine, an act, a performance. We can contextualize Burroughs within the tradition of knife-throwers hurling daggers toward captive women and compare him to contemporary magicians/illusionists such as Criss Angel and David Blaine who both successfully performed the bullet catch (a number of performers were killed even attempting it).

His work also challenges and destabilizes performative categories (e.g. what is the difference, if any, between *reading* and *performance*)? Are they completely separate, are they synonymous, or do they overlap? Are all readings performances, but not all performances readings? Are these terms insufficient or too limiting? What else can we use?

What we can say for sure is that the shooting of Joan was the pivotal event in Burroughs's life.[2] Although he did not feel himself strictly bound to his marriage vows with Joan, in the aftermath of her death, he operated outside of the confines of marriage and fatherhood. Their son, Billy, went to live with Burroughs's parents. Joan had always been a source of angst to him and he had not always been a paragon of fatherhood; now, he would no longer even have to keep up pretences or negotiate these relationships.

On the morning of 3 March 1981, Billy died from a failed liver transplant as a result of his alcoholism. Burroughs 'sobbed uncontrollably for half an hour'. He 'had been unable to mend the relationship in Boulder [Colorado] during the only sustained time they spent together' (Miles 2013: 558). According to Miles, 'Billy's illness forced Bill to confront the fact that he had been a lousy father and had badly neglected his son' (2013: 525), and Billy's illness was an occasion for deep reflection for William. Understandably, he may have also thought about Joan more than usual. Miles reports that 'Billy blamed him for everything' (2013: 558). He either did not know how to, or was unable, to have a relationship with his son. He truly could not grasp both how their relationship had got to this point – or rather how it had failed to reach any real point of closeness – and what to do about it. Burroughs was unable and, with a few intermittent exceptions, usually reluctant, if not unwilling, to perform in the role of father.

Shortly before his death, Burroughs wrote in his journal, 'Mother, Dad, Mort, Billy – I failed them all –.' This is an oft-quoted Burroughs phrase. What is not quoted so often is the name after the dash – 'Ruski', whom Burroughs calls 'the actor' (2000: 244). Ruski was Burroughs's favourite cat and one that he gave away to friends when its personality became too disagreeable because of other cats Burroughs had acquired (Morgan 2012: 624). Granted, Ruski allowed Burroughs to acknowledge and reciprocate feelings of tenderness, which was something he was not adept at doing.[3] However, it is striking that Burroughs acknowledges failing his mother, father, brother and son, but not Joan. He places more emotional emphasis on and directs more feelings of regret to a cat he gave away than to the wife he shot and killed. We might call this a *performative non-utterance*. By not acknowledging Joan, he does not bring her into being on the page. He strikes her from the record and converts her from death to non-existence and erases her. Mere oblivion. Sans everything. By not mentioning his first failure regarding her, he fails her yet again. Chillingly, at the end of this same entry Burroughs writes, 'how easy the new S&W. 22 8-shot slides out one to the head. Can mean end of argument' (2000: 244).

Burroughs was always conscious of the performance. In the sentence following his catalogue of failure, he asks: 'Can any actor fill the *living role?*' (2000: 244). After all, being oneself is a tough act (to follow). It is a general truth that everyone is dealing with something difficult. Despite the publicity and media attention given to Burroughs, his life demonstrates that the hardest performance is the one required by our own lives, the personal performance. And so, he plays his part.

Works cited

Birmingham, J. (2007), 'Burroughs Readings'. *Reality Studio*. Available at: http://realitystudio.org/bibliographic-bunker/burroughs-readings/ (last accessed 24 August 2014).

Birmingham, J. (2009), 'William Burroughs and the William Tell Legend.' *Reality Studio*. Available at: www.realitystudio.org/bibliographic-bunker/william-burroughs-and-the-william-tell-legend/ (last accessed 24 August 2014).

Burroughs, W.S. (1952a), 'TO ALLEN GINSBERG', 5 March 1952 in O. Harris (ed.), *The Letters of William S. Burroughs 1945–1959*, New York: Viking.

Burroughs, W.S. (1952b), 'TO ALLEN GINSBERG', 13 July 1952 in O. Harris (ed.), *The Letters of William S. Burroughs 1945–1959*, New York: Viking.

Burroughs, W.S. (1954a), 'TO ALLEN GINSBERG', 7 April 1954 in O. Harris (ed.), *The Letters of William S. Burroughs 1945–1959*, New York: Viking.

Burroughs, W.S. (1954b), 'TO ALLEN GINSBERG', 24 June 1954 in O. Harris (ed.), *The Letters of William S. Burroughs 1945–1959*, New York: Viking.

Burroughs, W.S. (1954c), 'TO ALLEN GINSBERG.' 13 December 1954 in O. Harris (ed.), *The Letters of William S. Burroughs 1945–1959*, New York: Viking.

Burroughs, W.S. (1955), 'TO ALLEN GINSBERG', 7 February 1955 in O. Harris (ed.), *The Letters of William S. Burroughs 1945–1959*, New York: Viking.

Burroughs, W.S. (1965), 'White Junk' in S. Lotringer (ed.), *Burroughs Live: The Collected Interviews of William S. Burroughs*, Los Angeles: Semiotext(e).

Burroughs, W.S. (2000), J. Grauerholz (ed.), *Last Words: The Final Journals of William Burroughs*, London: Flamingo-Harper Collins.

Burroughs, W.S. (2010), 'Introduction' in *Queer*, Twenty-Fifth Anniversary Edition, London: Penguin.

Davidson, M. (1989), *The San Francisco Renaissance: Poetics and Community at Mid-Century*, Cambridge: Cambridge University.

Ginsberg, A. (1966), 'Allen Ginsberg (1966)' in G. Plimpton (ed.), *Beat Writers at Work*, New York: Modern Library.

Miles, B. (2013), *Call Me Burroughs: A Life*, New York: Twelve.

Morgan, T. (2012), *Literary Outlaw: The Life and Times of William S. Burroughs*, New York: W.W. Norton.

Robinson, E. S. (2011), *Shift Linguals: Cut-up Narratives from William S. Burroughs to the Present*, Amsterdam: Rodopoi.

Schneiderman, D. (2014), 'William S. Burroughs at 100: Exploding Five Major Myths.' *The Huffington Post*. Available at: www.huffingtonpost.com/davis-schneiderman/william-s-burroughs-at-10_b_4713165.html (last accessed 24 August 2014).

Watson, S. (1995), *The Birth of the Beat Generation: Visionaries, Rebels, and Hipsters, 1944–1960*, New York: Pantheon.

The Stoop: Anne Waldman's Early Drama

Lisa Chinn

In 1964, Anne Waldman published her play *The Stoop* in a Bennington College literary magazine. Republished in Kevin Killian and David Brazil's *Kenning Anthology of Poets Theatre 1945-1985* in 2010, *The Stoop* is an artifact from Anne Waldman's earlier years of experimentation with various literary genres. 'Poets Theatre', according to Killian and Brazil, emphasizes a physical and sonic range which comes from privileging the performing body over the page on which a work of drama is written (Killian and Brazil 2010: i). In other words, for Killian and Brazil, the poet attempts to write into existence the body and minimize the role of the written word. Indeed, *The Stoop*, like many of Waldman's early forays into theatre, explores many of the preoccupations that Waldman will develop over the course of her career, most capaciously in her favoured genre, poetry.

The Stoop's early critique of 1950s and 1960s Cold War cultural conformity emerges at a time when 'containment culture', or the culture that idealized normativity (in every sense of the word) – most prominently displayed in depictions of the happy nuclear family – prompted reevaluation by Beat culture. Waldman, at the age of nineteen, astutely displayed the contradictions and willed blindness of such a culture. This play relies on a keen misunderstanding and flailing between two generations, figured in the characters of Mother and Father on the one side and Daughter and Son on the other. Waldman also questions gender normativity, which will be addressed in much of her work later in her career. The children resist gender definitions through their 'transgendering'. In other words, the children switch genders so that their parents misidentify their own children. The voice, then, plays a central role in 'displaying' gender in a way that visual manipulation misses. Such subversion of gender norms seems less radical today, but put in its historical context, this play serves as a way to read 1964 as a seminal year for experimentation in Beat theatre. (That same year, for example, Amiri Baraka [LeRoi Jones's] *Dutchman* opened at the Cherry Lane

Theatre in Greenwich Village. Baraka's play is often cited as one of the first creations to come out of the Black Nationalist movement that would sweep Black artists back to Harlem for the next decade.) Beyond its symbolism for the Beat movement, a movement that occluded women as much as it held up a particular type of masculinity, Waldman's play was foundational for her dramatic works, published and unpublished, up to the present day.

However, this emphasis on the voice is as polymorphous as the gendering of the bodies in *The Stoop*. *The Stoop* not only picks up on the relationship between body and voice, but also the vast diversity of vocal manipulation, a manipulation that leaves the voice dislocated from the body from which it originates. Here, I would like to suggest that a term coming from musicology and sound studies may help us understand Waldman's use of the voice, a term that has a long and variegated history: the *acousmatic*. The 'acousmatic', simply defined, is a sound that is cut off from its source (Schaeffer 1967: 92). However, as we shall see a bit later, the relationship between sound and sound source is complicated in Waldman's work by the disidentification of the corporeal body. Thus, while also referring to other early theatrical pieces found in Waldman's archive, my central focus on *The Stoop* shows the way in which gender, voice, and theatre 'perform' an aesthetic sensibility. I will suggest here how the field of sound studies may add an important concept to the foundations of gender studies (and Judith Butler's notion of 'performativity' in particular) and how Waldman constructed a more thorough understanding of gender performativity long before Butler.

Twenty-five years before the publication of Judith Butler's *Gender Trouble*, Waldman uses vocal and bodily dissonance to think about the gendered body. The body as the source of the voice plays a crucial role in subversion and articulation of gender that foreshadows Judith Butler's work on gender performativity. However, Waldman's understanding of gender is much more varied, nuanced, and fluid than Butler's. Waldman shows us that Butler's understanding of the body is only partially formed, because it elides the central place of the voice in the performativity of the physical body. What Waldman shows, well before Butler, is that emphasizing the centrality of the voice as a source from within the body displays a keen critique of gender normativity. In this sense, the Poets Theatre is the perfect venue for highlighting the resonances and nuances between body and voice; *The Stoop* is a central performative text for showing just how bodies materialize through the voice.

The detailed opening stage directions are indicative of the importance of sound and voice throughout the piece. In both the unpublished archival and published version, the work is subtitled 'A Play in One Act', indicating that the space and time of the play are restricted to a single 'scene': the whole play takes place on the stoop within a relatively short amount of time. The stage directions for the opening dialogue are extensive, leading up to the idea that the eight boys have commandeered a space of ownership confirmed by the presence of the mother and father: 'The eight boys are lounging on the stoop.... They curse loudly and lucidly at each other. One boy has a radio blasting rock n' roll' (Waldman 2010: 195). The boys 'curse loudly', causing the very public nature of their words to resonate as a public subversion of social politesse. The radio functions less as a tool for communication and more as a means to alienate passersby while holding their small community together. Thus, the social space of the stoop at once shows the liminality of the boys' existence as not yet adult, while also showing the complex relationship between private ownership and public space. While much of the play focuses on the interactions on the stoop, Waldman's play with interior/exterior, public/private spaces is complicated through the spoken word, which penetrates the dichotomies set up by this material and spatial staging.

The plot of *The Stoop* seems rather simple, if not a bit odd, upon first reading: 'rebellious' teenage boys loiter on the stoop of a New York City brownstone while Mother and Father attempt to extricate the delinquents from their property. Mother's single mission is to make sure the boys leave. The action begins when she returns home from the grocery store. Lugging grocery bags up to her brownstone, she stops to find the eight boys playing games and enjoying themselves on her property, which seems to be a regular occurrence. She appears agitated and overwhelmed by life in general, and upon seeing the boys she becomes even more agitated. The stage directions tell us that the mother is 'overburdened with packages from the local A & P. She has a metal shopping cart trailing behind her and several huge brown bags in her free arm' (Waldman 2010: 195). Yet, when using her voice to signal her own distance from the boys, she cannot articulate her dissatisfaction in words. Instead, she 'sighs and coughs, as if terribly ill with shopping duties' (Waldman 2010: 195). This cough signifies a larger problem: throughout the play, the mother, who is the one who urgently calls for the removal of the boys, is constantly undermined by the other characters in the play. Her sigh and cough signify both her tiredness and her desire for recognition. However, the cough and sigh also signify the mother's inability to make her words *do* anything: the boys do not move as she appears; they do not move when she threatens to call the police; and they do not move when the mother yells at them. Calling for the boys to 'listen' multiple times, the mother never succeeds in getting the boys to do just that.

Unlike the boys on the stoop, the mother is able to command her husband, but only when we do not see her. She enters the brownstone, commanding Father inside: 'Arthur! Come get the garbage ... And get those creeps off our stoop' (Waldman 2010: 197). This is the first instance in which we hear the mother's voice without actually seeing her. We next see the father come out the door with trash in hand. The boys give the father the same treatment. Here, we are to understand that Father has been in the brownstone throughout the first altercation. When the door is shut, we hear nothing from him. Yet we hear Mother grow even more emphatic as she closes the door to the home.

Father's attempts to persuade the boys off the stoop leave him vulnerable to the harassment that comes with his attempts to 'connect' with them by using a 'nice guy' rhetoric that makes him sound spineless. After heeding his wife's commands, Father apologetically descends the steps of the stoop while dropping pieces of garbage on the boys. As we see later, pleading for the boys to loiter elsewhere only makes him more of a target for their ridicule. In this sense, Father, who has the majority of the lines in the play, actually becomes more of a spineless, buffoon-like character the more he talks. While he speaks more than any other character, he also misunderstands and misidentifies his children later in the play, which ultimately leads to his unlawful arrest. This last moment, when Mother and Father are arrested for 'public perversion', is ironic: it is their children, who at the time of the arrest are making out with the boys on the stoop, who are overtly sexual. The parents can only look on, and in so doing, are arrested for the 'crimes' of their children. This last presence of the police recalls the policing of bodies in the 1950s. The paranoia surrounding 'deviant' sexualities, including transgendered bodies, recalls Cold War state apparatuses that still resonate within Waldman's work.

The most interesting aspect of this play is when the children of Mother and Father enter the scene. There is a disconnection between the two generations as the 'transgendering' of the children is not registered as such, and the inability of Mother and Father to recognize their son and daughter beyond their outward appearances triggers a much more nuanced commentary on generational gender politics. The Son enters the scene first, while Mother and Father argue about what to do about the boys on the stoop. Father is constantly rationalizing their presence, stating that 'Boys will be boys, you know'. Directly after this sentence, he uses his son, Morris, as an example: 'Why, look at Morris' (Waldman 2010: 197). Yet, the irony is apparent as soon as the Son enters: he is dressed like his sister. On the one hand, Waldman mocks Father by having him say 'look at Morris', as if 'looking' will tell us that the Son is someone who is indeed a boy who will be a boy. A 'look' tells us that Son is in fact *not* a boy who will be a boy. Father himself does not recognize his son in drag, thus, for him, 'looking' is indeed the *only* way of understanding who his son is. Yet everyone from the younger generation, including the boys on the stoop, the Daughter, and the police, understand Morris to be a cross-dresser.

It is unclear from the stage directions whether Son attempts to imitate the voice of a woman or if he keeps his own voice. Yet, with the direct and often heavy-handed stage directions, it seems as if the Son does not change his voice to 'match' his appearance. This would mean that Father cannot see beyond the surface of things; his surface interactions with members of his family cannot go any further. It also means that Father is 'tone deaf'. In this way, the voice becomes the central physical indicator that should tell us much about the relationship between it and the body. Waldman wants us not only to see, but also to hear, the disconnect between her parents' generation and herself; the voice provides the central source for representing such meaning.

Just as Mother leaves on another shopping trip to the grocery store, Daughter walks up to the stoop dressed like a man. Here, there is a stage direction for the Daughter to speak in a deep voice. This single stage direction tells us that, somehow, the masking of the daughter's voice so as to sound masculine is important to understand the already complex gender dynamics of the play. Daughter's first lines of the play are to ask the boys if she can play games with them on the stoop (Waldman 2010: 199):

(*Boys resume playing game comfortably. Daughter enters, dressed like a boy.*)

Boy   Here comes butch. (*Boys whistle and cheer, again in jest, not threatening.*)

Daughter   (*In a deep voice.*) May I join you guys?

Boy   Sorry, lover, it wouldn't do. A handsome cultured boy (*laugh*) like yourself.

Here, we recognize right away that the boys on the stoop have more of an understanding of gender fluidity than Father does. However, the daughter's shifting voice complicates her interactions with Father: if the male gaze is a form of *looking* at the female body, then what does it mean when the female cross-dresses not only her body but also her voice? Father, of course, does not see his daughter in front of him; rather, he sees Morris, his son. When Father calls his Daughter Morris and asks her to come inside away from the 'naughty boys', and Daughter tells Father that she doesn't want to (Waldman 2010: 199), there is no pushback from Father. The 'son' has more fluidity in saying what [s]he means and following through on those statements without repercussions.

Daughter's resistance to entering the home introduces the penultimate action of the play, when both Son and Daughter find themselves overwhelmed by their attraction for the boys on the stoop (Waldman 2010: 200):

> [*TENSION BUILDS . . . as SON caresses their hair, kisses and fondles them etc. BOYS protest: HEH, CUT IT OUT! HEH, QUEENIE, CUT IT OUT! DAUGHTER STARTS PLAYING CRAP GAME HERSELF. She puffs away on a cigarette, holds a beer can and exclaims: HOT SHIT! She is frighteningly like a man. Game and rock n' roll continue, as SON continues molesting. FATHER is frantic and protests greatly*]

At the very end, the parents are locked up for public displays of 'perversities' prompted by Mother and Father, even as Mother throws food at the boys to try and get them off the stoop. Such a chaotic last scene ends with the police officers taking the parents to another confined space: that of a jail cell. Yet what I find most fascinating about this story is the inability of generations to understand one another; this misunderstanding is put forth in terms of gender disguising.

We see here a performance of the generational divide between the parents and their children's contemporaries. For the father, Morris and Judy are exactly as they ought to be: Morris is a male and Judy is a female. For the boys on the stoop, and for us, the audience, the genders are switched: Morris pretends to be a female while Judy pretends to be a male. This reversal is even more interesting when we think about the spatial placement of the bodies in question. The mother, throughout this whole scene, is inside the home. We cannot see her. The father has negotiated the boundaries between inside and outside and has come out to negotiate the space between offspring and non-offspring. However, the father fails in almost every way: he fails to see that his son and daughter cross-dress; he fails to see the disconnect between his generation and the generation of the next 'teenager'; and he fails to see his own place in all of this. This dissonance between father and children is underscored by the boys who are supposed to be 'trouble-makers'; they 'get' that Judy and Morris have traded their normative gender roles. Judy and Morris finally have the last laugh when the voice is disembodied.

What is significant about this play is the way in which the generational divide can never be bridged, because the father and mother's understanding of the world does not allow them to see their son and daughter as they truly are. This overemphasis on gendered corporeality is structured and organized through the logic of the visual: the father and mother exclude the voice of their offspring as a significant component of the performance of gender. Waldman calls attention to this elision of voice in many of her plays, including *Signs* and *Plasma in the Casbah*.

This elision of voice by the mother and father foreshadows the major problem with Judith Butler's influential *Gender Trouble*. Thus, here, we see that a dramatic work can tell us much more about the provenance of the voice than perhaps even a theoretical work on the topic may produce. Butler's notion of performativity as fleshed out in *Gender Trouble* and her other work written in the 1990s elides *full* corporeality, relying on the logic of the visual to do the work of gender 'performativity' (Schlichter 2011: 33). Butler, focusing on the *picture* of gender as a totality of the corporeality of the dramatic performance, represses the voice. Even when discussing the spectacle of drag (Butler 1993: 121–142), she mutes the very voices that she wishes to highlight. Thus, Butler cannot help us fully unpack this play because she is tied to a type of Derridean *écriture* (to a primacy of the written text) at the heart of which is a logocentrism (primacy of the word). Such logocentrism cannot help in understanding the dramatic works of Waldman, because her works are tied to a polymorphous voice that erupts from her work. *The Stoop* is no exception.

The 'occlusion of sound', as Fred Moten has described it in writers such as Derrida, Lacan, and Edelman, all of whom work within a logocentric tradition, has produced a *phonocentric* deafness (Moten 2003: 43). If we invoke Butler's work in *Gender Trouble* and *Bodies that Matter*, we have an under-theorized marker of voice. We might turn to what Michel Chion and Pierre Schaeffer, in their works on voice in cinema and music respectively, would call the *acousmatic* voice (Chion 2010: 18; Schaeffer 1967: 300). This materializes as a split between the visual and the sonic; in an attempt to make voice and body cohere, the process of suturing a 'non-localized' voice to its bodily source leaves a scar. In *The Stoop*, we can make the relationship between voice and body return to the point that I made at the beginning of this chapter: the acousmatic voice is 'a sound that is heard without its cause being seen' (Chion 2010: 18). The acousmatic voice 'materializes' a split between the visual and the sonic; in Waldman's play, this split is the theme that underpins the whole play.

It is no coincidence that Chion is writing about cinema and our current subject is marked as theatrical. This emphasis on the theatrical can show us just how the physical body and material voice can come into tension with one another in such a way that words on a page cannot do it justice. In our play itself, the voice becomes a problem for the characters because of its disassociation from the visual body. This type of 'mechanic voice' only serves to confuse the father or mother.

* * *

The Stoop was written and published when Waldman was just 19 years old, one year before her transformative experience at the Berkeley poetry reading, in which she decided to dedicate herself to poetry almost exclusively. Yet, we see here the influences that have been present throughout Waldman's long career. She has recently returned to the theatre with plays like *Red Noir*, directed by Judith Malina of The Living Theatre. The production focuses on gender and the ways in which issues of gender fluidity are still relevant.

In an interview with Randy Roarke originally published in *Disembodied Poetics: Annals of the Jack Kerouac School*, Waldman says (2001: 35):

> I remember hearing my young woman – more like a girl – voice and thinking "This isn't the real voice." The real voice was deep inside in my *hara* – and it was a deeper, more seasoned and musical voice – an ageless voice. I realized I would eventually have to find the words to match it – the words would have to grow up to the voice and the wisdom of that voice. The poet's path. It's not that I have to "find my voice" – it's already there waiting for me. I've just begun to recognize it. It's always been there trying to wake me up.

In this passage, Waldman displays a type of unveiling or growing into the voice already existing within her. She alludes to another voice that is hidden or masked by the some sort of physical barrier: a true, almost spiritual, voice lingering within her body which attempts to 'wake [her] up' as if it exists in another dimension completely. Perhaps this is the true core of the quotation: that this ageless, musical, voice is in some sense a more powerful force within the poet's body that transmits the words on the page. She says, 'And I felt in a way once I was speaking the words and making these sounds they no longer were mine. My body was a receptacle. My voice was even woman's *cri de coeur*' (Waldman 2010: 35). In this way, this description of the 'real voice' is played out, some twenty years after writing *The Stoop*, in her well-known epic trilogy *Iovis*.

In this same interview, Waldman alludes to the trilogy when asked about her thought process: '*Iovis* is full of sound out of all those instances as well as structures within structures. And hidden agendas. And others' voices' (Waldman 2010: 42). Indeed, throughout the *Iovis* trilogy, Waldman's lines inspire an unpredictability that is fresh and that destabilizes the boundaries of both prose and epic poetry. For instance, throughout much of the series, from Book I to Book III, Waldman intersperses long lines with excerpts, and indeed at times whole letters, written mostly by her father or son. These letters work to resist traditional notions of a line of poetry and call into question the defining component of lyric poetry. That is, the 'overheard' quality inherent in the 'I/ you' apostrophe of lyric is subsumed under a more capacious category than the personal, intimate, letter provides. In other places, she uses the innovative line to mimic a multi-vocal 'dialogue'.

For instance, in *Iovis* I, Part XVIII, 'I Am the Guard', Waldman addresses Allen Ginsberg and Jack Kerouac in turn. Each section of the epic has its own introduction or synopsis for the section. In this introductory paragraph, she states that Ginsberg and Waldman 'both agree that the angelic writer had realized the first noble truth of suffering & composed his mind elegantly & spontaneously on the tongue to the page . . . She often heard his sound in her head, whole lines even, & many years later is invited to participate in a reading honoring his work at the local university' (Waldman 2011: 269). In this section, Waldman attempts to memorialize and capture the sounds, the 'whole lines even', that she constantly carries with her. The very first lines set up a dialogue, outlined on the page as one speaker speaking on the left, and the other speaker responding on the right. The quotation marks further underscore the dialogic nature of the passages, both of which disrupt traditional left-to-right reading. Reiterating Peter Puchek's keen observations in his essay on Waldman, we see 'subversive play with form, reveling in the polymorphous perversity of the page-as-body' (2002: 246). For example, the text reads (Waldman 2011: 269):

Stop the murder and the suicide!
All's well!
I am the Guard
    Jack Kerouac

                                    You are fun
                                    You are god
                                    You are
                          'Far -out-like-a-light'

Though we have a type of epigraph in the first three lines, attributed to Kerouac, we then have the subsequent four lines that go unattributed. Following the logic of the acousmatic – the poetic body infused with voices echoing throughout the page – we see a type of working through the voice through the medium of the page. This is only one of many instances of a reworking of the body and voice onto the page of poetry.

A final way to understand this reworking is to note the influence of Waldman's Buddhist practice. This includes the Madhyamika creation myth, about which she says (2001: 247):

[It] refutes the idea of solid existence and embraces the view of codependent or co-arising origination. Things do not come from themselves nor do they come from things other than themselves, nor do they arise from both these factors, nor do they come from neither of these factors. Where do they come from? We live in *Samsarodadhi*, or ocean-like world. The strands of our existence come together karmically.

Here, we see Waldman's break with western notions of solid existence. Such a creation myth perfectly captures what I have shown here, that neither voice nor body is rightly attached to a source. The question of a solid existence demarcates the body from the page, the body from the voice, and the voice from the page. Waldman attempts to get away from questions of demarcation, of boundaries, of structures of hierarchy. Rather, her poetics erase all such boundaries, freeing us from the strictures of the modern world.

Works cited

Baraka, A. [LeRoi Jones] (2010), *Dutchman*, in K. Killian and B. Brazil (eds), *The Kenning Anthology of Poets Theatre 1945–1985*, Chicago: Kenning.

Butler, J. (1990), *Gender Trouble*, London: Routledge.

Butler, J. (1993), *Bodies that Matter*, London: Routledge.

Chion, M. (2010), *Le Son*, Paris: Armand Colin.

Kane, B. (2014), *Sound Unseen*, Oxford: Oxford University Press.

Killian, K., and Brazil, B. (2010), 'Notes and Acknowledgements', in K. Killian and B. Brazil (eds), *The Kenning Anthology of Poets Theatre 1945–1985*, Chicago: Kenning.

Moten, F. (2003), *In the Break: The Aesthetics of the Black Radical Tradition*, Minneapolis: University of Minnesota.

Puchek, P. (2002), 'From Revolution to Creation: Beat Desire and Body Poetics in Anne Waldman's Poetry', in N. Grace and R. Johnson (eds), *Girls Who Wore Black: Women Writing the Beat Generation*, New Brunswick: Rutgers University.

Schaeffer, P. (1967), 'L'acousmatique" *Traité des objets sonore*, Paris: Éditions du Seuil.

Schlichter, A. (2011), 'Do Voices Matter? Vocality, Materiality, Gender Performativity', *Body & Society*, 17: 31–52.

Waldman, A. (2001), 'Go-Between Between', from *Vow to Poetry: Essays, Interviews, and Manifestos*, St. Paul: Coffee House.

Waldman, A. (2008), *Red Noir & Other Pieces for Performance*, Brooklyn: farfalle press/McMillan and Parrish.

Waldman, A. (2010), *The Stoop*, in K. Killian and B. Brazil (eds), *The Kenning Anthology of Poets Theatre 1945–1985*, Chicago: Kenning.

Waldman, A. (2011), *Iovis Trilogy*, St. Paul: Coffee House.

Waldman, A. (Unpublished manuscript, undated), 'Plasma in the Casbah' and 'The Signs', Box 22, Anne Waldman Papers 1945–2002, Special Collections Library, University of Michigan (last accessed 21 April 2015).

Part Two

The 'Afro-Beats'

Amiri Baraka's Revolutionary Theatre: Black Power Politics, Avant-Garde Poetics

Jimmy Fazzino

The first and only novel by Amiri Baraka (who then went by the name of LeRoi Jones), *The System of Dante's Hell* (1965), has its origins in the play *The Eighth Ditch*, which was performed as part of the inaugural bill of the New York Poets Theatre in the fall of 1961 (Diggory 2009: 243). Jones was a co-founder of the theatre along with Alan Marlowe, James Waring, and Diane di Prima, with whom he edited the 'newsletter' *The Floating Bear*. The New York Poets Theatre, like *Floating Bear*, was an important outlet and meeting ground for Beat, Black Mountain and New York School writers and artists. Jones, di Prima, Michael McClure, Robert Duncan, John Wieners and Frank O'Hara all had their work performed there or at its second incarnation in 1964 at the New Bowery Theatre.

The Poets Theatre is a prime example of how the Beat movement intersected with other key literary and artistic developments of the era: in particular how Jones and di Prima were integral in fostering what di Prima has described as 'one big jam session' (2001: 254). Jones's days in Greenwich Village were numbered, though, and his involvement with Poets Theatre would become just one step among many others over the course of a long and varied career whose only constant was constant evolution. The specific trajectory of this career – most notably the transition from LeRoi Jones to Amiri Baraka, from bohemian beatnik to black power revolutionary – has been the focus of much of the scholarship on Jones/Baraka and led to a periodization of his work. William Harris (1985: xvii–xxx) has written about Jones's Beat period during the late 1950s and early 1960s, his black nationalist period beginning in the mid-1960s, and his third-world Marxist period, which flowered in the mid-1970s and, to a certain extent, stayed with him for the rest of his life. Harris adds to these a 'transitional period' (1963–1965) during which time he produced some of his most important and widely studied poetry (*The Dead Lecturer*) and drama (*Dutchman, The Slave*).

Although Harris's categories are useful, I want, instead, to read Baraka's career dialectically (which is only fitting, considering his longstanding commitment to 'Marxism-Leninism-Mao Tse-Tung Thought' [Baraka 1982: 4–10]), charting the ways in which earlier themes and concerns are retained, even as they are transformed, in later phases of his career. Baraka's turn to black cultural nationalism required not only a rejection but also a sublation of his Beat and avant-garde aesthetics. Yet to emphasize continuity rather than disjuncture across Baraka's oeuvre is to go against the grain of conventional wisdom about the poet and playwright. This consensus view is well represented by Werner Sollors in his still-authoritative *Amiri Baraka/ LeRoi Jones: The Quest for a 'Populist Modernism'* (1978), where Sollors equates Baraka's youthful 'avant-gardism' with a petulant, apolitical narcissism that the author must outgrow before getting down to the serious business of cultural nationalism and world revolution.[1] According to Sollors, when Baraka leaves Greenwich Village for Harlem after the death of Malcolm X in 1965, his departure marks a clean break with his Beat peers and the avant-garde influences they once shared.

In Baraka's writing practice and self-conception as an artist, black cultural nationalism is not incompatible with the legacies of the European avant-garde; rather, the two continually reinforce one another. In this regard, Baraka can be compared to another African American poet associated with the Beat Generation: Ted Joans. A poet, painter and jazz trumpeter from Illinois, Joans made a name for himself as the archetypal hipster figure in the same Greenwich Village bohemian milieu that fostered Baraka's earliest work. He named Langston Hughes and André Breton as his spiritual father figures; he had the distinction of being a rare American (and the only African American) to be tapped by Breton to join the Surrealist group. As Michel Fabre writes (1993: 308): 'By defining himself as a black surrealist, Joans emphasized the link between the open, creative, *weltanschauung* proclaimed by the French avant-garde of the 1920s and the soul-expanding force of black power.' The affinities between his surrealist and pan-Africanist commitments are even more pointed than that. As Fabre notes (1993: 314), Joans 'was happy to learn that, during the 1931 Exposition Coloniale, the Paris surrealists had opened an anticolonial exhibit displaying European "tribal fetishes" like Bibles, crucifixes, and stereotyped images of blacks of the kind found on Banania cocoa boxes'. Joans's *Black Manifesto* (1971) deserves to be recognized as a major statement both of and on the black power era.

Racial politics and avant-garde poetics are similarly aligned in Baraka's work. Aldon Nielsen, who places Baraka at the centre of his encyclopaedic study of African American experimental writing, *Black Chant* (whose title comes from a line in Baraka's major poem 'Black Dada Nihilismus'), cites one interview in which Baraka explains (Nielsen 1997: 49), 'I was always interested in Surrealism and Expressionism, and I think the reason was to really try to get below the surface of things. . . . The Civil Rights Movement, it's the same thing essentially, trying to get below the surface of things, trying to get below the norm, the everyday, the status quo, which was finally unacceptable, just unacceptable.' For Baraka, concludes Nielsen (1997: 49), surrealism possesses 'a political as well as an aesthetic logic'. The greatest lesson taught by the avant-garde to Baraka and countless others, and what all true revolutionaries know, is that politics and aesthetics are inseparable. Baraka's time in Cuba showed him that radical art achieved without reference to an outside world is mere posturing. The Black Arts movement will be founded on the premise that radical politics without a sustaining vision provided by the arts will fail to awaken those who most need to hear its message. Baraka's work recapitulates the avant-garde's founding gesture of abolishing the distinction between art and politics; once this project is initiated, it will inevitably look beyond the United States alone, leading him instead to a critique of racism and imperialism wherever they occur.

Like many in his generation, Baraka eventually grew impatient and dissatisfied with the mainstream civil rights movement in the United States. His frustration dates at least as far back as his 1960 trip to Cuba. Travelling with a group of African American intellectuals under the banner of the 'Fair Play for Cuba' committee, his visit granted him a new perspective on the parochialism and ineffectualness of racial discourse back home. Also travelling with the group was Robert Williams, the controversial NAACP head from North Carolina who had recently made waves by arming the local African American community against threats from the Klan. Williams's 1962 book *Negroes with Guns* would inspire the Black Panthers. His militant philosophy was something that Baraka began to find more and more appealing as the 1960s wore on. His influence is clearly visible in Baraka's 1967 agitprop play *Arm Yourself or Harm Yourself: A Message of Self-Defense for Black Men*.

Baraka does not abandon civil rights so much as put it to more radical and provocative uses and the same can be said of his commitment to *la revolution surréaliste*. In Joanna Pawlik's study of Beat surrealism, she points out that Baraka, Joans and Bob Kaufman differ from their white Beat peers in that André Breton, not Antonin Artaud, makes a bigger impact on their work. She writes (2011: 223): 'For Joans, and to a certain extent for fellow black Beat writers Bob Kaufman and Amiri Baraka, it was not the private "limit experiences" suggested by Artaud's work and biography which underwrote the postwar currency of surrealist modernism, but the anti-colonialism and racial politics of Bretonian surrealism.' Citing Nielsen and others, Pawlik concludes (2011: 223): 'Black Beat writers' engagement with the movement was more explicitly political and marked by a keener internationalist sensibility than their white contemporaries.' While Baraka's conception of the Revolutionary Theatre and his productions at BARTS and Spirit House are all marked by the influence of Artaud, his most celebrated play, *Dutchman* (1964), is indeed deeply indebted to Bretonian surrealism.

The single act (with two scenes) of *Dutchman* centers on the sexually and racially charged interactions between Clay, a self-proclaimed 'Black Baudelaire,' and the white Lula on a New York subway car. Clay and the older woman begin flirting before Lula starts taunting him mercilessly. She calls him 'Uncle Thomas Woolly-Head' and 'liver-lipped white man' (2001: 32) and things reach a fever pitch until, at the play's climax, Clay explodes into a several-page-long soliloquy full of pure invective directed at Lula most proximally but really aimed at white America. It may be Clay who threatens bloody murder on behalf of all 'blues people' (2001: 36) but, in a final twist, it is Lula who takes the decisive action and stabs Clay to death. A brief denouement resets the action, so to speak, with another young black man, another Clay, boarding the train, emphasizing the much-remarked ritual atmosphere of the play.

Clay's monologue is remarkable for, among other things, how it translates into specifically racialized terms in Breton's infamous dictum from the *Second Manifesto of Surrealism* that 'the simplest Surrealist act consists of dashing down into the street, pistol in hand, and firing blindly, as fast as you can pull the trigger, into the crowd' (1969: 125). At the same time, he proposes a provocative theory of black art. He says: 'Charlie Parker? Charlie Parker. All the hip white boys scream for Bird. And Bird saying, "Up your ass, feeble-minded ofay! Up your ass." And they sit there talking of the tortured genius of Charlie Parker. Bird would've played not a note of music if he just walked up to East Sixty-seventh Street and killed the first ten white people he saw. Not a note!' (2001: 35). The notion that Charlie Parker's music (and Clay's poetry) is a sublimation of the artist's murderous impulses gives us a way to read the performative violence that fills Baraka's own drama and verse during the black nationalist period. He would repeatedly claim that he was advocating for *real violence* committed upon a racist society; in fact, he tells Werner Sollors that this is what sets him apart from Artaud and the Theatre of Cruelty: Artaud confines his violent spectacle to the stage, while Baraka calls for violence *in the streets*. Should we take his claims at face value? To the extent that Clay is a stand-in for Baraka himself at a crucial time in his progression as an artist and an erstwhile revolutionary, it is fair to say that Baraka means his Black Arts theatre to prompt a cathartic experience among his African American audience members.[2]

Baraka will refer to Clay along with other protagonists in his 1964 manifesto 'The Revolutionary Theatre' (2009: 237), writing:

> The Revolutionary Theatre must Attack and Accuse anything that can be accused and attacked. It must Accuse and Attack because it is a theatre of Victims. It looks at the sky with the victims' eyes, and moves the victims to look at the strength in their minds and their bodies. Clay, in *Dutchman*, Ray in *The Toilet*, Walker in *The Slave*, are all victims. In the Western sense they could be heroes.

The author appears to be mocking the West, and the tradition of Western tragedy in particular, for its long tradition of victim-heroes – at the end of his manifesto, he contrasts the 'new heroes' of the Revolutionary Theatre with 'the weak Hamlets debating whether or not they are ready to die for what's on their minds' (2009: 240–241) – although it is unclear how Baraka's theatre isn't guilty of a similar *ressentiment*. Dubious about Baraka's entire project as an artist and intellectual, Jerry Gafio Watts (2001: 172–173) asks, '[H]ow could a revolutionary theater be a theater of victims? Unlike revolutionaries, victims are the objects, not the subjects, of history. Victims are locked in a struggle for the recognition of their plight by their victimizers. The protest orientation of Jones's revolutionary theater gives his drama a victim-status orientation, even though Jones uses the word *victim* as a metaphor for the "oppressed"'.

I agree with Watts that it is difficult to square Baraka's emphasis on the victim status of his protagonists with the earthshaking ambitions of the Revolutionary Theatre – unless, that is, we read Baraka's intentions dialectically, whereby works like *Dutchman*, *The Toilet* and *The Slave* remain pre-revolutionary, with their 'heroes' victims to be redeemed by the properly revolutionary theatre to come. Watts's excoriation of Baraka's manifesto continues for several more pages, however, and, like the character in Prince Hamlet's play within a play, he protests too much. Werner Sollors has taken a different tack, reading Clay's significance in allegorical terms. Kimberly Benston (1976: 155–163) has also discussed the mythic and allegorical content of the play, but while Benston reads it as historical and religious allegory (e.g. Clay as Adam and apple-eating Lula as Eve), Sollors additionally posits a more intimate relationship having to do with the author's struggle to grow from Beat bohemian to black power revolutionary.

Sollors (1978: 123) calls *Dutchman* 'a drama of the self'. As such, it remains to some extent locked into the narcissistic concerns that define Baraka's early, 'expressive' poetry and prose. At the same time, what *Dutchman* dramatizes is the playwright's groping toward a future black art that moves him beyond white bohemia and its ineffectual (because it is merely cultural or aesthetic) protest against the bourgeois establishment. Sollors (1978: 127) sets up the core problematic: 'In the central scene of *Dutchman*, Clay, who once thought of himself as a Black Baudelaire, has become a Black Breton; and his address is not merely a racial address in the tradition of Frantz Fanon, but also shows strong affinities to André Breton's "Second Manifesto of Surrealism" ... Clay may thus be seen "surrealizing" Black nationalism and "ethnicizing" surrealism.' How, then, to read Clay's death? Does it represent Baraka's rejection of surrealism and the avant-garde – with the author of *Preface to a Twenty Volume Suicide Note* (1961) killing off a part of himself through the murder of his fictional avatar? To the extent, however, that Clay is a *tragic* figure, undone like Hamlet by his own lack of resolve and an unwillingness to enact the violence he threatens, his death instead announces Baraka's reaffirmed commitment to follow Breton's lead and 'make for [him]self a tenet of total revolt, complete insubordination, of sabotage according to rule', as Breton puts it in the 'Second Manifesto'.[3]

After the success of *Dutchman*, the promising young playwright was commissioned by the *New York Times* to write an essay on the contemporary theatre. What they got was evidently not what they were looking for, and the *Times* declined to publish. *The Village Voice* also rejected the piece called 'The Revolutionary Theatre' before *Black Dialogue* finally offered to publish it. The essay was reprinted in *Liberator* in July 1965 and appeared the following year in Baraka's influential volume *Home: Social Essays*. It's not hard to see why the *Times* refused to publish Baraka's essay. However, it is also ironic, considering that 'The Revolutionary Theatre' takes part in the venerable tradition of the avant-garde manifesto, whose founding father in many ways, the Italian futurist poet Filippo Tommaso Marinetti, had had his 'Futurist Manifesto' published on the front page of *Le Figaro* in Paris on 20 June 1909. Marinetti's manifesto (1991: 51), which urges readers: 'Come on! Set fire to the library shelves! Turn aside to flood the museums! ... Take up your pickaxes, and axes and hammers and wreck, wreck the venerable cities, pitilessly!' must have appeared just as shocking to readers of the venerable *Figaro* as would *Times* readers encountering lines like these from Baraka (2009: 238):

> [W]e will change the drawing rooms into places where real things can be said about a real world, or into smoky rooms where the destruction of Washington can be plotted. The Revolutionary Theatre must function like an incendiary pencil planted in Curtis Lemay's cap. So that when the final curtain goes down brains are splattered over the seats and the floor, and bleeding nuns must wire SOS's to Belgians with gold teeth.

For all its *épater la bourgeoisie* shock value, Baraka's manifesto is a major statement of the burgeoning Black Arts movement. As Jerry Watts admits (2001: 174), the 'essay functioned as a call to arms to black playwrights, writers, and scholars of all varieties'. It also laid the ideological, thematic and aesthetic groundwork for the Black Arts Repertory Theatre and beyond; in all of the above, Baraka's thinking continues to be shaped by avant-garde/surrealist influences, with Artaud, not Breton, now chief among them. Guillaume Apollinaire is credited with having written the first surrealist play, *Les mamelles de Tirésias*, in 1903 – just as he is credited with having coined the word *sur-réaliste* in response to another stage performance, Jean Cocteau's ballet *Parade* (1917). However, it is Artaud who remains most closely identified with the theatre. His conception of the Theatre of Cruelty has now inspired several generations of dramatists: *The Theatre and Its Double*, first published in 1938, is widely read today.

In choosing the stage at all, in terms of where the most important work of cultural nationalism is to be done, Baraka is following in the footsteps of avant-gardists of all stripes. From the early futurist *serate* (theatrical evenings) to the dada performances at Cabaret Voltaire during World War I to Artaud's Theatre of Cruelty, the stage had been a place where the most directly provocative artistic experimentation could take place. Drawing upon these and similar examples, Martin Puchner's study (2005: 25–26) of the avant-garde highlights their 'theatricality' and 'performativity'. Avant-garde art is theatrical for being over the top and also for attempting to create a space where a future or alternative world might be glimpsed. It is performative both for being achieved *in performance* and, in the more radical Austinian sense, for bringing something new into the world through the force of its utterance. That is to say, there were no futurists before Marinetti's manifesto announced their birth in *Le Figaro*. Puchner's study attends most fully to the avant-garde manifesto with its bombastic rhetoric and projective energy but, largely following Marjorie Perloff (1986: 90–91), he develops a concept of 'manifesto art' that includes poetry, painting, sculpture and drama. In Baraka's oeuvre, a manifesto function is as operative in the play *Dutchman* and the poems of *The Dead Lecturer* as it is in the Revolutionary Theatre manifesto.

Baraka's essay – and the Black Arts movement it helped inspire – thus takes part in a tradition of manifesto writing that stretches back to Marx and Engels and involves revolutionary politics as much as it does radical aesthetics. In terms of its content, though, his manifesto points straight back to those of Artaud for the Theatre of Cruelty and, in important ways, Baraka's proposal for a new kind of theatre can be read as an update or a rewriting of the Theatre of Cruelty: a 'fusion of aesthetic and racial avant-gardism' (to borrow from Sollors on *Dutchman* [1978: 127]). Baraka himself is equivocal about this 'fusion', though, when he writes (2009: 237) that 'the Revolutionary Theatre, even if it is Western, must be anti-Western'. Rather than a contradiction to be overcome, this central conflict within Baraka's own conception of a future black art is a source of strength. Borrowing a tactic from his poem 'Black Dada Nihilismus', in 'The Revolutionary Theatre', the author enlists Artaud to fight alongside Denmark Vesey and Patrice Lumumba in the struggle for black self-determination across the globe.

To the extent that Baraka's manifesto lays out a discernible aesthetic for his new theatre, it begins to sound remarkably like Artaud's programme for the Theatre of Cruelty, full of wild, convulsive gestures, dissonant sources and violent action all meant to stir the audience into action (e.g. 'The Revolutionary Theatre should stagger through our universe, insulting, preaching, spitting craziness' [2009: 236]). Among those who have written about Artaud's influence, there is a tendency to see that influence as limited to the aesthetic sphere; Baraka would seem to endorse this viewpoint when he tells William Harris, 'I was making [my work] more overtly political than Artaud. Artaud was to me the blind thrust against bourgeois sensibility and bourgeois consciousness. I wanted to make it much more overtly political and much more focused' (Harris 1985: 141). Baraka may want to distance himself from Artaud when it comes to the political content of his work, but his statement to Harris stems from the same blind spot discussed earlier regarding the 'apolitical' Artaud. It overlooks the manifest political content of his Theatre of Cruelty manifestoes, content that Baraka has, in fact, picked up on and developed in 'The Revolutionary Theatre'.

The majority of Artaud's second manifesto is, in fact, taken up by a sketch of a play to be entitled *The Conquest of Mexico*, and in response to this Theatre of Cruelty ur-spectacle, which was composed but never staged in Artaud's lifetime, Baraka writes (2009: 236): 'Even as Artaud designed *The Conquest of Mexico*, so we must design *The Conquest of White Eye*, and show the missionaries and wiggly Liberals dying under blasts of concrete. For sound effects, wild screams of joy, from all the peoples of the world'. For Baraka as for Artaud, the original sin of European imperialism *always* involves the present. Poised upon the historical moment of decolonization in Africa and elsewhere, Baraka's manifesto naturally draws upon the anti-colonial sentiment that animated Artaud's work.

The politics of Baraka's Revolutionary Theatre manifesto are resolutely internationalist. They anticipate the third-world turn in his thinking during the 1970s; they also point to an increasingly Pan-Africanist view of black nationalism. Baraka's *trans*-nationalist conception of struggle and liberation is, in fact, shared by earlier avant-garde groups such as the futurists who sprouted up across Europe in the years preceding World War II and the Dadaist dissenters who converged on neutral Zurich during the war, as well as the Communist internationals. When he writes for example, 'The Revolutionary Theatre is shaped by the world, and moves to reshape the world', (2009: 238) he is calling for a politically engaged art that indeed has the 'world' as its proper object. This *worlded* vision of a committed black art is central to the manifesto's powerful rhetoric and to the future work it inspired.

The word itself ('world') appears more than twenty times in the fairly compact essay. Near the beginning, Baraka appeals to a quasi-Hegelian *Weltgeist*: 'This should be a theatre of World Spirit. Where the spirit can be shown to be the most competent force in the world. Force. Spirit. Feeling.' The Revolutionary Theatre will endeavour to 'call down the actual wrath of world spirit' through the performative violence of its productions' (2009: 237, 241). Yet most often in Baraka's manifesto, the world, as such, is presented as the necessary field of play in a totalizing present defined by the capitalist world system.[4] The theatre must, therefore, become 'a weapon to help in the slaughter of these dimwitted fat-bellied white guys who somehow believe that the rest of the world is here for them to slobber on' in a society 'which sends young crackers all over the world blowing off colored people's heads' (2009: 237–238). Baraka's message is couched in terms that are anti-imperialist and anti-colonial as much as they are anti-racist, making his use of Artaud and the Theatre of Cruelty particularly significant.

Baraka ends his manifesto with a seeming nod back to Breton which keeps the broader surrealist and avant-garde context in view. In the second *Manifesto of Surrealism*, Breton (1969: 125) rounds out his 'simplest surrealist act' (firing blindly into a crowd) with this further provocation: 'Anyone who, at least once in his life, has not dreamed of thus putting an end to the petty system of debasement and cretinization in effect has a well-defined place in that crowd, with his belly at barrel level.' When, following Artaud's lead with *The Conquest of Mexico*, Baraka proposes a first production for his 'Revolutionary Theatre', he writes: 'The play that will split the heavens for us will be called THE DESTRUCTION OF AMERICA. The heroes will be Crazy Horse, Denmark Vesey, Patrice Lumumba, and not history, not memory, not sad sentimental groping for a warmth in our despair; these will be new men, new heroes, and their enemies: most of you who are reading this' (2009: 241). Watts points out (2001: 173) that there seems to be some confusion about who the real audience for the Revolutionary Theatre is intended to be. But in the spring of 1965, the Black Arts Repertory Theatre and School (BARTS) was founded to provide arts and education programmes for the black community in Harlem, making the rhetorical violence of Baraka's manifesto, which is aimed squarely at whites, necessary to first create a performative space in which the Black Arts could arise and develop.

The death of Malcolm X in February 1965 had been the final straw. In short order, Baraka left his wife Hettie and their two daughters and moved uptown. He writes in his autobiography (1997: 311): 'When Malcolm was murdered we felt that was the final open declaration of war on black people and we resolved to fight. The Harlem move was our open commitment to this idea. In our naive and subjective way we fully expected the revolution to jump off any minute.' The first play produced at BARTS was Baraka's *Experimental Death Unit 1*. It had premiered at St Mark's Playhouse – another marker of the continuity between his 'transitional' and black nationalist periods. The theatre and school were both in operation less than a year. After a summer of poetry and theatre in the streets of Harlem, BARTS lost its much-needed federal funding and was forced to close. Baraka moved back to Newark with his lover Vashti and before long began pulling together 'another edition of the Black Arts' (1997: 342) in the form of Spirit House. In 1966 and 1967, the Spirit House Movers and Players performed a number of Baraka's recent black nationalist and agitprop plays, including *Arm Yourself or Harm Yourself*, *Great Goodness of Life*, and *A Black Mass*.

A Black Mass, featuring the music of Sun Ra, is a retelling of the Black Muslim myth of Jacoub (Yakub), the scientist/magician who created the white race as a race of monsters and devils. Baraka's version stresses metaphysical themes of time and timelessness; in a twist on Adam and Eve's fall, Faustian Jacoub's creations are the bringers of time – and thus change – into a world of perfect harmony. The setting of *Black Mass* – the stage suffused with a 'blue or red-violet glow', the scene a 'fantastic chemical laboratory' with 'weird mixtures bubbling' and 'solutions that glow in the dark' (1998: 37) – is also decidedly futuristic, with a strong science fiction vibe that is enhanced by Sun Ra's score. These elements are fully in keeping with the long arc of Baraka's evolution as a writer. In a remark that explicitly connects surrealism, science fiction, and his later Marxist play *What Was the Relationship of the Lone Ranger to the Means of Production?* (1978) but also pertains to *Black Mass*, he will tell Harris (1985: 142–143): 'There were definitely some surrealist elements in some of those things, surreal or fantasy. My early reading was science fiction. So I have never felt constrained by quote "surface" realism.' He explains: 'I have always valued [surrealist techniques] as one approach to art . . . to actually create worlds in which strange things happen, but these strange things really relate to the real world.' In *A Black Mass*, Baraka infuses black nationalist subject matter with an avant-garde sensibility and stages an early example of what would now be called 'Afrofuturism'.

Tyrus Miller (2015: 145–177) has recently written about an 'aesthetic revolution' in 1960s America; the Black Arts constituted part of its vanguard. By the mid-1970s, inspired by his trip to Tanzania (which had close ties with

Maoist China) to attend the Sixth Pan-African Congress in 1974, Baraka had moved away from a nationalist toward a Marxist conception of black self-determination. He now affirmed his solidarity with the oppressed peoples of the third world and argued that socialism was the only solution. The rejection of black nationalist ideology by one of its most visible and outspoken ideologues was seen as a major breakthrough, and it alienated many of Baraka's supporters.[5] The shift to Marxism-Leninism-Mao Tse-Tung thought, however, represents not only disjuncture but also the logical extension of a radically internationalist impulse that, as we have seen, had informed Baraka's work for years. His *worlded* sense of political struggle and social change had been apparent since the Revolutionary Theatre manifesto a decade earlier. The internationalism of Baraka's theatre owes a great deal to its avant-garde forerunners.

With his death in 2014 at the age of seventy-nine has come renewed interest in the large body of work he left behind. As scholars and critics attempt to define his legacy, perhaps we can finally begin to look past the polemics or, better yet, situate his most incendiary proclamations and violent rhetoric within the panoply of performative tactics he made use of in his art. These tactics serve to unite the early Beat and avant-garde writing with the later Black Arts and Marxist work, revealing, in retrospect, the fundamental continuity that underlies his long career as a poet, dramatist, writer and activist. Baraka's final play, *Most Dangerous Man in America (W. E. B. Du Bois)*, which premiered the following year, finds Baraka grappling to the very end with the twin demons of racism and colonialism. Grove Press has recently published a substantial collection of his poetry, leaving one to imagine the possibilities of a similar collection of Baraka's dramatic works. A single volume encompassing everything from *The Eighth Ditch* to *Most Dangerous Man in America* would remind readers of the momentousness of those early years in Greenwich Village and the New York Poets Theatre. Such a collection would help clarify Baraka's importance to the development of Beat drama and to Beat literature as a whole.

Works cited

Artaud, A. (1970), *The Theatre and Its Double*, V. Corti (trans.), London: Calder and Boyars.

Artaud, A. (1971), 'Surréalisme et revolution,' *Oeuvres complètes*, vol. 8, Paris: Gallimard.

Artaud, A. (1988), *Selected Writings*, S. Sontag (ed.), Berkeley: University of California.

Baraka, A. (1964), *The Dead Lecturer*, New York: Grove.

Baraka, A. (1982), 'Nationalism, Self-Determination, and Socialist Revolution', *The Black Nation*, 2.1: 4–10.

Baraka, A. (1991), *The LeRoi Jones/Amiri Baraka Reader*, W. J. Harris (ed.), New York: Thunder's Mouth.

Baraka, A. [LeRoi Jones] (1997), *The Autobiography of LeRoi Jones*, Chicago: Lawrence Hill.

Baraka, A. (1998), *Four Black Revolutionary Plays*, New York: Marion Boyars.

Baraka, A. (2001), *Dutchman and The Slave*, New York: Harper.

Baraka, A. (2009), *Home: Social Essays*, New York: Akashic.

Benston, K. (1976), *Baraka: The Renegade and the Mask*, New Haven, CT: Yale University.

Breton, A. (1969), *Manifestoes of Surrealism*, R. Seaver and H. R. Lane (trans.), Ann Arbor: University of Michigan.

Bürger, P. (1984), *Theory of the Avant-Garde*, M. Shaw (trans.), Minneapolis: University of Minnesota.

Diggory, T. (2009), *Encyclopedia of the New York School Poets*, New York: Facts on File.

Di Prima, D. (2001), *Recollections of My Life as a Woman: The New York Years*, New York: Penguin.

Fabre, M. (1993), *From Harlem to Paris: Black American Writers in France, 1840–1980*, Champaign: University of Illinois.

Frazier, R. T. (2011), 'The Congress of African People: Baraka, Brother Mao, and the Year of '74,' in M. Marable and E. K. Hinton (eds), *The New Black History: Revisiting the Second Reconstruction*, New York: Palgrave, 135–54.

Harris, W. J. (1985), *The Jazz Aesthetic: The Poetry and Poetics of Amiri Baraka*, Columbia: University of Missouri.

Lee, A. R. (ed.), (1996), *The Beat Generation Writers*, London: Pluto.

Marinetti, F. T. (1991), *Let's Murder the Moonshine: Selected Writings*, R. W. Flint (ed.), Flint and A. A. Coppotelli (trans.), Los Angeles: Sun and Moon.

Miles, B. (2001), *The Beat Hotel: Ginsberg, Burroughs, and Corso in Paris, 1958–1963*, New York: Grove.

Nielsen, A. (1997), *Black Chant: Languages of African-American Postmodernism*, Cambridge: Cambridge University.

Oren, M. (1986), 'The Umbra Poets Workshop, 1962–1965: Some Socio-Literary Puzzles,' in J. Weixlmann and C. J. Fontenot (eds), *Studies in Black American Literature, Vol. 2: Belief vs. Theory in Black American Literary Criticism*, Greenwood, FL: Penkevill, 177–223.

Pawlik, J. (2010), 'Artaud in Performance: Dissident Surrealism and the Postwar American Literary Avant-Garde', *Papers of Surrealism* 8: 1–21.

Pawlik, J. (2011), 'Ted Joans' Surrealist History Lesson', *International Journal of Francophone Studies* 14.1–2: 221–39.

Pawlik, J. (2013), 'Surrealism, Beat Literature, and the San Francisco Renaissance', *Literature Compass* 10.2: 97–110.

Perloff, M. (1986), *The Futurist Moment: Avant-Garde, Avant Guerre, and the Language of Rupture*, Chicago: University of Chicago.

Puchner, M. (2005), *Poetry of the Revolution: Marx, Manifestos, and the Avant-Gardes*, Princeton, NJ: Princeton University.

Sollors, W. (1978), *Amiri Baraka/LeRoi Jones: The Quest for a 'Populist Modernism'*, New York: Columbia University.

Tietchen, T. (2010), *The Cubalogues: Beat Writers in Revolutionary Havana*, Gainesville: University Press of Florida.

Wallerstein, I. (2004), *World-Systems Analysis: An Introduction*, Durham, NC: Duke University.

Watts, J. G. (2001), *Amiri Baraka: The Politics and Art of a Black Intellectual*, New York: New York University.

Sounding Across the City: Ted Joans's *Bird Lives!* As Jazz Performance

Amor Kohli

This chapter aims to read the 'Bird Lives!' graffiti that appeared around New York City after bebop musician Charlie Parker's death in 1955 as a performance that embodies a jazz aesthetic. Such a reading works primarily when we think about how a jazz aesthetic operates, and when we shake loose from thinking about this graffiti primarily as the finished product (i.e., the written words 'Bird Lives!' on a wall or sidewalk). Plainly, 'Bird Lives!' might be read for a jazz influence in the way that some 'jazz literature' can, insofar as it references a real or fictional jazz musician. Like the most evocative of jazz-inspired art, the production of the graffiti expresses a deeply rooted connection to jazz. *Bird Lives!* as a performance is not only the sum of its parts, but importantly exposes a multi-fold process that includes those very parts, and the conceptualization and execution of the project.[1] Conceived by the Black poet and artist Ted Joans, *Bird Lives!* not only demonstrates what Joans has called his 'claim to jazz history' but is also indicative of how he engaged the example of jazz as a way of making art and moving through the world.

Often mentioned, but seldom discussed critically, the 'Bird Lives!' graffiti has been understood as straightforward memorialization. While not perhaps as aesthetically impressive as the graffiti that would appear around New York City 20-odd years later, *Bird Lives!* gives us particular insight into the aesthetic approach of its initiator, Joans. Despite the dominance of the memorialization reading, another way to understand 'Bird Lives!' is to interpret it as more meaningful than a singular act of graffiti, or as the 'writing on the wall'. I will argue that we more productively understand how the act exemplifies Joans' aesthetic by paying attention to how the writing on the wall (as both noun and verb) came to be. In other words, this chapter discusses the process by which '*Bird Lives!*', including the final product, emerges. *Bird Lives!* as conceptualized and produced is emblematic of Joans' commitment to a jazz aesthetic which crosses and combines genres. In its construction and execution, the graffiti is a process-centred conceptual performance in which

improvisation and motion are central to its achievement. With its connection
to the moving, living body, 'Bird Lives!' is a 'jazz-ed' performance that emerges
though writing and choreography – by which I mean the production of
bodies moving through space – while using the entire city, above and below
ground, as a canvas-stage. It is a fugitive choreography through which the
performers' bodies inscribe their presence through space while inscribing
their subject's spiritual presence all around the city.

Taken as a whole, this graffiti as an event expands out past the final result
most clearly evident to its viewers. The 'Jesus wept' of the hipster set, 'Bird
Lives!' was a two word slogan that became more than text; it became a
happening. It became more than prose, approaching performance through its
involvement with writing, space, movement, time. Generally speaking, the
written words 'Bird Lives!' have been understood as an end in itself. Of course,
they signify a celebration of the life and work of Charlie Parker on the occasion
of his death. We can reasonably infer, for instance, that those who wrote and
encountered the graffiti did not take this to mean that the news of Parker's
death was erroneous. It did not mean 'Bird did not die' (unlike, say, a graffito
that proclaims 'Tupac Lives!'). It could mean, as Joans would later imply, simply
that 'Bird's music still lives on'. Even as the graffiti takes Bird's death as its
subject matter, it does so by referring to an essentially different possibility.
Taking the words 'Bird Lives!' along with the graffiti as an event, we can see
that the city-wide performance of *Bird Lives!* says even more, speaking
poetically about loss, desire, and permanence. Going further, *Bird Lives!* is
situated in the midst of larger questions about Black recognition, life, death,
presence and where Black expressive practice fits in the context of quotidian
performance.

In 1959, Ted Joans, a friend and one-time roommate of Charlie Parker's,
wrote the words that appear in Robert Reisner's *Bird: The Legend of Charlie
Parker*: 'Bird died four years ago but he lives, he lives and now how do you
sound?' (Reisner 1962: 118). Four years earlier, on the occasion of Bird's
passing, graffiti began appearing around New York City, that said, repeatedly
and seemingly simply, 'Bird Lives!' It is well known that Parker and his music
served as a kind of lodestone for many of the Beat Generation writers and
artists with whom Joans both collaborated and connected. Jack Kerouac has
Bird commune with the Kerouac stand-in Leo Percepied in the novel *The
Subterraneans*. Bird is clearly in mind during Kerouac's manifesto on method,
'Essentials of Spontaneous Prose'. Many poets – Joans, Kerouac, and Bob
Kaufman among them – wrote stirring poems about Parker even before his
death, with Kaufman naming his son Parker after the important musician.
The 'Bird Lives!' graffiti quickly became a talking point, shorthand for the
fervour of Bird's fans. Ralph Ellison mentions the graffiti in his famous essay

(a review of Reisner's book), 'On Bird, Bird-Watching, and Jazz'. Ross Russell uses it for the title of his 1973 biography of Charlie Parker. It is, in fact, in a review of Russell's biography that Joans unveils himself as the architect of the original 'Bird Lives!' graffiti. Before that, he had remained publicly silent about his participation in that initial event. During that favourable review of Russell's biography, Joans also gives credit to his co-performers: 'But one thing I want to . . . turn the entire world onto, in print for the first time, is that Donald Brand[t], Joel Axelrod, Julien Josephson, and Ted Joans were the first four that rode subways in four different directions and did the historical graffiti manifest: BIRD LIVES!' (Joans 1973: 30). The graffiti became so closely associated with Joans that, upon his own passing in 2003, it was repeatedly mentioned in his obituaries. As one example, the *New York Times* obituary headline reads 'Ted Joans, 74, Jazzy Beat Poet Known for "Bird Lives" Graffiti' (2003: N43).

Joans' use of the famous two-word phrase in Reisner's book emphasizes Bird's music as a generative force, transforming how we now 'sound'. Parker's music had a profound impact on how many began to 'sound', across a variety of genres and expressive forms. How musicians played, how people spoke, how painters painted, and how poets wrote bore the mark of an influence that could be traced back, at least in part, to Parker. While this sometimes produced unfortunate effects, such as that which Benjamin Lempert has called 'the hyperactive excesses' of bebop-styled poetry (2015: 305), nonetheless, Joans' comment asks us to pay attention to how Bird still lives through his work's impact on 'you' and your 'sound'. For Joans, though, *sound* not only refers to aural activity. It also refers to ways of knowing and being, bringing together, among other things, writing, speaking, performance, and movement. In the repetition of 'he lives, he lives', Joans not only proposes that 'Bird did not die' or that 'Bird's spirit lives on', but also that Bird is free. The excesses that Bird's life was both celebrated and castigated for are expressed through this graffiti in another sense. It is his spirit that overflows its earthly container. Once again, as in his music, Bird subverts the demands of formal expectation, thwarting the finality of death. Moreover, as a Black man in mid-century America, his continued assertion of life-affirming creativity in the face of social death is recast as continued presence in the face of bodily death.

After the 1973 admission in the *Village Voice,* Joans would discuss how the graffiti came about a few more times, particularly in a series of autobiographical writings. Through reading Joans' own post-1973 recollections of how the graffiti came to appear across the city, we can see that it was not only a singular, momentary flash of inspiration, but also involved important elements of conceptualization and distinct, but linked, moments of bodily action. The words, the writing hand, and the moving body all meet in the initial performance of *Bird Lives!* As such, through this reading we can comprehend how the text, while integral, is only part of a more complex and consciously conceived embodied action. It is a 'doing' or a 'happening' with similarities to key elements of jazz.

Indeed, in an unintended and unwelcome but very real connection to jazz history, many of the times that Joans mentions 'Bird Lives!' is to insist upon credit for starting it. The need to demand, sometimes loudly and continually, credit for one's contribution and composition is well known to the Black originators, composers and arrangers of jazz. Impulse and technique cannot (yet) be copyrighted. Nor can influence. Those unnamed, unknown performers who contributed to developments in jazz history do not get credit. However, even those whose names we *do* know often struggled to get sufficient acknowledgement, especially while they were alive to enjoy it. Indeed, frustration with the lack of credit to Black arrangers, composers, and performers helped contribute to the shift from swing jazz to bebop, the very style of jazz that Parker is often credited with developing and which inspired the Beat Generation writers. Writing 'Bird Lives!' all over New York City reminds the spectator about his impact and legacy as much as it memorializes.

In 'Je Me Vois' (1996), Joans begins the discussion of the graffiti with a reminder about his own contribution that enfolds a theory and method for *Bird Lives!*: '... my claim to jazz history is of being the inventor and instigator for the graffiti "BIRD LIVES!" When I heard that Bird had gone on to his ancestors I organized three friends of mine to spread the two-word slogan that expressed that Bird would live and be reborn as long as his music was spiritually existing. I armed the three worthy constituents with chalk and charcoal (not spray paint!) and sent them in three different directions on NYC tri-boroughs subways. They chose the places to write "Bird Lives!"' (Joans 1996: 252). In a later piece, 'Jadis, je me souviens bien ... Once if I Remember Well', published in 2002, Joans provides more detail about the build-up to the graffiti, repeating some elements while expanding on others (2002: 91):

> When I heard that Bird had gone on to his ancestors, I put a stack of his 78 rpm recordings on my Philco as I shed inner and outer tears. While listening to his Dial and Savoy discs as I did, a series of frenzied automatic drawings just grew. Then I phoned some of my friends to meet me at Cafe Rienzi for some very important proposals. At the Rienzi I told three of the hipsters, Donald, Julien, and Joel my plan. I gave each man a piece of white chalk and a chunk of charcoal. We took subways in four different directions and along the route we wrote with religious fervor, two large words 'BIRD LIVES!'

These narratives lend credence to the idea of *Bird Lives!* as a performance piece and give the claim that Joans is 'responsible' for the graffiti important layers. The 2002 discussion from *Black Renaissance/Renaissance Noire* adds a critical factor to the instigation of the event: the coterminous grief and mourning as emotionally and physically rendered. This may seem obvious, yet the element of grief is barely addressed when Joans and the graffiti are mentioned together. More often, we find out, for example, that (as mentioned earlier) Joans and Parker were roommates at one point, or attended some party together. In Joans' recollection here, however, the emotional quotient is produced through grief and mourning in reaction to the news and funnelled into and through listening to Bird's records. In turn, this combination generates for Joans an energetically sourced and executed artistic expression: 'the frenzied automatic drawings' and their inspiration from surrealist methods. This, as Joans chronicles, inspires and initiates an even larger plan that is, while individually based, also collective and collaborative. Each individual – or what I have been calling 'performer' – will operate independently. Again, they 'chose where to write "Bird Lives!"' and do so when inspiration strikes, yet they operate collectively. Notwithstanding that they move in 'four different directions' across the city, they write and perform the 'Bird Lives!' event as part of an ensemble. Such a productive tension between the individual and collective performance is one of the key elements of the jazz impulse, and these forms of transaction generated within this particular performance mirror those found in a jazz music performance.

Joans seeks out three others to spread the spirit of jazz enacted through this example to the wider city. It need not always cohere in obvious, prescribed, and preconceived ways. Robin D.G. Kelley writes that jazz 'emerges often out of unexpected juxtapositions, even mistakes and mis-communication – what jazz critic A.B. Spellman calls "the Marvelous"' (2012: 10). The reference to the surrealist concept of the 'Marvelous' is crucial here, as for Joans the two practices of jazz and surrealism are deeply linked. Moreover, the idea that musical 'breakthroughs' burst forth from 'chance encounters, moments of miscommunication, confusion and mistakes … central to [the] process of discovery' as a hallmark of experimentation illuminates the way that a jazz impulse as a catalyst for experimental creation has had a hard time being contained (Kelley 2012: 10). In part, jazz's continual evocation of audacious and capacious movement shows how we might understand a performance that occurs while moving across a large space as bearing the hallmarks of a jazz impulse.

Like the music itself, this could not happen without the body. While this, too, might seem obvious, we might remember that a poetic line based on the long breath stems from an attempt at the translation of a jazz saxophone soloist's line, produced by the musician's breath and produced, of course, from the body. In this case, it is a Black body already and historically hemmed in by a battery of political, societal, and epistemological forces. The ways in which this body expresses freedom, joy, and a deeper sense of self-assertion is also fundamental to a jazz impulse that is developed through the embodied performance of *Bird Lives!*

The 'quality of embodiment', as Ronald Radano has written, 'sits at the very heart of [the] aesthetic value' of Black music, including jazz (2013: 126). Dance is one of the most evident connections of the body with the music; it's worth keeping in mind that the style of jazz with which Charlie Parker is most associated – known as bebop – was rebuked early on for its refusal to capitulate to the expectations of an audience who had grown to see jazz music and dance music as identical. As LeRoi Jones (Amiri Baraka) writes in *Blues People,* the response of disdainful listeners and critics was, 'You can't dance to it!' and meant it as a devastating, dismantling critique. The response of a young Baraka was to reverse the dismantling: '*You* can't dance to it!' (Jones/Baraka 2002: 199), producing through a rhythmic shift, a counter-criticism that brings together the moving body, knowledge, appreciation, and pleasure. Of course one could dance to bebop. People often did, simply responding to what the new music did with new organizations of the body in space and time.

Joans' many commentaries draw attention to his belief in jazz not only as a structural vocabulary, but also as a conceptual impetus for living and moving. Jazz, for Joans, like surrealism (his other principal inspiration), is 'not a return to a past age and outdated ideas' (Joans 1989: n.p.) but a path to reconceive ways of approaching social, aesthetic, political, and physical systems of organization. In his 'Last Statement of the Manifesto', apparently intended for the short-lived music magazine *The Cricket*,[2] he insists upon the profound connection between the music and the formation of a 'new political ideology. Perhaps it will be something similar to this Black music, Jazz. Perhaps it will be a way "unheard-of-before" or at least "not-done-thataway"' (Joans 1970: n.p.). Such newness would effect multiple freedoms that jazz produces, '[n]ot only in musics, but dance also' (Joans 1970: n.p.). In addition, he here celebrates the essentialness of the freedom to travel across the globe, writing that in this potentially emergent world, 'Freedom of unrestricted movement would be internationally applied' (Joans 1970: n.p.). While an unfettered dance that shares the impulse of jazz is key to Joans' ethos, this free movement includes the spaces through which the body moves *to* time and *in* time, but also *over* time.

Once he 'splits' Greenwich Village in the early 1960s, Joans undertakes a lifelong movement, becoming known as a 'tri-continental poet', a description that, while technically accurate, doesn't achieve the full quality of his peripateticism as it privileges place rather than his continual and purposeful moving within and through those spaces. With a seemingly boundless energy, even into his later decades, Joans makes action and energy core elements of his ethic and his aesthetic. For example, as A. Robert Lee notes, when in a poem like 'My Trip' from 1970's *Afrodisia,* Joans writes 'I have Moroccod/ Algiered/Tunised/Libyad/Egypted/ Mauritanied/Malied . . .' (Joans 1976: 64), 'place-names become active energies, verbs' (Lee 2004: 125). Motion and movement are central to his conception of the paradisal energy-space, 'Afrodisia', which will exist 'WHERE EVER BLACK PEOPLE MAKE MUSIC DO DANCES/MOVE BLACK BODIES . . .' (Joans 1976: 71). That is to say, everywhere.

Joans was known for his live performances, wherein his Black Body moved, and he recited poetry that made music. By many accounts, one could only truly appreciate Ted Joans by hearing and watching him perform. When he performed his poetry in front of an audience, his sounds and tones would dip, slide, stutter and smooth out, producing effects that that we might consider *jazzy.* Additionally, Joans brought to his poetry performances the cool, the activity, the power, the humour, the pain, the politics and the sexuality that many have heard and felt in jazz. This all made him a jazz poet or, as he would put it, a *jazzpoet.* The fusion of the two jazz action words marked, for Joans, a resolution of any breach between the two modes (jazz and poetry) and produced instead a singular identity in which one participated. It is, for Joans, a way of life and a mode of being in the world.

Just as jazz describes more than the music itself, performance need not only describe an event that occurs at one time in front of an audience, like a poetry reading. Moreover, his insistence that the *Bird Lives!* graffiti serves to earn him a place in 'jazz history' does not preclude thinking about the graffiti as method, concept, and event. Thinking of *Bird Lives!* as I am here complicates a hierarchy of values that understands a performance as an activity that occurs simultaneously and that can be taken in by one viewer at one time. *Bird Lives!* exists between the staggered moments of performance and the later moment during which the audience/viewer encounters the graffiti.

Omi Osun Joni Jones has, along with Sharon Bridgforth, recently articulated how the example of jazz has influenced what she calls a 'theatrical jazz aesthetic'. Tracing its lineage to the lessons Black dramatists took from the Black Arts Movement of the late 1960s and 1970s, Jones describes a theatrical practice that borrows and transforms ideas from jazz music. 'Theatrical jazz', according to Jones, refers to a 'wide range of performance experiences that have common impulses' including '"the break"– or the moment of improvisation and invention – as well as nonlinear narrative strategies, a fluidity of time and space, a nonmimetic gestural vocabulary, and a spiritual vitality that is variously expressed across performances' (Jones and Bridgforth 2014: 139). Although Jones is talking about a particular kind of theatrical event, this theatre celebrates, as does Ted Joans' graffiti event, distinct elements of a jazz aesthetic including process over artifactual product, improvisation, collaboration, an expansion of the performance space as traditionally conceived, and what Jones calls 'fluidity'.

It may very well be that Ted Joans, when imagining his graffiti act, drew less consciously from the jazz tradition than in the type of event that Jones describes. However, method, technique and artistic instrument are clearly important to Joans. In his comments on the graffiti, Joans shows a consciousness of *technique*, organized performance, and materials. In this city-wide performance piece, Joans begins as choreographer, director, composer, all the while allowing the improvisatory creativity of his performers to express itself in their movement. As he explicitly states, they choose where and when to write 'Bird Lives!' allowing the creative spirit to blossom where individually appropriate. He provides the broader framework for the piece, the opening 'key', the instruments used and not used (*not* spray paint!). A series of connected actions that coalesce into an event spanning city-space and time, *Bird Lives!* is, like much of the jazz music from which it takes its example, at once structured and left open to improvisation and flashes of personal inspiration. In this organized performance, the performance of the assertion 'Bird Lives!' is collaborative, at once individual and collective, raggedly temporal and spatial, ensuring a staggered entry of performance not set to any predetermined composition.

Again, key to understanding Joans' participation in a jazz aesthetic is in its privileging of process over product. The final product – the graffiti 'Bird Lives!' – is no doubt significant. However, in Joans' formulation, the final product is not actually final. In the initial event, the improvisation and individual decision over when and where to write ensures that the event, the *happening* as I am referring to it, is a continuous performance, consisting of not only the moment in which one of the performers writes, but also as each performer travels to the next writing space. Just as in one of Jackson Pollock's drip paintings, Romare Bearden's collages, or even Joans' lesser known 'jazzaction' paintings, we may not be able to see or faithfully replicate the movement of the bodies through space, but it is integral to the larger process of the piece. We must acknowledge the meaning of these bodies in motion in this performance, moving through the city – at street level and below it – with organized purpose and improvisatory possibility. The scrawling, the moving, the literal unawareness (especially pre-mobile phones) of when co-performers are writing, but the knowledge that they may be out there doing so at that very moment makes it clear that we see the importance of process here over mere 'final' product.

'Final' here deserves quotation marks as, again, the instruments the performers use are remarkable for their impermanence and flux. As we've seen, Joans' comments on *Bird Lives!* reveal that this project was conceived with thought given to technique and material. The choice to provide both chalk and charcoal takes into account a variety of potential surfaces and physical contexts on/in which they might appear. Joans' insistence, from the 1973 *Village Voice* review cited earlier, that they did 'not [use] spray paint!' as had been reported by others, including Russell (although Ellison got it right), evinces the artist's investment in making certain his audience knows the material was chosen purposefully. Spray paint may, of course, fade over a longer period of time. However, left unprotected to the elements and time, chalk and charcoal are remarkable here for how quickly they may change. On sidewalks, on sides of buildings, they transition and transform depending on external factors: rain, snow, wind, etc. Graffiti written with chalk and charcoal will blur and run. It changes form fast, both living and dying from moment to moment.

Jazz's ephemeral quality provides it with a meaningful sense of vitality. While I have concentrated here on similar aspects of the *Bird Lives!* event, and how it, too, celebrates a succession of linked but autonomous creative acts, there is, nonetheless, a deep value in making space for the pleasures of the audience/viewer's discovery after the creative act has occurred. Ted Gioia has written that jazz 'lives and dies in the moment of performance' (1988: 83). Privileging the immediacy of the moment as authentic expression, Gioia could very well be suggesting an essentially degraded character to any recording of jazz. There is, we might read here, no substitute to accessing jazz in the moment of performance. Such a view also suggests an authenticity of reception; the only listeners to get the true experience are those who were there. I would have loved, for instance, to have been at Birdland for the performance that ended up as the recording *Coltrane: Live at Birdland*. But the reality is that had I been there, at that moment in 'Afro-Blue' when John Coltrane re-enters (in the midst of Elvin Jones' 'thrashing and cursing' [Baraka 1998: 66]) with a soul-piercing shriek, I might've had someone bump into me at that moment, or be involved in ordering a drink, or in the bathroom, or sneezing, or so forth, and I would've missed one of my favourite points of that whole performance. When I listen now, though, I stop and prepare myself but can still never truly predict the quality of my physical reaction to it. It always surprises, even just a little. Baraka, in his liner notes for that album, also places himself and his own performance into the listening of that record: 'I got up and danced while writing these notes, screaming at Elvin to cool it' (1998: 63). We do not read the break in the note-writing, nor do we hear the aural screaming (that involves his body) or see his dancing body (that involves his voice) but we see that the jazz performance instigated Baraka's authentic response. Similarly, we imagine these four hipsters travelling, at Joans' instigation, separately yet together, acting in synch yet not necessarily simultaneously; we might not be able to render their exact movements, but we know they were moving across the city as their bodies wrote those words that sprung from the simultaneity of loss and presence: 'Bird Lives!' The graffiti is memorialization: it is also, though, the expression of a combined celebration and mourning that can't be faithfully replicated two, three, or ten days after first hearing about Bird's death. But that shock, sadness, and spirit of celebration that inspired that first performance of *Bird Lives!* should be counterbalanced by the delight and surprise Bird fans must have had upon coming across another expression of *Bird Lives!* Imagine being a lover of Bird's music and walking down the street, in an alley, underground in the subway and stumbling upon that celebration of the contradictions of mortal humanity/godlike artistry; loss/existence, impermanence/immortality in two words and an exclamation point. Perhaps something revelatory opened up, momentarily, and gave you a glimpse of the Marvelous, where the contradictions could fruitfully exist at the same time, where Bird could be dead and live; a revolutionary image that, as Aimé Césaire writes, 'maintains the possibility of the happy medium' (1996: 142). The search for similar moments of wonder, discovery, and surprise drove Ted Joans. It was a gift he celebrated and was determined to share.[3]

Works cited

Césaire, A. (1996), 'Poetry and Knowledge' in M. Richardson and K. Fijalkowski (eds), *Refusal of the Shadow: Surrealism and the Caribbean,* New York: Verso: 134–146.

Gioia, T. (1988), *The Imperfect Art: Reflections on Jazz and Modern Culture,* New York: Oxford.

Joans, T. (1970), 'Last Statement of Manifesto,' [unpublished manuscript], Box 16, Folder 11, The Ted Joans Papers, BANC MSS 99/244z, Bancroft Library, University of California, Berkeley.

Joans, T. (1973), 'Bird Lives!: A book by Ross Russell,' *Village Voice,* 6 December 1973: 30.

Joans, T. (1975), 'Ted Joans, Tri-continental Poet,' *Transition* 48: 4–12.

Joans, T. (1976), *Afrodisia: Old & New Poems by Ted Joans,* London: Marion Boyars.

Joans, T. (1989), 'I, Too at the Beginning: Beat Generation Segment' [unpublished manuscript], Box 14, Folder 1, The Ted Joans Papers, BANC MSS 99/244z, Bancroft Library, University of California, Berkeley.

Joans, T. (1996), 'Je Me Vois (I See Myself),' in S. Andrews, (ed.), *Contemporary Authors: Autobiography Series, 25*, Detroit: Gale Research: 219–258.

Joans, T. (2002), 'Jadis, si je me Souviens Bien . . . Once if I Remember Well,' *Black Renaissance/Renaissance Noire*, 4: 91.

Jones, L./Baraka A. (1998), *Black Music*, New York: Da Capo.

Jones, L/Baraka A. (2002), *Blues People: Negro Music in White America*, New York: Harper Perennial.

Jones, O. and Bridgforth, S. (2014), 'Black Desire, Theatrical Jazz, and River See,' *TDR: The Drama Review*, 58: 136–146.

Kelley, R. (2012), *Africa Speaks, America Answers: Modern Jazz in Revolutionary Times*, Cambridge, Mass.: Harvard University.

Lee, A.R. (2004), 'Black Beat: Performing Ted Joans' in J. Skerl (ed.), *Reconstructing the Beats*, New York: Palgrave/Macmillan: 117–232.

Lempert, B. (2015), 'Hughes/Olson: Whose Music? Whose Era?' *American Literature*, 87: 303–330.

Radano, R. (2013), 'The Sound of Racial Feeling', *Daedalus*, 142: 126–134.

Reisner, R., (ed.), (1962), *Bird: The Legend of Charlie Parker*, New York: Da Capo.

'Ted Joans, 74, Jazzy Beat Poet Known for "Bird Lives" Graffiti' [obituary] (2003), *New York Times*, 18 May 2003: N43.

9

Radical Ritual Performance in the Early Prophetic Poetry of Bob Kaufman

Thomas Pynn

Introduction

William Stafford, in one of his pithy aphorisms, states that '[m]any critics treat a novel or poem as a statement./But it is better considered as a performance' (2014: 46). Stafford's astute observation that a poem is not a statement suggests a way of performing language in order to communicate what cannot be spoken of in conventionalized direct discourse. Conventionalized discourse assumes, among other things, that our everyday use of language tells us everything we need to know about ourselves, others, and the world in which we live. Beat performative language, however, is influenced by the work of both Charles Olson and Robert Creeley in their development of open form poetics or 'COMPOSITION BY FIELD, [that is] opposed to inherited line, stanza, over-all form, what is the "old" base of the non-projective' (Olson 1997: 239). Projective verse assumes that ordinary uses of language cannot even begin to express the deeper significance of the human condition or the quest for freedom. A performative use of language, then, is an embodied performance contingent upon one's sensitivity to both the inner and outer land and soundscapes. Beat performative aesthetics demand a dynamic, unconventional and indirect embodiment of language that allows for rhythmic irregularity, displacement of the phrase, and episodic structure. Olson's formulation in 'Projective Verse' (1997: 242) is instructive: 'The HEAD by way of the EAR, to the SYLLABLE/The HEART, by way of the BREATH, to the LINE.'

This oft-cited couplet suggests not only grammatical alterations by which the open form poet will perform language but also that one develops an awareness of being part of a universal life force much larger than one's own self and sensitivity to life's spiritual (from *spiritus*: 'breath', 'spirit') qualities and mystery: imagination, vision, and prophecy, as one finds in the poetry and engravings of William Blake or the automatic writing of William Butler

Yeats. Furthermore, the poet building on the anagogic qualities of language as well as the movement of embodied vocalizations – for human language requires a living body – makes an oblique distinction between the use of the everyday language of getting and spending, calculating loss and gain, and calculated malice, opting instead for radical ritual communicative acts that invoke the sacred, thereby imagining a future in which life possibilities or eventualities are both expanded and enhanced.

Drawing on the pre-Christian tradition of the Bard as (re)inscribed in Romantic aesthetics by William Blake and the American Transcendentalism of Walt Whitman, Beat poets use both the expressive and communicative aspects of language in projective form in order to bring the prophetic voice of the poet to an America in need of spiritual, moral, and aesthetic regeneration. For Elizabeth Bell and others, this is 'the ritual model of communication' in which 'communication is not imparting information, but a representation of shared beliefs' (2008: 8). This model gives what is shared and participated in a central place in the human community; thus, revitalizing communication ritually restores both individuals and the community. Such ritual communication is radical when it challenges and confronts hegemony.

As the Bard occupied the centre of the community when that community was in danger of forgetting itself, in order to remind and awaken the people of and to their identity and place in the cosmos, so did Beat poets occupy spaces at the margins of urban America – coffee houses, strip clubs, bars, art galleries after business hours, low-income housing – calling America back to its purported values of freedom, justice and equality. Bob Kaufman is one Beat poet who performs 'the ritual view of communication [which] maintains that culture is created, maintained, repaired, and transformed in and through communication' (Bell 2008: 8). Through radical ritual communication, both space and time are newly opened in a transformation of consciousness, thereby energizing the participants' actions in a living community with a shared cache of meaning. Just as ritual uses language and movement in ways that cut crosswise to everyday practices of communication, so does Kaufman perform language in other ways than the purveyors of normative language, who speak what Allen Ginsberg referred to as 'officialese', whether academic, political, social, or religious (Knight 1987: xi). Ginsberg imagines that a new poetic energy will counteract 'the militarism and materialism of American civilization' (Raskin 2004: 16). It would be 'a return, as he put it, "to the original religious shamanistic prophetic priestly Bardic magic!"' (Raskin 2004: 17). It would, indeed, be a radical ritual performative act of expression and communication.

Performing at the margins of the power elite – academic, religious, political, social, economic – Bob Kaufman may be understood as illuminating the border that marks off the outward form of individual things co-opted by the dominant forces in society from the inward life of all sentient beings participating in reality. Kaufman performs poetry as a form of radical ritual communication in order to re-establish a living connection in each person with the very source of their personhood, thereby outwardly effecting a change in cultural awareness. In order to effect a radical transformation of American consciousness from living 'on the border of perpetual fright' that demanded conformity and obedience, some Beat culture artists became 'advocates' of a new America (Knight 1987: xi). Their roles, therefore, would include both prophetic and shamanistic strategies of performative creativity in order to confront the framing of consciousness by what C. Wright Mills (1956, 1959) identified as two new powerfully formative elements in American life in the 1950s: the white collar worker of middle management and the power elite constituted of the military, governmental, and corporate sectors who are engaged in 'the pain/of the work/of wrecking the world' (Snyder 1983: 92). Kaufman confronts the hegemony of consumerist America led by the new worker bees of middle management and the incestuous triangle of the power elite framing American consciousness. Performance as framing perception, Bell explains, summarizing part of the work of Gregory Bateson in his *Steps to an Ecology of Mind* (1972), operates in at least three significant ways: by delimiting messages in which one is directed to pay attention to this and not that; meta-communicatively by inventing and implementing systems of interpretation of those messages; and altering-framing consciousness (1998: 36). The Beats can be understood as confronting this frame and then breaking it, thereby performing a prophetic function in society. Or, at least, attempting to set Americans free from the dominant mode of consciousness – 'the official myth', as Kenneth Rexroth termed it (Rexroth 41).

Breaking the frame of American hegemonic consciousness

How, then, do Beat poets break the hegemonic frame of consciousness that reduces human consciousness to a subservient Moloch mechanism mind – *Urizen* – and then (re)frame consciousness in ways conducive to a living and humane human being? In her *Postmodern Theatric(k)s: Monologue in Contemporary American Drama*, Deborah R. Geis states that 'performative discourse' when it relies upon 'physical or gestic language' can become 'interpersonal discourse'. This has the 'power to command the ear as well as the eye' (1993: 1). What she terms 'autoperformance' in the context of postmodern dramatic performance can include, as I hope to demonstrate, the performative poetry of Bob Kaufman insofar as his work blurs the line between character and actor; fiction and non-fiction; telling and reporting; and the conscious and subconscious in an 'ironic crossing of boundaries' (Geis 1993: 4). Indeed, one might say that in the case of the Beats, autoperformance is autobiography meeting art – a living art. The performance of Beat religious consciousness through their respective art signals a form of radical ritual communication that is distinctly prophetic. For Kaufman, autoperformance – 'a semiautobiographical mode' – manifests in the role of prophetic poet (Geis 1993:4).

Kaufman's autoperformances are living performances that open out consciousness to new vistas of reality toward a new trans-American imaginary. They do this by blurring the boundaries between poet and reader/listener, body and language, and life and art. Performative transformation is dependent on the orality emphasized in Beat performance. T. J. Anderson underscores the importance of the spoken versus the written word in Kaufman's performative aesthetic when he observes that '[s]ince most of his work was performed orally, Kaufman sought to return poetry back to its original roots as an oral art form first and foremost' (2004: 72). For Anderson, Kaufman's Beat orality is necessarily, though not exclusively, tied to jazz, but jazz 'in a sacred and religious context' (2004: 94). For the purposes of this chapter what I'd like to follow (more than Anderson's observation about Kaufman's linking of jazz performance with spiritual consciousness) is the importance Anderson places on the overall significance of Kaufman's religious performance. Anderson states that just as Kaufman contributed to the development of jazz poetry by 'his innovative use of scat phrasing . . . [which] brought attention to the musical possibilities of poetry when language goes beyond "meaning" . . . he infuses his work with a heightened sense of spirituality that goes beyond the secular implications of music and poetry' (2004: 94–5). That 'heightened sense of spirituality', I suggest, is the prophetic imagination.

Beat art generally and the prophetic early poetry of Kaufman specifically performs at the margins of normative society and challenges hegemonic assumptions about human identity; human relations with both human and non-human life forms; and the everyday trap of trivial, daily existence. While Gillian Thompson has written about Joyce Glassman (Johnson) and Elise Cowen as female Beat artists, what she says about the female Beats being at the margins holds true but in a different way for Kaufman. Kaufman, too, performs 'from a unique perspective' in a 'performance of survival' (Thompson 2011: 2), but unlike these and some other Beat women artists, Kaufman was not excluded from the circles of Beat authorial authority. Yet despite Kaufman's voluntary association and sought-after participation with both the San Francisco Renaissance and Beat culture artists, he nonetheless had to 'create an identity for' himself (Thompson 2011: 2). Kaufman is excluded from America's white supremacist milieu as part of the rejection of African-Americans generally and joins the rest of the ethnically diverse Beat counterculture artists at the margins. As Anderson points out, 'By refusing to specify his race and by having a recognizably Jewish last name, Kaufman became the quintessential outsider' (2004: 72). From the margins, Kaufman offers Americans a new vision of what both human beings and America can be contra its sentimental nihilism, direct and indirect forms of violence, aggressive caricatures of masculinity and its return to a spirituality that sees the sacred in relation to existence. Kaufman uses his prophetic poetic performances to reconfigure the normative, 'the norms which constitute our status as subjects' (Thomason 8) – in other words, our consciousness.

Like the Romantics, Transcendentalists, Dadaists, and Surrealists before them, Beat culture artists generally and the poets specifically had an active interest in consciousness. Joanna McClure has stated that 'we were more concerned with new consciousness than with spirituality' (Charters 2001: 632). Ann Charters reiterates McClure's observation and adds that 'We were more interested in a state of consciousness, rather than a sense of spirituality – or we felt that they were one and the same. We felt that consciousness and spirituality were equally sacred' (2001: 632). This interest reveals that at least part of the Beat project was just as spiritual as it was aesthetic and as concerned with justice – racial, sexual, political, environmental – as it was with expanding their own experiences as artists. 'Critical of this country on the one hand', Arthur Knight explains (1987: xi):

> the Beats were at the same time its strongest advocates, wanting us to recognize our strengths and failings so that we could function as humanly (and humanely) as possible in a society that had become increasingly desensitized, one in which the areas of consciousness had increasingly narrowed down.

Radical ritual performance opening out onto new vistas of consciousness is a creative act that is closely connected with the function of religious ritual or with the very role of religion itself. In her essay entitled 'Performance', Catherine Bell calls for expanding the practice of ritual performance and communication. Her rubric allows us to see how some Beat culture artists like Kaufman involved in the production of a countercultural discourse make use of performance in order to rectify 'the devaluation of action that occurs when it is contrasted with thought' (1998: 206). In this sense, then, Kaufman can be understood as engaging in radical ritual communication and prophetic performance that enhances and '*creates* culture, authority, transcendence, and whatever forms of holistic ordering are required for people to act in meaningful and effective ways' (1998: 208).

Bob Kaufman: American Beat Prophet

In his ground-breaking *The Prophetic Imagination*, Walter Brueggemann states that those who would engage their respective communities prophetically 'nurture, nourish, and evoke a consciousness and perception alternative to the consciousness and perception of the dominant culture around us' (1978: 13). The key similarity here is that a Beat poet such as Kaufman and a religious prophet have a shared purpose: consciousness itself. Brueggemann trenchantly observes that our reduction of the prophet to social justice has eclipsed the much more radical function of dismantling one view of reality 'in order to permit a new reality to appear' (1978: 21). The prophet and Beat poet engaging in radical ritual performative acts of communication both make use of poetry's indirect saying to accomplish the shared purpose of consciousness transformation. The prophet, like the modern artist, however, is not left unscathed in the process of prophetic performance. Maria Damon points out that 'Kaufman's circle has not been slow to associate the Christic attribute of humility, of giving up one's physical integrity and personal claim to sacredness to die in obscurity, with Kaufman's withdrawal and decline' (1993: 42). Furthermore, she reports (1993: 44) that:

> According to many who knew him in his North Beach years, Kaufman does not call so much on the relatively modern Western spiritual and literary tradition's notions of mortifying the flesh to feed the spirit, as he does on the older and more inclusive tradition of the poet as shaman, who mediates the spirit world through body as well as through mind, and who often undergoes a near-fatal illness as part of her or his initiation into shamanism.

As Damon shows, it has been conventional in both Beat history and scholarship to associate Kaufman with the figure of Christ and/or the ancient tradition of the shaman. Kaufman, himself, often made the analogy between being a poet and the crucifixion as he does in 'The Poet': 'THE POET NAILED TO THE/BONE OF THE WORLD' (1981: 68). In what follows, however, my intention is to suggest that it may also be useful to add another interpretive layer in understanding Kaufman's poetic role in Beat countercultures as prophetic according to Brueggemann's work on the prophetic imagination.

Reading the prophetic-visionary element in Kaufman's early poetic performances entails that in this chapter, I set out some of the prophetic attributes that appear in his first collection of poems, *Solitudes Crowded in Loneliness* (1965). The volume's opening poem, 'I Have Folded My Sorrows', is a prime example of how, according to Brueggemann, the prophetic imagination speaks from and in '*the language of grief*' for grief is nothing less than the sorrows of the heart in its unfolding perfection steeped in suffering (1978: 46). This prophetic-poetic trajectory in the poem consists of three stages which serve as a structure for the poem itself and as an order of remembrance as prophecy: the unfolding sorrows of past injustices, what he has learned along the way, and the ramifications of the prophetic-poetic journey 'space in time' (Kaufman 1965: 3). Thus, 'I Have Folded My Sorrows' serves both as a brief glimpse at significant features of the poetic-prophetic journey and as an epigraph for the poems that follow.

In the poem's first triad we are offered an image of folding that also implies a simultaneous unfolding: a folding of 'sorrows' into the unfolding 'mantle of summer night' (1965: 3). Folding 'sorrows' is both an act of putting away and remembering; hence, in folding 'my sorrows into the mantle of summer night' the poem's I-consciousness looks back upon the life lived as a kind of *memento mori* thereby introducing what is to follow and foreshadowing 'the funerals of the poet' referred to in the poem's closing couplet (1965: 3). Each sorrow is a 'brief storm' forming the 'catastrophic histories buried in' the speaker's 'eyes' (1965: 3). The opening lines are composed in the language of grief in so far as the poet speaks out of, communicates from, a 'space in time' demarcated by suffering (1965: 3).

The second triad of lines anaphorically announces that in the folding/unfolding rhythm of 'catastrophic histories' constituting 'sorrows' the space-time continuum is left undisturbed yet the prophet–poet bearing witness is not. In the unfolding of 'space in time' in which 'each brief storm' is 'allotted space in time' the 'Cosmic Game' is playing itself out regardless (or even heedless of) human suffering (1965: 3). The material world is unchanged. Yet, what has been altered is consciousness. Kaufman shifts into surrealistic imagery to express and communicate, *perform*, an act of radical ritual communication of self-unfolding: 'the shingled hippo becomes/the gay unicorn' (1965: 3). 'The shingled hippo' is an animal capable of horrific violence. It is one of the few mammals that will fight to the death; however, despite the violence the hippo represents, it is transformed, in the crucible of the creative and prophetic imagination, into 'the gay unicorn', a medieval Christian symbol of the purity of Christ consciousness, of the sacred and virgin heart. Thus, in three lines, Kaufman has leapt from sorrow and suffering to gaiety and a purified consciousness. In doing so, he offers the reader and/or listener a vision of a radically altered and new consciousness. This new vision serves the dual function of both setting out an attainable image and energizing the reader/listener with hope – though this transformation of consciousness will necessitate that one look directly at one's own existence, not allowing the power elite to distract one from the reality of birth and death.

Following from the playful imagery of 'the gay unicorn' the speaker declares that his 'traffic is not with the addled keepers of yesterday's disasters', thereby effectively separating himself from fear mongers and other assorted authorities who fan the flames of vengeance for past-perceived wrongs, consequently inciting the cycles of violence, those 'seekers of manifest disembowelment on shafts of yesterday's pains' (1965: 3). 'The prophet', Brueggemann reminds us, 'does not scold or reprimand' (2001: 46). While Brueggemann is writing of the prophets of the *Tanukh*, what he states here is analogous to what Kaufman and others are doing in post-war America. As Americans experience the continuation of the wartime economy and vast amounts of wealth are produced, the middle class expands as the white collar worker takes the helm of middle management. An expansion of affluence occurs unlike at any other time in American history. Middle-class America becomes satiated through conspicuous consumption, complacent in the protection of their own status and passive aggressively denying the same rights and affluence to others, particularly minorities. While the ancient prophets addressed primarily the Kings of their respective times, Kaufman and Beat counterculture must address the American people at large because hegemony diffuses the central power of the elite to encompass a greater portion of the populace than simply those at court.

Yet, prophetic consciousness is not necessarily immune to the demands and illusions of the power elite. The poet avers, 'yes, I have searched the rooms of the moon on cold summer nights/And yes, I have refought those unfinished encounters./Still they remain unfinished./And yes, I have at times wished myself something different' (1965: 3). It is characteristic of prophets to experience doubt and anxiety about, and discontent with, their suitability to the task of intervening in human beings' tendencies to get trapped in patterns of forgetting and remembering; however, what is not in doubt is the veracity and timeliness of the work. Since prophetic consciousness is not the consciousness of a God-realized master, the prophet–poet is also liable, at times, to be overwhelmed by self-forgetting and despair. The difference, or at least one difference, then, between the prophetic imagination and ordinary consciousness is that the former has access to creativity. Poetry composed concretely in '*the language of grief*' will sometimes appear as 'Blues come dressed like introspective echoes of a journey' (1965: 3); again the important thing here is that the sorrow of a blues song like Kaufman's poem may leap out of that grief and into an imaginative hopefulness, even joy. It is true that 'The tragedies are sung nightly at the funerals of the poet' (1965: 3) because poetry, as prophecy, marks a kind of death, but the death of self-deception, not the death of one's true self. It is this anticipation of dying while one is still living that the prophet–poet re-awakens in us.

One of the most recognized functions of the poet–prophet is performing in the role of moral authority. Not in the limited sense of being a guardian of normative codes tacitly assumed by society, but in the wider and deeper sense of justice, the voice crying in the wilderness. In 'Benediction' we are offered the voice of the poet–prophet calling our attention to injustice, prophesying atonement, and revealing false prophets. Benediction, usually the utterance of a blessing and a devoted wish for the happiness, prosperity, and success of a person or enterprise, is being used ironically *and* in the sense of Christian prophetic witness: the poem is an indictment of American violence both at home and abroad. Kaufman was raised an African-American Roman Catholic in New Orleans and knows that the priest at the end of mass sends congregants out into the world by benediction. In Kaufman's poem, however, the benediction takes on the form and tone of the prophet crying out in the urban wilderness. Composed in two stanzas, the first and shortest of the two makes a direct reference to both the biblical event of the arrival of Moses in the Pharoah's court to request that he set free his people, and to the nineteenth century spiritual 'Go Down Moses': 'Pale brown Moses went down to Egypt land/to let somebody's people go' (1965: 9). That Moses is 'Pale brown' may be a rejoinder to the amazingly successful Cecil B. DeMille 1956 release of *The Ten Commandments* starring Charlton Heston: Moses very likely was not Caucasian. Kaufman's use of the phrase 'somebody's people' is telling because, in both the Biblical narrative and the song, we know exactly whose and which people, but in the poem, the ambiguity provokes us into asking if there is a new situation in which people are being enslaved. As it turns out, they are in Florida where '[t]he poor governor is all alone,/[w]ith six thousand illiterates' (1965: 9). It might be the case that Florida stands in for an America in which there had been over one hundred race riots in the twentieth century alone, and 'the poor governor' as the now notorious governors – Alabama's John Malcolm Patterson and George Wallace, Georgia's Marvin Griffin and Ernest Vandiver, South Carolina's Strom Thurmond – all of whom acted in office to obstruct integration and perpetuate racial inequality.

The second stanza continues the ironic tone established and sustained by the repeated phrase 'America, I forgive you ... I forgive you' (1965: 9). While the sincerity of the forgiveness is certainly up for debate, the cataloguing of atrocities is not. Kaufman puts on the mantle of prophetic poet, illuminating the violence towards both the domestic and foreign Other towards which too many Americans have turned a blind eye: 'Nailing Black Jesus to an imported cross/Every six weeks in Dawson, Georgia', 'Eating Black children', and 'Burning Japanese babies defensively' (1965: 9). These images refer us to the lynchings, Jim Crow laws and forced segregation pervasive across America, not only in the South, throughout the first half of the twentieth century as well as the nuclear massacre of hundreds of thousands of Japanese civilians. The prophetic voice of the poet knows exactly the kind of violence the prophet is called to confront: 'the barriers and pecking orders that secure us at each other's expense, [and] the fearful practice of eating off the table of a hungry brother or sister' (Brueggemann 1978: 46). Furthermore, such social oppression, let alone outright murders, is a denial of some African Americans' access to decent education, nutrition, and healthcare.

The religious significance of the poem evokes blood sacrifice and declares that America should offer up her murderous self-interest as a holocaust. This contrasts sharply with America's 'generals [who] have mushrooming visions', and with the Truman administration's official excuse for dropping the atomic bombs on the Japanese: that it saved thousands of American lives, thus suggesting not only racist motivation but also a denial that Japanese people are human beings (1965: 9). The poem presents the antinomy of conditioned versus unconditioned hospitality, but whereas an antinomy calls for sustained reflection in humility on the promise of America – the 'beautiful thoughts' on the minds of America's 'ancestor' (in reference to Thomas Jefferson if not all of America's Enlightened founders) ironically amounts to little more than 'beautiful thoughts' (1965: 9). Instead of the pursuit of the core value of freedom, America, 'Every day your people get more and more/Cars, televisions, sickness, death dreams' (1965: 9). America, rather than becoming free, has enslaved itself to a penultimate aspiration called the American dream. In the poem's last two lines Kaufman rejects the Whitmanesque optimism of mythic American progress by concluding, 'You must have been great/Alive' (1965: 9).

It is, however, in his most extensive and expansive religious poem, 'Second April', that Kaufman deepens the theme of calling Americans, including the power elite, back to self-awareness and freedom by engaging 'their experiences of suffering to death' (Brueggemann 20–1: 41). The poem, first published as a broadside by City Lights Press in 1959, is an eclectic, religious text based primarily in Judeo-Christian and Mahayana Buddhist texts and teachings linked by the emphasis on mind and the Christ-Bodhisattva ideal of a saviour who works for the salvation of all sentient beings. 'Second April' is a prophetic epic framed by the teachings of both the Judeo-Christian tradition and Mahayana Buddhism. Its prophetic dimension is a complex dream-vision that begins with an invocation, but it is not a Greek or Roman mythological epic in which the Muses are invoked; rather, it is a spiritual invocation of the inner life: 'O man in the inner basement core of me' (1965: 65). It is also a call to all human beings to smell 'futures of green anticipated comings, pasts denied, now time to thwart time, time to frieze illusionary motion on far imagined walls, stopped bleeding moondial clocks, booming out dead hours' (1965: 65). In short, it is a call for each American, each human being to awaken and emerge as the wise and compassionate beings living in peace with one another. This is the call to be 'gone . . . gone . . . gone . . . gone . . . on to second April' (1965: 65). Kaufman's allusion is to the *Heart Sutra's* 'mantra of the perfection of wisdom' *tadyathagate, gate, paragate, parasamgatebodhisvaha*! (Dalai Lama 2002: 61). 'Second April', then, can be understood as both the literal arrival of the spring season and a metaphorical spiritual spring, Nature awakening from winter's sleep and a mind awakening from its own sleep. The prophetic call in the poem's opening section reminds us that as we move through our experiences of suffering we are to keep our eyes on 'green anticipated comings', that is to say on newness, a transformed and renewed consciousness, that is the liberation from and cessation of all suffering.

Apocalyptic in its imagery of the upheavals of consciousness, the poem's eschatology, the old consciousness, is being replaced by the new vision/ consciousness. Just as prophets like Isaiah and Paul had to use 'symbols that are adequate to confront the horror and massiveness of the experience that evokes numbness and requires denial' (Brueggemann 2001: 45), so does Kaufman make use of both expressionistic and surrealistic forms of language in his Beat autoperformance of radical ritual communication in order to awaken Americans from their slumber.

Kaufman's use of surrealist aesthetics in 'Second April' informs the symbolism of transformation necessary to the prophetic imagination. For Andre Breton, 'the *liberation of the mind* [is] the express aim of surrealism' (1978: 115). Surrealism would, Breton and others maintained, bring 'the solution of the principal problems of life' (1978: 122). They saw art as effecting a form of awareness that could lead to social change. Awareness coupled with uses of language that emerged from the depths of the human psyche announced a fundamental break with existing modes of communication and the conventional manner in which one perceives and accepts the exterior world. Hence, Kaufman and other Beats utilized surrealist aesthetics to help free the self, as Jeffrey Falla points out, 'from the socioculturally influenced sense of self that imprisons everyone as social subjects through internalized images of normative identity (be it racial, gender, sexual, national, or psychological)and, indeed, internalized images of normalcy in general' (2002: 187). Karsten Harries has observed that 'a considerable part of what is called surrealism has as its goal the descent to a more immediate level of experience by means of a destruction of our superficial understanding of what is real' (1968: 116). Thus, the emphasis in Kaufman's early prophetic poetry on surrealist uses of language offers him 'symbols that are adequate to confront the horror and massiveness of the experience that evokes numbness and requires denial' (Brueggemann 2001: 45).

An example of surrealist technique employed in 'Second April' appears in the third stanza (Kaufman 1965: 66): 'the spoon is a cop, the door is closed, I hope Rimbaud bleeds all over my stolen pants, pants, that's a thing, they watch.' One way that surrealism evokes image-emotions from the depths of the subconscious mind is by expressing the irrational by effecting a synthesis out of opposite meanings, to see and associate objects and other phenomena without preconceived interferences. Within Kaufman's surrealist language are such juxtapositions of unfamiliar objects, as in the line 'the spoon is a cop' (1965: 66). Yet, it is not a completely irrational phrase that leaves no anchor for communicative action. It is an example of what David Sterritt terms a 'pararational' mode of thought (1998: 38). The para-rational mode of thought is 'an alternative way of conceptualizing and employing reason and retains enough intellectual and psychological coherence to have (according to its proponents) significant value as an aid in reaching personal and/or social change' (1998: 38–39). Thus, not only does the juxtaposition of 'spoon' with 'cop' jar our normalized consciousness allowing new vistas of awareness to open out onto a new way of seeing the world, but also allows access to rational meaning-making. '[T]he spoon is a cop' can be read as an image associated with 'they', the guardians of normalcy.

Maria Damon notes that the poem 'juxtaposes assertions of "thingness" ... against the refrain "look out for green"—the static known of material fixity versus the unbounded energy of life/death and constant change' (Damon 1993: 55). More often than that, however, images of 'thingness' are drawn out to their horrifying ends as in the image of projecting one's self into a future and not living in the present: 'Future, that's a thing, future men with three penises seducing future women with vaginas in their armpits, future children with lavender eyes between their toes, wiping crazy fallout from the ass on their future skulls, a thing, future' (Kaufman 1965: 67). The future as a thing is detailed in cubist and surrealist imagery highlighting an apocalyptic nuclear future that both calls attention to the present situation of the 'they' who are in control of nuclear weapons and the consequences of life under the control of the 'they' who 'watch' and are constantly 'looking for things' (1965: 66). Things can be read in a number of ways, but one layer of meaning can be made as an image of a static, as opposed to a dynamic, reality. A static reality is one that is not only unchanging but can also be brought under control. A thing is a thing to be manipulated, controlled, possessed, consumed, and kept under surveillance. One of the principal goals of surrealism is 'to present interior reality and exterior reality as two elements in process of unification, of finally becoming *one*' (Breton 1978: 116). The above passage and many others in 'Second April' make it clear that man's inner and outer lives are radically disharmonious. As the conflict between internal and external life intensifies, so do the attempts by the power elite to control and surveil.

Although hegemony is emerging as the order of things in 1950s America wherein even the religious dimension of human culture is co-opted by the power elite and we have become 'trapped in modern icons', the 'Third eye remains basic' (Kaufman 1965: 70). Throughout the poem, as Damon notices, the destructiveness of the 'they' is countered by renewal, resistance, refusal, and even humorous uses of the creative imagination presented in the language of surrealism, the appropriate use of symbolism in the nuclear age. Even though 'death you is our woman now' we are enjoined by the prophetic voice to 'look out for green', which is to say the continuity of existence in its birth–death cycle (1965: 71). Furthermore, the prophetic imagination is also at work in the midst of horrendous suffering. In 'Second April', the prophetic voice is intercessory: 'God give us new, we ate fire last time, be cool, God' (Kaufman 1965: 73). Even though the power elite has turned the world topsy-turvy and brought humankind to the brink of nuclear annihilation, the prophetic voice, speaking in hipster language, asks the Divine to renew life without destroying it. For Kaufman and some of the Beats, as it was for the Romantics and Transcendentalists, it is the artist who, through the act of the creative and prophetic imagination, can give humankind a vision of a vital world without destruction, the very opposite of the life-threatening power elite. In the poem's closing stanza there are signs of hope in the midst of despair. The prophetic imagination's vision ends, and the poet–prophet emerges from the dream-vision state, 'Kissed at wintertide' and back into the world of conformity, 'alone in a lemming world' (Kaufman 1965: 74). It is a world unlike the apocalyptic world in his vision: a world suffused in green. With the iteration of green we are left energized by a vision of hope and regeneration.

Conclusion: Beat religious consciousness, Beat spiritual legacy

Engaging in radical ritual performance pre-supposes a religious consciousness that cuts cross-wise to the dominant mode of consciousness. Kenneth Rexroth, one of the earliest critics to recognize the religious and/or spiritual dimension of Beat counter-discourse, referred to the dominant mode of consciousness as 'the official myth' (Rexroth 41). In his essay 'Disengagement:

The Art of the Beat Generation', Rexroth observed that 'Against the ruin of the world, there is only one defense – the creative act' (42). Those who were setting about the work of ruining the world in 1950s America, the white collar worker and the power elite, did so in two main ways: offering a static view of life and human existence and numbing people to all aspects of existence. Thus, America in the 1950s is set on a course of affluence, oppressive social policy, and static religion, the effect of which is to (re)frame consciousness to the dominant narrative about the meaning and purpose of life (Brueggemann 2001: 26–37). Disengagement, then, is Rexroth's term for the only way that a creative artist can exist and work in a world that has been subsumed in 'an absolute corruption' (49). By disengaging from American culture rather than participating in the parade of satiated, self-destructive somnambulence, the creative artist can then function to act as a counterpoint to American hegemony. For Rexroth, central to disengagement and the 'Art of the Beat Generation' is a set of values – 'Social disengagement, artistic integrity, voluntary poverty' – that 'are not the virtues we [Rexroth's generation] tried to inculcate—rather they are the exact opposite' (56).

Stephen Prothero has written about Beat religious consciousness and reaches similar conclusions to Rexroth. For him, the Beats, despite their use of doomsday imagery, 'sought to move beyond predictions of social apocalypse and depictions of individual sadness to some transcendental hope' (1991: 210). That the Beats rejected 'the pragmatic functionality of social structure' and tended to blur the arbitrary distinction between the sacred and the profane did not necessarily contradict or counteract their insistence on the 'sacrality of human interrelatedness or *communitas*' (1991: 211). The Beats lived out their spiritual quest 'on the edge' such that expression and communication of religious consciousness through their respective arts signaled a form of radical ritual performance that continued to unfold through the 1960s, giving the younger generation and their adult allies a model upon/from which to develop their own unique responses to American materialism, consumerism, militarism, racism, and sexism.

My point is not to suggest that Kaufman can be considered a prophet who is also a poet, but rather, that he is first and foremost a poet who shares some significant affinities with the Judaic conceptions of prophethood as characterized in the work of Brueggemann. In poems such as 'Second April', Kaufman uses surrealist language to wake us up to the fact of reification. Just as Brueggemann, writing of contemporary America, notices that 'everything has become a commodity and there are no more neighbors!' (2014: 13), so do Kaufman and the Beats also notice the increasing commodification of everyday life. Brueggemann has termed this phenomenon 'the liturgy of consumerism', a radical form of coveting 'a posture and practice of acquisitiveness, the capacity and readiness to acquire what properly belongs to another, and so to place the well-being of the other in jeopardy' (2014: 70). Yet, even in this kind of situation, the 'third eye remains basic' (Kaufman 1965: 70). What's needed is for the prophetic poet to re-awaken us so that we can open the inner eye that sees the true nature of things.

Works cited

Anderson, T.J. (2004), *Notes to Make the Sound Come Right*, Lafayette: University of Arkansas.

Bell, C. (1998), 'Performance', in M. C. Taylor (ed.), *Critical Terms for Religious Studies*, Chicago: University of Chicago, 205–224.

Bell, E. (2008), *Theories of Performance*, Los Angeles: Sage.

Breton, A. (1978), *What is Surrealism? Selected Writings,* F. Rosemont (ed.), D. Gascoyne (trans.), New York: Monad.

Brueggemann, W. (2001), *The Prophetic Imagination*, 2nd edn, Minneapolis: Fortress.

Brueggemann, W. (2014), *Sabbath as Resistance: Saying No to the Culture of Now*. Louisville: Westminster John Knox.

Chandler, D.R. (2007), 'The Beat Generation and Buddhist Religion', *Asia Journal of Theology* 21(2): 312–324.

Charters, A. (ed.), (2001), *Beat Down to Your Soul: What Was the Beat Generation?* New York: Penguin.

Charters, A. and S. Charters (2010), *Brother Souls: John Clellon Holmes, Jack Kerouac, and the Beat Generation*, Jackson: University Press of Mississippi.

Damon, M. (1993), *The Dark End of the Street: Margins in American Vanguard Poetry*, Minneapolis: University of Minnesota.

Dass, R. (2004), *Paths to God: Living the Bhagavad Gita,* New York: Harmony.

Falla, J. (2002), 'Bob Kaufman and the Invisible Double', *Callaloo* 25.1:183–189.

Geis, D. R. (1993), *Postmodern Theatric(k)s: Monologue in Contemporary American Drama*, Ann Arbor: University of Michigan.

Harries, K. (1968), *The Meaning of Modern Art*, Evanston: Northwestern.

Kaufman, B (1965), *Solitudes Crowded with Loneliness*, New York: New Directions.

Kerouac, J. (1995), *Selected Letters: 1940–1956*, Ann Charters (ed.), New York: Penguin.

Knight, A. and K. Knight (1987), *The Beat Vision: A Primary Sourcebook*. New York: Paragon.

Lama, D. (2002), *Essence of the Heart Sutra: The Dalai Lama's Heart of Wisdom Teachings*, Boston: Wisdom.

Mills, C.W. (1956), *White Collar*, Oxford: Oxford University Press.

Mills, C.W. (1959), *The Power Elite*, Oxford, Oxford University Press.

Olson, C. (1997), *Collected Prose*, Berkeley: University of California.

Prothero, S. (1991), 'On the Holy Road: The Beat Movement as Spiritual Protest', *Harvard Theological Review*, 84(2): 205–222.

Prothero, S. (1995), 'Introduction', in C. Tonkinson (ed.), *Big Sky Mind: Buddhism and the Beat Generation*, New York: Tricycle, 1–20.

Raskin, J. (2004), *American Scream: Allen Ginsberg's HOWL and the Making of the Beat Generation*, Berkeley, University of California.

Snyder, G. (1983), *Axe Handles*, San Francisco: North Point.

Stafford, W. (2014), *Sound of the Ax: Aphorisms and Poems*, V. Wixon and P. Merchant (eds), Pittsburgh: University of Pittsburgh.

Strerritt, D. (1998), *Mad to be Saved: The Beats, the '50s, and Film*, Carbondale: Southern Illinois University.

Thompson, G. (2011), 'Gender Performance in the Literature of the Female Beats', *Comparative Literature and Culture*, 13.1. Available at: http://docs.lib. Purdue.edu/clcweb/vol13/iss1/ (last accessed 24 January 2015).

10

Adrienne Kennedy: A Kindred Spirit to the Beats

Nita N. Kumar

Two references to the Beat writers in Adrienne Kennedy's work appear mystifying as well as suggestive and seem like a good starting point for an exploration of the presence of Beat elements, world view, and aesthetics in Kennedy's writings: 'While Eddie Jr. plays outside I read Edith Wharton, a book on Egypt and Chinua Achebe. LeRoi Jones, Ted Joans and Allen Ginsburg [sic] are reading in the Village. Eddie comes every evening right before dark. He wants to know if I'll go back to him for the sake of our son.' (Kennedy 2001: 64); 'Jack Kerouac's book: THE SUBTERRANEANS' (Kennedy 1987: 109). A quick recall of the Kennedy chronology in connection with the Beat movement may be in order here. Born in 1931 in Pittsburgh, Pennsylvania, Kennedy grew up in Cleveland, Ohio and moved to New York in 1954 having married Joseph Kennedy. Her husband was at graduate school at Columbia University and Kennedy cared for their children, while also attending creative writing courses at Columbia from 1954–1956. In *People Who Led to My Plays*, her highly innovative autobiographical work, she talks about her meeting with people 'at gatherings around Columbia University' (Kennedy 1987: 81). In the 1950s, the Beat action may be said to have moved to the Village, but the environs of Columbia University, where Jack Kerouac, Allen Ginsberg, William Burroughs, Lucien Carr, Joan Vollmer and Edie Parker had first met, were perhaps still resonating with the presence of Beat writers there about a decade earlier.

Kerouac's *The Subterraneans* was published in 1958, the year after *On the Road*. Kennedy's mention of this book in *People Who Led to My Plays*, in the first quotation at the beginning of this chapter, is left conspicuously incomplete with the hanging presence of the colon, without the explanatory note that is present for most other entries in this uniquely crafted autobiography. So what in *The Subterraneans*, a semi-fictional account of Kerouac's relationship with a black woman named Alene Lee, would have left its mark on Kennedy? Its unconventional, spontaneous prose narrative which attempts to capture lived experience, the style that had already made its mark with *On the Road*? Its rather shallow depiction of women? Its stereotyped portrayal of African Americans, both in the character of Mardou Fox as well as in other elements in the novel? The depiction of women as well as of African Americans in *The Subterraneans* could have bothered Kennedy, as she was thinking deeply about race and gender identity issues at this time. Generally, the Beat writers' attitudes towards and depiction of women are too well known to need any gloss here. *The Subterraneans* was widely criticized for its depiction of African American characters. The famously biting remarks of Kenneth Rexroth (who held a grudge against Kerouac) in his review give us a flavor of the criticism (1959: n.p.):

> In the last three years Jack Kerouac has favored us with his observations about hitchhiking, riding freights and driving other people's fast cars across country. It would seem he did these things poorly and that doing them frightened him severely. Next he gave us his ideas about jazz and Negroes, two subjects about which he knew less than nothing; in fact he knew them in reverse. In this reader's opinion, his opinions about Negroes are shared only by members of the Ku Klux Klan. Jazz, he seems to believe, is throbbing drums and screaming horns, pandemonium in the jungle night over a pot of missionary fricassee.

Kennedy's silence beyond the colon in her entry on *The Subterraneans* is perhaps expressive of both her conflicted response to the novel and her refusal to engage with the conflict within the text of *People Who Led to My Plays*.

The second excerpt at the beginning of this chapter is from *A Movie Star Has to Star in Black and White*. Spoken in the play by Columbia Pictures Lady, it is nonetheless very evocative of Kennedy's reflections about her own life in New York City. In the section on 'Marriage and Motherhood' in *People Who Led to My Plays*, she observes: 'Caring for him [her son] in dark winter twilight hours or on long summer days by its solitary nature helped me become perhaps more myself than I had ever been. The books I read while sitting in Riverside Park, *Crime and Punishment*, Gorki's *Childhood*, burned deeply in my mind in contrast to the kafeeklatsch [sic] conversations of the other young mothers' (1987: 82). Though the time Kennedy spent in New York before she left for West Africa and Europe in 1961 was mainly spent privately, this was clearly a period of extensive reading, experiments with writing and angst about her life and role. Her entries about this period in *People Who Led to My Plays* show her to be soaking up contemporary culture, both literary and popular. A statement such as 'LeRoi Jones, Ted Joans and Allen Ginsburg [sic] are reading in the Village' expresses the longing she seems to have felt to be part of the action, to write and perform, and, as she says, to have 'my family on the stage (like the family in *Our Town*)' (Kennedy 1987: 81).

The point of these reflections is to set the context for an exploration of Adrienne Kennedy as a playwright very close in the spirit of her work to the Beat writers. Certainly, there are obvious and overt differences between the profiles of Adrienne Kennedy and the most well-known Beat Generation writers. She: an African American woman raised in Cleveland, Ohio who later moved to New York, a rather private person even after she achieved renown as a playwright. They: prominent Beat writers, mostly male and white, some of whom gave up their privileged lives to experiment with radical, counter-cultural modes of living, experimenting with drugs, crime, and alternate forms of sexuality. Yet, much as Adrienne Kennedy appears to be markedly different from these writers, there is still congruity in the spirit of their work. Growing, living and writing in the 'Howl Generation,' Kennedy writes plays that are certainly an integral part of the broad counter-cultural movement of the period. There are deep resonances of the cultural, social, political, and philosophical attitudes embodied in the Beat culture as well as of the artistic expressions and experiments of the movement. That is not to say that there is any evidence of a direct influence on Kennedy beyond a conjectural one; rather, it is more a matter of similarity between Kennedy and the Beat writers regarding their socio-political and artistic responses to the prevalent conditions in America in the 1950s and 1960s. The Beats certainly could have had an influence on the development of Kennedy as an artist, but even when her growth trajectory was different, her work displays qualities that are, at times, stunningly close to the seminal expressions of Beat literature. In her Introduction to *The Philosophy of the Beats*, Sharin N. Enkholy observes that the 'Beats initiated a radical break with the old formalistic forms of expression, introducing a new relation to power and language, particularly the poetic voicing of personal experience and the articulations of positions of marginality' (2012: 3). Nearly all the elements in this description of the Beat Generation are equally true of Adrienne Kennedy's work, notwithstanding the differences in their subject matters and the specifics of their style. It is with these that this chapter is now concerned.

While the Beats were initially seen as apolitical, recent criticism has recognized the political resonances in Beat writing. Kennedy's work is intensely personal, but again there is now common agreement that political/social concerns are never far away from her work. As in the Beat writers, the social and the political in Kennedy are experienced as intensely personal: there is a complete turning inward. But the inner is constituted by, and in conflict with, what is evidently outside – the conditions created by the prevailing social, political, gender, race, power relations in post-war America. The Beats enact a rejection of normative American culture, for instance of materiality and acquisitiveness (among other things) as in *Howl*, or dictatorial cultural control and authoritarianism through the metaphor of addiction in *Naked Lunch* (to name one idea). Kennedy's work similarly exhibits an intense psychological reaction to issues of race and gender in America. The artistic processes at work in these pieces have a similarity: the political and the social are experienced as psychological and visceral. Kennedy's Negro-Sarah in *Funnyhouse of a Negro* and Clara in *The Owl Answers* could well be the subjects of Ginsberg's *Howl*. Suzanne, in *The Alexander Plays*, is an extremely intelligent, sensitive and creative woman destroyed by a culture of sexism, racism, and authoritarianism. The other striking resemblance Kennedy has with the Beats is that – notwithstanding the intense recoil from, and rejection of, the prevailing conditions – neither Kennedy nor the Beat writers have any doctrinal social/political programme or vision. Their works dramatize the conflicts, the lived experience, the rejection and the condemnation of post-war American values and imply a longing for alternative modes of being. However, neither overtly nor through implication do these works offer a solution, a world-order, a well-(or indeed even vaguely) thought-out structure or system. Like Beat literature, Kennedy's works contain a state of intensely experienced and often anguished being, rather than offering a pointed or satirical commentary. Kennedy has disavowed being a 'feminist' writer or being outspoken in her politics. She has repeatedly claimed that autobiographical work is the only thing that interests her. Writing, for her, is the process of trying to 'struggle with the material that is lodged in your unconscious, and . . . bring it to the conscious level' (Kennedy 1977: 42). However, in grappling with the intensely personal, she reveals the complex interworking of sexuality, race and colonization as the determinants of the consciousness of her black, female protagonists. Her plays delve into the unconscious and forcefully bring home the point that the personal is political; they do so in the sense in which Teresa de Lauretis defines the equation between the personal and the political, by maintaining the 'tension between them precisely through the understanding of identity as multiple and even self-contradictory' (1986: 9).

The 1940s and 1950s saw the spread of avant-garde movements to the United States, particularly New York. In order to express her view of the world, Kennedy, like the Beats, jettisons the use of realistic methods and invokes non-linear, non-rational, and often surrealistic methods to carry her intensely personal take on the world. Surrealism is a very broad term, its meaning stemming from the European surrealist movement led by Breton and the others. Elsewhere I have argued that Kennedy's brand of surrealism is markedly different from Breton's. To quote very briefly from that piece, I argue that '[w]hile in Breton, the dissolution of contradictions that produces surreality is a joyous state of "absolute reality," in Kennedy, surrealism is a sign and symptom of deep individual and racial pain and traumas, and does not lead to any form of resolution of contradictions. . . . Whereas Breton celebrates surrreality and looks forward to the joy of its possession, Kennedy's protagonists are destroyed by their experience of the dissolution of the structure of dream and reality, and are unable to achieve any resolution of these states' (Kumar 2005: 59–60).

Kennedy's early plays such as *Funnyhouse of a Negro* and *The Owl Answers* are as focused on enacting the raw experience of a conflicted existence as any Beat writing. In its formal aspects, Kennedy's work is closest to William Burroughs's, especially *Naked Lunch*, though the subject and the focus of the works are vastly different. However, in both Kennedy and Burroughs, the assumption of an ordered and unified self is discarded in favour of decentred configurations of identity. In both, a substratum of social and political ills is presented through the disjointed, nightmarish experiences of amorphously defined characters. Both employ anti-realistic devices such as multiple personas, transformation of characters, mixing and merging of time and place. As Mary McCarthy says, the 'action of *The Naked Lunch* takes place in the consciousness of One Man, William Lee' (2001: 358). So, too, the action of Kennedy's works takes place within the consciousness of characters that, if anything, are even less accessible and less well-defined than William Lee. *Funnyhouse of a Negro* is a non-linear and anti-realistic play, with characters moving in and out of themselves, across space and time. Sarah, who is described as 'Negro', includes within herself other personas – Duchess of Hapsburg, Queen Victoria, Patrice Lumumba and Jesus – with each one described as 'One of Herselves'. The other characters are The Mother, Landlady who is the 'Funnylady', and Raymond, who is the 'Funnyman'. In terms of chronological sequence, the play seems to begin just a little before the end when Sarah/Negro hangs herself. In her first appearance, we see her already with a hangman's rope about her neck, with 'red blood on the part that would be her face', and at the end, we see her hanging figure on the stage (Kennedy 2001: 13). In between, we catch disjointed but deeply revealing glimpses of Sarah's life and her multiple selves: 'She is a faceless, dark character with a hangman's rope about her neck and red blood on the part that would be her face. She is the NEGRO' (Kennedy 2001: 13). Here are two excerpts from one of her speeches:

> Part of the time I live with Raymond, part of the time with God, Maxmillian and Albert Saxe Coburg. I live in my room. It is a small room on the top floor of a brownstone in the West Nineties in New York, a room filled with my dark old volumes, a narrow bed and on the wall old

photographs of castles and monarchs of England. It is also Victoria's chamber. Queen Victoria Regina's .... When I am the Duchess of Hapsburg I sit opposite Victoria in my headpiece and we talk .... She wants me to tell her of royal world where everything and everyone is white and there are no unfortunate black ones.

(Kennedy 2001: 13–14)

[...]

He pleaded with me to help him find Genesis, search for Genesis in the midst of golden savannas, nim and white frankopenny trees and white stallions roaming under a blue sky, help him search for the white doves, he wanted the black man to make a pure statement, he wanted the black man to rise from colonialism. But I sat in the room with my mother, sat by her bedside and helped her comb her straight black hair and wove long dreams of her beauty.

(Kennedy 2001: 20)

Sarah's identity is not only multiple, but also transcends the boundaries of time, space, gender and class in assuming the identities of the Duchess of Hapsburg, Queen Victoria, Patrice Lumumba, and Jesus. The external is subsumed in the self. This gives a tremendous reach, dynamism and symbolic power to the category of the 'personal'. Burroughs in *Naked Lunch* employs a similar surrealistic style, mixing up the real and the fantastic. In the section 'AJ's Annual Party', after Mary has mutilated Johnny's face and genitals and Mark has tied her on the platform, the narrative reads thus (Burroughs 1959: 89):

He [Mark] jerks her to her feet and tightens the noose. He sticks his cock up her and waltzes around the platform and off into space swinging in a great arc... 'Wheeeeee!' he screams, turning into Johnny. Her neck snaps. A great fluid wave undulates through her body. Johnny drops to the floor and stands poised and alert like a young animal.

He leaps about the room. With a scream of longing that shatters the glass wall he leaps out into space. Masturbating end-over-end, three thousand feet down, his sperm floating beside him, he screams all the way against the shattering blue of sky, the rising sun burning over his body like gasoline, down past great oaks and persimmons, swamp cypress and mahogany, to shatter in liquid relief in a ruined square paved with limestone. Weeds and vines grow between the stones, and rusty iron bolts three feet thick penetrate the white stone, stain it shit-brown of rust.

As Jones Irwin says of the excerpt from Burroughs quoted above, '[t]his delirious surrealism then moves back to what appears to be a more realist or sociopolitical critique, highlighting once more the hybridized nature of Burroughs's text' (2012: 274). The lyrical surrealism in both Kennedy and Burroughs alternates; some parts are nightmarish, others are more realistic and socio-political, precluding any easy positioning of the text. Like the Beats, Kennedy is able to break away from the constraints of 'realism', yet retains the power of a 'moral' perspective on socio-cultural issues, bringing alive the possibility of her works being read as powerful comments on social and political conditions.

However, while the critique that these works offer has to be inferred, their inner dynamic is focused on capturing the moment of lived experience in all its rawness, contradictoriness and intensity, without any concessions to the rules of logic or rationality. The ideas of theatricality and performativity are as central to Kennedy as to the Beats. One can see a great commonality in the way their texts are inherently performative, and resist narrativity. Kennedy's plays are impossible to summarize because they have no plot outlines and no progressive action. The drama lies in the multiple, contradictory elements in the conflicted consciousness of her characters. While Burroughs's *Naked Lunch* is a novel, it has often been called 'anti-novelistic'. It consists of loosely related vignettes – what Burroughs himself called 'routines' – which are really dramatic pieces born out of what Alfred Kazin (1971) called Burroughs's 'marvelously episodic imagination'. As Jennie Skerl describes it, routines 'are dramatically realized fantasies consisting of monologues, dialogues, plot episodes, scene descriptions, and collage passages of associative imagery' (1985: 43).

This statement could also describe Kennedy's work. Kennedy had long been trying to write 'memory' plays in the tradition of Tennessee Williams, but finally found her expression in the short, intense, one-act form. Her plays redefine every element of drama – character, plot, dialogue – to produce works that capture the very essence of drama: conflict. Just as characters merge in an enveloping consciousness, which then is revealed to be multiple and fractured, so dialogue becomes indistinguishable from monologue. There is repetition, accretion, layering, rather than linear progression. The intersubjective spaces disappear. Characters repeat each other's lines, bringing a new resonance to the same words. At its heart, the world of Kennedy's plays is performative, even though they do not subscribe to the conventional pieties of drama and are difficult to stage. A dream-like atmosphere prevails – or perhaps nightmarish is a more appropriate word. Place and time change and transform. The setting of *The Owl Answers* 'is a New York subway is the Tower of London is a Harlem hotel room is St. Peters' (Kennedy 2001: 29). This method of superimposing elements upon each other liberates the text and adds ever-expanding meanings; it is the key to the metaphorical power of her work, as it is in Burroughs's *Naked Lunch*. Commenting on *Naked Lunch*, Mary McCarthy says: 'The scene shifts about, from New York to Chicago to St. Louis to New Orleans to Mexico to Malmo, Tangier, Venice and the human identities shift about too, for all these modern places and modern individuals (if that is the right word) have interchangeable parts. Burroughs is fond, too, of the word "ectoplasm". The beings that surround Lee, particularly the inimical ones, seem ectoplasmic phantoms projected on the wide screen of his consciousness from a mass séance' (2001: 359).

Part of the fascination of Tangiers for Burroughs was the fact that, for him, it appeared as a dream city. As Phil Baker says, 'it seemed to exist on "several dimensions", so the walker could always find streets, parks and squares that they had never seen before … a place where fact merges into dream and dreams erupt into the real world' (2010: 86). Indeed, dream and nightmare are central to the works of Kennedy and Burroughs. In his book *My Education: A Book of Dreams*, he reflects on the reality of dreams (1996: 2):

> The conventional dream, approved by the psychoanalyst, clearly or by obvious association, refers to the dreamer's waking life, the people and places he knows, his desires, wishes, and obsessions. Such dreams radiate a special disinterest. They are as boring and as commonplace as the average dreamers. There is a special class of dreams, in my experience, that are not dreams at all but quite as real as so-called waking life and, … if one can specify degrees of reality, more real by the impact of unfamiliar scenes, places, personnel, even odors.

Kennedy's plays exist in the pervading atmosphere of dream and nightmare, assuming a reality far more potent than mere waking life. *Funnyhouse of a Negro* opens with a 'WOMAN [who] dresses in white' walking across a stage suffused in a strong white light which is 'unreal and ugly' 'carrying before her a bald head', the curtain is 'ghastly white' (Kennedy 2001: 13). The characters are haunted by the fear and the experience of losing hair that lies on their pillows when they wake up. The word 'dream' is used in all its senses repeatedly in the play. A line spoken with modifications by characters says: 'It is my dream to live in rooms with European antiques and my Queen Victoria, photographs of Roman ruins, walls of books, a piano, oriental carpets and to eat my meals on a white glass table' (Kennedy 2001: 14). In this surreal atmosphere, freed from the tyranny of rationality, Kennedy is able to expose the deepest fears and longings of her characters, whose worlds are still visibly constituted by the real-time issues of race, class, gender, culture, and politics. Despite their surrealism, Kennedy's plays do not create a fantasy world, they merely reveal the pain and trauma of the real one. The personal, the eccentric, the unconventional in Kennedy, as in the Beat writers, is always hemmed in by, and defined as such, by the context of a harsh reality outside. Kennedy, too, achieves 'a sort of nakedness of mind, and ultimately, of soul: a feeling of being reduced to the bedrock of consciousness' – the words used by John Clellon Holmes to describe the nature of Beat writing (2001: 223).

More than anything else, however, the Beat movement was a cultural phenomenon; the lives and the works of the Beat generation writers became symbols in popular imagination and the stuff of cultural lore. Kennedy's life, persona, and work, on the contrary, have been more private and esoteric; her work has found its place primarily in an academic tradition rather than a popular one. It is, therefore, even more striking to recognize that popular culture holds a central place both in Kennedy's work and her imagination. *People Who Led to My Plays* defines the self as a composite of innumerable influences; all the elements are treated almost on a par with each other. Parents, family, friends, teachers, books, historical figures, dreams are all there, as are influences from popular culture. Kennedy is captivated by popular stories and myths and enamoured of film stars and prominent figures. The title of the play *Funnyhouse of a Negro* derives from an amusement park in Cleveland that featured a 'funnyhouse' with 'two huge white figures perched on either side, bobbing back and forth and laughing hysterically at the confused patrons within' (Bryant-Jackson and Overbeck 1992: 72). While all her plays include elements of popular culture, the one that foregrounds it is the play *A Movie Star Has to Star in Black and White*. The play mixes the story of Clara, her brother, mother and father with scenes and characters from the movies *Now Voyager*, *Viva Zapata*, and *A Place in the Sun*. Bette Davis, Paul Henreid, Jean Peters, Marlon Brando, Montgomery Clift, and Shelley Winters are listed as characters. The play also uses the Columbia Pictures Lady and music from the movies. While the Beat writers created a spectacle out of their lives and performed it in full public view, the Kennedy characters are dazzled by the popular and the spectacular, and live out their fantasies in the intensely private arena of their minds.

There is now a substantial body of writing that recognizes the international influence on and the trans-national character of Beat writing. The extensive travel that the Beat writers undertook played an important role in the development of their consciousness. Nancy M. Grace and Jennie Skerl, in their introduction to the book *Transnational Beat Generation*, argue that 'travel both within and outside the United States for many Beat writers – including Jack Kerouac, Allen Ginsberg, William S. Burroughs, Lawrence Ferlinghetti, Gary Snyder, Joanne Kyger, Philip Whalen, Janine Pommy Vega, and Anne Waldman – characterized a method for fusing life and art and vice versa' (Grace and Skerl 2012: 1). Adrienne Kennedy's experience of both travelling and living in West Africa and Europe had a profound and formative influence on her as a writer. She published her first story in *Black Orpheus*, a West African journal in which Wole Soyinka and Chinua Achebe were also being published in the early 1960s. Her first play, *Funnyhouse of a Negro*, was written during her stay. Her discovery of masks in Ghana gave her an insight into an extended notion of character. In *People Who Led to My Plays*, she says, 'Not until I bought a great African mask from a vendor on the streets of Accra, of a woman with a bird flying through her forehead, did I totally break from realistic-looking characters' (Kennedy 1987: 121). The discovery of the mask opened up the possibility of exploring the many parts of the self by turning them into different people. It gave her the freedom and means of dealing with what interested her the most: the conflict within the self and the need to use historical characters as extensions of her main characters. Kennedy also claimed that her stay in the newly liberated Ghana and her travels through the beautiful landscapes of Africa gave her 'strength in being a black person and a connection to West Africa' (Betsko and Koenig 1987: 249). She discovered African theatrical forms and read writers such as Soyinka and Achebe. It also strengthened her understanding of the issues of race and colonization, and put American culture into a wider perspective. Her play *She Talks to Beethoven* is an intricately woven piece in which a number of contexts are embedded one within the other, contexts which are widely removed chronologically but have innumerable strands connecting them. It brings into conjunction a mythic time in which the story of Beethoven's opera *Fidelio* is set, Beethoven's Vienna of the 1820s with the Napoleonic war in the background, the newly liberated but politically troubled Ghana of 1961, and the contemporary African American world in which Kennedy is writing. Each of these contexts reverberates on the other, commenting, enlarging and enriching the central concern of the play, the relationships between the aesthetic, the social and the political.

Adrienne Kennedy's plays show that she is a kindred spirit of the Beat writers and are clear, vibrant articulations of the angst of the 'Howl' generation. Their works share not only an inner turmoil, but also a quest for meaning, an individualism, a rejection of the banalities of society, a willingness to put their inner conflicted selves out there, and, finally, a determination to create performances out of the material of their lives.

Works cited

Baker, P. (2010), *William S. Burroughs*, London: Reaktion.
Betsko, K. and R. Koenig (1987), *Interviews with Contemporary Women Playwrights*, New York: Beech Tree.

Bryant-Jackson, P. and L. More Overbeck (eds) (1992), *Intersecting Boundaries: The Theatre of Adrienne Kennedy*, Minneapolis: University of Minnesota.

Burroughs, W.S. (1959), *Naked Lunch*, New York: Grove.

Burroughs, W.S. (1996), *My Education: A Book of Dreams*, Harmondsworth, Middlesex: Penguin.

de Lauretis, T. (ed.), (1986), *Feminist Studies/Critical Studies*. Bloomington: Indiana University.

Enkholy, S.N. (2012), *The Philosophy of the Beats*, Lexington: The University Press of Kentucky.

Grace, N.M. and J. Skerl (2012), 'Introduction to Transnational Beat: Global Poetics in a Postmodern World' in N.M. Grace and J. Skerl (eds), *Transnational Beat Generation*, New York: Palgrave Macmillan.

Holmes, J. C. (2001), 'This is the Beat Generation' in Ann Charters (ed.), *Beat Down to Your Soul: What Was the Beat Generation*, Harmondsworth, Middlesex: Penguin.

Irwin, J. (2012), 'William Burroughs as Philosopher: From Beat Morality to Third Worldism to Continental Theory' in S.N. Enkholy (ed.), *The Philosophy of the Beats*, Lexington: The University Press of Kentucky.

Kazin, A. (1971), 'He's just wild about writing', *The New York Times on the Web* (12 December 1971). Available at: www.nytimes.com/books/00/02/13/specials/burroughs-wild.html (last accessed 4 July 2015).

Kennedy, A. (1977), 'A Growth of Images', *The Drama Review* 21.4: 42–48.

Kennedy, A. (1987), *People Who Led to My Plays*, New York: Alfred A. Knopf.

Kennedy, A. (2001), *The Adrienne Kennedy Reader*, Introduction by W. Sollors, Minneapolis: University of Minnesota.

Kumar, N.N. (2005), 'Dramatic Transformations: The Surrealism of Being Black and Female in Adrienne Kennedy's *The Owl Answers*', *The Journal of American Drama and Theatre*, 17(2): 59–70.

McCarthy, M. (2001), 'Burroughs' *Naked Lunch*', in Ann Charters (ed.), *Beat Down to Your Soul: What Was the Beat Generation*, Harmondsworth, Middlesex: Penguin.

Rexroth, K. (1959), 'Discordant and Cool', *The New York Times on the Web* (29 November 1959). Available at: www.nytimes.com/books/97/09/07/home/kerouac-mexico.html (last accessed 4 July 2015).

Skerl, J. (1985), *William S. Burroughs: Twayne's United States Authors Series*, Boston: Twayne.

Part Three

Poets Theatre and the Beats

Bunny Lang and the Cambridge Poets' Theatre in the 1950s

Heidi R. Bean

Playwright, producer, actor, publicist, costume designer, director, and tireless advocate, Violet Ranney (V. R.) 'Bunny' Lang was a driving force of the Poets' Theatre of Cambridge, Massachusetts in the 1950s. From the group's founding in 1950 until her own untimely death of Hodgkin's disease in 1956 at the age of 32, Lang helped to shape the course of post-World War II American poetic theatre. Along with Lyon Phelps, the Harvard graduate and unpublished poet who had founded the group, and Mary (Molly) Manning Howe, the Irish-born writer and actor who directed drama at Radcliffe's Idler Theatre, Lang was one of three guiding personalities of the Cambridge Poets' Theatre in its important early years, when it was primarily a workshop for dramatists interested in forging a new American voice that would awaken its audiences via the merging of poetry and theatricality.

Lang was born in 1924 and grew up in Boston, the last of seven children. Her mother was a rich and beautiful Boston socialite; her father a musician, composer, and conductor. As a student, she attended the Hannah More Academy, then the University of Chicago, though she did not graduate. She was considered unusually alluring, if not a beauty, and when she had her debut into society in 1941, her future may have seemed charmed. However, Lang was not one to be idle. Serving two years in the Canadian WAC (the US organization would not take her at the age of 18), she first worked as a typist and filing clerk and then on a newspaper. She wrote poetry and short stories and worked on an historical novel before eventually turning to playwriting. While Lang had grown up amongst servants, her family's wealth had slipped away over the years. By the time she joined the Poets' Theatre in 1950, her mother had recently died after a long illness, and Lang was living with and caring for her ageing father in the no-longer-quite-elegant home she grew up in.

Some of Lang's stature in the Poets' (as the group was known) came from her ability to bring together the disparate worlds of Boston society and underground theatre as though they'd always been bedfellows. She was fiercely loyal to all. She was an active member of Newbury Street society, a member of the Charlotte Cushman Club (chairing their charity ball in 1954), and she had been 'brought up in a society so small', according to Poets' Theatre member and memoirist Alison Lurie, 'that to give someone's name was a sufficient description [of who they were]' (1975: 7). What distinguished Lang from the rest of her society peers, however, was that she extended this familiarity and coterie mentality in all of her affiliations, from fashionable elites to bohemian artists. Despite her pedigree, Lang was egalitarian in her social dealings. She was also completely at ease working with an experimental theatre that operated on a shoestring budget, and she dressed the part. Her regular uniform for Poets' Theatre meetings and rehearsals was a man's sweatshirt, torn sneakers, and a faded, dirty trenchcoat. At least as much by personality as by circumstance, she was equally comfortable with respectable Boston society, Harvard intellectuals, and bohemian artists, and she embraced them all.

When the Poets' Theatre came together in 1950, Lang quickly became one of its most active members. Officially, she was the group's secretary (Phelps was its president and Howe its vice president), but her involvement went far beyond this title. Peter Davison has called her 'the Mae West of the troupe' (1994: 26): she was energetic, seductive, and outrageous, and everyone who came into contact with her succumbed to her charm. Her work with the Poets' Theatre was hardly without conflict, however. Lang was known to be pushy and controlling, and the production in 1952 of her second play, *Fire Exit*, nearly brought the group to financial ruin, even as critics cautiously admired it. Though this strained her relationship with the Poets' it didn't end it, and her Beat-inspired third play, *I Too Have Lived in Arcadia*, produced in 1954, was by all accounts the Poets' Theatre's most popular production to date.

Lang's plays represent some of the best work produced by the Poets' Theatre in its early years, and the controversies that surrounded her participation with the group shed light on the clash of literary and theatrical values that not only characterized the Poets' Theatre during this time but were also playing out across American theatre and poetry in general. While most of the group's members esteemed Lang's work as a shining example of the new direction of poetic drama in the post-World War II period, not everyone agreed. And when Lang passed away prematurely in 1956, the Poets' Theatre began to head off in a very different direction, ultimately abandoning the plan to be a writerly project for would-be poet-dramatists in favour of becoming a producer of more 'serious' dramatic works.

The Poets' Theatre began in the summer of 1950 with a fireside chat in the home of poet and Harvard professor Richard Eberhart. In the academically orientated and critically celebrated poetry scene of Cambridge and Boston in the 1940s and 1950s, a group of Harvard-affiliated poets gathering together to discuss writing not poetry but drama might seem intentionally subversive. But thanks to such writers at T. S. Eliot, Christopher Fry, W. H. Auden, and Archibald MacLeish, verse drama had become a popular and viable form. It had become so popular, in fact, that Fry's *The Lady's Not for Burning* played in London's West End for nine months in 1949, while the following year, Eliot's *The Cocktail Party* ran on Broadway for 51 weeks and earned a Tony award for Best Play. At least one Cambridge critic, however, was suspicious of this public hunger for verse drama, remarking contemptuously that it simply 'fulfill[ed] a public need in a philistine era – to assuage the audience's feelings of guilt for not reading poetry: a guilt that [audiences wrongly felt] could be dissolved by the penance of seeing Fry's *The Dark Is Light Enough*' (Sayre 1995: 96). Notably, the poet-dramatists of the Poets' Theatre, while grateful for the renewed interest in poetry that verse drama had fostered, did not consider themselves the artistic inheritors of Eliot and Fry but rather found inspiration in Samuel Beckett, Alfred Jarry, Jean Cocteau, Bertolt Brecht, and Federico García Lorca, as well as in poets 'who had not written for theatre as yet', as Lyon Phelps put it in a 1958 interview (Discussion 1958: 13).

Despite Phelps's limited expertise – he had never published a poem and had no experience of writing for the theatre – his idea for a theatre dedicated exclusively to poetic drama 'caught on like wildfire' as Eberhart later remarked (1955: 19). Phelps's lack of experience was offset, however, by Howe's theatre credentials. Writer, actor, drama and film critic, and life-long friend of Samuel Beckett (as well as the mother of poets Susan and Fanny), Howe had performed at the Abbey Theatre, where she worked with Yeats, and at the Gate Theatre before moving to Cambridge with her husband who had joined the faculty at Harvard Law School and directed plays at Radcliffe College. Despite Howe's list of accomplishments, it was Lang who was the Poets' Theatre's most influential member in its early years; she was certainly one of its most colourful. She was the only member who had no affiliation with Harvard. Her poetry had already been published in *Poetry* and *The Chicago Review*, which earned her the respect of the other poets in the group, whose work had so far appeared only in the *Harvard Advocate*, from their alma mater institution (Lurie 1975: 13). Just as importantly, Lang had passion and flair; she championed theatricality and even embraced a certain kind of raw anti-professionalism. Although she wasn't present at the initial gathering in Eberhart's living room, she served as actor, director, costume designer, and especially promoter of the Poets' Theatre from its very first night. As several members recount, Lang's influence was everywhere.

Together, Phelps, Howe, and Lang personify the competing drives of the
early Poets' Theatre. It was not strictly a venue for poetry, 'serious' theatre, or
entertaining theatricality but rather a merging of those interests. Lang was
considered by some to be its visionary. It was Lang, for example, who brought
the poet Gregory Corso to the theatre, where he was originally hired to sweep
up (see Sayre 1995: 2001). While Lang was passionately encouraging young
writers and embracing anti-professionalism, Phelps was busily drawing up
formal procedures for the selection of plays to be produced. Meanwhile,
Howe served as the group's 'theatrical conscience ... [knowing] better than
any of her young colleagues what was playable, what would or wouldn't work
onstage' (Sayre 1995: 196). Under this joint tutelage, with a bit of bumping
and scraping, the Poets' Theatre began to stage its first performances.

The inaugural event was a programme of readings by ten poets quickly
put together to raise interest. Afterwards, Phelps delivered a speech on the
vision and goals of the Poets' Theatre in which he emphasized the importance
of poetic language over visual effect. While the venture was largely conceived
as a writerly project, Phelps also argued that '[T]he training of an audience is
inseparable from the training of ourselves as poet-playwrights' (1951: 5). On
26 February 1951, three months after that initial evening of poetry readings,
the Poets' Theatre presented its first official programme of plays at Cambridge's
Christ Church Parish House where Lang made her performance debut. The
free evening premiered Frank O'Hara's *Try! Try!*, John Ashbery's *Everyman*,
Richard Eberhart's *The Apparition*, and Lyon Phelps's *Three Words in No
Time*. Promotional illustrations were designed in the signature style of
O'Hara's Harvard dorm-mate Edward Gorey, who later earned a lasting
reputation for his macabre children's stories and illustrations such as *The
Gashlycrumb Tinies* (and who penned plays for the Poets' about such topics as
a teddy bear sneaking into the nursery to commit a murder). Lang directed
and starred in *Try! Try!*, written by her close friend O'Hara. Though she was
not known to be a good actress, 'it was', according to her friend Lurie,
'marvellous [sic] to watch her on the stage. She could save a bad play
sometimes simply by walking out and smiling at the audience: the less the
lines meant, the more she could put into them' (1975: 17–18). She favoured
slightly tattered costumes of flowing white folds, and while a show was
running she could invent new costumes nightly. Unlike other members of the
Poets', who, according to Lurie,were motivated by a desire to get their poetry
published or to achieve some measure of local fame, Lang used the Poets'
Theatre to 'express herself, to present herself' (Lurie 1975: 19). In her stage
debut with the group, she delivered O'Hara's lines with an ironic weightiness
that both heightened the play's humour and invited the audience to share in
the joke.

According to Phelps, Lang's direction of *Try! Try!* was 'subtle, conscientious, and serious', and he credited Lang's use of stylized gestures adapted from Noh, along with O'Hara's writing, for the play's comic success. Bringing the audience into the play – often by breaking through the theatrical illusion and sometimes also by thematizing the audience and the act of spectatorship – was an explicit, though somewhat controversial goal of the Poets' Theatre in its early years, a goal which Phelps traced back to the programme notes on Noh theatre that Lang wrote for the premiere production. Howe, meanwhile, protested that explicit appeals to the audience broke through the necessary illusion of theatre. This disagreement was part of a more general clash over theatrical values that continued to play in the background as the group grew and shifted in its first several years; this often found its way into Lang's plays.

It was within the context of this early explicit interest in the audience training that the first of Lang's three plays was produced by the Poets' Theatre – the Noh-inspired *At Battle's End* (1952). The play begins with the appearance of the stage manager (changed to the 'Interpreter-Chorus' in a later version of the play) who embarks on an explanation of the style of theatre the audience is about to see. In the initial draft of the play, the stage manager disparages Western realist theatre, which invites passivity, remarking that 'theater-going in our culture is the very antithesis of art' because art requires an audience to participate actively and give something of themselves (Lang typescript n.d.: n.p.). Rather than seeking mere entertainment and relaxation, the audience should be 'disciplined', actively working with the drama to reveal its meanings. In the later, published, version of the play, Lang toned down her criticism of the audience and instead emphasized Noh's use of theatricality and symbolism, rather than realist staging, and its convention of an official Spectator, 'who sat on the stage and set, for the audience, an example of perfect and unbroken concentration' (Lang 2010: 53).

Written entirely in verse, *At Battle's End* is not built around action, but around, as the Interpreter-Chorus puts it, 'Situation' (Lang 2010:53). The poetic texture gives the familiar story of a husband returned from the war (which was also the situation of O'Hara's *Try! Try!*) new purchase. After seven years on the front lines, Jack comes home seeking his wife Melpomene, but he has trouble finding her and enlists the assistance of Wong, a local gardener. Melpomene has not been happy to have been left alone for seven years, with a mother-in-law to care for, a house to keep, and no one to help. When her mother-in-law began stealing chickens and creating a general nuisance in the neighbourhood, Melpomene 'did away' with her, presumably sending her away to let 'charity' take care of her, and she now threatens that 'when [Jack] comes back, he'll get his' (Lang 2010: 55). Not surprisingly, then, the reunion between the couple is tense. Melpomene seems mostly interested in the gifts that Jack has brought, while Jack ruminates on all that has changed in his absence and on his regret at being taken away from his wife so quickly. Caught up in his own philosophizing about how war has changed him, Jack fails to notice Wong re-enter as a kind of grim reaper figure who causes Melpomene to drop dead immediately (the 'Supernatural Event' that, as the Interpreter-Chorus has instructed us, resolves a piece of Noh theatre). Eventually, Jack realizes what has happened and drops dead himself, after which Wong moralizes, somewhat cryptically, that 'man is like a pumpkin. For a while his cheek/Is ruddy like the pumpkin. Then he clings to vine./ When his stem is sturdy, everything is fine./But when he grows too fat and big—he breaks the twig' (Lang 2010: 59).

Lang's use of the stage manager to chastise the audience into greater discipline and responsibility (or of the Interpreter-Chorus in the later version to instruct the audience in the conventions of Noh theatre) was part of a larger emphasis on the role of the audience playing out in the poetry world. This was, after all, the era of Donald Allen's 'New American Poetry,' and performance poetics had taken hold across the nation. Emerging from multiple locations, including Berkeley, San Francisco, Boston, New York, and Black Mountain, the 'New American Poetry' challenged academic verse with a living practice that reached audiences directly through performance. Beat readings were infamously participatory, with poets either heckling one another or simply drowning each other out. The influence of the Poets' Theatre was more than circumstantial. Several of the 'New York-based poets' associated with Herbert Machiz's Artists' Theatre in the mid-1950s, for example, had only recently relocated from Boston and been actively involved with the Cambridge Poets. While Sayre asserts that the most lasting influence of the Poets' Theatre is its contribution to the development of a 'natural speaking voice' for poetry, she also argues that it can be seen as a spiritual predecessor to the later Off-Off Broadway movement and mid-century American avant-garde theatre companies and experimental clubs, such as La Mama. The intentionally anti-professional merging of poetry, art, and theatricality to which theatre historian Stephen Bottoms attributes the success of New York-based poets theatres was preceded by the similarly productive collaborations of the Poets' Theatre a decade earlier.

In *At Battle's End*, for example, Lang's Interpreter-Chorus figure explains that Noh plays are built around situations rather than actions: 'The Situation is *described* in lyric circumstances by poetic thoughts and stately movements. The audience comes to see how a story they all know very well is displayed by suggestive verses, subtle and philosophical commentaries and asides, and of course music and dance' (Lang 2010: 53). A decade later, New York's Off-Off Broadway and underground theatre scene would stage in cafés and makeshift venues highly theatrical performances that were built around a similar central emphasis on a particular moment instead of the development of themes and a linear narrative. As Bottoms describes it, these performances 'tended to stay in one place – literally, the small space of the stage – and to view that place prismatically, creating a variety of perspectives on the central dramatic circumstance by "riffing" improvisationally around it. They keenly felt the need for a central, theatrical image around which a play could cohere', focusing on what they found most visually exciting (Bottoms 2004: 125).

As a conceptual merging of poetic language and performance, poet's theatre worked to disrupt the conventions of both poetry and theatre. As theatre, poets explicitly brought 'reality' into contact with 'imagination'. It used bodies as art material, turned spectators into actors and actors into spectators, and drew attention to the conventions of theatrical representation, such as stage, frame, props, etc. As poetry (building off poetic trends in the 1940s), poet's theatre explored the arbitrariness of the symbol, made the 'subject' of the piece the shifting relations between author, narrator, world, and language, self-consciously explored the evolving processes of art-making and meaning-making, and employed linguistic artifice and the materiality of language to undermine absorption into the conventions of theatre. Many poets of the 1940s saw themselves as agents of cultural change and understood poetry to be a more 'real' experience for its wedding of imagination with reality – what Sarah Bay-Cheng and Barbara Cole have called 'the hallmark of truth within the theatrical illusion of realism' (Bay-Cheng and Cole 2010: 21).

One method of blending the poetic with the theatrical involved incorporating popular theatrical forms with verse dialogue. Lang's second play to be produced by the Poets' Theatre was built around a community of vaudeville and burlesque performers. *Fire Exit*, a loose adaptation of the Eurydice and Orpheus myth and subtitled 'Vaudeville for Eurydice', turns Eurydice, or Eury, as she's known in the play, into a performer-in-training. Eury is being raised after her mother's death by her aunts and uncles, all of whom work the Vaudeville circuit as performers and concessionaires. She attends a convent school, but during the breaks, the family trains her as a dancer and performer with the hope that she will join the family profession. But Eury doesn't feel that this is work of which she can be proud. When she meets Orpheus, he is a classical pianist working in a hotel lobby; by the time he returns for her several years later (after she has graduated from school, turned down a marriage proposal, and passed on a chance to join a travelling midget show to wait for him), he has become a hugely successful 'serious' professional musician. Unfortunately, Orpheus is not interested in Eury's career, or even in her desires and happiness. As his fame and fortune increase, he wants her simply to follow him, quietly waiting and doing nothing. Eventually, he leaves her behind on an ill-fated bicycle tour through the French countryside; when he returns to find her, she's gone. He looks for her for years, eventually assuming she's dead, only to learn from a Vaudeville comedian that she works as a house chorus girl and occasional stripper in an unremarkable town – Hades as burlesque theatre. He comes to take her back, promising that her past doesn't matter, but Eury refuses to return. 'Perhaps it was better this way', she remarks at the end to the comedian who has become a kind of father-figure to her: 'I wanted him to look at me' (Lang 1975: 252).

The play was produced by the Poets' Theatre in 1952; Lang starred in the role of Eurydice. In 1951, Lang had worked a several-month stint as a chorus girl at the famed 'Old Howard', the Howard Atheneum, a long-standing Boston burlesque theatre, to pay off a debt. Even after the debt had been repaid, Lang continued in the chorus for several months. Her room in her father's home prominently displayed the photos and notes the regular company gave her upon her departure and her closet held a number of used burlesque costumes. She wrote *Fire Exit* in part as a tribute to the friends she'd made at the Old Howard (Lurie 1975: 40). Her friends from the Poets' Theatre all went, sometimes regularly, to see her perform. Lurie described the standard Old Howard evening's entertainments in this way: 'A short opening number, often with a patriotic theme, presented the cast, and then the individual acts began: a vaudeville scrap bag of comedy bits, strippers, chorus numbers, and specialties which might include a tap dancer, an acrobat or sentimental popular songs to the accompaniment of candy-box colored lantern slides' (Lurie 1975: 39). In *Fire Exit*, Lang positions such popular theatricality as a foil for 'serious' performance; this clash itself becomes the ethical dilemma of modern life.

Lang's experiences as a chorus dancer inspire the play's themes, especially the conflict between the supposed social betterment encouraged by true 'art' and the profane pleasure aroused by popular entertainments. Eury's Vaudeville family members love, respect, and take care of themselves and each other, and they take pride in their work. Orpheus lives in a world of adulation and isolation rather than love and community; his single-minded pursuit of his art renders him incapable of love and compassion for another person. The difference seems not to be 'art vs. entertainment' but whether one believes in what one is doing. Eury tells her uncle that she'll never be a performer because she doesn't 'believe' in it and she could never be proud of it. Hurt, her uncle explains how he and his wife have built up their bird act, training the birds themselves, and creating the show from scratch. Orpheus, by contrast, has talent but little depth. He mocks his own audience, makes career choices out of a sense of competiveness rather than devotion, and seems not to enjoy his own successes.

Like *At Battle's End*, *Fire Exit* thematizes the role of the audience, and it critiques popular audiences of all classes. Eury cringes at her experience with Vaudeville audiences, who, emboldened by their ability to hide in the darkness, laugh and mock the performers they've paid to see. 'I hate the audience', she announces coldly (Lang 1975: 162). Orpheus, on the other hand, is advised by his manager not to cater to popular tastes. He doesn't, but, bewilderingly, his music is adored by popular audiences, who misunderstand his intentions. 'I wrote *The Melancholy Magic of Your Smile* as a joke, do you understand?' he protests, to no avail, as his audience chases him, not comprehending his music but treating him like some sort of prize or object (Lang 1975: 196). Audiences, the play implies, are both ignorant and cruel. Popular performers are caught between the jeering of the working-class spectators and 'college boys' who come to 'laugh at what is publicly contemptible' (Lang 1975: 245) and the bafflement of high society who can't understand why they don't try to 'better' themselves. The play might even be taken as a subtle swipe at the behind-the-scenes conflicts of the Poets' Theatre itself, where Lang, O'Hara, Phelps, and others supported the playful theatricals being produced by many of the young poet-playwrights and Howe, Catharine Huntington, and others advocated more 'serious' theatre.

Whereas *At Battle's End* is written entirely in verse and uses poetry as one of several theatrical elements to heighten the symbolic impact of the play, *Fire Exit* uses poetry rhetorically to emphasize key themes and critiques. When Orpheus returns to Eury to reaffirm his love and marry her, Eury and her family launch into satirically stilted verse, drawing attention to the unreasonable hopes they place in her betrothal to a man of social standing (Lang 1975: 177–178):

Eurydice   So long to the scullery hopes and the dismal weeks
  That wore and that told, that scrabbed and screeched!
Now for the weather, the pitch and the plume,
The place of the precipice, Orpheus has come!

Mrs. Blanche   Now she will no longer weep and snarl,
  Now she will no longer creep or wail!

Eurydice   There shall be nothing that I will not understand,
  There will be no attention that he will not grant!
  We shall be cared for and coveted, justified at last,
  With all the bright what-have-you that we love the best!

Mrs. Robelle   No longer abide her silly ancillary decisions,
Now she knows where she is.
Reward us her aunts our precipitant persistence,
He is hers, she is his.

Part of what we see in this mockery of poetic elevation are Lang's own deeply ambivalent feelings about marriage. Poetry reveals this young love-at-first-sight as an overwrought performance of form with no substance. Rather than a tale of the beauty of a doomed but undying relationship, the story of Orpheus and Eurydice becomes here a biting critique of our cultural belief in the transformative power of love.

In the end, *Fire Exit* was controversial not for its subject matter but for the way Lang took control of the play, defying other board members and racking up costly bills. She directed the play herself because, according to Lurie, she couldn't find any other director agreeable enough (a promotional flyer listed the director as 'Madeleine Paget', an apparent pseudonym). While Lang was rumoured to have argued that the play was worth $300 in promotion for the Poets' (Accounts 1952: n.p.), the one-week run at Cambridge's Brattle Theatre ultimately ended up putting the Poets' Theatre several hundred dollars in debt, possibly due to unusually high advertising and production costs that Lang had approved. However, reviews of the play were positive overall. The *Christian Science Monitor* praised its imaginative dialogue in 'the hard task of bringing new poetry to the stage', but it ultimately found both the writing and performing uneven (Nordell 1952: 10), singling out for criticism the play's 'undisciplined' merging of realism and stylized acting. The *Harvard Crimson*, on the other hand, deemed the play 'thoroughly entertaining' with 'some very interesting characters', an 'original interpretation' and a 'fine cast'. It was a great improvement on the 'spotty poetry and confusing physical gyrations' of past productions, the review asserted, concluding that *Fire Exit* offered renewed hope for the Poets' Theatre (Maccoby 1952).

Having been nearly driven to financial ruin by *Fire Exit*, however, the Poets' Theatre changed tack in 1953, producing only three plays, all by established authors – *Agamemnon* by Harvard literature professor William Alfred, and *This Music Crept by Me upon the Waters* and *The Trojan Horse*, both by Pulitzer Prize-winning poet and Harvard faculty member Archibald MacLeish. Howe directed all three with Phelps acting as producer. Rounding out the season was a much-celebrated reading of *Under Milk Wood* by the Irish poet and playwright Dylan Thomas. The following year, the Poets' offered a mixed season of work by both new and established authors; Lang again became active as director, actor, and playwright. The season included plays by Phelps, the budding American poet James Schuyler, American poet and academic Reuel Denney, French poet René Char, Irish playwright Denis Johnston, and the American literary critic and poet I. A. Richards. This was also the season in which Lang presented her third and final play, *I Too Have Lived in Arcadia*. In a letter to Bradley Phillips, whom Lang married in 1955, Hugh Amory wrote (Amory 1956: n.p.):

> Without laboring the point, I don't know as she ever regarded the Poets' Theatre as her friend, in the sense that I think they were opposed to much of what she believed in, and still are. The big battle, of course, was over *Fire Exit*, on which the Poets' Theatre has since meanly claimed the credit. All I can say is that she conveyed a sense of honor even in returning to a theatre which had none, and did not regard it as opportunism to have *Arcadia* produced here, the more so, after all, since she did not receive the production she wanted.

Whatever happened behind the scenes, Lang did eventually return; *Arcadia* was, by all estimations, her best work.

This time Lang stayed out of the production, which was directed by Phelps – a production which Lurie calls 'first-rate, professional but unpretentious' (Lurie 1975: 55). The plot revolves around Damon and Chloris, who have left their 'beat', 'bugged', 'hung-up', and false lives in the city to live on an island near Newfoundland, raising food and sheep, loving themselves and each other. When Damon's former lover Phoebe comes to the island to take him back to his urban life of music, art, and nightclubs, Damon, who is easily swayed and never fully honest with himself, follows her back. The plot is simple but the play is infused with poetic musings on evolution and love. It also includes a talking dog named Georges, Phoebe's sidekick (perhaps a former lover who now follows her slavishly, the play seems to imply), who speaks in French translations of American jazz slang – the dog riffs on 'dig' with the French words *creuser* and *bêcher* and finds Chloris's naiveté hilarious when she doesn't understand him. Lang later implied that she wrote the play to get revenge on a former New York boyfriend who had dumped her.

Unlike *At Battle's End* and *Fire Exit*, *Arcadia* neither thematizes nor critiques its audience. Instead, it is Damon's superficiality and lack of self-honesty that are lambasted here. Damon is a trumpet player who gives up his ideals of an 'honest' life to return to his unfulfilled desires as a nightclub musician. Poetic dialogue heightens the power of the play's conflicts, and expositions and philosophical ruminations replace action. The central dramatic circumstance plays out with fantastical elements – in *At Battle's*

End, it is the grim reaper figure who causes both Jack and Melpomene to drop dead; in *Arcadia*, it is the talking dog with the Beat vocabulary. A poetic quality imbues all of the play's dialogue, but it is neither as symbolic as *At Battle's End* nor as plot-driven as *Fire Exit*. Instead, the play attempts to bring poetry and drama together into a balanced presentation of dramatic situation, language, and action.

The production, which included recorded jazz interludes and was preceded by a playlet by Alfred de Musset called *A Door Must Be Open or Shut*, premiered to a packed house in October of 1954. While the *Harvard Crimson* complained that the straightforward story was 'smothered by form and language that was far too complex' (Schoenberg 1954), the *Boston Herald* admired Lang's 'originality and genuine poetic talent', though it also felt it presented 'a challenge both exasperating and stimulating' (Hughes 1954). Mixed reviews were the norm for the Poets' Theatre, however, and *Arcadia* was arguably the most popular play the group had produced its first five years.

This success only underscored what several members of the Poets already believed – that Lang's work represented some of the best new poetic writing being produced for the theatre. *Arcadia* was enthusiastically nominated by the Poets' Theatre to be published in Harvard University Press's *Poets' Theatre* series, which had been founded in 1953 explicitly to publish, annually, a play that represented the best work produced by the Poets in the previous year. Though the series was a remarkable institutional vote of confidence in the experimental theatre company, conflicts between the press and the theatre over differing goals for the series slowed down publication. Lang's *Fire Exit* had been recommended for publication in 1954, as the second volume in the series, but it was rejected by the Press. Perhaps submitting Lang's *Arcadia* along with a proposal for a revised selection process was a hopeful calculation. Certainly, submitting a second play by Lang after one had already been rejected indicated a particular vote of confidence in her work. Richard Eberhart wrote a letter supporting *Arcadia*'s publication on the grounds of its contemporariness, pointing out that the Poets' Theatre was especially interested in showcasing plays with modern themes and characters that would appeal to young audiences. Then, too, this was the third play of Lang's to be produced by the Poets', and each had been more critically successful than the last. While *Fire Exit* had run for four nights at the 200-seat Brattle Theatre, *Arcadia* had run for an initial week and then been extended for another week at the 50-seat Palmer Street Theatre that had recently become the Poets' Theatre's home. In a second letter in support of *Arcadia*'s nomination to the Press, Hugh Amory, using the pseudonym Willis Wayde, estimated that 'at least 400 of this 800 [who saw the play] wanted to read it, from conversations in the lobby. Their feelings were so new, I think, that they wanted to confirm them to see if they were right' (Wayde n.d.: n.p.).But *Arcadia* was ultimately rejected by the Press on literary grounds.

Meanwhile, Archibald MacLeish had been working quietly to secure a Rockefeller grant to support a Poets' Theatre artist residency. The grant was approved in 1954, and the first residency was jointly awarded to Lang and O'Hara for the first six months of 1956. This included 'money for a tape recorder and travel expenses of poets coming to Cambridge' (Poets' Theatre, 7 Sept 1954: n.p.). It also included a stipend of $1,500 each. While some complained that O'Hara drank his residency away in Boston-area bars, and Lang spent half of hers on a honeymoon in Europe, the joint selection of O'Hara and Lang demonstrated the Poets' Theatre's vision of poetic drama as a new form in which poetry served not as merely a 'texture' for traditional dramatic form but as a new unity of poetry and drama that would give drama a new form. Lang died, however, just two weeks after her residency ended.

Over the course of its first six years, under the shared guidance of Phelps, Lang, and Howe, the Poets' Theatre grew in both reputation and respectability, partly through its own efforts and the quality of the plays it produced, partly through increasing cultural interest in verse drama. Harvard faculty and students who had previously seen the theatre as beneath them began to flock to the productions. Harvard sponsored its own symposium on verse play at the Harvard Summer School in 1955, and though it did not officially enlist the Poets' Theatre to present its work, at least some of the panelists were members.[1] The reputation of the Poets' Theatre spread regionally too. WGBH, a local Boston radio station, broadcast its productions of MacLeish's plays in May of 1954, and by early 1955, Wheaton, Bard, and Bennington Colleges, as well as the Artists' Theatre in New York, were all requesting permission to produce their plays.

Although interest grew, funding did not keep pace. The Rockefeller grant was prestigious and not ungenerous, but it was used to support writers in residence, not the costs of operating the theatre itself. There was talk of creating a summer school, in acting, dance, or stage movement, to raise funds. By 1955, the Poets seemed to be experiencing a crisis of identity as a direct result of its own success. While some, like Lang, saw it as primarily a lab for writers, others, like Howe, saw it as a professional theatre.

In the end, the biggest blow to the Poets' early experimentalism was a confluence of several events – including Lang's passing, their growing popularity, formal recognition from the Harvard University Press and the Rockefeller Foundation, and the enormous audience draw of more traditional events and readings, such as Thomas's reading of *Under Milk Wood* and poetry readings by Dame Edith Sitwell and Sir Osbert Sitwell. From 1956, until its demise in 1968,[2] the Poets' produced a wealth of modern theatre that included both new poetic plays as well as 'classics' by such figures as Beckett, T. S. Eliot, Lorca, and Eugène Ionesco, but its vision of a truly new poet's theatre had faded even as its name had remained. Direct instruction of the audience vs the necessity of illusion continued to be a point of contention in the early years of the Poets' Theatre, but as its productions of new plays by young writers increasingly gave way to 'classic' plays by established artists, its explicit attention to audience training began to recede.

Still, because of some of its early performances in New York as well as the relocation there of some of its early members such as Ashbery and O'Hara, the legacy of the Poets' Theatre that Lang had helped to build lived on – a legacy that could be found not only in New York's poets theatres of the 1950s and 1960s, but also in less obvious places, such as the work of The Living Theatre, in the San Francisco Poets Theatre in the 1970s and 1980s, and even today in works by several poet-playwrights producing new theatre.

Works cited

Accounts letter (1952), *Fire Exit*: printed material, Folder 403, Poets' Theatre Collection.

Amory, H. (1956), Letter to Bradley Phillips, 15 October 1956, Folder 92, V. R. Lang Papers (MS Am 1951), Houghton Library, Harvard University.

Bay-Cheng, S. and B. Cole (eds) (2010), *Poets at Play: An Anthology of Modernist Drama*, Selinsgrove: Susquehanna University.

Bottoms, S. J. (2004), *Playing Underground: A Critical History of the 1960s Off-Off-Broadway Movement*, Ann Arbor: University of Michigan.

Davison, P. (1994), *The Fading Smile: Poets in Boston, from Robert Frost to Robert Lowell to Sylvia Plath, 1955–1960*, New York: Knopf.

Discussion between Lyon Phelps, Mary Manning, and Jack Rogers concerning the history of the Poets' Theatre (1958), typescript carbon transcript, Folder 567, Poets' Theatre Collection.

di Prima, D. (2001), *Recollections of My Life as a Woman*, New York: Viking.

Eberhart, R. (1955), 'Poets' Theatre II', *Center: A Magazine for the Performing Arts* 2.3: 19–21.

Howe, M. M., C. Huntington, and W. Hunt (1955), Letter, 8 December 1955, Miscellaneous Papers concerning season 1955–1956, Folder 557, Poets' Theatre Collection.

Hughes, E. (1954), 'Poets' Theatre: *A Door Must Be Open or Shut, I Too Have Lived in Arcadia*,' *The Boston Herald*, 27 October 1954.

Janssen, M. (2010), *Not at All What One Is Used To: The Life and Times of Isabella Gardner*, Columbia, MO: University of Missouri.

Lang, V. R. [Bunny] (n.d.), 'At Battle's End: A Verse Drama in the Manner of the Noh,' Typescript, Folder 3, V. R. Lang Papers (MS Am 1951), Houghton Library, Harvard University.

Lang, V.R. [Bunny] (1975), *Fire Exit* and *I Too Have Lived in Arcadia*, in *Poems and Plays*, New York: Random House, 151–252; 253–97.

Lang, V.R. [Bunny] (2010), *At Battle's End*, in K. Killian and D. Brazil (eds), *The Kenning Anthology of Poets Theatre, 1945–1985*, Chicago: Kenning, 52–59.

Lurie, A. (1975), 'V. R. Lang: A Memoir', in V.R. Lang, *Poems and Plays*, New York: Random House, 3–71.

Maccoby, M. (1952), 'The Playgoer: *Fire Exit* at the Brattle', *Harvard Crimson*, 2 December 1952.

Nordell, R. (1952), '*Fire Exit* by Poets' Theatre', *Christian Science Monitor*, 2 December 1952: 10.

O'Hara, F. (1951), '"Try! Try!" Poets' Theatre Reading with John Ashbery, Richard Eberhart, and Lyon Phelps', Audio recording, The Listening Booth, Woodberry Poetry Room, Harvard University. Available at: http://hcl. harvard.edu/poetryroom/listeningbooth/poets/ohara.cfm (last accessed 26 July 2015).

O'Hara, F. (1960), 'Try! Try!' in Herbert Machiz (ed.), *Artists' Theatre: Four Plays*, New York: Grove, 15–42.

Phelps, L. (1951), 'The Objectives of the Poets' Theatre', Typescript, Folder 542, Poets' Theatre Collection.

Poets' Theatre (1952), Executive Committee, Meeting Minutes from 25 September 1952, Folder 8, Poets' Theatre Collection.

Poets' Theatre (1954), Meeting Minutes from 7 September 1954, Folder 9, Poets' Theatre Collection.

Poets' Theatre Collection, Poets' Theatre (Cambridge, Mass.) Records, 1936–1989 (MS Thr 833), Harvard Theatre Collection, Houghton Library, Harvard University.

Sayre, N. (1995), *Previous Convictions: A Journey through the 1950s*, New Brunswick, NJ: Rutgers University.

Schoenberg, R. J. (1954), '*I Too Have Lived in Arcadia* at the Poets' Theatre', *The Harvard Crimson*, 28 October 1954.

Senelick, L. (2000), 'Text and Violence: Performance Practices of the Modernist Avant-Garde', in J. Harding (ed.), *Contours of the Theatrical Avant-Garde: Performance and Textuality*, Ann Arbor: University of Michigan, 15–42.

Tytell, J. (1995), *The Living Theatre: Art, Exile, and Outrage*, New York: Grove.

Wayde, W. [Hugh Amory] (n.d.), Correspondence with Harvard University Press, Folder 171, Poets' Theatre Collection.

Diane di Prima as Playwright: The Early Years 1959–1964

Nancy M. Grace

Anyone who has followed the career of the poet Diane di Prima is aware that she's an autodidact and a Renaissance individual. Many know her as the author of the erotic *Memoirs of a Beatnik* and of the poems *Loba*, 'Rant, from a Cool Place', and 'A Brass Furnace Going Out: Song after an Abortion'. Standard biographies of her report that in the early 1960s she was a co-founder/editor of *The Floating Bear* newsletter with LeRoi Jones (the late Amiri Baraka) and soon thereafter, co-founder with her then-husband Alan Marlowe of The Poet's Press. Sometimes wedged between these is the often-overlooked fact that in the early 1960s she also co-founded the New York Poets Theatre.

The confluence of these streams is significant because they speak to the dynamism with which di Prima began and has remained faithful to a poetics that refuses narrow categorization of genre, aesthetics, and authorial presence. Even the founding of the New York Poets Theatre represents this post-World War II bohemian blurring of boundaries – and for di Prima was one of many projects to which she devoted considerable energy, including writing, editing, acting, translating medieval Latin love poems, and, equally integrated with the others, raising two daughters as a single mother. The founding of the Poets Theatre in spring 1961, however, has remained a significant touchstone in her life. As she wrote in *Recollections* of *My Life as a Woman*, her 2001 memoir of her early years in New York City, it was one of those moments '. . . that in happening, immediately stamp their imprint on the gullible stuff of our brains, whispering "This is important. Remember this"' (2001: 255). In her mind's eye, that 'bright and gusty' day, five intrepid young artists – she, James Waring, John Herbert McDowell, LeRoi Jones, and Alan Marlowe – walked in 'to a notary's office, to complete the first steps in the process of founding the New York Poets Theatre' (2001: 255). The dancer Freddie Herko – one of di Prima's dearest friends – was also a co-founder but did not accompany them that day, although he remained involved until his suicide in 1964. Despite the passage of time, or perhaps because of it, di Prima remembers that for the most part the Theatre fulfilled their optimistic vision, 'stand[ing] out in its harmony and seeming unity of purpose' (2001: 256).

Recollections testifies to di Prima's serious involvement in New York's emerging avant garde theatre, to which she contributed not only as a co-founder of a company but also as an actor, playwright, and artistic director (Killian and Brazil 2010: 553). Even after leaving New York permanently for California in the late 1960s, she continued to work in theatre, finishing her full-length *Whale Honey* in 1975. As editors Kevin Killian and David Brazil remark in *The Kenning Anthology of Poets Theater 1945–1985*, her 'influence on poets theatre has been lasting and deep' (2010: 552).

Despite such an accolade, her work as a playwright has received little historical or critical attention. I speculate that there are several major reasons for this. First, sad to say, there remains a long-standing academic blindness to the literary significance of Beats and Beat texts, both still considered by many to be uneducated, scruffy rip-offs of others' genius. Then, too, *Zipcode*, the text in which she compiled most of her plays, published by Coffee House Press in 1991, has been out of print for years and is not available in many college or university libraries. The anthology is also often omitted from easily accessible online bibliographies of di Prima's works. Fortunately, original typescripts of all of her plays are available from the University of Louisville archives, so scholars as well as devotees can access this treasure trove, all of which bear witness to the care with which di Prima has preserved this critical period of her life and that of post-World War II theatre and dance culture in the United States. Plays in the Louisville collection date from late 1959 to 1980. Di Prima carefully attached Post-it® notes to the archival materials with dates of composition, identification of typesetting copies for *Zipcode*, and dates and places of some production. The focus of this chapter is a sub-set of di Prima's plays from 1959 through to 1964, when the New York Poets Theatre closed – arguably the period during which she was most devoted to the theatre.

Di Prima's earliest play is *The Discontent of the Russian Prince*, which she dated circa 1959, noting that it was produced in 1961 by the New York Poets Theatre. *Russian Prince* was one of three that constituted the debut programme of the Theatre on 29 October 1961, in a space called the Off-Bowery Theatre. The other two were *The Pillow* by Michael McClure and an excerpt titled 'The Eighth Ditch' from LeRoi Jones's *The System of Dante's Hell. Rain Fur* was also written in 1959; it was never produced but is published in Killian and Brazil's anthology .She wrote several plays in 1960: *Paideuma*, performed as a staged reading at the Living Theatre in New York in 1960; *Like*, a one-act play in four scenes produced at the American Theatre for Poets in New York City in 1964; and *Murder Cake*, performed as a staged reading at The Living Theatre and directed by the dancer/choreographer Jimmy Waring in 1960. It was performed as a full production at the New York's Poets Theatre on 21 March 1963, and published in *Kulchur* magazine in the spring of 1963.[1] *Poet's Vaudeville* is a short libretto that di Prima composed in 1962 and produced at New York's Café Cino in March 1965. She wrote several other short plays during this formative period, in addition to the first three acts of *Whale Honey* in 1962. However, the subset identified above, all one acts written in their entirety from 1959–1962, provides an excellent lens through which to observe di Prima's development as both experimental playwright and poet.

In *Recollections*, di Prima describes this period as a mix of aesthetics and ideas: 'Everything from Burlesque to Bauhaus was playing itself out on our stage, in our company and the work was richer and more exciting for it; though it was also—it had to be—uneven and infuriating' (2001: 280). In the New York Poets Theatre alone, participants and playwrights included Waring, Marlowe, Frank O'Hara, Wallace Stevens, Gertrude Stein, John Wieners, Barbara Guest, Robert Duncan, Kenneth Koch, and dancers from Merce Cunningham's company – an eclectic set of play bills, to say the least.[2]

Fittingly, di Prima's plays reflect this greater egalitarian yet cantankerous amalgamation. *Poet's Vaudeville*, while not her first play, makes an excellent case in point. It features a set of characters simply named 'People', 'Animals', 'The Seasons', 'Love' and 'Death'. Reminiscent of vaudeville as an early twentieth-century form of popular culture entertainment presenting disparate and unrelated acts, these characters deliver a hodge-podge of truisms (e.g., 'Magic is merely the practice of coordination,' 5), insider *avant garde* jokes (e.g., 'Confusion confuses Freddie [Herko] less than order,' 1), children's songs (e.g., 'No more pencils no more books/No more teachers dirty looks', 4), animal sounds (e.g., 'Woof-Woofs'), and meta-discourse (e.g., 'I think the thing to do with this section is you write the music first & then I'll make words', 2). Reflecting post-World War II nihilism and despair more so than *fin de siècle* vaudevillian silliness and sentimentality, the play ends with the dark existential pronouncement, 'And we/Whom death pulls down to earth/Are bones & ashes/And no more' (8). *Poet's Vaudeville* is more tightly unified thematically than a vaudeville programme and resists the grotesque qualities of vaudevillian circus with its fondness for gratuitous sexual titillation; simultaneously, the play revels in its progenitor's emphasis on whimsy, language play, and irreverence, often aimed at overcoming class and other prejudices – all of which di Prima and many of her compatriots fostered during those heady years in New York's Lower East Side/East Village avant garde.[3]

Di Prima's theatrical productions, like those of many of her Beat contemporaries, adhere to two major criteria by which Killian and Brazil assembled their Poets Theatre anthology. In the context of western literary/

theatrical histories, Poets Theatre texts, as Killian and Brazil interpret them, are coterie productions intended to destabilize more conventional theatrical forms in the process of affirming both the social scene in which the performance takes place and the poetic integrity of the work itself (2010: xiv). As such, they are often highly experimental, produced in low-budget venues, and rarely see the media light of mainstream productions – all qualities nurtured, if not revered, by di Prima and her coterie. In fact, Joseph LeSueur, editor of the special play issue of *Kulchur*, the 1963 volume that included di Prima's *Murder Cake*, stated in his brief introduction that 'no straight realistic or naturalistic play is included. So we might as well draw a conclusion, an optimistic one of course: as long as an "opening-up" exists, a climate which either occasions or permits new forms, the non-commercial theatre is still very much alive' (di Prima 1963: 1). Moreover, Killian and Brazil reject the facile definition of a poets' theatre as 'a play written by a poet' (2010: xii), concluding that a more accurate criterion is the fact that these plays were important but non-identical to the works upon which the author's reputation was based.[4]

While her plays fit within this broader category of poets' theatre – hence her well-earned inclusion in the Kenning anthology – particular threads, topical and aesthetic, demarcate them as hers – and hers alone. Few, for instance, could mistake a di Prima play for a LeRoi Jones play with its super-realistic characters, homophobia, and jazz/race-inspired language of anger, defiance, and violence aimed at middle-class, white Americans; a Wallace Stevens play with its clear, serene, male-centred and symbol-laden portraiture featuring haute-coterie anaphoric dialogue; or a Michael McClure play with its misogynist, beast-like humans screeching 'beast language' caricatures of primal babble. Any number of others could be added to this list, including women writers, such as Gertrude Stein, V.R. 'Bunny' Lang, or ruth weiss, although all three can be aligned more closely with di Prima's aesthetics since their plays, as do hers, at times defy the traditional male gaze.

What, then, distinguishes a di Prima play as a di Prima play? Generically, it is a persistent devotion to a feminist/surrealist/absurdist vision that speaks not only to a twentieth-century, Euro-American dissemination of radical politics and the arts, but also to di Prima's private world of aesthetic, historical, and mystical influences. Di Prima reified this particular personalized hybrid differently depending on the genre in which she was working. For example, one can discern in just about any di Prima text her indebtedness to Keats and Pound – especially her focus on light – expressed not only through her reliance on the visual image but also what Anthony Libby calls the 'white light of traditional mysticism' (2002: 63) or the 'magick' of a number of transcendental practices, including writing. However, several key elements are noticeably absent from the early plays but are reflected in her first book of poetry, *This Kind of Bird Flies Backwards* (1958), and in her experimental *Dinners and Nightmares* (1961). The plays do not revel in Black-inspired Beat and hipster language: rarely does one come across the scatological, the obscene, the dirty, or terms such as 'chick', 'swing' 'beat', 'wow', or 'dig' – instead, the apostrophic and definitely old-world European 'O' dominates. For the most part, the plays also eschew the realistic vision of the Lower East Side/ Greenwich Village as the hodge-podge of roach-infested pads and bars that *Dinners* highlights. Nor do the plays foreground the Poundian economy of language, especially typewriter abbreviations such as '', 'wd', 'w/', that one finds in di Prima's poems and letters.[5] Missing as well is the violence and horror bred of anger at, on the macro-level, the mid-century world gone mad with near-apocalyptic war and, at the micro-level, the injustices women and other marginalized groups have faced. These raw emotions permeate *Dinners* and *Bird*, exemplified in the former by the often quoted 'Nightmare #4', which expresses the speaker's brutal killing of a cat (*Selected Poems* 4). Such naked honesty is barely discernible in the plays, suppressed between the lines and under the surface of Bahktin-like language play.

The vision that she used for the plays was not birthed whole cloth, but it did emerge quickly over the five years during which she practiced sustained playwriting. Perhaps the most direct way to discern the personal thread is through the characters that populate her plays. A detailed, although not absolutely comprehensive, mapping of them looks like this: British Romantic Writers (e.g., Byron and the Shelleys), British Historical Figures (e.g., Richard Lovelace), The Seasons (e.g., Winter, Spring, Fall, and Summer), Numbers (she loved and worked easily with mathematics), Classical European Authors (Dante, read to her by her grandfather), Nursery Rhyme Characters (e.g., Jack and Jill, Tom Thumb), Characters from Fictional Works in the Anglo-American/Greco-Roman Literary Tradition (Emma, Olimpia, King Minos, Childe Harold), Plants (Trees), Animals (e.g., Dogs), Types (e.g., Archeologists, Girl, Boy, Man, Woman, Child), Abstractions (e.g., Love and Death), and Gender-identified names (e.g., Bessie, Kit). This list does not imply that a reader or audience can't identify or *identify with* her characters, but rather that they constitute the syncretic vision created from her experiences as a reader, writer, female, bi-sexual, Italian American, post-war 20-year-old, daughter, friend, student, *avant garde* poet, mother, scholar, mystic, anarchist, comic, and other identities. As characters, they mediate authorial and narrator perspectives like an encyclopaedic rubric or *topoi* of American/British/European histories.

On the trans-Atlantic plain is di Prima's deep indebtedness to the impact of Modernist practices and philosophies on mid-twentieth century poetics. *Modernism* itself can be a vexed term, and rightly so, if one approaches it as a movement or school. However, it is neither, despite the fact that it is associated

Beat Drama

with a literary period.[6] Di Prima's cultural world, specifically the Modernism with which she was most familiar, was fundamentally American/Anglo-Eurocentric.[7] In her plays, we most often find vestiges of Dadism, Vorticism, Expressionism, Feminism, Absurdism, and Surrealism, the dramatic structures representing uninhibited appropriation, apparently as the mood struck her, of the mesmerizing swirl of ideas permeating the American art scene in the post-war years. However, di Prima's art, beginning with her earliest poetry, continuing in other mediums, and solid as ever in her most recent book of poetry, *The Poetry Deal* (2014), rests firmly upon a search for 'prime matter' or 'the real', which exists beyond language and is thus accessed by tapping into the unconscious, an apparently magical process (or alchemical as she later came to view it through her study of Paracelsus) by which the individual moves outside the boundaries of human cultures to experience the spiritual essence of cosmic creation (Leslie 1997: 16).

To this end, the poetics of influence as di Prima articulates it works dialectically as all writers not only draw upon those who have come before them but also sculpt a reader's visions of those very precursors through aesthetic appropriation of them. Defying the trope of Western art coming from 'a broken, an incomplete, tradition' to which we remain blind, di Prima credits Western poets with the practice of recognizing 'a precision of lineage' and frequently addressing it in their art/lives (di Prima 2011: 2). As she explains in her book on H.D. [Hilda Doolittle]'s influence on Robert Duncan's poetry, the poem 'stands at a juncture of planes – of whatever lineages have become manifest at a given point' (2011: 3). As exemplars of this philosophy, her plays frequently rely upon the following junctures of identifiable modernist practices:

a) engaging with and creating a multi- and inter-disciplinary forms of art (Dadism, Surrealism);
b) seeking the truth by disengaging from cultural norms of time and space, that is the linear and the rational, in favour of the dream or the nightmare (Depth Psychology, Dadism, Surrealism, Vorticism, Absurdism);
c) relying upon randomly composed or found constructions (Dadaism);
d) placing objects in unfamiliar contexts to produce new meanings (Dadaism, Surrealism);
e) juxtaposing and piling up of language to create a brutal barrage of primal (most real) sensory data (Surrealism, Absurdism);
f) dematerializing the art object (Dadaism);
g) using materials to reveal the Greater Spirit, which leads to the Good (Expressionism);

h) foregrounding the subjective in moods and ideas (Expressionism);

i) returning to the apparently risk-free world of childhood (Surrealism; Romanticism);

j) locating truth and beauty within the realm of the subject rather than that of the object (Surrealism, Romanticism);

k) opening a creative space – pre-verbal or alchemical – where everyone could be transformed into an artist (Dadaism);

l) emphasizing the material realities of women's lives and the essentialist nature of the female (First-wave and Second-wave Feminisms);

m) valuing ideas, events, philosophies from modernity, which sometimes involves repudiating past European practices in favour of elements from American popular culture, such as jazz and Vaudeville (Imagism, Feminisms, Eccentrism);

n) relying on common speech, creating new rhythms, and disengaging language from conventional syntax (Romanticism, Imagism, Surrealism, Absurdism); and

o) seeking the authentic self (Existentialism, Feminisms).

In *toto*, these Modernist threads do not appear systematically in di Prima's plays. There is no carefully contrived philosophy of post-war theatre, but rather a plastic set of devices, some of which she seems more fond of than others. Not surprisingly, considering the socialist/anarchist/spiritualist bent of many Beat writers, Futurism, with its mechanical and brutal turn toward fascism, is an invisible and often unnamed threat against which the other philosophies operate, as is an Existentialist/Absurdist vision in the meaninglessness of the universe. Also rejected is the turn-of-the-century Constructivist anti-art and pro-technology polemics, along with, perhaps more unexpectedly, the Imagist principle that the highest form of poetry should use the 'exact' word ('only those that contribute to the presentation,' according to Ezra Pound)[8] despite the fact that Pound, one of the major proponents of Imagism, was a major influence on di Prima's art.[9] Finally, and more difficult to discern, is the apparent absence of early-to-mid-1960s 'New Realism', that it, the application of Dada-inspired cut-ups and appropriations stunningly exemplified in *The Tennis Court Oath* (1962) by her colleague John Ashbery.

What does emerge in keeping with all of these movements/schools is a brazen revolt against the despotism of the still-revered Aristotelian paradigm for appropriate theatrical productions. The implied objective of a di Prima play is not action or finely constructed plot; neither is it the well-rounded character, dialogue, spectacle, or the conveyance of a tightly built concluding message. Rather, it is poetry itself. Di Prima describes them as 'word scores' 'with no plot, no stage directions' (2001: 376), a recognition of the more ancient foundation of poetry that is, music, or what Northrop Frye called *melos* and Pound called *melopoeia*. As one reads the plays, many of them metamorphose into a compilation of sounds functioning like a symphony or other formal musical texts, such as ancient charms and chants that by destroying logos reveal new meanings through *melos*. To this end, the plays dramatize that which Martin Esslin identified as the principal objective of the post-war Theatre of the Absurd: 'to convey a poetic image or a complex pattern of poetic images' or an 'essentially static' conveyance of a 'central idea, or atmosphere, or mode of being', through 'a critique of language, an attack above all on fossilized forms of language which have become devoid of meaning' (Esslin 1965). In these contexts, then, di Prima's plays say just as much about the Modernist influences on Beat writers as they do about di Prima as a Beat playwright.

Di Prima has spoken about the way her writing processes grew out of these earlier radical art movements. In a 1989 interview with poet Tony Moffit, she explained that 'all those European elements that we'd been cut off from during the war, late Surrealism . . . were all there. You'd see [Jean Cocteau's] *Blood of a Poet* six times, eight times' (*Breaking* 2004: 98). She credits Dadaism with promoting her reliance on 'non-random randomness', realized as 'looking at the wall and letting the images arise and following any image only as far as it went, not trying to make sense out of it, not trying to complete the sentence and holding on to whatever next image arose' (*Breaking* 2004: 99). These processes remain central to di Prima's writing, influenced as well by Jack Kerouac's theory of spontaneous composition, John Cage's aesthetics, and Jimmy Waring's choreography (*Breaking* 2004: 103). The history of her focus on the rights and powers of women is detailed in *Recollections*.

Interestingly, the extent to which di Prima's plays may have been collaboratively 'devised', that is, constructed through rehearsal, or improvised in performance – much like street theatre or Kerouac's literary practices – is not entirely clear, but the multiple versions of the plays, from original typescripts to final copies for *Zipcode*, suggest that she was working fundamentally as a solo playwright, with a script written in advance of any staged readings or performances. At that point, she turned them over to the director – as she did with Jimmy Waring when he directed *Murder Cake* for the Judson Poets Theatre – 'to do with as s/he will[ed]' (Judson; di Prima 2001: 376).

At this juncture, I have discussed di Prima's plays in the collective sense, but as I noted above, this particular vision was not static. It evolved, and with considerable alacrity. The seeds of that process are embedded in her first play, *The Discontent of the Russian Prince*, which stands out as being more conventional than the word scores that followed. The first 27 typed lines of the archival copy, approximately two-thirds of the page, present traditional stage directions, establishing the setting (a cluttered bedroom in a Bohemian pad), characters (Kit and Bessie), ambient sound (rain, alarm clock, sobbing), and action (Kit and Bessie getting out of bed). Based on these lines alone, a reader may well assume that di Prima eschewed transformative theatrical poetics, the extremely detailed stage directions throughout the remainder of the one-act supporting that claim. With *The Discontent of the Russian Prince*, di Prima as neophyte playwright was exerting considerable control over the performance.

She also fashioned the play with conventional characters: a male and female with conventional names, Bessie and Kit, who for the most part act like realistic adults, engaging in conversation with each other, making breakfast, and performing morning ablutions. Their relationship is fraught with tension as the play comments on the troubled reality of conjugal bliss, allegorically mirrored in wet, black sheets and periods of rain, both of which the couple repetitively confronts. The male character, or the Russian Prince (although he's never identified as such), can't face the day without sobbing, displaying not only discontent but also fear, distrust, low self-esteem and a privileged tendency to dominate his more domestically captive partner. Focused on character exposition rather than plot, the play's conclusion is open-ended – no easy denouement as Bessie and Kit ultimately find themselves stuck together in a dreary apartment, each isolated in an existential crisis: Bessie paces and mutters; Kit dances. Authenticity, and certainly primal reality, eludes them both, their fictional actualities clearly structured upon a recognizable theme – the dirty realities underlying the myth of heterosexual romance – and message – there are no reliable scripts in the search for the genuine self: you have to make it up.

The characters and plot are recognizable, no doubt for decades of theatre goers, but di Prima, even at this early stage in her writer's life, willingly mixed it up. First, what is fundamentally realistic dialogue between two adults occasionally breaks into surrealism. The most dramatic example occurs approximately one-third of the way into the play: Kit and Bessie have a conversation about hanging the sheets out to wash in the rain, Kit asking her three times to do it and Bessie each time responding with a non-sequitur. The initial one is a succinct reference to herself as subject, *not* to the requested act: 'No, I wasn't'; the second refers to green as a good colour of icing; and the third focuses on an unidentified 'he' whose father speaks 'fluent Egyptian.' Stage directions then instruct Bessie to remove the dirty sheets Kit is sleeping on and take them outside – as she does so, 'things' keeping falling out of them (4). What 'things' are presumably left to the discretion of the director. After this, she makes the bed with the wet black sheets that she'd brought in off the clothesline. This short scene disrupts the reality of early morning rituals and throws the characters as well as the audience into a dislocated diegetic universe. Both characters, however, are whipped back to the previous time-space continuum by Bessie asking Kit if he wants scrambled eggs. Granted, the couple continues to deliver several non-sequiturs, but a semblance of the introductory realism is restored as they shower, brush their teeth, and Bessie heads to the kitchen. The fragility of this universe, though, is quickly revealed as Bessie returns to announce that the eggs themselves have refused to scramble: acting out of their own agency, they have told her, she reports, that '[t]hey don't want to mingle. They say they're too young. They fear to lose what can never be regained'. And 'they hate poetry'. The egg scene draws to a close with Bessie holding the eggs aloft and Kit then placing them 'side by side' on the bed, each character moving on to other morning activities (9).

The egg scene is humourous, but more than that, pivotal in understanding di Prima's integral connection of Surrealist or Dadaist discourses and actions with two additional narrative components: identity/gender-bending as performance and meta-discourse. The former, a not-uncommon theme in Modernist art but apotheosized in Modernist history, recurs on the second page of the original typescript.[10] Kit is identified as a boy and Bessie as a girl, with the phrase 'or vice versa' written underneath, three simple words that obliterate the play's foundational paradigm of heteronormativity. The names themselves are not androgynous, although Kit more so than Bessie, but the reversal creates a wobbling effect as a reader of the typescript can't avoid seeing the male through the feminine name 'Bessie' and female through the masculine name 'Kit'. In reverse, Bessie also becomes the dominating, discontented prince and Kit the more subservient female partner. Bessie sobs and recites poetry while Kit makes the bed with dirty sheets and reports on eggs with agency. In effect, the play in production could have multiple gender-bending possibilities. If the audience is not privy to 'or vice versa' the gender hierarchy most likely remains in place; if male and female actors are cast in the opposite sex role, the gender hierarchy is explicitly destroyed and replaced with its counterpart. If the audience is aware of the possibility of role switching but the roles are cast in compliance with the convention of hetero-male over hetero-female, the potential for reversal is present throughout the play – hence the wobbling, or an optical illusion effect, as neither binary holds steady – and a more transgender world opens up to replace the binaries. These effects are enhanced by the fact that neither character ever calls the other by his/her/their name, an absurdist technique that undermines their identities to greater or lesser degrees depending on how a director chose to stage the production. Overall, then, *The Discontent of the Russian Prince* speaks to the injustices inherent in the naturalizing of gender identity and expression and to the role of language itself in denaturalizing such identities and expressions.

The denaturalization process, whether implicit or explicit in the reading or the viewing of the play, calls attention to the way in which all identities are to some degree performances. With Bessie the boy and Kit the girl, long before Judith Butler troubled gender as a drag performance, di Prima's first play demands that we see heterosexual bodies *performing* as the opposite gender and, potentially, other genders. The performance aspect is introduced in the first few exchanges between Bessie and Kit, Kit blaming his/her/their weeping on audiences, a vague reference, to which Bessie simply declares 'Dont' [sic] (1). Twelve lines later, however, Kit directly blames his sobbing on the audience of the play itself, to whom he/she/they now points per di Prima's stage directions – an aside or breaking of the fourth wall.

Kit and Bessie then briefly discuss the fact that they as characters and the others as audience are basically the same, implying that all human beings act out roles. The two then half-heartedly re-begin the day, which includes the surrealist dialogue prior to the eggs-with-agency passage. At that point, Kit shrieks as he confronts his physical image in a mirror, only to disengage from the image and then to paint a beard and dark eye circles on his face, an altered self reflected back at him in the mirror. These actions, both surreal and comic, speak to the way human identity is both 'othered' and 'performed', that is, through various kinds of mirrors (human and otherwise), but also to the gendered reality of those identities as performances acted out in front of others or mirrors.

Kit's exposure of the fallacy of the autonomous 'real' self is highlighted soon thereafter with the eggs-with-agency encounter, which ends with Kit asking for coffee and Bessie angrily replying, 'I am not going *offstage* for one more thing!' (10, emphasis added). Again, the mid-twentieth-century Bohemian diegesis is torn asunder: the home, or the world of domesticity, is a stage after all, a message carried forward in an intriguing way: Kit says it will be the last request, Bessie wants to find out if that is indeed true, and Kit responds by saying that can't be done because '[t]he playwright isn't up yet!' (10). The exchange of meta-discourse affirms explicitly the scripted reality of what the audience/reader encounters and implicitly calls out the scripted realities *of* the audience/reader. The play mocks the audience/reader as naïve, if not ignorant, of greater ontological truths, and it is this lesson that brings the play to a close: Kit and Bessie want to start the day yet again, since their domesticity has eroded into discord. But they can't – because, as Bessie points out, the audience won't let them. The script of the theatre goer demands that it's time for the play to end. Kit and Bessie have to acknowledge that their very being as they know it depends on the presence of an audience. As such realization sinks in, the world of discordant technological sound – alarm bells and radio programmes – erupts around them as one dances and the other paces, each in isolated discontent, acting out yet again another human script.

Di Prima's next play, *Rain Fur* (circa 1959, as is *Russian Prince*), reveals that while modelling more traditional forms she was also delving deeper into experimental theatrical structures to explore the themes of gender, identities, and expression, as well as the plasticity of time and space.[11] *Rain Fur* was written in a day, and in her e-mail correspondence with Killian and Brazil, di Prima remembers that after finishing it she 'threw it in the waste basket. Didn't like it, I guess. Can't remember. What I do remember is Jimmy Waring came by for a visit. He never missed a thing. Pulled the short mss out of the wastebasket & said, 'What's this?' Read it and told me to keep it' (Killian and Brazil 2010: 552).

Most noticeably for a reader of the script, *Rain Fur* eschews characters as realistic individual personalities. Instead of Bessie and Kit, the cast is comprised of three mathematical forms of A: A itself, A' (prime), and A1 (sub-prime).[12] This set signifies a cohesive unity of similarity within uniqueness, not the least of which is a playful reference to the multiple selves of the author: A Prime or, when reversed, Prime A – prima.[13] The other characters in the one-act play are a doctor, a tree, two archeologists, King Minos, in addition to a girl, horse, woodsman, court poet, and some maidens.

Again in juxtaposition to the *Russian Prince*, *Rain Fur* includes some stage directions or exposition and has settings identifiable in logical time and space. However, both features are considerably scaled back. Scene One is set simply in an 'Afternoon. Someplace' (di Prima 2010: 167) Scene Two opens with the archeologists dressed as cowboys in a western movie set in the evening. Scene Three is set back in time several thousand years to a temple in Crete. Exposition throughout is sporadic, terse, and focused on actions such as characters entering and exiting, bowing, dancing, sitting, and brandishing an axe.

Killian and Brazil describe *Rain Fur* as 'a rolling cast of characters' in 'a quest for identity . . . di Prima has written, or perhaps appropriated, for them' (2010: 553). They point out as well her use of the 'no exposition' technique that we see in *Russian Prince*: the characters' names appear in the script, but the characters never identity themselves or others by these names, thus forcing audience members to create identities or give them up entirely. Several characters do, however, call out other names, apparently directed at others on stage. Girl, for example, appears to address King Minos, who has already identified herself as a female, with masculine names: Julius, Ben, John, and Angelo (di Prima 2010: 168), although she could also be addressing the archeologists, who enter just ahead of Minos. Small clues in a couple of stage directions hint at character types, such as Woodsman who is instructed to swing his axe and Court Poet who plays a lyre; one character, Doctor, actually in dialogue reveals his profession to another character. These moments are rare, so unless there is an 'extra-diagetical' device, such as a programme (Killian and Brazil 2010: 553), or a director who through costuming or other means provides clues for identification, an actual theatergoer would find it extremely challenging to distinguish one from another.

In fact, in the case of the mathematical set of A's, without assistance, that actual theatre goer could *not* identify them as anything even approximating mathematics. They open the play in unison with the incongruous line, 'We agree about nothing'. A follows with the ironic 'Isn't that true!' and likewise A sub-prime with 'You're so right!' (di Prima 2010: 167). They then, in unison, 'smile, bow, back away from each other and start dancing' per the stage directions. Each then delivers a soliloquy.

Killian and Brazil describe these soliloquies and those of the other characters as well, as 'dense and flowery speeches' (2010: 553). David Hadbawnik reads these speeches as more like Gertrude Stein and Ezra Pound who, he writes, 'offer models of a fragmented, collage approach to language' (2010), which more aptly depicts the free verse structure di Prima used instead of prose dialogue. Killian and Brazil's description is a vague, impressionistic interpretation, and while image-laden lines, such as '[Jasmine] flowed over my brain like a watercress salad, leaving soggy bits of petals sticking here and there to the membranes' (di Prima 2010: 168) delivered by A,[1] may strike one as 'dense and flowery', more accurately, they are akin to Pound and Stein, comically surrealistic in tone, functioning in accordance with the polemics of poetic surrealism.

Most notably, the play exemplifies the truth-seeking process that Andre Breton set forth in his first Surrealist Manifesto. This is a process that must 'free both interlocutors from any obligations of politeness. Each of them simply pursues his soliloquy without trying to derive any special dialectical pleasure from it and without trying to impose anything whatsoever upon his neighbor' (Kolocotroni 1998: 310). I do not know whether di Prima ever read Breton's manifesto, but *Rain Fur* also illustrates his description of dialogue as 'remarks' intended to defy the development of a thesis. A remark should be 'disaffected', and its reply 'totally indifferent to the personal pride of the person speaking. The words, the images are only so many springboards for the mind of the listener' (Kolocotroni 1998: 310). This is exactly what we find in *Rain Fur*, which in technique is a reversal of *Russian Prince*, *Rain Fur's* surrealist soliloquies far outweighing moments of realistic discourse exchanges. When the latter do occur, they are banal clichés, representing the vacuity of many discursive practices and the mechanical nature with which human beings use them. A wonderfully humourous example is the line 'Howdy, partner', delivered to Doctor by First Archeologist costumed as a cowboy playing poker (di Prima 2010: 168). What could be more of a cowboy western cliché than 'Howdy, partner'? Only a riding-off-into-the sunset remark, which also appears (di Prima 2010: 170–71).

Many of the characters, but especially the A's, who perform throughout like a jazz refrain or riff, allude to the provocative power of the belief in the autonomous self as the genesis of being. Their lines sometimes defy grammatical syntax, unlike those of the other characters, thereby forcing a reader/audience into a linguistic realm that undermines common connotations. The process begins with their introductory soliloquies, followed by each A repeating a word sound: 'slurp', 'di', and 'sh-' (di Prima 2010, 168).[14] In Scene Two, A and A[1] deliver three short lines and A1 two short lines. The three sets are arranged horizontally across the page, implying that they are spoken as equals and that the lines can be delivered either across or down. If the former, we get 'ably aiding the easily eliminating only a rose I bring you' in line two. If the latter, spoken by A, we get 'ahem/ably aiding the/ aggressor is not art'. The first is grammatical garble, the second an intriguing claim about the timeless nature of art. Later in the scene, the A's swap words, articulating them faster and faster per stage directions so that, for instance, 'rug', 'red', 'new', 'visit', and other words as fillers of grammatical slots are sufficiently blurred into the primal sound of something that can spelled as 'rrnedvwisgewiredt' and any number of other ways – and its pronunciations are virtually limitless (di Prima 2010: 171).

The concept of transformation, or the undermining of arbitrarily routinized boundaries as exemplified in the A's' word swapping, drives the play from its beginning when we are introduced to King Minos who has transitioned into a young girl. She eventually opens Scene Two hanging from the Tree. All the while, the two archeologists scribble nonsensically in notebooks, while Woodsman yells 'Free Ezra Pound', amongst other non-sequiturs (di Prima 2010: 171). The A's don't appear in this scene, but the characters in Scene Two, as do the A's, clearly shatter the space-time continuum in direct position to the stage directions dictating ancient Crete as the setting.

The play concludes with King Minos pontificating on her own beauty, using language to transform her body into flowers, which then shift into images of power and beauty: 'the snakes, the earthquakes, the white/racing cars' (di Prima 2010: 172). In an unrhymed couplet, she declares, 'I am the tides./I shall be heard of, in song' (di Prima 2010: 172), the lines evoking belief in primordial female/genitive powers linked in the primordial *melos* of poetry. However, these lines fail to convince the archeologists that there's anything of value in a Crete ruled by a female. They exit the stage, leaving Tree to ask Minos if they should meet for dinner. Provocatively, Minos replies, 'I have a date'. Unity, in other words, is at least temporarily aborted through the repetition of a code for romantic foreplay – the tease of the unattainable.

The reversal of sex and gender roles here also suggests that trans movements are quite natural but that the naturalizing of sex/gender roles remains in words as well as actions a code that for millennia has thwarted code breakers. Ultimately, *Rain Fur* stands as a wild romp backwards through time and out of time, in a pantheistic, gender-bending world in which thought naturalized as action in language remains at odds with its fundamental magical (that is, transformative) propensities.

Di Prima's next several plays suggest that she dared to make a profound commitment to poets' theatre, departing from more conventional scripting, plotting, characterizations, and settings, while remaining true to her feminist, surreal, absurdist use of language. Over the years, she moved from the one-act plays that dominated the New York Poets Theatre productions to full-length plays, such as *Whale Honey* and *Discovery of America*, but in structure and content, she never looked back. Take, for instance, the typescript of *Like*, her short one-act in three scenes circa 1960. It features one extremely brief stage direction, '*enter woman*', which appears in scene three (9). The characters are types and nursery-rhyme figures – Man, Woman, Child; and Jack and Jill, respectively, moving freely out of time and space. These five engage each other in conversation, but their language frequently slips from everyday banalities into surreal, poetic discourse. In fact, like *Rain Fur*, the dialogue in *Like* is arranged on the page as free verse, not as prose lines.

Throughout, the play foregrounds the Romantic belief in the inherent wisdom of children and reveals the Woman's dissatisfaction with the roles of nuclear family members. In scene three, the Man and Child discuss the Woman, who has been absent for a week, the Child, who seems to miss her more so than does the Man, uttering in an adult-like voice the semblance of a riddle, 'if you were a piece of paper crumpled and blowing/on the steps of the public library,' which the Man completes: 'I would wait/whatever the winds said'.(9). Just prior to the Child's conditional 'if' statement, the Woman has entered, unseen, thus standing with them but as a ghostly presence of absence, that which completes the triangular romance of the family in which the Man and Child, and perhaps the Woman herself, believe, yet existing with her own integrity and agency beyond the confines of prescriptive roles based on sex and gender. The image, captivating as a tableau on a Grecian urn, roots the ancient past in the present, a sweeping reversal and thus a troubling of our modern sense of time. Simultaneously, the tableau narrows its scope to di Prima's personal history: her decision to have and raise a child without a husband.

Like's focus on characters as generic categories is complemented by what may be di Prima's most-often produced play, *Murder Cake*, which features a surrealistic collage of characters from both history and fiction: Childe Harold, Emma, Mr Knightley, Olimpia, Richard Lovelace, and Dante. This grouping suggests dissatisfaction with the status quo, righteous indignation, morality, sexuality, mythology, and female power – themes found in her other plays from this period and now classic themes in her poetry. The play's original typescript contains no exposition whatsoever, except for the names of the characters – and not a single character ever refers to or is referred to by their names or public/private roles. More confused than *Rain Fur*'s audience if it had had any, *Murder Cake*'s audiences would have needed the extra-diegetical device of a programme to comprehend the Anglo-European literary/historical ménage performing for them.[15] Most of the characters, a few of whom interact with each other, have extended speeches that read as soliloquies rather than dialogue; most follow Breton's description of poetic surrealism. The lines themselves are arranged on the page in block paragraphs rather than free verse, thus reading at times like prose poems. In form and content, *Murder Cake* exists in an unrecognizable, because essentially invisible, diegetic realm.

Their speeches, I think more so than in the earlier plays, resemble the Bakhtinian heteroglossia of the novel, a play of different voices and discourses, routinized speech patterns signifying the various beliefs, perceptions, and values of the characters, narrators, and the author. To be more specific, it is Bakhtin's hybrid utterance that drives *Murder Cake*, the single speaker whose voice reveals multiple kinds of speech. Thus primarily within, but also across, individual characters, the play draws extensively upon twentieth-century colloquial languages, mixed with parodies of the original languages and historical moments that gave birth to the characters. For instance, Richard Lovelace, a sixteenth-century royalist convicted of crimes against the state, opens the play as an unabashed phony (di Prima 1963:1):

> Uninjured I have evolved out of cruel presentiments, out of cold jello, in fact, to appear before you in this guise of a meek nobleman who spends his time twiddling twats and that in public too. Well, let me tell you it ain't so unpeopled this globe, I could cite a few instances, but annihilation presses, as always.

Here, the language of the Renaissance or Enlightenment court (e.g., 'cruel presentiments') butts up against a modern phrase suggesting an inexpensive, manufactured dessert as a protective substance ('cold jello'). 'Well, let me tell you it ain't so unpeopled this globe' presents a contemporary trope of general opposition carrying the ubiquitous 'ain't' of the British aristocracy prior to World War II. 'Cite a few instances' suggests argumentative discourse. In effect, the voice of each character takes on a unique quality while simultaneously creating a comic tone that destabilizes the illusion of language as emanating as original from any human source. Who needs to know that it is Richard Lovelace, or his avatar, that speaks when his language exposes the composite reality of all human discourse? Is it even possible in an existential sense, the play subtly asks, for human beings to create their own essence if language has already done that long ago? As a follow-up, how does one move beyond that mechanical image of humanity?

It's Emma who speaks most forcefully in hybrid utterance, echoing di Prima's deep commitment to feminist art and positing a possible answer to the existential nihilism exemplified by Lovelace and other characters. Emma speaks a collage of stereotypic images of woman as saint and whore, as life and death, as a body void of mind, yet she mocks, pities, and confronts with disgust these prescribed visions of female reality, an effect enhanced by the threading together of romance novel, epithets, colloquialisms for aging, and other bits of discourses. The following is from her last long speech in the play (di Prima 1963:6):

> Whom nothing has loved, in the blue sea or in heaven, I stand before you, a girl with the mouth of a seagull and spidery-eyed. My long limbs are dripping water. Hell, what do you know about it. Do you remember, have you time to remember, when airplanes were even silver and worth looking up for . . . Do not imagine that I am giving birth . . . I was almighty, but funny, pretty funny. What a blemish. I was put to pasture at an early age, when eventually I found it necessary to go up the river to spawn. . .The mouth of a clam. Kissing it . . . Naked except for her pearls, spasms of glee sat on her fermenting eyelids. Birds of prey.

Emma's 'I' and 'she' persistently merge and separate in a highly romanticized, and thus unreal, irrational post-World War II critique of Jane Austen's *Emma* as well as the young girl, E.C. (Emma Cleary), that James Joyce's Stephen Daedalus transforms/objectifies as both a grotesque whore and an ethereal bird in *Portrait of the Artist as a Young Man*. Di Prima's Emma, unlike her literary predecessors, is clearly aware of her subjugation, resents it – 'Hell, what do you know about it.' – and understands its destructive powers on the body and the mind. By speaking such feminist truths through the constellation of surrealistic images and language, di Prima aims straight at the heart of oppression, daring to strike out against its very life – a premeditated killing, in other words, a Murder.

All of these plays illustrate the complex palette of dramatic techniques with which di Prima was working in the late 1950s and early 1960s. However, it is *Paideuma*, from this same period, that most explicitly illuminates the larger philosophical vision directing her work. The very title tells us so, which is why I have reserved discussion of the play for last – an ideal topic to bring closure to this period in di Prima's life.

Paideuma is a direct reference to Ezra Pound, a major influence on di Prima as a poet as I've already noted. The term appears in his book *Guide to Kulchur* and comes from the nineteenth century German ethnologist Leo Frobenius, who defined it as the way in which culture imprints itself on human beings. For Pound, however, 'paideuma' was a tangle or complex of in-rooted ideas (assumptions, biases, habits, etc.) of any period that humans carry within them and is thought moving into action. The opposite of ideology, 'paideuma' is the naturalizing of thought and of any given age is best revealed, or denaturalized, through study of literature, myth, and history (Tryphonopoulos 2005: 125). It is similar to di Prima's description of poetic influences as 'a juncture of planes' existing at any given moment.

Di Prima's *Paideuma* consists of four scenes, and the characters are ordinals, First through Sixth. In other words, like the A's in *Rain Fur*, they are signifiers of a place in a sequence and also a form of transfinite forms in a set. Brief, handwritten stage directions on the earliest typescript say that the characters 'come out and get hats and sit down'. No other texts specify time and place. Each character begins by speaking a dictionary definition of an unidentified term. First, for instance, says 'ability to act, capacity for action or being acted upon. Capable of undergoing an effect'. Third says, 'figuratively, anything that festers and corrupts like an open sore'. First's lines define 'power' and the Third's 'ulcer', although these nouns are never identified in the play. Thus the audience/reader immediately encounters the irrationality of only half of a syllogism, the empty space negating rational meaning, encouraging the substitution of multiple signifieds and suggesting that the ordinals speak their own language, almost reading each other's minds.

The ordinals consistently indulge in non-sequiturs, silly limericks, onomatopoesis, maxims, nursery rhymes, encyclopaedic lists, clichés, direct references to Pound's *Guide to Kulchur*, lines appropriated from Shakespeare's *Romeo and Juliet*, lines in French, and other genres and forms of language from various historical periods. Handwritten production notes on the typescript used for a staged reading at The Living Theatre identify the historical period and/or tone of voice for some of the lines. Here's a short sample from Scene 3 (the bracketed language represents production notes, which may or may not be di Prima's):

First   Ashbery.
        Burroughs.
        Finstein.
        Leroi.
        Bremser.

Sixth   Imposter. 548.3
        Sciolist. 493.2 (*offhand*)

Fifth   The most ill-conditioned of all the soldiers?

First   A sound mind in a sound body. (*sensible*)
No excellent soul is exempt from a mixture of madness. (*pity and wisdom*)
Whom the gods would destroy they first make mad. (*mad*)
. . .

Fifth   Whew! I managed to get away with him. Ha. Ha. (5)

No gendered or identifiable human characters emerge, but instead an asexual or blurry same-sex rendering of a panoply of voices out of body, space, and time, and, at least on paper, mostly in dialogue with only themselves or the audience – not with another ordinal. The set breaks under the weight of its own absurdity, suggesting that even mathematics – the most universal of languages – is an imposter, certainly not the ultimate truth.

Insinuating as much are the last three speakers in Scene Three – ordinals Third, First, and Fifth. Third points out the non-communal reality of man playing god; First, in disgust according to production notes, riffs on the term 'Buddhism', and Fifth appropriates the last two lines of the first stanza of Rudyard Kipling's poem 'The Liner She's a Lady' (1894), a transparent allegory for the power differential between the British military/aristocracy and the average British citizen. Fifth's last line bears the same message, appropriating another Kipling passage, this one from *A Book of Words*, a lecture delivered to young seaman in which he brutally called them out as abject servants in 'a packet of assorted miseries which we call a Ship' (Kipling 1894: n.p). The language of numbers, then, parodying human discourses, tosses up presentiments about the human condition: Buddhism's belief in *satori* and nothingness is the equal of Existentialism's faith in humankind's ability to create itself, which is the same as poor sods on a ship learning about their subjugation. The truth may appear to lie somewhere in between, but ultimately resides outside and beyond such human constructs.

Amidst other cultural pronouncements of wisdom, all suspect as fallacies in this absurdist world, the play concludes with ordinals Sixth and Third verbally assaulting the patriarchy, embodied in allusions to a generic father and a generic 'him'; the latter could substitute for both father and a male object of desire for either or both ordinals. Sixth declares that 'My father' taught that one should constrain the mind rather than letting it flow. Third, who speaks the last line, expresses desire for the 'him', but states that Third's father employs the 'him', hinting that the father's economic power over 'him' destroys the power of both Third and 'him'. The play leaves the ordinals and the audience/reader in a state of suspension, caught in patriarchy's power while cognizant of the trap in which we have long resided. One can assume that these are di Prima's imaginings of the materials of her own mid-twentieth-century *paideuma*, thought – naturalized to *appear to be* primal forms of expression – transformed into action by the play itself, which expresses through the exposure of threads of cultural discourses across time and geography mild bewilderment at the realities of the human condition.

In conclusion, all of di Prima's plays, especially *Paideuma*, function as prototypes or artistic exercises for her later endeavours. The plays stand alone, without question, but in them reside the seeds of the surrealist, absurdist, and feminist themes and forms that distinguish her poetry as political and spiritual, aligned with that of other Beat writers yet uniquely hers. Certainly, in what has become her most important work, the great long poem *Loba*, she acts on the desire to merge the oppositional impulses of historicity and vision through a recovery and restructuring of a Poundian tangle, or paideuma, of habits, assumptions, beliefs, maxims, and mantras. In *Loba*, through the transmogrifications of a Native American legend about a wolf, there lives in full resurrection every dramatic character di Prima ever created – the A's, the ordinals, Bessie, King Minos, Keats, and others into infinity – a mass of primal light twinkling far beyond the cacophony of human words.

Works cited

Ashbery, J. (1962), *The Tennis Court Oath*, Middletown, Conn.: Wesleyan University.

di Prima, D. (1963), *Murder Cake, Kulchur*, 3.9:48–54.

di Prima, D. (1992), *Zipcode*, Minneapolis, Coffee House.

di Prima, D. (2001), *Recollections of My Life as a Woman: The New York Years*, New York: Viking.

di Prima, D. (2010), *Rain Fur*, in K. Killian and D. Brazil (eds) *The Kenning Anthology of Poets Theatre 1945–1985*, Chicago: Kenning, 167–173.

di Prima, D. (2011), *R.D.'s H.D.* New York: City University of New York.

di Prima, D. (2012), *Murder Cake*, Big Night in Buffalo, YouTube. Available at: www.youtube.com/watch?v=jLgGMHjjfEQ> (last accessed 12 August 2015).

Esslin, M. (1965), 'Introduction,' *Absurdist Drama*. Available at: www.samuel-beckett.net/AbsurdEsslin.html (last accessed 28 July 2015).

Grace, N. and R. Johnson (2004), *Breaking the Rule of Cool: Reading and Interviewing Beat Women Writers*, Jackson, Miss.: University Press of Mississippi.

Hadbawnik, D. (2002), 'Diane di Prima in Conversation with David Hadbawnik,' *Jacket Magazine* 18, Available at: http://jacketmagazine.com/18/diprima-iv.html (last accessed 3 August 2015).

Hawbahnik, D. (2010), 'On Diane di Prima's *Rain Fur*,' Kenning Editions, 24 March, 2010. Available at: www.kenningeditions.com/kenning-editions/previews-supplements-david-hadbawnik-on-diane-di-primas-rain-fur/ (last accessed 30 July 2015).

Judson Poets Theater, *Judson Memorial Church*. Available at: www.judson.org/judsonpoetstheater (last accessed 5 August 2015).

Killian, K. and D. Brazil (eds) (2010), *The Kenning Anthology of Poets Theater 1945–1985*, Chicago: Kenning.

Kipling, R. (1894), 'The Liner She's a Lady' and *A Book of Words*, Poetry Lover's Page. Available at: www.poetryloverspage.com/poets/kipling/kipling_ind.html (last accessed 30 July 2015).

Kolocotroni, V., J. Goldman, and O. Taxidou (eds) (1998), *Modernism: An Anthology of Sources and Documents*, Chicago: University of Chicago.

Leslie, R. (1997), *Surrealism: The Dream of Revolution*, New York: Smithmark.

Libby, A. (2002), 'Diane di Prima: "Nothing Is Lost: It Shines In Our Eyes" in R. Johnson and N. Grace (eds), *Girls Who Wore Black: Women Writing the Beat Generation,* New Brunswick, New Jersey: Rutgers University, 45–68.

Pawlik, Joanna (2013), 'Beat Literature and the San Francisco Renaissance,' *Literature Compass* 10.2: 97–110.

Tryphonopoulos, D. P. D. and A. J. Stephen (eds) (2005), *Ezra Pound Encyclopedia*, Westport, Conn.: Greenwood.

Susoyev, S. and G. Birimisa (eds) (2007), *Return to the Caffe Cino*, San Francisco: Moving Finger.

Wolf, R. (1997), *Andy Warhol, Poetry, and Gossip in the 1960s*, Chicago: University of Chicago.

13

Homely Persons, Rude Speeches: Camp Personalities, Cold War Sensibilities and Dystopian Impulses in Frank O'Hara's *Loves Labor, an Eclogue*

Jason Lagapa

Of the three one-act plays put on between 14 February and 27 March 1964 by the New York Poets Theatre, Diane di Prima, a founding member of the theatre group, has said that Frank O'Hara's contribution, *Loves Labor, an eclogue*, was 'the pièce de résistance' (2002: 376). Di Prima's praise was not merely an instance of one playwright admiring the work of another's but an indication of the close friendship that di Prima enjoyed with O'Hara. The friendship also marked a collaborative relationship that joined two distinct literary movements of the time, di Prima's Beat Generation and O'Hara's New York School Poets. Despite divergent poetics between the counter-cultural, visionary Beats and the ironic, Dadaist-influenced New York School Poets, the New York Poets Theatre was a venue where di Prima's and O'Hara's interests in experimental theatre would coincide. Di Prima, who served as the assistant director for at least one of the productions of *Loves Labor*, found much to appreciate in O'Hara's work. Of the many facets of *Loves Labor*, di Prima especially liked the play's liveliness, its host of actors, and the grand scope of its production: 'In contrast to the small cast in my play and in Wallace Stevens', Frank seemed to require a cast of thousands' (2002: 376). Di Prima further praised O'Hara's play by suggesting that with 'twenty or more people cavorting separately on that little stage', *Loves Labor* was a 'great demonstration of the harmony of chaos' (2002: 376).

Though di Prima herself admired *Loves Labor*, she would also subsequently admit: 'of course, many folks who had come along with us thus far absolutely *hated Loves Labor*' (2002: 376). One might explain the divergent responses to *Loves Labor* – a theatrical event alternately experienced as magnificent and repellent – as consequences that O'Hara had hoped and aimed for in writing the play. Philip Auslander, in his early account of the New York School Poets' playwriting, questioned if O'Hara did not intend both to 'm[ock] the pretensions of those who advocate a return to ... high seriousness in the theatre' and to 'att[empt] to elevate kitsch to the status of art' (1989: 57). In *Loves Labor*, such aesthetic tensions between frivolity and seriousness are readily apparent. O'Hara addresses the inherently destructive tendencies of humankind, positing the end of civilization as inevitable, yet he does not depict such dystopian degeneration solely in dour terms. Instead, O'Hara renders such loss with spectacle and campy humour. As di Prima would say, 'Frank had given us the entire Decline of the West in less than four typewritten pages of hilarious poetry' (2002: 76). With *Loves Labor*, O'Hara offers up a stark depiction of social entropy, yet everywhere within the play O'Hara employs both Dadaist techniques and camp sensibilities to provide a counterpoint to the prevailing pessimism that his subject of decline would seem to engender.

Loves Labor centres on Arcadia as a pastoral ideal, and while such common pastoral elements as a shepherd and his sheep, natural beauty and a tranquil setting open the play, there is a predominant sense that the placid conditions will soon go awry. The programme that accompanied the evening of one-act plays put on by the New York Poets Theatre hints at the impending dissolution of the idyllic scene. O'Hara explains that *Loves Labor* 'is not "about" something; depressingly it is something. And secondarily, it is a way of looking at man and his human nature as the only source of the violence which has come closer and closer to destroying the race. It is a view which has no bridge' (1964: n.p.). The destructiveness that provides the premise for *Loves Labor* gives the play a dystopian, apocalyptic quality. Indeed, the Cold War fear of world-wide annihilation and 'ongoing concern with Soviet-American foreign relations' that Michael Davidson has noted elsewhere in O'Hara's poetry (2004: 68–69) surface as well in *Loves Labor*, insofar as the play depicts humankind's ruination and abandonment of Arcadia as an allegory for the dangers of O'Hara's own time period of the 1960s. In contrast to such a willful human destructiveness, O'Hara had wanted to present an alternate existence akin to the one in the Garden of Eden, a place where 'there was peace because man had no consciousness of himself nor any knowledge of sex or his separateness from plants or other animals. It is this peace I intend to recreate' (1964: n.p.).

The initial stage directions for *Loves Labor* reinforce O'Hara's interest in recreating an Edenic scene: 'A rocky pasture on the side of a mountain of lapis-lazuli, and below a gentle stream fringed with boksage. Morning dew' (O'Hara 1978: 155). However, the first lines of the play betray O'Hara's ambivalence about the ability of humans to inhabit this pristine setting. With the play written in absurd and loosely related speeches, O'Hara quickly introduces a campy malaise to his pastoral scene; his shepherd balks at the darkness of morning upon which the sun has yet to rise (1978: 156):

> It is night, I guess, and we are asleep.
> Or are [we] looking after our sheep?
>   I don't care.
>   I can't see a thing,
>   not even a bird.
>   The day is done.

The shepherd's effete dismissal of his responsibilities quickly transitions from an apathetic response to husbandry to a more forbidding pronouncement that the day, just beginning, is already over. The inclusion of despairing elements within O'Hara's initial pastoral scene should not be altogether surprising, as the pastoral tradition often entailed expressions of dismay and anguish at how remote perfection is from actual existence. As Walter W. Greg writes, Italian Renaissance Pastoralists, for example, routinely used the pastoral genre as a means of registering a social critique as they alluded to the hardships of their lives and the shortcomings of their present society (1959: 51–52):

> They could not, it is true, believe in an Arcadia in which all the cares of this world should end – the golden age is always a time to be sung and remembered, or else dreamed of, in the years to come, it is never the present – but if they cannot escape from the changes and chances of this mortal life, if death and unfaith are still realities in their dreamland as on earth, they will at least utter their grief melodiously, and water fair pastures with their tears.

O'Hara's campy, listless shepherd is thus of a piece with a pastoral tradition that bemoans the troubled nature of human existence and records the degree to which paradise seemed beyond human reach.

O'Hara himself labelled *Loves Labor* an 'eclogue', which the *Princeton Encyclopedia of Poetry and Poetics* defines as a short pastoral poem that contains dramatic elements like dialogue or soliloquy and whose 'setting, the *locus amoenus* ("pleasant place"), is Arcadian (later Edenic)—rural, idyllic, serene …' (Preminger and Brogan 1993: 317). Despite the eclogue's calm, rural setting, the *Princeton Encyclopedia* goes on to explain that 'its ends are far from primitive or serene' and quotes George Puttenham as saying that the eclogue is: 'not of purpose to counterfeit or represent the rusticall manner of loves and communication, but under the vaile of homely persons and in rude speeches to insinuate and glaunce at greater matters' (Preminger and Brogan 1993: 317). The gravity and true subject matter of the eclogue thus routinely led to 'criticism of political or religious corruption. Elevation of the rustic life implied denigration of urban' (Preminger and Brogan 1993: 317). The serious import of the eclogue and its resource to 'homely persons' and 'rude speeches' are not at odds with O'Hara's own purposes: declarative speeches by the characters – many of whom are self-serving, vapid and coarse – advance O'Hara's grave critique of humankind's harmful and destructive tendencies by showing individuals at their worst.

Throughout *Loves Labor*, O'Hara depicts Arcadia in an ambivalent fashion, as indicated by his characters' excited outbursts that marvel at the idyllic landscape and their subsequent indifferent and prosaic accounts of their environs. For instance, Venus, the goddess of love and a familiar presence in pastoral literature, sounds alternately bored and delighted in her observations of Arcadia (1978: 156):

Aren't we old-fashioned to be up and about?
I waken each morning with such a sense of the air!
which is my own faintly luminous skin
still snoring slightly and aware of yesterday's scent.
My heart cries 'It would be passionate to be there!'

Venus's impressions of Arcadia chronicle a lively, astonishing atmosphere, yet for all of Arcadia's stunning natural characteristics, these sublime attributes may simply be signs of Venus' own divinity, mere manifestations of her 'faintly luminous skin'. Though Venus exclaims loudly about the beauty that surrounds her, an odd sense of separation marks her experience as she seems simultaneously immersed in and detached from the scene she witnesses.

If Venus is both amusingly bored and filled – campily – with excitement, another character – the Irish Film Star, as she is listed in the playbill – is likewise split in her reaction, sounding impressed and sceptical at once: 'Well I declare! And is it Arcadia truly?' (1978: 157). The Irish Film Star, who later identifies herself as Mavourneen O'Sash, immediately reacts to her surroundings by sending off a telegram expressing her misgivings about her latest film project in Arcadia (1978: 157):

To James Actiun, Esquire Hotel Zabaglione, Rochester New York. Dear pot: Sam has signed me for the Princess, p, r, i, n, c, e, s, s, as in potato, ranch, incest, navel, caesarean, erupt, Sonia, sap, in 'Tower Pot'—do you think I can say the lines? Help me, my own. Love, (signed) Mavourneen O'Sash. Have you got all that?

The mixed responses to Arcadia by Venus and the Irish Film Star indicate O'Hara's interest in showing Arcadia in decline, less a pastoral wonder than a site undervalued by its bored and uninterested inhabitants.

The Irish Film Star's speech also allows for a consideration of the style and form that O'Hara adopts in *Loves Labor*. Tellingly, the droll indifference of the Irish Film Star not only details a lack of appreciation for the paradise that is Arcadia but also reveals the Dadaist influence on *Loves Labor*. It is with the spelling out of the word *princess* that O'Hara invokes a Dadaist technique premised upon nonsense and the irrational: 'p, r, i, n, c, e, s, s, as in potato, ranch, incest, navel, caesarean, erupt, Sonia, sap' (1978: 157). The absurd listing of unrelated words reads like a Dadaist exercise in automatic writing, an 'erup[tion]' from the unconscious that juxtaposes a plant tuber with human anatomy, sexual taboos, a medical procedure and a proper name. The nonsense words deftly relate the actress' vacuity and reinforce the degree to which *Loves Labor* revolves around expressions of absurdity.

Marjorie Perloff has written of the influence of early twentieth-century avant-garde literary forms on O'Hara's work, arguing that the 'lessons of Dada and Surrealism ha[d], after all, been learned' early in his career, the result of which was the employment of 'witty modulations and sudden polarization of images' recurrently within his poetry (1998: 125–26). For the Dadaists, their experimental techniques sought not only to challenge traditional art forms but also to criticize and subvert a society they believed was too rigid in its mores and too bureaucratically and rationally ordered. As Kenneth Coutts-Smith writes, Dadaist procedures steeped in randomness linked art with the unconscious and battled against the prevalent beliefs of society: 'The Dadaists, for their part, explored and exploited the irrational, an unconditional landscape of images in which they saw not only artistic and creative freedom but also the complete existential freedom of [humankind] shackled in a society whose concepts and assumptions appeared to be totally arbitrary and meaningless' (1970: 38). *Loves Labor* works upon a similar aesthetic premise of liberating the unconscious and critiquing a society that O'Hara felt was courting its own demise. Non-sequiturs and absurd references in the characters' lines thus not only serve to add humour to the play but also disrupt the sense that society is actually proceeding on a sane, rational course – especially if its progress includes nuclear armament and devastation of the environment.

While Dadaist elements figure prominently in *Love's Labor*, camp posturing also proves to be integral to the play. Indeed, a central achievement of *Love's Labor* is O'Hara's fusion of camp aesthetics with Dadaist techniques, all of which enhance his play's humour and reinforce his repudiation of an all-too-rational Cold War society. The campy extravagance of O'Hara's characters amplifies and draws attention to the irrational utterances that they make. Such theatricality, Susan Sontag has argued, is a central tenet of camp, wherein 'Camp is the glorification of "character"' (1966: 285). As Sontag further explains: '[w]hat Camp taste responds to is "instant character" (this is of course, very eighteenth century); conversely, what it is not stirred by is the sense of development of character. Character is understood as a state of continual incandescence – a person being one, very intense thing' (1966: 286). In accordance with camp style, O'Hara's characters are not fully realized and become emblematic of a self-involved type; in this way, the characters in *Loves Labor*, all of whom are full of pomp, bombast, and self-importance, help fuel O'Hara's social critique. O'Hara will have us understand that his characters are not to be taken seriously but instead exemplify a world run amok.

Metternich, a character in *Loves Labor* who epitomizes campy histrionics and spouts Dadaist non-sequiturs, helps to establish O'Hara's concern with social entropy and the downfall of Arcadia. Metternich, based presumably on the conservative Austrian politician Klemens von Metternich, initially lauds what Arcadia has to offer. Metternich's place in Arcadia is a privileged one; he pines sententiously for the pastoral scene that he occupies, aligning both his self and voice with Arcadia (1978: 158):

and here when I speak you will believe
in me, for my voice is an Arcadian violin
which in the other world's despised
as an ambition or pride. Near
these blue hills I could have lived
pure as flames, far from others, free of
their laborious envy and the gnats

With declarative, grandiose words ('and here when I speak'), Metternich attempts to establish himself, imperiously claiming a would-be integrity that is 'pure as flames'. Moreover, Metternich's disdain for the world outside of the secluded sphere of Arcadia is readily discernible: Metternich pompously rejects the realm beyond Arcadia and assures himself that others resent him without reason. O'Hara thus presents Metternich as a figure not unlike one of the 'homely persons' who deliver 'rude speeches' in Puttenham's account of the traditional eclogue. Indeed, Metternich's ambition and arrogance is at odds with the tranquility and purity of Arcadia, and the play offers a critique of willfulness as it caricatures Metternich's desperate drive to fulfil his every need 'far from others'.

Metternich's yearning speech about the glories and perfection of Arcadia, though, functions merely as a precursor to its imminent destruction. His wistful desire for the 'blue hills [in which he] could have lived' already acknowledged Arcadia's remoteness from a real, viable existence and hinted at its inevitable downfall. Metternich comes to this sober recognition just a few lines later (1978: 159):

Our crystalline Arcadia
is ended, our last refuge shattered,
soon we shall seem interesting
because the landscape is disgusting,
and we are rapidly becoming human.

Amidst Metternich's campy outbursts ('the landscape is disgusting') and his burgeoning consciousness of his own humanness, O'Hara alludes to the shift common to the evolution of the eclogue where Eden substitutes for Arcadia. All of the human characters must soon confront their lapsarian status. O'Hara's larger argument is that humankind is responsible for the destruction of Arcadia/Eden.

O'Hara, consequently, portrays his characters seeking less a remedy for the demise of Arcadia than a novel place to inhabit (1978: 160):

Paris   But surely one thing is as good as another.

Metternich   I shall go elsewhere.
       And speak rather more plainly.

Irish Film Star   I shall be a great success.
       Truly, I don't know anything.
       I'm not even particularly unhappy.

The droll remarks of Paris, Metternich and the Irish Film Star reach a zenith of camp indifference to Arcadia. Compared to the characters' longer speeches, the brevity of these lines serves to underscore an inherent selfishness of humankind and to reinforce the characters' alienation and separateness from each other. Arcadia is gone, though the significance of its loss hardly registers amid the characters' all-consuming preoccupation with their own individual existences.

O'Hara wants to lay blame squarely on humankind for being indifferent to its environment and unable to rise above self-regard in order to promote love of one another. Accordingly, the gods who preside over Arcadia find fault with the self-centred behaviour of the human beings. Minerva, for instance, chides Venus for despoiling Arcadia (1978: 160):

> You have enlivened the situation,
> Venus, by your decorative power,
> but in introducing the outsider
> you've set fire to your own purity,
> and the palace of the gods.

The outside element to which Minerva negatively refers is humankind, yet what is particularly pernicious to the viability of Arcadia is humanity's belief that it is apart from nature and above all other forms of life. O'Hara's gods know what the humans do not: the peace of Arcadia will be eclipsed by the vain actions of people ignorant of the impact of their behaviour. Minerva says (1978: 160):

> You, and we, have become the whim
> of love, whose momentary passion
> is the painful memory of this serenity,
> a gasp followed by a shower.

Minerva ends her speech mocking human behaviour as mundane and remarking that that the 'whim/of love' and orgasmic 'gasp' only results in the unfortunate ruination of Arcadia's 'serenity'.

O'Hara's apparent dismissal of sex and its orgasmic conclusion in Arcadia would seem a prudish stance for a writer who has written provocatively and graphically about sexual activity in many of his poems. Such prudishness would also seem at odds with the campy aesthetics of *Loves Labor* itself. O'Hara's real target, I would argue, is not sex or love, but the violence and aggression that he thinks is inherent in human behaviour. To return to the previously quoted comments in *Loves Labor*'s programme, O'Hara conceives of 'human nature as the only source of the violence which has come closer and closer to destroying the race'. The violent nature about which O'Hara speaks stems from personal and social conflict. In *Loves Labor*, the origins of such discord can be traced to the type of petty actions and selfish demeanours of characters like Metternich, the Irish Film Star and Paris. The actual import of *Loves Labor* – a condemnation of humankind's bellicose tendencies – finds direct expression in Minerva's exchange with Paris, whose actions had lead to the Trojan War (1978: 160):

Minerva   What do you see in my eyes?

Paris   I see the towers of Troy illuminated.

Paris thus epitomizes the fallibility of humankind whose shortsightedness is as destructive as it is self-indulgent. Troy is illuminated by fire and by war, and O'Hara laments that such aggression is a human tendency.

The invocation of the fall of Troy amidst all of the other lines about the end of Arcadia contributes to the dystopian characteristics of *Loves Labor*. While eclogues often carried out a critique of urban existence to accompany their praise of nature, O'Hara's particularly gravitates towards the somber as the play is ending. Indeed, *Loves Labor* takes on an especially dark tone when Metternich announces: 'The day has become a destruction' (1978: 161). Such an ominous mood is consistent with another of O'Hara's eclogues, *Amorous Nightmares of Delay*. *Amorous* is a play that centres on a beloved teacher who presides over and leads a discussion among a group of students. Much like *Loves Labor*, the characters in *Amorous* make vague, unrelated speeches, as both students and teacher talk past each other, waxing philosophically and often absurdly outside a schoolhouse. The ending of *Amorous*, though, is what primarily proves relevant to *Loves Labor*, for it concluding scene also offers an apocalyptic vision. The students gather as they mourn their teacher who has died, yet the play ends as the scene shifts to a nightclub where the students perform in front of a group of patrons whom they address in a rambling speech (1978: 84–85):

> ... how are you folks? we didn't know you were there until just now so put the touch on us while you can we're the forever fading into the future type of dancing doll ... you're all from out of town, eh? baby, and that trap door there's not just for the corpse, we've got to follow our little old teacher into the dark where we spent the rest of our time ... just cause we smile doesn't mean the lights are going back on, get on your back or your knees so your head won't come off when the trouble starts which is like blowing up in a hot place ... and if everything we say aint true the hereafter's going to wear us like a stole ... Oops! that's all, folks.

An uneasy mix of vaudeville theatrics, morbidly frank speech and Cold War imagery combine to make *Amorous* a meditation on death and the hereafter. O'Hara's impulse in *Amorous*, as in *Loves Labor*, is to alert the audience to the potential destructiveness of humankind. Though the teacher's demise occupies the foreground, the references to protective positions as 'the trouble starts' and to things 'blowing up in a hot place' suggest a larger and starker reality in store for civilization should it proceed on its current course. As Davidson has contended about O'Hara's references to wind in 'Poem (Kruschev is coming on the Right Day!)', the description of blowing wind in *Amorous* hearkens to the image of nuclear fall-out, for the violence of the wind 'carries with it hints of a more recent western wind produced nuclear tests' and an atmosphere 'neutralized by the atomic age' (2004: 68). In *Loves Labor*, the kids might be cavalier in their speech, but their campy, cartoonish farewell, reminiscent of Porky Pig's send-off –'Oops! that's all, folks' – also brings with it a chilling finality.

From the internecine wars of the *Iliad* to a future burdened by Cold War tensions, O'Hara's eclogues engross themselves in death and potential destruction and thus feature a warning of the destruction of civilization at the hands of humankind. O'Hara has visited similar subject matter before; particularly in his poem 'Ode to Joy', he railed against mortality and the frailty of human existence, urging in the poem's refrain that there be 'no more dying' (1995: 281). If *Amorous* and *Loves Labor* read as dystopian warnings about bellicose tendencies and nuclear warfare, 'Ode to Joy' instead drives towards a utopian future in which death no longer wields its power over humanity: 'We shall have everything we want and there'll be no more dying on the pretty plains or in the supper clubs' (O'Hara 1995: 281). In lieu of death, O'Hara will construct his utopia as an urban enclave where 'buildings will go up into the dizzy air as love itself goes in/and up the reeling life that it has chosen for once or all' (1995: 281). In his vision, O'Hara betrays a distinctly cosmopolitan, urbane sensibility, and though the scope of O'Hara's project is grand, it is also remarkable for its straightforwardness, simplicity, and optimism: peace might begin with something as small as the intimacy between a congregation of friends and a fundamental agreement to commune amicably together.

Despite the utopian impulses of 'Ode to Joy', the poem concludes with an insistent plea for death to cease in its very last line. 'Ode to Joy' thus oscillates between hope and despair, between sex and death, and between camp frivolity and dread. Reading the alternating camp and morbid rhetoric of 'Ode to Joy' alongside *Loves Labor* allows for an understanding of the play as likewise contrapuntal; though *Loves Labor* seems steadfast in its representation of the destructive tendencies of humankind, O'Hara's use of camp provides a humorous counterpoint to what could be an altogether too somber dystopian message. O'Hara's characters, who blithely and campily dismiss the end of Arcadia, augment the play's amusing qualities, yet their vapid demeanour also contributes to O'Hara's warning of the decline of civilization and his satirical observations of human behaviour. The result of *Loves Labor*'s combination of camp and dystopian elements is a play that is both comical and disheartening. *Loves Labor* thus follows a fundamental principle of camp that disregards treating grave matters too seriously. As Sontag writes, the 'whole point of Camp is to dethrone the serious. Camp is playful, anti-serious. More precisely Camp involves a new, more complex relation to "the serious." One can be serious about the frivolous, frivolous about the serious' (1966: 288).

The conjunction of frivolity and seriousness especially made their mark in Alan Marlowe's production of *Loves Labor*. As Stephen J. Bottoms relates, Marlowe's direction of *Loves Labor* 'turned the piece into a kind of outrageous, farce . . . [featuring] a wild, campy cast including [John] Vaccaro, Fred Herko, and the drag queen and freak-show artist Frankie Francine . . . With the forgetful Francine constantly looking for his lines, written onto various parts of his costume, this was a flagrantly tacky display of queer excess' (2004: 64). Such campy unruliness can be entertaining, not only provoking amusement in, and appreciation by, the audience but also calling attention to absurdities of human behaviour. Marlowe's direction of *Loves Labor* thus heightens the campy elements of the play in such a way that O'Hara's dystopian rebuke of humankind's destructiveness is counterbalanced by the frivolity and excess of the actors playing their parts. Though O'Hara's warning about the human propensity for violence and a corresponding decline of civilization remains intact, *Loves Labor's* performative elements leaven such a message, and the characters' campy selfishness transform into a recognizable – and entertaining – critique of humankind.

Joe LeSueur, O'Hara's close friend and one-time roommate, relates an anecdote in the introduction to O'Hara's *Selected Plays* about Hal Fondren, another of O'Hara's friends, who attended O'Hara's play *Try! Try!* at the Poets' Theater in Cambridge, Massachusetts (O'Hara 1978: xi):

> Unlike most members of the audience, [Fondren] found many of the individual lines hilarious and saw no reason to suppress his laughter. At the end of the performance, an irate Thornton Wilder rose from his seat and, looking straight at Hal, sternly rebuked the members of the audience who had laughed; he pointed out that what they had just seen was a serious work, possibly an important one.

It is entirely possible that Fondren's reaction to the campy elements of the play *and* Wilder's plea for the seriousness of O'Hara's work are both correct. In *Loves Labor*, O'Hara does reconcile outrageous humour with the play's grave concerns about war; the play's dystopian themes – embedded as they are within the pastoral genre – give rise to a camp sensibility meant to draw attention to and combat our human tendency for destruction.

Works cited

Auslander, P. (1989), *The New York School Poets as Playwrights: O'Hara, Ashbery, Koch, Schuyler and the Visual Arts*, New York: Peter Lang.

Bottoms, S. (2004), *Playing Underground: A Critical History of the 1960's Off-Off Broadway Movement*, Ann Arbor: University of Michigan.

Coutts-Smith, K. (1970), *Dada*, New York: Studio Vista – Dutton.

Davidson, M. (2004), *Guys Like Us: Citing Masculinity in Cold War Poetics*, Chicago: University of Chicago.

di Prima, D. (2002), *Recollections of My Life as a Woman: The New York Years*, New York: Viking Penguin.

Greg, W. (1959), *Pastoral Poetry and Pastoral Drama*, New York: Russell & Russell.

LeSueur, J. (1978), 'Introduction' in Frank O'Hara, *Selected Plays*, New York: Full Court Press.

O'Hara, F. (1964), 'Program Notes (1964)', Pastelgram.org Available at: http://l.pastelgram.org/features/282/event/311 (last accessed 12 November 2014).

O'Hara, F. (1978), *Selected Plays*, New York: Full Court Press.

O'Hara, F. (1995), *The Collected Poems of Frank O'Hara*, Berkeley: University of California.

Perloff, M. (1998), *Frank O'Hara: Poets Among Painters*, Chicago: University of Chicago.

Preminger, A. and Brogan, T.V.F. (eds) (1993), *The New Princeton Encyclopedia of Poetry and Poetics*, Princeton: Princeton University.

Sontag, S. (1966), *Against Interpretation and Other Essays*, New York: Farrar, Straus and Giroux.

14

Outlaw Tongues: The Stimuli for Michael McClure's *The Beard*

Kurt Hemmer

Most contemporary readers can flip through Michael McClure's most ambitious and notorious drama, *The Beard*, and be baffled that something so ostensibly perplexing and tautological could have caused such uproar in the 1960s. Police arrested the actors Billie Dixon and Richard Bright after separate performances in San Francisco and Berkeley in August 1966, the California Senate called for an investigation after a production at Fullerton State College in November 1967, and the actors Bright and Alexandra Hay were arrested fourteen nights in a row in Los Angeles in January and February 1968 (C. 2011: 1). According to McClure scholar Rod Phillips, 'All in all, nineteen court cases centered around [sic] the play, with charges including obscenity, conspiracy to commit felony, and lewd and dissolute conduct in a public place' (2003: 27). As McClure himself explains, 'People have said that *The Beard* cases were to the theater what *Howl* was to poetry and *Naked Lunch* was to the novel' (1994a: 295).

The play actually began as a poster. McClure became interested in boxing through his friend Norman Mailer, and had a vision of a boxing poster promoting a match between Billy the Kid and movie actress Jean Harlow. He had professional posters (and even tickets for the fake bout) made and displayed them throughout San Francisco. After that, he claims, the Kid and Harlow 'entered [his] consciousness' and performed the play as he typed it (1994a: 286). Self-published in 1965, first performed after playwright Harold Pinter suggested the Actors' Workshop look at McClure's work and director Mark Estrin chose it, the play premiered at the Encore Theater on 18 December 1965 in San Francisco. It was republished in 1967. *The Beard* has gone generally unheralded because of the demands it makes both on its readers and its audience. Though it was made into a film by Andy Warhol in 1966, McClure was not a fan (Warhol had also filmed a spoof of Harlow called *Harlot* in December 1964) and McClure's attorney, the notorious Melvin Belli, sent Warhol a letter warning him never to screen it (C. 2011: 3).

The Beard is recognized today more for the stir it caused in the courts in the 1960s than as a dramatic piece worth reinvestigating. Yet, arguably, McClure's play is indeed – to reuse McClure's own analogy – as important to Beat drama as 'Howl' is to Beat poetry and *Naked Lunch* is to the Beat novel. To better understand what McClure was attempting with *The Beard*, it is important to re-historicize the play in terms of the challenge the Frankfurt School theorist Herbert Marcuse presented to McClure, and the influence of surrealist French dramatist Antonin Artaud. McClure attempted to resist the co-optation of the counterculture by mainstream society, a dilemma portended in the work of Marcuse, through a radical philosophy of theatre inspired by Artaud. Though often read allegorically as a sexual parry between the male and female libidos, as Norman Mailer does when he states that the play's theme is 'the nature of perverse temper between a man and a woman' (1967: n.p.), *The Beard* can simultaneously, and more interestingly, be read as a statement for avoiding ecological annihilation. In making such a statement, McClure unwittingly wrote his characters out of the existential hell of Jean-Paul Sartre's *Huis clos* (famously known in English by Paul Bowles's evocative but misleading translation *No Exit*). *The Beard* is a radical revelation of American sexual repression in the 1960s and, as such, part of the war against the imagination, which, as Diane di Prima claims in her poem 'Rant' (1985) and McClure echoes in his poem 'Beginning with a Line by di Prima' (1991), is the only war that matters.

McClure's fascination with Billy the Kid began, as with many members of his generation, as a child reading pulp Westerns and listening to Western radio shows but, like a *Magicicada*, it resurfaced. In 1958, with public fascination growing over the supposedly recent phenomenon of juvenile delinquency, and white middle-class American youth spending their allowances on Hollywood's latest depiction of existential angst, Warner Brothers decided to turn Billy the Kid into the recently deceased James Dean. The film *The Left Handed Gun* (a misnomer derived from the mirror image of a ferrotype photograph – the only authenticated image of the Kid), was essentially Dean's *Rebel without a Cause* (1955) redone as a B Western with a novice Paul Newman playing the Kid. Stephen Tatum, in his study of the changing images of Billy the Kid, says of *The Left Handed Gun*, 'Instead of the outlaw-hero who seeks redemption for his sins by means of an honorable social commitment, the Kid resembles a Southwestern rebel without a cause, a James Dean figure shuffling through Fort Sumner and learning the bitter lesson that society is weak, deceitful, treacherous, and tyrannous, ultimately desirous of denying his existence by capturing him in handcuffs or in dime novels' (1982: 135).

McClure would later befriend Dennis Hopper, who worked with Dean in *Rebel without a Cause* and *Giant* (1956), and who was slated to play Billy the

Kid in the Los Angeles production of *The Beard* in 1968 before he had a falling out with the play's producer. *The Left Handed Gun* was directed by Arthur Penn, who would become famous a decade later for ushering in the New Hollywood era that challenged the Hays Code ethics of post-Harlow films with *Bonnie and Clyde* (1967); the Leslie Stevens screenplay was based on a teleplay by Gore Vidal. McClure saw the film with underground filmmaker Kenneth Anger (McClure 1999c), whose film *Scorpio Rising* (1964) would enmesh Dean with homosexuality and biker sub-culture, and whose book *Hollywood Babylon* (1965) would feature the suicide of Harlow's husband Paul Bern. McClure himself would get the chance to portray a Western outlaw named Plummer in Peter Fonda's classic Western *The Hired Hand* (1971), which Frank Mazzola, who had acted with Dean in *Rebel without a Cause,* famously edited with his signature montage scenes. Bob Dylan, who had given McClure an autoharp which McClure played at the Human Be-In on 14 January 1967 and used to compose 'Come on God, and Buy Me a Mercedes Benz', portrayed Alias in Sam Peckinpah's famous *Pat Garrett and Billy the Kid* (1973). Dylan, and Hopper and McClure's protégé Jim Morrison, were great admirers of James Dean.

On 30 September 1955, the 24-year-old Dean died in a car crash (Riese 1991: 298). A week later, on 7 October, McClure gave his first public poetry reading at the 6 Gallery in San Francisco to 'an audience consisting of an almost secret, semi-outlawed slice of America' (McClure 1999b: 35). At this reading, with Jack Kerouac yelling encouragement and Neal Cassady in the audience, Allen Ginsberg read the first parts of his poem 'Howl'. During the negotiations for the film version of Kerouac's novel *On the Road* in 1958, the idea of Dean Moriarty, Kerouac's character based on Cassady, dying in a car wreck at the end, like Dean, was tossed around and even considered by Kerouac (Brinkley 1998: 60). But according to Lawrence Ferlinghetti, who was also present at the Six Gallery reading, Cassady 'moved and talked like a speeded-up Paul Newman …' (1981: vi). By the late 1950s, McClure was beginning to see the Kid as a countercultural icon and a signifier who could be better cast as a Beat poet-seer rather than Newman's illiterate, mixed-up Kid of *The Left Handed Gun* – something more than a simulacrum of James Dean. Within a year, McClure had completed a draft of his first play, *The Blossom or Billy the Kid.*

Very little attention has been paid to the rigorous artistry and the deft cultural work of *The Beard.* According to Richard Cándida Smith: 'As the Vietnam War intensified, McClure came to equate sexual repression with the American history of westward expansion through conquest, and [*The Beard*] seemed to have a providential role in the growing antiwar movement. In his mind, helping Americans confront the construction of sexual pleasure and identity was essential to end the Vietnam War and Cold War militarism' (1995: 340). As *The Beard* continued to be censored, McClure believed that it was viewed as a threat to the dominant culture because it exposed the sexual repression that led to national aggression. When asked what the place of the poet is in society, McClure responded, 'The same as any other artist – to maintain the thoroughfares, to maintain the pathways of the imagination in a society that would close down the pathways of the imagination' (1994a: 254).

While McClure was making his initial attempts to maintain the pathways of the imagination in his poetry and drama, Marcuse was making a philosophical critique of an American society that was closing down the pathways of the imagination. It is interesting to note that McClure (who admired Marcuse) went to one of his lectures in San Francisco. Marcuse then attended one of McClure's poetry readings, and they had a brief correspondence (McClure 1999d). In *One-Dimensional Man* (1964), Marcuse argues that advanced industrial society eliminated the difference between private and public existence and that this led to the acceptance of the interests of industrial capitalism. He writes: 'The people recognize themselves in their commodities; they find their soul in their automobile, hi-fi set, split-level home, kitchen equipment' (1964: 9). As individuals increasingly identify with merchandise and the demands of consumerism, they become one-dimensional, unable to critique the dominant ideology, because it is always-already embraced. The dominant culture appropriates and co-opts the counterculture, which was one of the symptoms of this one-dimensionality that threatened to diminish the radical ambition of the Beats. McClure felt that one way his work could resist the one-dimensionality of the American consciousness would be to disrupt its complacency. In his poem 'Listen Lawrence', written as an attempt to move Lawrence Ferlinghetti away from socialism and toward McClure's biologism (Phillips 2000: 118), McClure exclaims, 'MARCUSE was right!' (1983: 40). In his struggle against the one-dimensional society, McClure tried to develop a poetics of drama that would resist co-optation.

Marcuse explains in his 'Political Preface' to the 1966 edition of *Eros and Civilization* (1955), 'It was the thesis of *Eros and Civilization*, more fully developed in my *One-Dimensional Man*, that man could avoid the fate of a Welfare-Through-Warfare State only by achieving a new starting point ... "Polymorphous sexuality" was the term which I used to indicate that the new direction of progress would depend completely on the opportunity to activate repressed or arrested *organic*, biological needs: to make the human body an instrument of pleasure rather than labor' (1966: xiv–xv). Influenced by Marcuse, McClure developed the idea, present in many of his works, but finding its source in *The Beard*, that the body should not be thought of primarily as a means of production but primarily as a means of pleasure.

McClure's attempt to re-conceptualize the body in a similar manner to that proposed by Marcuse was additionally stimulated by Artaud's philosophy of drama. Artaud was a proto-Beat. In the 1920s and 1930s, his experimentation with peyote and other drugs, his fascination with the indigenous cultures of Mexico, his involvement with Buddhism, and his faith in the value of spontaneity made him a precursor to the Beats, made it easy to see how he became one of their heroes. Artaud's theory of drama was the impetus for McClure's radical theatre which confronted what Marcuse called the 'one-dimensionality' of American culture. Like Marcuse, Artaud emphasized transforming the human condition rather than aligning himself with a particular political stance. Artaud inspired McClure with a theory of drama that spoke to using the body as part of the delivery of art. At times, when writing his early poems, McClure even imagined himself as Artaud, using his body, while he composed (1999a: 165).

Artaud believed that an authentic theatre would be experienced viscerally. The theatre should not be considered an exclusive place separated from the lives of the audience, but rather should be used to violently rip the audience out of its complacency. Rather than viewing theatre as a remote artifact, the audience should experience drama as a spontaneous biological eruption without the possibility of intellectual anticipation of the scenes performed. Artaud's theory of 'alchemist theater' called for the transmutation of the common substance of life into an event of transformative value. Theatre should aim to turn banal subject matter into the 'gold' of visceral, 'magical' experience. This primal, or archetypal theatre, as Artaud would call it, would be a 'virtual reality', more poetic than philosophic, and one that would ideally change the lives of its audience. According to Artaud, the primal theatre would cause 'states whose keenness is so intense and so total that we feel the underlying threat of chaos through their quivering music and forms, as decisive as it is dangerous' (1974: 36).

The immediacy of the conclusion of *The Beard*, performed with such a degree of authenticity as to have the actors arrested repeatedly, was intended to be an unfiltered image that could not be dismissed or filed away intellectually, but had to be dealt with emotionally and spontaneously. For Artaud, the action of the theatre is necessarily disruptive and cruel. In describing the attributes of his Theater of Cruelty, he writes, '[W]e will try to centre our show around famous personalities ...' (1974: 65). Using Billy the Kid and Jean Harlow, famous personalities familiar to most of the audience in the 1960s, performing a sexual act considered by many people at the time to be degenerate, McClure created a modern myth that revealed to the audience, through their struggle to come to terms with what they experienced, their own subconscious concerns. The archetypal figures of the Kid and Harlow were used to tap into the collective unconsciousness of the audience to bring shared conceptions about the symbolic significance of the characters portrayed and the act they perform so that the performance becomes an anti-cathartic jolt of awakening.

Artaud's Theater of Cruelty is concerned with mass reaction rather than personal interpretation. The goal is to inspire the audience at a sub-conscious level. McClure's use of pop culture icons is an attempt to spark shared points of recognition in his audience. The intent is to bring the audience's collective unconscious to the surface. Elaborating on the multifarious signs he calls for to induce the audience to experience theatre as an intense collective dream, Artaud writes: 'We must take inflection into account here, the particular way a word is pronounced, as well as the visual language of things (audible, sound language aside), also movement, attitudes and gestures, providing their meanings are extended, their features connected even as far as those signs' (1974: 68). McClure's concern in *The Beard*, with only two characters on a sparsely set stage, is primarily with the signs of '[r]hythm, volume, intensity, and timbre' (1994a: 18). Changing our ways of listening and reading so that we can properly interpret the multiple signs of McClure's new use of language is necessary to fully grasp his conception of the play: 'I'm talking about the split between what we say we're talking about and what we're speaking of' (1994a: 17). In following Artaud's dictum to eliminate the gap between life and theatre, McClure reproduces a quarrel that appears on the surface to be painfully mundane. Ostensibly, *The Beard* is an argument between the Kid and Harlow in which the outlaw is trying to seduce the movie star. Yet we need to try to read what is being expressed both inside and outside the language to fully understand the drama.

In addition to this subtle use of emotional or spatial language, McClure uses iconic figures in *The Beard* to develop a modern myth for his audience. McClure discovered Artaud in 1958, the same year he saw *The Left Handed Gun*, and was inspired to extend to the world of theatre the sense of revitalization the Beats were trying to bring to poetry. However he did not write *The Beard* until 1965. In the interim, McClure developed an intense interest in Billy the Kid and Jean Harlow and spent a great deal of time meticulously researching their lives. Or, as he put it, 'Billy the Kid and Jean Harlow became obsessed with me, and stood by my desk and performed a play as I wrote it down' (1999a: 166). After the promulgation of the Hays Code of moral conduct in motion pictures in 1934, Harlow represented a type of untamed sensuality for McClure that was subversive compared to post-war depictions of silver-screen sexuality. In his autobiographical novel

The Mad Cub (1970), McClure's persona describes Harlow's significance to him: 'Jean Harlow died stinking in bed of uremic poisoning with the stench of a rat's cage all around her. Jean Harlow was all soft beauty and tenderness and wistfulness to everybody . . . all goodness and sweetness and whorishness and utterly soul and clawless and a bringer of pleasure and higher sights of being' (1995: 223). In his 1961 poem 'La Plus Blanche', McClure writes of Harlow, 'For you are the whole creature of love!' (12). As the embodiment of love, she becomes the supreme symbol of the female for McClure: triumphant and warm, simultaneously seductive and regenerative. When Harlow died, McClure was not yet five years old. Yet this film star would become for him the ultimate image of female sensuality – defying the contained domestic suggestiveness he would encounter as a teenager and young adult on the silver screen.

The male counterpart to Harlow in McClure's mythos is Billy the Kid. McClure chose the Kid as a symbol that would resist the co-optation which, Marcuse argued, was the fate of the counterculture in the one-dimensional society. Marcuse's pessimistic analysis ruled out any possible mass resistance to the consumer culture: 'The new bohème, the beatniks and hipsters, the peace creeps—all these "decadents" now have become what decadence probably always was: poor refuge of defamed humanity' (1974b: xxi). Yet it is important to recognize that here Marcuse is probably referring to the 'beatniks' created by the mass media, not the Beat artists like McClure. As part of his concern with effectual resistance, McClure became fascinated with the Hell's Angels as a potential symbolic reincarnation of the essence of the Kid. The task now was to create a figure that would inspire the threat of the Angels, yet embody the political attributes of the Beat poets.

When the Hells Angels became a national phenomenon in the mid-1960s, some counterculture intellectuals like Hunter S. Thompson and Ken Kesey viewed an alliance with them as the potential antidote for the ineffectualness of the counterculture. The Angels symbolized liberating violence in the same way that the Kid did for McClure. Tom Wolfe writes in his account of Kesey and the Merry Pranksters, *The Electric Kool-Aid Acid Test* (1968), 'The Angels brought a lot of things into synch. Outlaws, by definition, were people who had moved off center and were out in some kind of Edge City. The beauty of it was, the Angels had done it like the Pranksters, by choice' (1999: 152). A poster for *The Beard* is even mentioned by one of the characters in Wolfe's book: 'it's a poster for a production of "The Beard" and has "Grah roor ograrh . . . lion lioness . . . oh grahr . . ." (like that) printed on it . . . and for that moment I understood exactly what was being said' (1999: 277). The Angels must have seemed like the incarnation of the cowboy outlaw heroes the Beats and neo-Beats had seen or imagined on radio shows, in the dime novels, comic books, movies, and television dramas of their youth. From Thompson's perspective, the Angels themselves were products of 'Celluloid outlaws' (1996: 330), 'Western movies and two-fisted TV shows' (1996: 332). To counterculture intellectuals, the Angels represented not only a return to the mythic ideals of the Western outlaw hero, but also embodied a legitimate threat to the dominant culture, something Marcuse had not seen in the beatnik counterculture itself. If the Beats and their allies could join forces with the Angels, then perhaps they would become a disturbing presence in a way that had eluded them in their poetry readings and art exhibits. McClure would use the Kid to symbolize the visceral energy that the Angels embodied and that some of the Beats found sorely lacking in the mid-1960s counterculture. McClure himself would play a motorcycle outlaw in Norman Mailer's film *Beyond the Law* (1968) while *The Beard* was being directed by Rip Torn in New York. It was during this time that McClure met Jim Morrison, who wanted to play Billy the Kid in a film of McClure's play; sadly it was never produced.

Henry McCarty, later known as Kid Antrim, then William H. Bonney and finally, Billy the Kid in the last few months of his life, was born, strangely enough, in New York City in 1859. One legend has him murdering 21 men, one for each year of his life, but he was probably involved in only nine to ten deaths. After being involved in a number of vengeance slayings and being hunted by the law, the Kid made a deal with Governor Lew Wallace for his testimony on other crimes, but Wallace was either unable or unwilling to honour his side of the deal. Pat Garrett, a former acquaintance of the Kid, and a recently elected sheriff and deputy US marshal, captured the Kid in December 1880. After being sentenced to death, the Kid made a miraculous escape, killing his two guards. Garrett found him in Fort Sumner at a friend's house, and waited for the Kid in a bedroom on the night of 14 July 1881. As the Kid entered the room, he apprehensively asked 'Quién es?' several times. They were his last words, and would fascinate Beat author William S. Burroughs and poet Charles Olson (who would question whether the Kid was actually a cold-blooded murderer at all). Garrett shot the Kid in the chest [1967: 139]).

McClure shared Olson's sympathetic understanding of the Kid, based on Walter Noble Burns's influential depiction of the outlaw as 'an American reincarnation of Robin Hood' (Utley 1989: 200). Rather than seeing the Kid as a villain, McClure, like Burns, reads the Kid as a noble outlaw killing out of principle rather than blood lust. In *The Mad Cub*, McClure's persona states his conception of the Kid: 'Billy the Kid was a seer, a mystic . . . a visionary – whatever you want to call it. . . . Like the French kid poet Rimbaud he sensed something beyond what other men of his day felt—he was prophetic' (1995: 222). To call the Kid a 'seer', a 'mystic' and a 'visionary' aligns him with the

Beat poets in the Blakean tradition. While McClure's Harlow seems to be and see infinite beauty, her counterpart sees infinite violence; she becomes, for McClure, a symbol of a particular American violence. McClure's Kid is neither the villainous freak of his detractors nor the rebel-without-a-cause Hollywood hero. He is more complex. Destroyed by the madness of his portentous visions, like the best minds of Ginsberg's 'Howl', the Kid is twisted by apocalyptic images. McClure also compares the Kid to the Beat hero Rimbaud, further connecting the outlaw with McClure's social milieu that prized youth in the face of an oppressive society they viewed as being controlled by an out-of-touch older generation. Like Rimbaud, the Kid also becomes for McClure a symbol of visionary youth committed to radical social change. The Kid, like Rimbaud's poetry, will heal by fire, not through mercy. The cover of McClure's anti-Vietnam War poem *Poisoned Wheat* (1965) is a picture of the Kid crossed out by an X. It symbolically condemns the US government for acting like the outlaw by poisoning wheat in Cambodia. McClure explains, 'In *The Beard* and in *The Blossom* ... murder is glamorized ... In *Poisoned Wheat* I felt "This is enough of glamorizing Billy the Kid for that" ... And I said "I'm canceling him; I'm canceling what I said about The Kid earlier. I don't love Billy the Kid any less, but I'm canceling what I said earlier"' (Phillips 2007: n.p.). For McClure it is no contradiction for the Kid to be simultaneously the symbol of righteous rebellion (which McClure promotes) and atrocious inhumanity (which McClure detests).

McClure was not the only writer involved with the San Francisco Renaissance to find Billy the Kid a potent cultural symbol of resistance to the dominant American culture of the 1950s. Jack Spicer used the Kid during the same period, yet offered a very different reading around the time of the release of *The Left Handed Gun* in the spring of 1958. Spicer's *Billy The Kid* (1959), with illustrations by Duncan's companion, the renowned artist Jess, begins, 'The radio that told me about the death of Billy The Kid' (1959: n.p.). As if a child listening to a Western radio show, Spicer hears of the death of the young anti-hero and desires to create an imaginary place of refuge for the Kid, and himself. McClure enjoyed Spicer's work, but recognized a crucial difference in their conceptions of the Kid. McClure explains, 'Jack's Billy the Kid is a Billy the Kid of the mind; in it Jack is listening, letting the persona create himself through his listening ... It has no historical foundation, as far as I can tell. My Billy the Kid stepped out of the Lincoln County Range War, and then became another kind of creature—but he stepped out of research' (1994a: 119).

This crucial aspect of writer-cum-scholar is made apparent in McClure's first artistic treatment of the Kid. This was begun in 1959, the same year as the publication of Spicer's book, but it was not brought to the stage until 1963, and not published until 1967. For McClure, an understanding of the historical Kid is crucial in interpreting his use of the Kid as a modern myth. McClure's play *The Blossom or Billy the Kid* (1967) was eventually dedicated to Jim Morrison, lead singer of The Doors, a friend and protégé of McClure's. A first performance of the drama was produced by Diane di Prima in New York City in 1963 and was accompanied by a 1947 recording of Artaud's *Pour en finir avec le jugement de dieu*. A second version of the play was performed at the University of Wisconsin-Milwaukee on 10 January 1967, but was closed down by the Regents of the University. Written using Kerouac's method of spontaneous prose combined with Olson's conception of projective verse, the play was the first of what McClure calls his 'outlaw dramas'.

The Blossom is set in 'eternity' with the Kid, his mother, his employer Tunstall, Tunstall's friend McSween, and McSween's wife unable to remember their deaths and forgetting their former relationships. Richard Cándida Smith mistakenly describes it as 'Billy the Kid, his employer, his employer's wife, and the two men who killed him are trapped in eternity reliving the emotions they felt at the time of their deaths' (1995: 332). Stephen Tatum writes, 'Since there is in the play an explicit metaphorical union of a flower, the Kid's phallus, and the Kid's gun, the blossom which the play describes is at once the process of a flower erupting from the earth to daylight, the phallus swelling to an erection, and the gun exploding in violence ... As in Spicer's poem, the Kid's creativity causes pain, but it leads to new visions' (1982: 148). The visions that the play leads to are not necessarily pleasant. Rather than being a redemptive force, as in Spicer's poem, the violence of the Kid in *The Blossom* is an ominous sign of the times. Cándida Smith writes, 'At the center is the Kid, "an idealistic mystic", according to McClure, who understands that death is more natural than life and that murder is his way of asserting presence in the universe. Paradise for the Kid was reliving that intense feeling preparatory to murder without break or diminution' (1995: 332). What Smith does not notice is that the characters the Kid kills in this 'eternity', Tunstall, Alexander McSween, and Susan McSween, are his former friends from life. Trapped in eternity, the Kid is unable to stop the violence within him, even when it is directed at allies. The eternity McClure places his characters in is a hell, especially for the Kid. McClure has the Kid rant, 'OH COLD PAIN FROM ICE ACHE DEATH FIRE!/IN ... / OH!/HELL! HELL! HELL! INFERNO!' (1967: 10). All of the characters articulate agony and are unable to connect with each other. (McClure's stage directions have each character speak alone and they do not look directly at each other.) The 'blossoming' of the Kid is not the surge of an empowered flower, but more the scourge of an angry god. As Tunstall envisions it, 'THE FLOWER RISES UP OUT OF THE EARTH BRINGING FIRE FROM COLD BLACKNESS' (1967: 11).

Tunstall's words seem to be directed at the Kid, coaxing him to free himself from the blackness and to bring colour into the darkness of eternity through violence. 'OH MURDERED LOVE-GOD', chants Tunstall, 'RISE FROM BLACKNESS./ ... FREED OF THIS—THE DESIRE/IS ACT AND BLOSSOM/ ... OH MURDERED, REPRESSED, RISE/TO MURDER!' (1967: 17). The Kid's blossoming is an act of violence freeing him from the stagnation of the dark eternity.

According to Artaud, whom McClure discovered the year before he began writing *The Blossom*, all action is cruel and disruptive, but necessary for life. Echoing Artaud, the Kid states, 'without heat of action all is a cold/LAUGH' (1967: 20). But the 'HORROR BLACK ACT' (1967: 21) of the Kid's visions is both 'A CONFUSION' and a 'LOVELINESS' that is violent (1967: 21). Murdering his friends in eternity, the Kid breaks through the darkness and inaction of death and back into the action of life, but loses his friends. The Kid tells his audience, 'I see into the black coldness, into the lighted/space beyond, to see myself locked in murder—my hand frozen forever in the act,/radiating the heat of anti-love. The gun/in my hand becomes immortal as a seed./ALL, all, all done without point except the exact point of life' (1967: 30). Paradoxically, the Kid's actions are both horrific and life affirming. 'In the play *The Blossom*,' writes McClure, 'the Kid is the prophet of death; he's a mystic of death. ... But the manner of it and the brutality of it and the numbers killed, and the style, is like a preview of the twentieth century. What he's doing is still beautiful, still is auric. That makes him like a visionary for the future' (1994a: 136).

According to McClure, human beings enjoy the destruction we wreak on the earth, and perversely it is both beautiful (because it is part of the affirmation of our nature) and insipid (because it leads to our own destruction). The only way McClure believes anything constructive can be done to change our course is to first admit our attraction to destruction. McClure writes (1994a: 25):

> If we see that, then we say: Oh, that's what we love to do, that's what we like to do, we like to do that. We love to kill big animals. Then we say: But if we like to do that, if we go any further, we are not going to have mammal brethren left at all. But first of all, you can't righteously take a stance that this is wrong, this is evil, this is not human. This is, in fact, entirely human, this *is* our nature. Then we say: Ah, but our nature has *other* possibilities. If we acknowledge that this is our nature, what *other* possibilities does our nature have?

McClure's argument here helps us understand the difference between his Billy the Kid in *The Blossom* and his Billy the Kid in *The Beard*.

While *The Blossom* is a prophetic work of a possible apocalyptic catastrophe, *The Beard* was written to transcend such a cataclysm. The Kid's soliloquy concluding *The Blossom* reads, 'PAIN, TORTURE, AGONY AS JOY WITHOUT JOY./NO! Oh solid solid vastness of/body. LOVE—NO! DESIRE! ALL IS/swelling at once to one eternal/last final act swelling./OH GOD, OH CHRIST, OH AGONY,/forever in bright darkness/here …' (1967: 31). Then a woman's voice 'like a musical note' – BLOSSOM' (1967: 31). If Billy the Kid's penis is metaphorically his gun; and his orgasm is the firing of his gun; and the Kid himself is the nineteenth-century, solitary embodiment of the mass destructive force to come into the twentieth century; then the orgasmic 'blossom' of the play's conclusion is a prophetic metaphor of the doomsday bomb. Such an outcome can be avoided, according to McClure, if the human imagination is free to choose an alternative nature to the self-destructive one embodied by and embedded in the Kid.

Beneath the surface of the mundane verbal battle of *The Beard* is an unconscious revisioning of Jean-Paul Sartre's *No Exit* (1944). David A. Ross, director of the Whitney Museum's *Beat Culture and the New America: 1950–1965* 1995 exhibit, writes, 'Beat culture offered an open road to a generation that feared itself lost in a no-exit world' (1995: 13). In his dissertation on Ferlinghetti's and McClure's plays, Thomas Whiteford Boeker astutely points out, '[*The Beard*] is the opposite of Sartre's *No Exit*, celebrating the alternative of creating Paradise rather than Hell out of human closeness' (1978: 165), but Boeker does not elaborate on this important connection between these plays. McClure states, 'I see that what both Sartre and Camus did in founding Existentialism is extremely important to my work and to the work of my friends and to the work of many whom I admire' (1994a: 9). 'Sociologically', argues Lisa Phillips, 'the Beats were the first large, self-conscious, and widely publicized group of middle-class dropouts and have sometimes been called American existentialists. They indeed shared a sense of acute alienation, of the absurd, and a belief in the importance of individual action with their European counterparts' (1995: 29). Yet, through the influence of Artaud, McClure rejected writing the type of philosophical dramas created by Sartre.

No Exit deals with the frustrated desires of three characters whose existence in hell is contingent on their relations with one another. The ultimate philosophical statement in the drama is Garcin's lament, 'Hell is—other people!' (1976a: 47). Yet Sartre explains, 'But "hell is other people" has always been misunderstood. It has been thought that what I meant by that was that our relations with other people are always poisoned, that they are invariably hellish relations. But what I really mean is something totally different' (1976b: 199). According to Sartre, we can break free from the gaze of the Other, but exactly how is unclear. In *Being and Nothingness* (1943),

Sartre writes, 'I am possessed by the Other; the Other's look fashions my body in its nakedness, causes it to be born, sculptures it, produces it as it *is*, sees it as I shall never see it. The Other holds a secret—the secret of what I am' (1956: 364). To escape the oppressive, defining gaze of the Other, Sartre claims we try to be loved in order to be valorized rather than contained by the Other's gaze. The problem, according to Sartre, is that the fear of the Other awakening from the sleep of love causes constant anxiety in the beloved, thus stymying one's satisfaction in the face of love.

The Beard can be read as finding a way out of Sartre's hell. Thus it simultaneously presents a disturbance to Marcuse's one-dimensional containment culture. While Sartre's play revolves around a philosophical idea (hell is the gaze of the Other), McClure's play is a poetic crescendo leading to a climatic, liberating image. Rather than the stark setting of the Second Empire-style drawing-room of *No Exit*, *The Beard* is set, as the surrealist Artaud would have appreciated, to provoke the eyes. An orange light shines on characters surrounded by blue velvet sitting beside a table covered with furs. Describing the sensations he wanted to stimulate, McClure says, 'It's a field of velvet; "Velvet Eternity" is the eternity that we touch with our fingertips, that we smell with our nose, that we feel with the seats of our buttocks when we sit on a chair, when we hear the sounds of someone else who's speaking' (1994a 17). Harlow's pale blue gown with plumed sleeves is worn in contrast to the simplicity of the Kid's tight pants and boots. Significantly, unlike in *The Blossom* where the Kid carries his shotgun in eternity, the Kid of *The Beard* has no gun. This is one of the signs that the Kid has come to represent something quite different for McClure than he had in the earlier play. Without his gun, the Kid becomes a figure who is capable of using language rather than violence – though it is a new language. Both the Kid and Harlow have small beards of torn white tissue paper. McClure explains, '"Beard" is Elizabethan slang, and it means to quarrel with someone; it means to pull his beard when you "beard" someone' (1994a: 17). The Kid and Harlow, however, are not in a struggle against one another but in relation to one another. Their choices will determine if their eternity is a Sartrean hell. The final image of *The Beard* suggests that it is not.

McClure believes, 'When they succeed, my plays are poems and they do not come from the idea of plot or ideas of dialogue or rhetoric; they come from an image' (1994a: 270). Finding themselves trapped together in an afterworld, like Sartre's characters, the Kid and Harlow do not know if they are in a heaven or a hell. Harlow says to the Kid, 'Your eyes are crazier than Hell! They stare!' (1965: 13). Harlow and the Kid are potentially in a Sartrean hell, contained by each other's gaze. As the play proceeds, it becomes apparent to the Kid that the choice is up to them. 'We're in Heaven', announces the Kid

(1965: 49). Yet it will only become a heaven if the Kid can convince Harlow to give in to desire and lose the gaze. The Kid implores, 'IF WE DON'T DO WHAT WE WANT–WE'RE NOT DIVINE!' (1965: 60). After tearing her panties and playfully biting her, the Kid remarks, 'A toothmark goes away in Heaven or Hell' (1965: 51). Harlow's view of his actions will determine where they are. Heaven and hell are not places that are, but places that are enacted. To evade Harlow's gaze is not enough; to make the eternity free of the gaze's oppression the Kid must lose his gaze as well. Since the anxiety of love makes it a poor substitute for the gaze, the Kid acts rather than thinks. With his head between her thighs, his attention is completely on giving her pleasure, thus he loses the gaze that threatens to contain her. (To McClure's credit, this actually aligns with the historical Kid, who was known to be an 'unfailingly seductive' lover [Utley 1989: 15]). As she starts to orgasm, Harlow ecstatically assures him, 'YOU'RE NEXT!' (1965: 70). Her final moans are the repetition of the word 'STAR', signifying both her heavenly bliss and the loss of her gaze on the Kid as she concentrates on the pleasure surging through her body.

'Billy the Kid and Jean Harlow', writes McClure, 'would not go away after the scandal over the play, *The Beard*, died down. They stood at my bed late at night till I wrote down "*The Sermons of Jean Harlow* & the Curses of Billy the Kid"' (1999a: 166). In this group of poems, Harlow's voice is the embodiment of a beautiful narcissism, exuberant and overflowing with life: 'OH GOD, HOW SUPERB IT IS, TO BE INFINITELY BEAUTIFUL!' (1968: n.p.). The Kid says of those who kill that he will torture them 'in Hell!!!' (1968: np). Yet the voices of Harlow and the Kid merge in the final poem of the series, suggesting that they complement one another and that each is necessary: 'ETERNALLY … FROZEN *FOREVER* …' (1968: n.p.). The Kid would return one more time, reprising his role as a backward and forward-seeing seer in *Range War* (1978), still trapped in eternity and haunted by visions— Pleistocene people killing a giant ground sloth and Green Berets setting fire to a Vietnamese thatched roof: 'I CAN SEE INTO THE PAST WHEN THE BIG CREATURES DIED AND … INTO THE FUTURE! … THERE'S NOTHIN THERE BUT PEOPLE KILLING PEOPLE' (1978: 16). Perhaps the optimism of *The Beard* had left him. But in 1965 McClure put his characters in a sexual situation that was uncomfortable, particularly at the time the play was performed, because of the positions his characters were in. It is this image of the masculine Kid on his knees, his head pressed between Harlow's spread legs, his tongue doing his talking for him, that McClure used in his theatre to 'cruelly' jerk his audience out of their complacency, and initiate a countercultural stance resisting co-optation. One of the general themes of the play is roughly akin to the countercultural slogan 'make love, not war', which came about roughly around the same time the play was conceived. But McClure's message is a little more radical, because it does not simply substitute male violent aggression with male sexual gratification. It asks its viewers to exchange the perpetuation of violence for the goal of giving pleasure – which is truly radical.

Works cited

Artaud, A. (1974), *The Theatre and its Double*, in *Antonin Artaud: Collected Works Volume Four*, V. Corti (trans.), London: Calder & Boyars.

Boeker, T. W. (1978), 'Two Playwrights of the San Francisco Renaissance: Lawrence Ferlinghetti and Michael McClure', Dissertation, University of Georgia.

Brinkley, D. (1998), 'In the Kerouac Archive', *The Atlantic Monthly* 282.5: 49–76.

C., Gary (2011), 'Andy Warhol, Michael McClure and *The Beard*', Warholstars. org. Available at: www.warholstars.org/beard.html (last accessed 18 May 2015).

Cándida Smith, R. (1995), *Utopia and Dissent: Art, Poetry, and Politics in California*, Berkeley: University of California.

Ellingham, L. and Killian, K. (1998), *Poet Be Like God: Jack Spicer and the San Francisco Renaissance*, Hanover, NH: University Press of New England.

Ferlinghetti, L. (1981), 'Editor's Note', in N. Cassady, *The First Third*, San Francisco: City Lights.

Mailer, N. (1967), Foreword, in *The Beard* by Michael McClure, San Francisco: Coyote.

Marcuse, H. (1966), *One Dimensional Man: Studies in the Ideology of Advanced Industrial Society*, Boston: Beacon.

Marcuse, H. (1974a), *Eros and Civilization: A Philosophical Inquiry into Freud*, Boston: Beacon.

Marcuse, H. (1974b), 'Political Preface' in *Eros and Civilization: A Philosophical Inquiry into Freud*. Boston: Beacon.

McClure, M. (1961), 'La Plus Blanche' in *The New Book/A Book of Torture*. New York: Grove.

McClure, M. (1965), *The Beard*, published privately by Michael McClure.

McClure, M. (1967), *The Blossom or Billy the Kid*, Milwaukee, WI: Great Lakes.

McClure, M. (1968), *The Sermons of Jean Harlow & The Curses of Billy the Kid*, San Francisco: Dave Haselwood.

McClure, M. (1970), 'William H. Bonney' in *Star*, New York: Grove.

McClure, M. (1978), *Range War, New Wilderness Letter*, 1.3–4: 1–17.

McClure, M. (1983), 'Listen Lawrence' in *Fragments of Perseus*, New York: New Directions.

McClure, M. (1994a), *Lighting the Corners: On Art, Nature, and the Visionary*, Albuquerque: University of New Mexico.

McClure, M. (1995), *The Mad Cub*. New York: Blue Moon.

McClure, M. (1999a), 'After Thoughts' in *Huge Dreams: San Francisco and Beat Poems*, New York: Penguin.

McClure, M. (1999b), 'Painting Beat by Numbers' in H. George-Warren (ed.), *The Rolling Stone Book of the Beats: The Beat Generation and American Culture*, New York: Hyperion.

McClure, M. (1999c), Telephone interview, 28 April.

McClure, M. (1999d), Telephone interview, 13 August.

Olson, C. (1967), 'Billy the Kid' in Donald Allen (ed.), *Human Universe and Other Essays*, New York: Grove.

Phillips, L. (1995), 'Beat Culture: America Revisioned' in *Beat Culture and the New America: 1950–1965*. New York: Flammarion.

Phillips, R. (2000), *'Forest Beatniks' and 'Urban Thoreaus': Gary Snyder, Jack Kerouac, Lew Welch, and Michael McClure*, New York: Peter Lang.

Phillips, R. (2003), *Michael McClure*, Boise, ID: Boise State University.

Phillips, R. (2007), *A Fierce God and a Fierce War: An Interview with Michael McClure*, Binley Woods, Coventry: The Beat Scene.

Reynolds, F. as told to M. McClure (1967), *Freewheelin Frank: Secretary of the Angels*. New York: Grove.

Riese, R. (1991), *The Unabridged James Dean: His Life and Legacy from A to Z*, New York: Wings.

Ross, D. A. (1995), 'Director's Foreword' in *Beat Culture and the New America: 1950–1965*, L. Phillips (ed.), New York: Whitney Museum.

Sartre, J-P. (1956), *Being and Nothingness: An Essay on Phenomenological Ontology*, H. E. Barnes (trans.), New York: Philosophical Library.

Sartre, J-P. (1976a), *No Exit*, in *No Exit and Three Other Plays*, S. Gilbert (trans.), New York: Vintage.

Sartre, J-P. (1976b), *Sartre on Theater*, F. Jelline (trans.), M. Contat and M. Rybalka (eds) New York: Pantheon.

Spicer, J. (1959), *Billy The Kid*, Stinson Beach, CA: Enkidu Surrogate.

Stenn, D. (1993), *Bombshell: The Life and Death of Jean Harlow*, New York: Doubleday.

Tatum, S. (1982), *Inventing Billy the Kid: Visions of the Outlaw in America, 1881–1981*. Albuquerque: University of New Mexico.

Thompson, H. S. (1981), *Hell's Angels: A Strange and Terrible Saga*, New York: Ballantine.

Thompson, H. S. (1989), *Fear and Loathing in Las Vegas: A Savage Journey to the Heart of the American Dream*, New York: Vintage.

Utley, R. M. (1989), *Billy the Kid: A Short and Violent Life,* Lincoln, NE: University of Nebraska.

Wolfe, T. (1989), *The Electric Kool-Aid Acid Test*, New York: Bantam.

Poetry Takes Centre Stage: John Wieners' *Still Life* at the New York Poets Theatre

Erik Mortenson

John Wieners (1934–2002) is best-known in Beat circles for his collection *The Hotel Wentley Poems* (1958), composed while he was living in San Francisco. His one-act play *Still Life* (1961–1962) may be a less-recognized work of an even less-recognized Beat writer, but both its composition and its staging share the very Beat concerns of spontaneity and an openness to chance that was the hallmark of the New York Poets Theatre. Wieners' work, along with other plays by poets in the Beat and underground milieus, sought to forge a new conception of theatre governed as much by artistic collaboration and audience interaction as by standard conceptions of plot or staging. Produced within the very loose structure of the New York Poets Theatre, Wieners' play raises more questions than it answers, creating a production that is more event than performance. By forcing its audience to create meaning out of gaps and fissures, *Still Life* exemplifies an underground theatre movement that sought to apply Beat as well as other post-war aesthetic practices to dramatic productions to challenge notions of theatre prevalent in mid-century America.

Between Black Mountain and Beat

Wieners was an ideal writer for this new type of experimental theatre. Steeped in both the Beat and Black Mountain traditions, Wieners was a liminal figure who drew on both in his work. Born in Milton, MA, Wieners attended Boston College before going on to study at Black Mountain College from 1955–1956. He became interested in the college having heard Charles Olson read in Boston, and he would go on to regularly correspond with the poet. Wieners' time at Black Mountain is important; many of the faculty were interested in performance, and several alumni would later work in the field. Wieners was clearly influenced by his time at the college, even naming one of his characters in *Still Life* 'Cage', a reference to the composer John Cage whose 'Theatre Piece' (1952), performed at Black Mountain, would become a touchstone for the Off-Off Broadway community. Wieners himself worked as both an actor and a stage manager at Cambridge's Poets' Theatre upon returning from Black Mountain. He was also part of the Beat movement. During his two-year stay in San Francisco from 1958–1960, Wieners was familiar with Beat circles and spent time with Michael McClure, who also shared an interest in dramatic productions. Returning to the East Coast, he struck up a friendship with Diane di Prima, one of the founding members of the New York Poets Theatre, who claimed 'John was one of my tightest friends for about ten years' (di Prima 2001: 272–73). Wieners' interest in both groups can be seen in the journal he edited from 1956–1958, *Measure*, which published selections from many Black Mountain writers along with the Beat work of Jack Kerouac, Gregory Corso, and one of the first excerpts of William S. Burroughs's *Naked Lunch*. Wieners also published two poems alongside Kerouac, Allen Ginsberg, and Burroughs in *Chicago Review*'s spring 1958 issue devoted to the 'San Francisco Poets'. Wieners' involvement in both movements was an important catalyst for his work, and *Still Life* owes a debt to both Beat and Black Mountain traditions.

Despite this familiarity with many Beat figures, Wieners has traditionally been left out of the Beat canon. His omission from Beat registers is somewhat surprising, since his work shares an interest in capturing the passing moment in all its intensity, something of a hallmark of Beat aesthetic practice. In his *Hotel Wentley Poems*, Wieners writes in 'A poem for record players,' 'Details/ but which are here and/I hear and shall never/give up again, shall carry/with me over the streets/of this seacoast city,/forever' (1958: n.p.) The collection is filled with such observations of the passing moment, as Wieners attempts to chronicle the people, places, and objects around him in numinous detail. In his journal entries during the period, collected in *The Journal of John Wieners is to be called 707 Scott Street for Billie Holiday 1959*, he remarks (1996: 126):

> absolute reality is all I am interested in, the light shining on the silver edge of these keys, the magic formation of the letters in rows upon the green field of the paper, looking like the shadowed corner of a garden, elaborating on none of this, entering into communion with it, picking up speed as I go further in, looking out that nothing disturbs me from it, this place, which cd. be called magic, but which is not, is only here, 707 Scott Street, San Francisco.

Such attention to how the mind perceives as images and thoughts well up into consciousness caught the attention of Allen Ginsberg. In his foreword to

Wieners' *Selected Poems 1958–1984*, Ginsberg praises Wieners for his attention to such detail: 'There is a disciplined effort of spontaneity wherein we can read his mind. He leaves evidence of it in the casual conscious breaks in the verse – the urgency to remember what is being thought, capture the flash of enchantment in the mind pictures that pass, leaving words behind, arranged on the page the way they came' (Ginsberg 1986: 15). For Ginsberg, Wieners' work clearly falls within a Beat aesthetic.

Wieners' thematic preoccupations are Beat as well. His marginalized, outsider status can be seen in the titles to his *Hotel Wentley Poems*. 'A Poem for tea heads' describes a drug user waiting with his pusher to score, while 'A Poem for the insane' chronicles the trials and tribulations of living in San Francisco's underground scene. His *Journal of John Wieners* is replete with thick descriptions of a drug 'pad' with people tying up for shots. Starting in 1960, Wieners was hospitalized numerous times for mental health issues and is known to have received shock therapy. He was also a gay man living in a highly homophobic post-war society. 'A poem for suckers' takes on the difficulties of living a homosexual lifestyle in the 1950s: 'Well we can go/in the queer bars w//our long hair reaching/down to the ground and/we can sing our songs/of love like the black mama/on the juke box after all/what have we got left' (1956: n.p.). The poem was originally titled 'A poem for cocksuckers' and in the Harry Ransom Center's signed copy Wieners has handwritten the word 'cock' to correct the censored title. According to di Prima, who first encountered the poet through the *Hotel Wentley Poems*, his 'Boston catholic family had had him committed for being gay, and using dope, maybe junk, now, all those shock treatments later, he was more than a little crazy' (di Prima 2001: 272–73). While the Beats were not the only ones on the margins of 1950s society, Wieners' life and writing was certainly in the Beat vein.

Despite close affinities with the Beats, Wieners was somewhat critical of them. In a 2 February 1959 letter to Olson, Wieners discusses drinking with Jack Kerouac in 'The Rok bar', describing the successful author of *On the Road* as 'An "Irish" lush. Jan says he looks like a bum. And he does. But more. With a gleam in his eyes. & $300 in the bank. And a *Life* reporter smiling his white teeth' (Wieners 2012: 19). Wieners appears ambivalent here, admiring Kerouac while simultaneously noting the contradiction between his 'Beat' persona and the reality of his fame and financial success. While other Beat writers were able to turn these marks of outsider status to their advantage, Wieners was less comfortable with flaunting his marginality. In another letter written later that month to Olson, Wieners discusses his thoughts on Ginsberg. Claiming to have read 'as far as I could into his long mother poem' before commenting that the line he remembers most from *Kaddish* is 'the dropping of the mind on the page', Wieners concludes in a 10 February 1959 letter to Olson, 'But it's this lack of the original which ultimately bars him. Bores me. I mean all poets inhabit the instantaneous the immediate but all we beat suffer from lack of joy, inability to lift above ourselves' (Wieners 2012: 24).[1] Wieners appears to feel an affinity with a poet trying to capture the workings of his own mind as it encounters the world. Nevertheless, Wieners feels that something is missing from Ginsberg's work. His poetry shares much with the confessional Beat style of Ginsberg, but prefers to delve further into the personal feelings such observations raise. While Wieners did become more political in the early 1970s, before that, his poems tended to be more introverted and lyrical. The play *Still Life*, with its elliptical style, exemplifies his unique brand of observation and reflection.

A theatre for poets

Founded by Alan Marlowe, Diane di Prima, James Waring, LeRoi Jones, Herbert McDowell, and Fred Herko in 1961, The New York Poets Theatre was designed to provide a space for artists working across various media to collaborate and display their work. A glance at the plays, readings, musical performances, and dance programmes that the theatre put on reveals the eclectic nature of the group. From its founding in 1961 until its dissolution in 1965, the group hosted plays by Wallace Stevens, Robert Duncan, and James Waring, among others, poetry readings by Burroughs, Ginsberg, Jones, McClure, Philip Whalen, and Gary Snyder, film screenings of work by Brian di Palma, Kenneth Anger, Stan Brakhage, Bruce Conners, Andy Warhol, and Jack Smith, musical performances by The Fugs, and happenings by Allan Kaprow, along with numerous other events. In a later prospectus, issued after reorganizing themselves as The American Theatre for Poets, Inc. in 1964, the organization declared that it 'is devoted to the development of new work in the theatre and dance, to the combining of the various art forms, and to encouraging poets and painters to work in the theatre' (Prospectus 1965). Though the group would fall foul of the law and would ultimately close a year later, they remained true to their word, producing a series of events that challenged expectation.[2]

The New York Poets Theatre was not alone in its inter-disciplinary approach to the post-war arts scene. The group was part of a larger zeitgeist which challenged the rigidity of early Cold War culture with an invigorating mix of spontaneity, chance techniques, and improvisation. In the field of drama, the example was set by The Living Theatre. Founded by Julian Beck and Judith Malina, it began in 1948 when the couple 'rented a cellar on

Wooster Street to put on a series of Japanese Noh plays translated by Ezra Pound', then re-launched in 1959 with an infamous production of Jack Gelber's *The Connection* (Little 1972: 29). The New York Poets Theatre quickly picked up on the 'chance theatre' being developed by John Cage and others in the Black Mountain circle, and was deeply influenced by The Living Theatre. In a 1965 programme, Camille Gordon's piece 'Musique Concrete and Chance Theatre' discusses the historical development of the sort of theatre that di Prima's group was presenting. Gordon relates that, around 1950, those at the Black Mountain College began experimenting with simultaneous performances based on chance which are typically credited with being the first 'happening': 'So Merce Cunningham danced, while Tudor played the piano, while a Kline painting hung, while various poets read, while Cage carried on his activities, and so on' (1965: n.p.). This sort of improvisational approach to theatre was meant as a challenge to the more traditional, crafted, Broadway production which aimed for clarity and entertainment. The New York Poets Theatre picks up on many of the same techniques, as we shall see with the staging of Wieners's play *Still Life*.

Because it was illegal to perform in bars that lacked a cabaret licence or in outdoor spaces such as Washington Square Park, the café quickly became the place where art flourished in New York (see Bottoms 2009: 18). The New York Poets Theatre was not a café per se, but partook in the atmosphere of a quasi-legal space where plays, films, and concerts could be performed and artists could mingle and discuss their work. Such spaces were charged with an aura of transgression. Richard Pepperman, the actor who plays the role of 'Cage' in *Still Life*, describes the theatre where the play took place as very intimate and charged with an undercurrent of sexuality. Jack Smith's black and white photographs hung on the walls, and drug use regularly occurred (Pepperman 2015). The New York Poets Theatre was an informal space where theatre and a sub-culture mingled; while most probably did not consider themselves 'Beat', a space charged with the aura associated with the Beats was nevertheless created.[3]

Still Life

Wieners' play opened Sunday 10 December 1961 at the New York Poets Theatre's Off-Bowery Gallery at 84 East 10th Street, New York City.[4] The play ran for 12 performances, sharing a bill with James Waring's *Nights at the Tango Palace*, an absurdist play concerning an upcoming masquerade that develops into a play-within-a-play featuring characters called 'Wrestler', 'Dracula', 'Cowboy', and a radio which speaks to the audience. The New York

Poets Theatre also staged the fourth act of Robert Duncan's infamous *Faust Foutu* that evening: a comical work with Faust as a main character and including Brunhilde and Greta Garbo, among others, with topical references throughout. Duncan had staged the play as early as 1955 at San Francisco's Six Gallery with a cast of artists such as Helen Adams, McClure, and Jack Spicer; Duncan himself rose and stripped naked at the end of the performance (Killian 2010: v, ix). But the fourth act, titled 'An Epilogue', was far less comical: a sort of final tribute to Faust as he muses on what has befallen him. According to di Prima, 'The plays were dark, the way that time of year is dark, as the sun sinks to its lowest point, and in New York you are boxed in by shadows' (2001: 279). With its somber tone, *Still Life* fit the bill perfectly.

Wieners' correspondence leading up to opening night demonstrates both the speed with which the New York Poets Theatre worked as well as Wieners' attitude toward the play. As late as 21 November 1961, Wieners wrote to di Prima asking for 'an actor's copy, so I could see what's up, and thereby give you my permission to go ahead with it' (Wieners 1961a: n.p.). This discussion over permissions only a few weeks before opening night is emblematic of the flexibility of Off-Off Broadway. Yet the main reason Wieners asked for a copy is that he had no recollection of the play. As he related to di Prima, 'The strange thing about this play is that I have no memory of ever having written it, either its title or anything of its subject matter' (1961a: n.p.). The reason for this lacuna is uncertain, though Wieners' drug use and subsequent hospitalization may have been to blame. In any case, Wieners himself was apparently not involved in the production. In a letter to Olson on 5 December 1961, Wieners states 'Will go to New York this weekend for opening of play at Poets Theatre. I hope you got the flyer. I knock on wood that all will be successful. I can't worry about the play, as I know nothing about it; it's just the trip down that worries me, where to stay, etc' (Wieners 2012: 38). The poet seems more concerned with his recent institutionalization, including his poem 'Acts of Youth' in the letter to Olson: 'Pain and suffering. Give me the strength/to bear it, to enter those places where the/great animals are caged. And we can live/at peace by their side. A bride to the burden' (Wieners 2012: 41–42). But Wieners was certainly pleased to see his play performed, attending the opening performance and writing to di Prima that 'it's an ambition come true' (Wieners 1961a: n.p.).

Still Life, like the majority of plays produced by the New York Poets Theatre, is less interested in telling a story on stage than it is in presenting unique characters with idiosyncratic language that challenges the notion of traditional dialogue. The play constantly gestures at meaning, only to undercut it once it appears that a discussion might be taking place. Here is a typical 'dialogue' from the script (1961b: 105–106):

Shirley   Nine.

Sarah   It's nine o'clock?

Cage   Jew.

Sarah   Blow out the candle.

Cage   I'm blank.

Sarah   Don't shoot no guns off in here, I'm warning

Cage   You.

Billie   Queen.

Girl in Patchwork Green   Asp bit me on Fifth Avenue.

This exchange could be parsed. It begins with the character Billie's request for a number, but ultimately devolves into confusion as each character reacts to the previous line with her or his own train of thought. Dialogue typically moves the plot forward in drama, but in *Still Life* it stalls the action, highlighting individual lines or even particular words or phrases in the process. The result is a play that seems to continually begin anew, as characters struggle to communicate but remain trapped in their own line of thinking.

If meaning does not reside in the interaction of the characters, neither does it occur within a character's own lines, which are often as fragmented and elliptic as the conversations in which they engage. Consider a monologue by the character Sarah (1961b: 98–99):

Heavy "with Romanesque pomp." Come home to the ruins. Stand for the dead-Tired. Pearls don't mean a thing, now. Where's the fire? Look at it. I haven't had this dress on since Capone. Someone's gonna pay for this, rose. Bird's dead. A double H is all I see on the street. Blown up. Blue balls and the doctor says Just one more parade before South St. Bend over, Mrs. Frank. Thanks for us. How many trays. Trash heap. If you see me passin' push over another leaf torn from the page. Rings a bell his name does just to hear it through the ashes. I don't care what grows. Donna. The iris in me smokes. Scratch dust, dear. There are no bones left in my heart to break. Where are the lights? I won't go wear this forest green again.

Sarah's monologue reveals the difficulty of comprehension even within the speech of a single character. Her lines do not build on one another to arrive at a final point; rather they read more like a passage from a stream-of-consciousness novel than a line from a character in a play. Yet even as an index to her thoughts, Sarah's words reveal little about her character, and are often enigmatic. What, for example, is 'Heavy with Romanesque pomp', and why is the phrase in quotation marks? The lines are best understood as non-sequiturs, poetic statements more interesting for their own sake than what they reveal about plot or character. *Still Life* shares much, then, with Wieners' own poetic work. The lines are often imagistic observations or highly personal thoughts and reflections that open possibilities rather than close them.

What little cohesion there is in *Still Life* results from oblique themes that are sometimes picked up across characters and conversations. In Sarah's monologue, names such as 'Mrs Frank' or 'Donna' do not appear elsewhere in the play, nor are they related to cast members, but her reference to 'rose' is (perhaps) a nod to the flower and herb imagery that runs throughout the play. The character titled Girl in Patchwork Green, as her name suggests, is connected to spring imagery. She declares, 'Remember what turns up here is April. Lilacs, petunias, orange grooves in the brown wood' (1961b: 96), and enjoys punning on the constant reference to herbs in the play: 'Thyme to the left, Oregano out back. Bear down with the mace' (1961b: 106–107). But again, the nature imagery, puns, and the many internal rhymes in characters' lines are not used to create patterns that lead to greater comprehension. Such devices exist for their own sake in the play, highlighting individual phrases rather than producing larger meanings.

The play's numerous topical references hold the possibility for themes to emerge. Drug references, for instance, occur throughout the play. The Girl in Patchwork Green begins the play by declaring: 'The joint's glass. Listen. Are the bells in? The lights turned on? Well I'm not. Mother earth. Just a girl in green watch it make flowers out of Mary's hair. (*The lights fall.*) Get high. See love bare on the stage. Here is Cage' (1961b: 95). Though *Still Life* hints at drug use, it prefers to keep its options open. What does 'joint' refer to here: the space of the theatre, a marijuana cigarette, male genitalia, or all three? Wieners follows up the reference with another ambiguous phrase, asking if the lights are 'turned on' and then having the Girl in Patchwork Green respond 'Well I'm not'. Is 'turned on' referring to getting high or becoming sexually excited? Both are possible, and both are kept in play when the girl ends her monologue with 'Get high. See love bare on the stage. Here is Cage.' Sarah's monologue mentioned above picks up on the drug theme with 'A double H is all I see on the street', a possible reference to heroin, and 'Bird's dead' speaks to the admiration the Beats had for Charlie Parker, as well as his drug dependency.

But since these sorts of references are not organized into a coherent pattern, the play cannot be said to be addressing the issue of drug use in the manner of Jack Gelber's *The Connection*. Rather, *Still Life* invokes the theme of drugs as a potential topic only to leave it behind in the next line of dialogue.

Dramatic performance offers extra-literary possibilities for corralling meaning, but even here, *Still Life* resists explication. Stage directions, for example, offer little clue as to how a character is to be performed. At one point, Wieners' stage directions inform us: '*Sarah whirls, Hair flies, Cage thinks*:"At night"' (1961b: 101). But how would thinking "at night" possibly be represented on stage? Even if it were, what would it add to the play? At other points, Wieners offers commentary that is enigmatic at best, as when he instructs Billie, '*Dog, child, Chris, cough and wheel*' (1961b: 102). Are these directions for the actors? If so, how do they function? What could this possibly mean as a guide? As Stephen Bottoms observes, playwrights were not 'writing their plays as self-contained literary entities that had to be interpreted "correctly" by directors and actors', but rather were 'creating one-act pieces cohering around distilled, emblematic images or confrontations, which often had as much in common with performance poetry or visual art as with conventional drama' (2009: 5). Yet staging choices affect reception in unseen ways. The character of Sarah, for example, was played by the 'beautiful mulatto actress' Ann Holt sitting in a box, leading di Prima to speculate that she 'might well have felt herself in a box most of the time' (di Prima 2001: 279). But according to di Prima, Holt was also the mistress of Barney Rosset and a lover of the father of di Prima's children, LeRoi Jones (2001: 279), thus the character of Sarah would probably have had different resonances for each audience member familiar with the off-stage relationships of the group, including the actor herself. Thus the actors, as well as the audience, were forced to make sense of a play that was intentionally resisting linear narrative and psychological characterization.[5]

While *Still Life*'s poetic quality makes it highly insular, at the same time it employs meta-dramatic elements that create extra-textual moments. Using the name 'Cage' is the most obvious sign of this desire to signal to the audience, given the enormous reputation enjoyed by John Cage in underground circles. Wieners' play is filled with topical references that jolt the viewer outside the play. At one point, Cage remarks, 'All right. I'll be Lucien Midnight for', (1961b: 107), a probable reference to Kerouac's long narrative poem named after his friend Lucien Carr that was eventually published as *Old Angel Midnight* (1973). The play also references famous figures like Al Capone and Vivien Leigh without offering reasons for their inclusion. Numerous other proper names, geographical places, and specific events are referenced in *Still Life*, and while they typically do not appear elsewhere in the play or directly reference other characters or even cast members, given the sort of coterie audience many Off-Off Broadway theatres enjoyed, they could very well reference members in attendance.[6] The actors Richard Pepperman, George Linjeris, Ann Holt, and Jaime Heidt, while not involved in other plays produced by the New York Poets Theatre, were all cast members in the other plays that evening, adding another layer to the performance. The play itself is also aware of its own status as a performance. The Girl in Patchwork Green opens and also closes the play, announcing at the end: 'Lights fade and die' (1961b: 109). Despite these extra-textual gestures, the play offers no overall context for their use, forcing the audience to draw their own conclusions.

The play's title captures the ironies that Wieners' text and its performance manifest. *Still Life* is an odd title for a drama that runs in time and moves across space. The most obvious reference is to painting, where the term refers to the representation of inanimate objects on the canvas. Yet *Still Life* could also be read as 'nevertheless' life, or as a type of quiet, peaceful existence. But life, in this play, is anything but still. Despite the inward focus of many of the characters and their lines, the play constantly pushes its spectators to produce their own meanings in the gaps and fissures that Wieners' work creates. The play's action may seem still, but the true movement resides in the audience (and the actors themselves), who must remain highly alert to follow Wieners' poetic flights and to catch his subtle references and undercurrents. Life is not so still, nor so stilted, after all.

Conclusion: critics respond

Still Life is emblematic of the sort of plays produced by the New York Poets Theatre. The group's focus on the lyricism of the characters' lines over more traditional dramatic elements such as plot, theme, and characterization sparked debate in the drama community. Peter Share, writing in the *Village Voice*, discussed a production of Wallace Stevens, Frank O'Hara, and Diane di Prima in 1964. Share's review captures the issue at the heart of the debate surrounding poets' theaters at the time: 'the major problem ... is whether ... [O'Hara's and di Prima's pieces are] plays at all or just examples of virtuosi putting down images. ... They are poets; are they playwrights?' (1964: 11). Share puts his finger squarely on the issue raised by the New York Poets Theatre and others like it on the Off-Off Broadway scene: can drama consist of well-crafted words that do not contribute to themes, plot, or characterization? The point is worth considering. If such poets' theatre is more interested in the linguistic properties of the lines themselves, why not simply present closet dramas or readings of the plays rather than full productions? These questions would continue to reverberate in the responses to the New York Poets Theatre, as critics tried to come to terms with a theatre that was clearly doing something different.

It was certainly not for everyone. Theatre critics such as Jerry Tallmer, who coined the term 'Off-Off Broadway', railed against the incoherency and amateurism of many of the productions. In a *New York Post* review of the same production Share discusses, Tallmer invidiously compares what he calls the 'theater of non sequitur' to the more accepted avant-garde 'Theater of the Absurd' (Tallmer 1964: n.p.). Tallmer's description of the New York Poets Theatre is basically apt. These poets' plays are meant as experiments, and are typically more concerned with the poetic quality of the lines than with coherence of plot or action. Tallmer does seem to understand this novel perspective, and, despite such denigration, finds brighter moments. But for critics like Tallmer accustomed to plays that 'made sense', the New York Poets Theatre was bound to disappoint. Plays like *Still Life* often left such ambivalent impressions, especially for those expecting a play that followed the 'rules' of more traditional, or even traditionally avant-garde, productions.

Yet other critics found something to enjoy. Ruth Herschberger, writing in the *New York Voice*, provided a strongly positive review of both *Still Life*'s bill and the play itself. Herschberger writes of the productions, 'This poets' theatre goes in for scary sensationalism, and it makes the grade' (1961: n.p.). Herschberger picks up on the 'dark' tone that di Prima believes characterized the performances. Her one critique is with the production of Duncan's work, claiming that Nikola Cernovich at the Living Theatre had directed it better a couple of years before. The New York Poets Theatre seems to have suffered from this unevenness in the quality of its productions. Of course, when a theater group operates on a low budget and draws on the expertise (or lack thereof) of a wide range of creative people, some of whom have never worked in the theatre before, there will always be mistakes. But Herschberger singles out *Still Life* for praise, commenting: 'Still Life' is a fascinating and somber play' (1961: n.p.). Di Prima certainly agreed. In her memoir, she observes that 'John Wieners' work *Still Life* was the most haunting, though I am not quite sure that his amazing words were truly realized' (2001: 279). Wieners would go on to have even more success with his play *Asphodel, in Hell's Despite*, produced in September 1963 at the Judson Poets Theatre. Sharing the bill with Gertrude Stein's *What Happened* and benefitting from a rock score by John Herbert MacDowell and set design by Andy Warhol, *Asphodel* was praised by numerous critics (see Bottoms 2009: 79–80).

Given the ephemeral nature of its writing and the speed of its production, it comes as little surprise that John Wieners' *Still Life* is seldom discussed and difficult to find in print. But the value of such Off-Off Broadway plays cannot simply be measured by their longevity. The play typifies the sort of work done in the Off-Off Broadway scene in the early post-war years. The New York Poets Theatre was more interested in providing a space for artists to create and collaborate than in producing works destined to survive as dramatic classics. Improvisation, chance, and spontaneous reactions to the needs and conditions of the present were the driving force behind *Still Life* and productions like it. This focus on process over product was very much 'Beat'. *Still Life* draws on Wieners' lyrical style, presenting characters whose lines contain a poetic quality that commands attention through his unique brand of detailed observation and thoughtful reflection. In the end, Wieners' desire to place poetry on the stage challenges both audience members and those involved in the production to broaden their ideas of what makes drama meaningful – a question that is certainly worthy of further consideration.

Works cited

Bottoms, S. J. (2009), *Playing Underground: A Critical History of the 1960s Off-Off Broadway Movement*, Ann Arbor: University of Michigan.

di Prima, D. (1964), 'Fuzz's Progress', *The Nation*, 4 May, 1964:463–65.

di Prima, D. (2001), *Recollections of My Life as a Woman: The New York Years*, New York: Viking.

Ginsberg, A. (1986), 'Foreword', in R. Foye (ed.), *John Wieners Selected Poems 1958–1984*, Santa Barbara, CA: Black Sparrow.

Gordon, C. (1965), 'Musique Concrete and Chance Theatre', Program, Box 1, File 7, Harry Ransom Humanities Research Center, Austin, Texas.

Harrington, S. G. (1964), 'City Puts Bomb under Off-Beat Culture Scene', *The Village Voice*, 26 March 1964: 1.

Herschberger, R. (1961), 'Poets Theatre at Off-Bowery', *New York Voice*, 14 Dec. 1961, Box 2, File 3, Harry Ransom Humanities Research Center, Austin, Texas.

Killian, K., and D. Brazil (eds) (2010), *The Kenning Anthology of Poets Theater 1945–1985*, Chicago: Kenning.

Little, S. W. (1972), *Off-Broadway: The Prophetic Theater*, New York: Delta.

New York Poets Theatre (1964), *The Village Voice*, 6 August 1964, Newspaper clipping, Box 2, File 2, Harry Ransom Humanities Research Center, Austin, Texas.

Pepperman, R. (2015), Telephone interview by author, Austin, Texas, 12 Jan. 2015.

Press Release (1961), New York Poets Theatre, 4 December 1961, Box 2, File 1, Harry Ransom Humanities Research Center, Austin, Texas.

Prospectus (1965), New York Poets Theatre, Box 1, File 6, 1 Jan. 1965–31 Dec.1965, Harry Ransom Humanities Research Center, Austin, Texas.

Rainer, Y. (2015), E-mail interview by author, 7 January 2015.

Share, P. (1964), 'Theatre: di Prima, O'Hara, Stevens', *Village Voice*, 20 Feb., 1964, Newspaper clipping, Box 2, File 3, Harry Ransom Humanities Research Centre, Austin, Texas.

Tallmer, J. (1964), 'Stevens, O'Hara, di Prima in N.Y. Poets Triple Bill', *New York Post*, 21 February 1964, Box 1, File 6, Harry Ransom Humanities Research Center, Austin, Texas.

Wieners, J. (1958), *The Hotel Wentley Poems*, San Francisco: Auerhahn.

Wieners, J. (1961a), Letter, 21 November 1961, Special Collections, University of Delaware Library.

Wieners, J. (1961b), *Still Life* Manuscript, Box 1, File 5, Harry Ransom Humanities Research Centre, Austin, Texas.

Wieners, J. (1986), *John Wieners Selected Poems 1958–1984*, Raymond Foye (ed.), Santa Barbara, CA: Black Sparrow.

Wieners, J. (1988), 'Memories of You', in *Cultural Affairs in Boston: Poetry & Prose 1956–1985*, Raymond Foye (ed.), Santa Rosa, CA: Black Sparrow.

Wieners, J. (1996), *The Journal of John Wieners is to be called 707 Scott Street for Billie Holiday 1959*, Los Angeles: Sun and Moon.

Wieners, J. (2012), *Lost & Found: The CUNY Poetics Document Initiative*, 3.3.ii: 19.

Part Four

Early Off-Off Broadway Theatre

Evenings of Bohemian Cruelty: The Living Theatre in the 1950s

Tim Good

The Living Theatre's connection with the Beat poets is long and complex. They made art and love together throughout the 1950s, when Living Theatre founders Judith Malina and Julian Beck worked with modernist texts by Gertrude Stein and William Carlos Williams, and with fellow Beat revolutionaries such as Kenneth Rexroth and Rochelle Owens, among many others. The Living Theatre took the poetic scripts of these writers as leaping-off points for ensemble creation and, as such, the particular 'poet's theatre' that Malina and Beck established throughout the 1950s, especially in staging the work of Beat writers, led aesthetically to the liberating work that made them world famous, starting with the opening of Jack Gelber's *The Connection* in 1959. The weaving together of Beat values and aesthetics with those of Antonin Artaud created what we now recognize as 'The Living Theatre'.

In Artaud's essay 'The Theatre and the Plague', he compares theatre to the bubonic plague, in an effort to open up new possibilities for what theatre can become. When all of our societal organizations have broken down, only then are we able to see the true possibilities of heroic action committed by individuals. Normal people end up committing exceptional acts. The plague, according to Artaud, 'invites them to take, in the face of destiny, a superior and heroic attitude they would never have assumed without it' (Artaud 1958: 32). The goal of Artaud's plague is heroism, not painful, agonizing death; enacting the plague is hardly even about cruelty.

The Living Theatre continues to enact their 'plague' to turn the theatre act into an incubator for individual heroism. Starting with *Mysteries and Smaller Pieces* in 1964, up until the present *Day in the Life* collective creations, The Living Theatre has enacted Artaudian plagues in the theatre. It starts with a few people coughing, as if there were some scratchy throats left over from the recently passed winter. Slowly, almost imperceptibly, the sound of the coughing increases, both in the number of people and in the severity of each individual cough.[1] Bit by bit, each person who was coughing also shows signs of feeling internal pain. Sores seem to appear on the skin as the infected people look in horror at their own arms, legs, and torsos. Moans become cries of agony as the infected turn to the healthy, using their last bit of energy to crawl toward the unaffected. The sick die loudly and grotesquely among the living. This can take anywhere from five to 40 minutes, depending on the context.

From an Artaudian perspective, what should happen during this theatrical plague is that some (and eventually all) audience members will be motivated by the extreme moment to stand up and try to save the dying actors, or, at least, to comfort them. In *The Theatre and its Double,* Artaud clarifies the primary purpose of comparing the theatre to the plague (1958: 31–32):

> The action of the theatre, like that of plague, is beneficial, for, impelling men to see themselves as they are, it causes the mask to fall, reveals the lie, the slackness, baseness, and hypocrisy of our world; it shakes off the asphyxiating inertia of matter which invades even the clearest testimony of the senses; and in revealing to collectivities of men their dark power, their hidden force, it invites them to take, in the face of destiny, a superior and heroic attitude they would never have assumed without it.

The result of the plague is either death or cure; the cure requires heroism. For Artaud, the theatre should be like the plague, in which the inherent cruelty of every act is revealed and faced honestly. The result will be that normal people will take 'a superior and heroic attitude they would never have assumed without it [the plague]'.

The initial commitment of The Living Theatre in the 1950s was to discover a new artistic form, to create a 'poet's theatre' that would never cease being a part of 'the revolution of the word' (Beck 1965: 6–7). They respected and produced dramatic poetry from the past, but their aim was to create a theatrical form that would speak directly to the audiences of their time. So this initial Living Theatre period is marked by experiments with form, by a feeling that old structures were not working, but also by uncertainty about what a more meaningful new structure might look like. It was from this desire to create an entirely new theatrical form that The Living Theatre decided to make Gertrude Stein's *Dr. Faustus Lights the Lights* one of their first productions. Beck wrote that they were attracted to Stein because her work 'never ceased being part of the revolution of the word' (1965: 7). The play opened at the Cherry Lane theatre on 2 December 1951.

The language structure of the play is clearly a break with the realistic theatrical traditions of the time. Stein's play is cubist in structure, in that it tries to walk around the ideas of an identity and the existence of the soul. It then gives those ideas a form so that the audience can see all sides of these ideas at once. This play is also a play in the mind, an attempt to portray the flow of ideas in a mind. It is therefore expressionistic in its portrayal of the imagination, and Cubist in its rhythmic and intellectual structure of that portrayal.

For The Living Theatre, *Dr. Faustus Lights the Lights* was a clear rejection of what they saw as the old, dead, aesthetics of American realism, and a bold statement of the new theatre form for which they were searching. The portrayal of Hell in this play was a prime example of their values and still-forming aesthetic. In contrast to Marlowe's Faust, who was dragged screaming to Hell by demons, and in contrast to Goethe's Faust who was 'saved' by an angelic woman, Stein's Faust merely disappeared into a black hole. For Stein, and for The Living, the greatest crime was to suppress or crush another human being's individuality; the penalty for that was to become nothing. This drop into nothingness was Hell for Stein and The Living.

Modernist poet William Carlos Williams was another early influence on Malina and Beck. He was a Living Theatre supporter and fan, as well as collaborator. As early as 1948, they were planning to work together, a year after the legal incorporation of The Living Theatre, and three years before their first Living Theatre production. In a letter from May 1948, Williams declared to Malina and Beck, 'Here's to the future full of rose edged clouds' (Malina 1984: 41, 43–4, 55–6).

The Living Theatre produced in four different venues in New York City from 1951–1963: their living room, the Cherry Lane Theatre, a loft space on 100th Street and Broadway, and the Living Theatre building on 14th Street and 6th Avenue. In August 1951, invited audiences experienced 'Theatre in the Room', with short plays by Paul Goodman, Gertrude Stein, Bertolt Brecht, and Federico Garcia Lorca. This was followed by a residency at the Cherry Lane Theatre from December 1951 to August 1952. It was here that The Living Theatre forged alliances with writers to create a 'poet's theater' that would eventually fold in the writer as one of the co-creators of a performance. Malina and Beck found themselves woven into the fabric of the early years of the Beat generation in New York, both in the work, and in its recreation. At the Cherry Lane Theatre, according to Bill Morgan, works staged there also included Kenneth Rexroth's *Beyond the Mountains*, as well as plays by Stein, T.S. Eliot, Pablo Picasso, and many others (1997: 62).

Williams wrote an effusive letter to The Living Theatre after he experienced *Doctor Faustus Lights the Lights*. This described the sensual mise-en-scène that The Living was developing: 'I swear it lives in a different air from the ordinary Broadway show, it is as fresh as a day in the country, the first really serious, really cleanly written, produced and acted play that I have seen, well, in a long time ... I can't tell you how important it is for the theater that you want to CREATE new plays. It is the most thrilling thing that can be done on the stage today' (Malina 1984: 197).

The intersection of The Living Theatre with Beat values and aesthetics deepened with their production of *Beyond the Mountains* by Kenneth Rexroth. Rexroth explained the underlying attitudes of the time: 'This is the world in which over every door is written the slogan: "The generation of experiment and revolt" is over. Bohemia died in the twenties. There are no more little magazines"' ('A Brief Guide' 2004). It was during this time, when Rexroth was moving between the San Francisco and New York scenes, that The Living Theatre produced his work *Beyond the Mountains,* which opened on 30 December 1951, at the Cherry Lane. This script featured the Greek stories of Phaedra, Iphigenia, Hermaios, and Berenike in verse form, directed by Beck, with Malina playing Iphigenia, Phaedra, and Electra. Initially, Rexroth was against The Living playing all four stories in one evening, but eventually he relented. Malina said of his objections, 'He has no idea how ambitious we are' (1984:192).

The Living Theatre continued working out of The Cherry Lane through late 1952, when the Fire Department closed the theatre for fire code violations, the first step in building The Living Theatre as a bona fide anti-establishment, revolutionary movement. During this time Malina and Beck continued their political activism by protesting the proliferation of nuclear weapons. They produced plays written by avant-garde artists, such as *Desire Trapped by the Tail* by Picasso and *Ubu the King* by Alfred Jarry. Malina and Beck spent the next year and a half looking for a new venue and raising money for future productions (Brown 1965: 37).

In early 1954, the Living Theatre found a new home in a loft on 100th Street, around the corner from Malina and Beck's apartment on the Upper West Side. During the next 19 months they performed seven new productions, including Strindberg's *Spook Sonata* and Racine's *Phèdre.* They turned the loft into a theatre by jamming in as many chairs as they could at one end of the room and erecting a stage at the other end, creating a sort of chamber theatre. During this time Beck further developed his integration of directing and set design into a single aesthetic, and Malina extended her experience as an actor, especially when she played the title role in *Phèdre.* This space was closed by the Building Department in late 1955 because it had put too many audience members in too small a space (Beck 1965: v–vi, 7; Brown 1965: 37).

With the productions at 100th Street, they continued their dedication to an all-encompassing artistic experience, rooted in the senses. As Stephen Bottoms puts it, 'The Becks had a shrewd awareness that plays using abstract language and imagery tended to dictate little about their actual staging, and were thus wide open to creative innovation. Their objective, which again set important precedents for off-off-Broadway, was to mount collaborative, multidimensional events, with the playwright's text functioning as a starting point in the creation of productions that belonged, uniquely, to their participants' (2004: 25). They produced there through 1954–1955, continuing their collaboration with Williams and with writers from the Beat and Black Mountain movements. Their reading of Williams's *Many Loves* in November of 1955 was the last performance in the 100th Street space. That too was closed by the Buildings Department in New York City, further solidifying their credentials as revolutionaries (Malina: 1984). Instead, they used this play to open their new space at 14th Street and 6th Avenue in July 1959. This was an old department store that they had renovated, and, during this time, The Living Theatre building became an artistic and cultural centre for the neighbourhood, hosting poetry readings every Monday night, often by Beat poets; it also housed the Merce Cunningham dance company.

On 6 November 1959, The Living Theatre opened *The Connection* by Jack Gelber. The play-within-a-play structure created the illusion that a film crew was recording actual heroin addicts in real time. This is arguably the first production that brought wider acclaim to The Living Theatre, and opened soon after they read Mary Caroline Richards's translation of Artaud's *The Theatre and It's Double*. Much has been made of The Living Theatre's 'misinterpretation' of Artaud, as if some pure 'Artaud' aesthetic exists somewhere, but the importance of The Living Theatre, Beat poets, and Artaud weaving together during this time cannot be overemphasized. Beck clarified the significance of their work leading up to 14th Street (1965: 17):

> At the Cherry Lane we made our initial statements. At One Hundredth Street we set out to develop our craft. On Fourteenth Street we tried to establish a theatrical institution which, by gathering together, could assemble the forces needed to begin to tunnel through. The work at the Cherry Lane and at One Hundredth Street was mostly preparation; through the work we were storing up energy; we made mistakes there; we always make mistakes and sometimes learn from them; we began to show and then to shed, dispose of, early notions of staging, moving from rigidity toward a certain fluidity.

The work of The Living Theatre leading up to and including the 14th Street period would serve as a foundation for everything that would eventually make them world famous.

The Connection received the kind of attention that serves to establish a cult phenomenon. It was initially excoriated by daily reviewers, then almost universally praised by weekly periodicals. After an initially sluggish box office, the show became a 'must-see' by word of mouth, and remained the foundation of the repertory for most of the 14th Street period. *The Connection* also mapped the transition of The Living Theatre from utilizing written scripts by poets to the move they would soon make into collective creation. This was true in material reality, as well as in the aesthetic and political development of the company. The success of *Many Loves* kept *The Connection* afloat after initial poor reviews; the ensuing popular success of *The Connection* kept the theatre solvent and thriving as a cultural and artistic centre for many years. Bernard F. Dukore described The Living Theatre as 'New York's flourishing citadel of theatrical bohemia' and three years into the run of *The Connection,* offered this assessment, 'Every time the "play" (actually, play-within-a-play) emerges as an artificiality, the play itself (the total performance) is made to seem real rather than the artificiality it actually is. The two levels (play and play-within-a-play) merge into one level of reality and illusion. We are finally presented with a successful slice-of-life achieved not by eschewing theatricalism, but by blending it with naturalism' (1962: 151).

Two different versions of *The Connection* help to illustrate this point. In 1959, the 14th Street production of the play was hailed as a new form of theatre, playing on manipulated levels of reality in a conscious decision to blur the lines between art and life. Using a theatrical structure similar to *Six Characters in Search of an Author, The Connection* shocked the audience by creating the illusion that real heroin junkies were onstage, and a film producer and his assistant were trying to capture the gritty reality of the drug world for a film documentary. The Living Theare had led up to *The Connection* with other fiction/reality blurring productions in the 1950s, such as Pirandello's *Tonight We Improvise.* This was the kind of Theater of Cruelty that The Living Theatre achieved. Reviews of the time talked about audience members' visceral reactions, their discomfort with the hyper-realism of the event. No one actually got up to help any of the heroin addicts on the stage, which would have been a logical outcome of a successful Theater of Cruelty event. However, this production did prompt people to connect what was happening in the theater to what was happening in real life.

So when The Living Theatre announced that they were going to remount *The Connection* in 2009, they hoped for a similar impact. The 2009 production also manipulated reality, but in a completely different way than 1959, and one that depended on their own history as a theatrical enterprise. This production made *no* effort to make the audience think that what was happening was actually real. The house opened to reveal one naked green bulb, and four actors talking in the dark onstage. Piano and drums waited mutely stage right. Judith Malina sat house right in the front row. There was a big Living Theatre poster behind the instruments on a wall on the set. The poster was all in French, depicting their first period in exile in France in the mid-1960s, after *The Brig* events at 14th Street and 6th Avenue in 1963. The harsh lighting design contributed to the understanding that this was not a 'real' room for heroin addicts. They were not trying to be shocking in the same way as 1959; this production interrogated need in terms of making us aware of our own addictions. The play was not updated to try to create any of the previous meta-theatrical blurring of reality and fiction. The audience sat down in the house, the lights went down, the play began. An actor entered and played a 45 rpm record of a jazz saxophone. The use of the 45-inch single signalled immediately that this was not an updated *Connection*. This was a new production commenting on its own history.

For instance, the Living Theatre poster on the upstage wall referred to events of 1965, and another poster on the set advertised, 'The Greatest Jazz Concert Ever' on Friday 15 May 1953. So, while the actors seemed to be set in 1965 (or so), the musicians in the play were professional jazz musicians, just as in the 1959 production. In fact, the leader of the 2009 onstage combo was the son of the leader of the 1959 combo. So, we had actors set in an amorphous past, with musicians with whom they were interacting set in the present. The intentional layering of reality took on other meanings, especially for The Living Theatre. As the audience entered the playing space, Judith Malina sat in the front row. She would later rise from her seat to play Sister Salvation in the play. With her positioning in the present as Judith Malina combined with her past of the previous production, as well taking on an acting role in the 2009 production, she was commenting on the history of the company itself.

In 2009, to bring the play more directly to the audience, references were added to the script which pointed to actual establishments on Clinton Street that audience members could patronize at intermission and after the show. Despite some 'real' intrusions, we always knew that this was a play. The Living Theatre has always remained true to taking personal risks to find the treasure of deeper truths for their audiences. Malina wrote, 'Some of the actors have got the clue to the trick, how to let yourself into your self – into your loaded-up self and get it out ... some go out there on that tightrope. A tightrope because if such excesses don't work they are laughable, it's either successful or silly ... The actor, like a diver, sinks into the excesses of the style and comes up with a horrid truth' (Malina 1991).

Malina's assertion that *The Connection* is about addiction could be turned around as an object lesson for The Living Theatre. The new space on Clinton

Street depended almost entirely on revivals of past Living Theatre successes. *Eureka* was the first new play by the company, performed in the space in 2008. While trying to resist the weight of their own history in an attempt to move forward artistically and politically, the Living Theatre may find that they have become addicted to the success of their own past.

The need to fill seats is a norm for most theatre companies, but this has not normally been a limitation for The Living Theatre. However, this new performance space added material commitments that necessitated success after success in a financial sense. However, even such widely acclaimed productions as *The Brig* (2006) did not bring the much-needed income to keep the theatre afloat in that space. Despite selling Malina's and Hanon Reznikov's apartment on the Upper West Side and despite being able to sell the Living Theatre archive to Yale, the theatre once again found itself in financial disarray. Perhaps the most important discovery of the 2009 production of *The Connection* was that the Living Theatre's addiction to its own past may not have been very healthy after all. The last production in the Clinton Street space was *Here We Are* in 2013. This marked the longest period of time that The Living Theatre had operated in the same space in New York City. The heroic action resulting from *The Connection* may have been to abandon the material restrictions that limited the artistic, personal, and political growth of the company.

Artaud called for a performance space that erased the barriers between spectator and performer, and made the spectator an integral part of the theatrical event (see the discussion in Barish 1981). When the actors of the Living Theatre adopt a character onstage, they do not stop being themselves. Malina has said that while she was playing Antigone, she was Judith Malina telling the story of Antigone through a dramatic form. The Living Theatre transitioned from the overt role-playing and mimicry of their early years without losing the communion with the audience that they had always sought. Julian Beck wrote that he felt bad about lying to the audiences in New York in productions such as *Tonight We Improvise* and *The Connection* (1965). They were always moving toward a more complete, visceral, sensual experience for everyone together in a performance. They found it in the ideals of Artaud. Beck clarified the connection between Artaud and the Living Theatre (*Signals* 1983):

> Artaud's desire to bring to the theatre the outcry, the great scream, as the Greeks tried to reach for that moment of scream. It was the protest, the way of the voice breaking out of the inhibition. Do I dare raise my voice? It was that specific attempt. And Artaud wanted to smash the whole prison of society with this outcry, with this scream.

The members of The Living Theatre were well aware of the cultural norms in their artistic and political arenas in 1963, and indeed had assumed positions of legitimized authority in both. For all their protest, they seemed to be acutely aware of how economics influenced their every action. The 14th Street space was shut down and occupied by the Revenue Department in 1963 for non-payment of taxes. They staged a last, very dramatic, performance of *The Brig* in 1963, breaking in through a back door to perform for audience members who snuck in with them. They were then taken from the artistic brig to the real brig, and were later tried and sentenced to short terms for contempt of court. This last clash with government authorities cemented their reputation as avant-garde revolutionaries on the barricades of a progressive and liberating movement. But The Living Theatre had kept their organization afloat in rented theatre buildings since 1951; they were well aware of how money affected everything else they did. For all their artistic and political achievement, they let something as obvious as rent and taxes sink their ship (see news stories in Smith 1963 and Harrington 1964).

One possibility is that Malina and Beck let the 14th Street theatre sink on purpose. If they hated money as they said, why not then find a way to subvert it? Jack Gelber laid out the revolutionary tactics of self-destruction (1986: 11, 19):

> I think the role of embattled revolutionaries, misunderstood artists, and disturbing theatre people was more importantly cultivated by Julian as a tool of survival. Every revolutionary movement needs its mythology; and as a leader, Julian promoted this fighting underdog image ... Julian had a way of courting financial disaster even in the midst of a successful run [*The Brig*] and chalking it up to ideological struggle.

Perhaps Beck did know exactly what he was doing. Perhaps he and Malina were looking for a useful way to move on to a new way of working, and this revolutionary exit from the 14th Street building purposefully fed the legend of The Living Theatre. Beck concluded, 'We were not prepared for nor did we calculate the great strength of established power' (*Signals*: 1983).

The Living Theatre's connection with Beat artists had deepened during the 14th Street period; and they mutually enhanced each other's work. These newer writers were attracted to working with them this is exemplified in the early development of the work of Rochelle Owens. She worked with The Living Theatre during this time, and was affected by the experimental approaches of Malina and Beck. Owens wrote about this in her 'Autobiography' (Owens 2015):

In 1959, I wrote my first play, *Futz*... Because of the success of *The String Game* and *Istanbul*, which had garnered a Village Voice Obie, I acquired an agent, and in 1965 *Futz* was produced as a work-in-progress under the auspices of the Office of Advanced Drama Research at the Tyrone Guthrie Theatre and the University of Minnesota. Two years earlier, the Living Theatre had planned it for production. The project was cancelled because of tax difficulties the company encountered.

Futz became one of the iconic plays of the off-off-Broadway movement in the 1960s. Her play *Homo* extended these initial Bohemian values into a more visceral experience. The Living Theatre had *Futz* in rehearsal when their 14th Street space was closed by the Department of Revenue; *Homo* was under consideration for a future performance, as evidenced by a handwritten note by Julian Beck on a typescript which Owens had given to the Living Theatre.

The Living Theatre had lived, loved, and worked with Beat writers throughout the 1950s and into the early 1960s, until they left for Europe in 1963. Their collaborations positively affected both groups moving into the cultural revolutions of the 1960s. What had started as a desire to produce a theatre of poetry matured into a total visceral theatrical experience that knitted together both the imagination and the expansive possibilities of the Beat poets (among others) with the intensely sensual total theatre envisioned by Artaud. Much of the aesthetics and values of both The Living Theatre and the Beat generation have become so enmeshed in popular culture that it becomes difficult to remember how groundbreaking they were in their time –both individually and together. The work they did with each other in the 1950s laid the foundation for a world where, as Malina claimed, 'We thought we were going to change *everything*' (*Signals*: 1983). They did.

Works cited

'A Brief Guide to the San Francisco Renaissance' (2004), Academy of American Poets: *Poets.org*, 28 May 2004. Available at: www.poets.org/poetsorg/text/brief-guide-san-francisco-renaissance (last accessed 12 June 2015).

Artaud, A. (1958), *The Theater and its Double* (1938), M.C. Richards (trans.), New York: Grove.

Barish, J. A. (1981), *The Antitheatrical Prejudice*. Berkeley: University of California.

Beck, J. (1964), Handwritten note, *Homo* by R. Owens, unpublished manuscript.

Beck, J. (1965), 'Storming the Barricades', in K. Brown, *The Brig*, New York: Hill and Wang, 1–36.

Bottoms, S. J. (2004), *Playing Underground: A Critical History of the 1960s Off-Off-Broadway Movement,* Ann Arbor: University of Michigan.

Brig, The (2007), performance, K. Brown (script), Judith Malina (dir), The Living Theatre, New York City, 26–27 May.

Brown, K. (1965), *The Brig,* New York: Hill and Wang.

Connection, The (2009), performance, J. Gelber (script), J. Malina (dir), The Living Theatre, New York City, 8 February.

Dukore, B. F. (1962), 'The New Dramatists: Jack Gelber', *Drama Survey* 2.2: 146–157.

Eureka (2008), performance, H. Reznikov and J. Malina (script), J. Malina (dir), The Living Theatre, New York City, 22–23 October.

Gelber, J. (1957), *The Connection.* New York: Grove.

Gelber, J. (1986), 'Julian Beck, Businessman', *The Drama Review* T-110: 6–29.

Harrington, S. G. (1964), 'Jury Finds Becks Guilty in Emotional Court Scene', *The Village Voice* 28 May: 5, 12.

Here We Are (2013), performance, J. Malina (script and dir), The Living Theatre, New York City, 2 February.

Malina, J. (1984), *The Diaries of Judith Malina 1947–1957.* New York: Grove.

Malina, J. (1991), Unpublished Diary, 22 May, Living Theatre Records, Box # 17, Yale Collection of American Literature, Beinecke Rare Book and Manuscript Library, New Haven, CT (last accessed 4 March 2014).

Morgan, B. (1997), *Beat Generation in New York: A Walking Tour of Jack Kerouac's City,* San Francisco: City Lights.

Owens, R. (2015), 'Autobiography', *rochelleowens.org.* Available at: http://rochelleowens.org/autobiography.php (last accessed 15 July 2015).

Signals Through the Flames: The Story of The Living Theater (1983), S. Rochlin and M. Harris (dir and prod), Mystic Fire, VHS.

Smith, M. (1963), 'Living Theater Goes Broke; Becks Brigged by Feds', *The Village Voice* 24 October: 1, 6, 8, 14.

Eas[ing] the Possible Past the Expected: A Restaging of Hettie Jones

Tatum Petrich

Introduction

Hettie Jones is not usually included in conversations about the New York City theatre scene of the 1960s, except perhaps as the 'inspiration' for Lula, the white murderess in *Dutchman* (1964) and for Grace, the ex-wife in *The Slave* (1964), two ground-breaking plays authored by her then-husband, LeRoi Jones/Amiri Baraka.[1] An author and poet in her own right, Jones, like other women Beats such as Joyce Johnson, Brenda Frazer, and Carolyn Cassady, is best known for her relationship with a key male figure of the Beat Generation. Indeed, most of Jones's critical attention was garnered from her 1990 memoir *How I Became Hettie Jones*, which centres on her marriage to Baraka and her experiences as a wife, mother, and aspiring poet during that time. Notably, the aesthetic achievements of her memoir and her award-winning poetry have been the subject of critical essays, which give important attention to Jones's literary achievements which surpass the documentation of her relationship with Baraka.[2] However, such scholarship is sparse and overlooks her formative experiences in the theatre. Thus, in much the same way that Jones sought to 'ease the possible past the expected' as a young woman in the 1950s and 1960s, this chapter seeks to push past – to revise and expand – what readers 'expect' of her as a Beat Generation wife and memoirist (Jones 1990: 27). That is, I offer here a 'restaging' of Hettie Jones: it furthers the recovery of her life and work by exploring how her connections to the theatre go beyond the playwriting achievements of her husband and, in fact, helped to shape her development as a Beat writer.

To date, Jones has not published any original plays, nor has she made a name for herself as a producer or stage actress; however, her affinity for and experiences with the theatre can be traced back to her childhood and continue through the height of the Beat period. Jones was immersed in the theatre before she made her way into the Village Beat scene; in fact, the theatre was the site of her earliest creative and artistic development. Once a part of the nascent New York City Beat community, though, Jones shifted her focus from her own work to that of others; she then played an integral role in what soon became the prolific Beat literary scene, which included fostering the work of experimental playwrights. In her capacity as the co-editor and co-publisher of *Yugen* and Totem Press, for example, she helped to publish the work of playwrights such as Kenneth Koch, and sporadically appeared on and behind the stage during this period. Further, Jones helped to support the work of her husband as he made a name for himself as a revolutionary playwright in the mid-1960s.

As this brief overview suggests, the theatre was a constant, if peripheral, presence in Jones's life leading up to and during the Beat period. It shaped her personal and creative life in undoubtedly significant ways and was integral to her formative years as a writer. In the mid-1950s, Jones's refusal to adhere to hegemonic social and cultural norms drew her to the countercultural Village scene; however, her resistance to such norms was complicated by the male Beats' perpetuation of mainstream gender roles. So, while Jones attempted to support herself financially and to become a writer, she was paradoxically expected by Baraka and the general misogyny of the male Beats to put her roles as wife, mother, and secretary first. As such, we need to understand the evolution of the theatre in Jones's life and work within the context of her struggles to break out of the hegemonic and countercultural expectations for women in the 1950s and 1960s.

Early work

Despite the wide range of Jones's work (see Petrich 2012), most critical attention has focused on her memoir *How I Became Hettie Jones* (1990). The memoir is set within the New York City Beat community, the jazz culture of the time, the Civil Rights movement and the beginning of the Black Power movement. As such, it provides useful insight into the Beat period and its surrounding contexts while it reveals Jones's struggle within this literary scene to actually become a writer. In her essay on women Beats' memoirs, Nancy M. Grace highlights how 'Jones uses the memoir to pick at the question of whether she is a writer, and if so, what kind' (2002: 157). Deborah Thompson focuses on the function of naming in Jones's memoir; she reads *How I Became Hettie Jones* alongside the autobiographies of Jones's husband and daughter 'in order to historicize white American identity shifts relative to shifts in African American and biracial American identities' (2002: 84). The scholarship by Grace and Thompson is undoubtedly important in drawing attention to Jones in her own right and, more specifically, in situating her memoir within larger discussions of the genre of life writing as well as of the history of race in post-war American culture. Barrett Watten argues that Jones's memoir is 'an exemplary account of the relation of poetry to knowledge' as he examines 'the divergence of the possibility of poetry as material practice' (2002: 98).

Conspicuously absent from Jones's wide-ranging body of work is playwriting. The theatre was a considerable presence in Jones's life beginning with childhood stints on the stage and continuing through both her undergraduate and graduate careers. However, the more active Jones became in the role of editor and publisher and the more demanding her life became in these roles in addition to those of a wife and mother, the more the theatre – and her own development as a writer – shifted into the background. As a young student and aspiring artist,, Jones immersed herself in theatre studies: she majored in drama at Mary Washington College and pursued (though did not complete) an MFA at Columbia University's School of Dramatic Arts.

In her memoir, Jones recalls that as a young student she had hoped to eventually 'write the plays of Lorca', but she 'began with poems' (1990:13). Her first published works in her college's literary magazine, the *Epaulet*, were poetry and short prose. Nevertheless, as a drama major, Jones performed in several plays and musicals, including George Bernard Shaw's *Arms and the Man* and Thornton Wilder's *Our Town*, studied stagecraft such as 'carpentry and electricity', and was a costumer.[3] She also worked in children's theatre at this time. In her undergraduate thesis, 'The Verse Form: A Prediction for Expression in Modern Drama' (referred to in her memoir as 'The Poet in the Theater' [1990: 13]), Jones argues that: 'What is necessary for the playwright to find is a form of language which will be an instrument for the expression of poetic experience' (Collected Papers). Signalling her overlapping interests in the theatre and poetry, Jones's thesis considers the artistic impetus of the playwright as well as the effect of a play's language on the audience in her argument for experimentation with contemporary verse forms in the theater. Additionally, for her playwriting coursework as an undergraduate and graduate student, Jones would write both original plays and play adaptations, several of which feature key themes of her life and work: the figure of the artist and of the independent-minded woman.

At least one of Jones's original plays, *Café au Lait*, was written and performed during her undergraduate studies (in 1952). Set at the titular sidewalk café and its surrounding streets on the left bank of Paris, the play takes place over the course of one day and intertwines two central themes: the experience of the struggling young artist and the vibrancy of city life and its culture. The early spring setting establishes a mood of 'beginning or awakening,' and, accordingly, the play concludes with a revelation of sorts (Collected Papers 1952: 1). From the start of the play, Jones introduces plenty of locals – businessmen, models, aspiring dancers, street artists, streetcleaners, flower girls, etc. – all of whom express enthusiasm for an upcoming contest at which 'the great Monsieur de Chapeau' will choose a local Paris girl to be a fashion model in his world tour (1952: 2). The energy that this event has engendered among the locals serves as the backdrop for the struggles of artist Andre Beauchamp. Andre happens upon the café in a 'sad and dejected' state and proceeds to discuss his creative block with Pierre and Michelle, the father and daughter proprietors of the café (1952: 4). He explains that he has been working on a portrait that 'has no soul' and he has been doing this in isolation in his garret in an effort to have complete concentration and to avoid distractions (1952: 6). Pierre and Michelle try to convince Andre that the inspiration for his art can easily be found on the city streets – in the people and culture of Paris. The city abounds with energy and beauty, in creative inspiration that cannot be found if the artist confines himself to solitary concentration. At Michelle's urging, Andre attends the modelling contest that evening, and there he indeed finds the soul of the city and thus the soul for his painting in 'the people – the streetcleaners, the scrubwomen,' '[t]he businessmen,' '[t]he flower girl,' '[t]he children,' and '[t]he artists' (1952: 13). '[T]he soul of Paris' has now become the soul of Andre's painting, and his artistic creativity is renewed (1952: 13).

Though somewhat banal, the play's resolution points to an irony that in many ways epitomizes Jones's experiences as a woman Beat writer. The play depicts a direct correlation between a city's atmosphere and an artist's creative output. Once Andre opens his eyes to the city, its street artists and other locals, he finds inspiration for his painting. It seems the answer to his artistic block was merely a matter of letting in the world around him. A few years after she wrote this play, however, Jones's own experiences as a developing writer would take shape quite differently. Jones and Baraka's various downtown apartments were, in many ways, home to the exploding Beat literary scene. The production of *Yugen* and Totem Press, for example, took place largely on their kitchen table, and the couple were constantly hosting parties for – and in fact informally boarding – other poets and artists. Whether on Fourteenth, Twentieth, or Morton Street, their apartment and the city outside of it was teeming with like-minded artists and poets, yet Jones kept her writing private at this time – from her husband, who would often criticize her for not writing, as well as from other women Beat writers. In her memoir, she claims that she lacked confidence and was ashamed of what little writing she struggled to produce during the Beat period – writing that she considered 'not only bad but worthless' (Petrich 2012: 24). What is interesting about *Café au Lait*, then, is more than just the insight it offers into Jones's early playwriting. One of her earliest creative works, it draws attention to the paradox of how, unlike Andre's epiphanic experience, when Jones was at the centre of the Beat scene full of aspiring, avant-garde writers, her creative voice was stifled and hidden, if not suppressed, for years to come.

Prior to this, though, Jones continued writing plays as a graduate student at Columbia. In the fall of 1955, for example, she wrote an adaptation of John Van Druten's 1943 *The Voice of the Turtle*, specifically, a 'Scenario for Act II, Scene I'. The original three-act comedy centres on Sally Middleton, a 22-year-old theatre actress living in New York City during World War II, who struggles with the conservative sexual mores of the period but ends up engaging in a new love affair over the course of the play's weekend timeline. In her abridged adaptation of the play, Jones begins *in medias res* when Bill comes over to pick Sally up for the evening. They have drinks and some light conversation and spend a few minutes reading and rehearsing Sally's new script before heading out to dinner. During this brief and lighthearted scene, Bill kisses Sally a couple of times, and this little bit of physical contact embodies a combination of the pair's genuine interest in and uncertainty about one another as they have only just met. In her reimagining of the play, Jones portrays a pivotal moment in Sally's life – when she is on the precipice of an unexpected sexual and romantic affair. Jones neither focuses explicitly on Sally's sexual exploits nor on the actress' efforts to reconcile what she – and Jones – consider society's conservative expectations with Sally's actual acts of sexual adventurousness. Rather, Jones depicts Sally just before she will ultimately follow her instincts and sleep with Bill – breaking, for the third time in her life, society's standards for 'ordinary girls' (Van Druten 1971: 18). In this adaptation, Jones again focuses on the figure of the artist, but in this case, she also offers a glimpse into Sally's protofeminist sexual identity just as it is developing within the New York City theatre scene.

Another of Jones's graduate school play adaptations centres on a sexually liberated young woman. For her reworking of Henry James's *Daisy Miller* (1878), Jones took apart and reassembled the text to write a carefully crafted, tightly focused version of James's story. She cuts through much of the original narrative to highlight Daisy's free-spirited, rebellious nature before she falls victim to Roman fever. On the actual assignment that Jones submitted, her professor offers high praise: 'This is one of the most original and [the] strongest treatments submitted. The action is extraordinarily well-managed, clean, and direct. And the set … is highly imaginative' (as cited in Jones, *Collected Papers*). Despite such accolades, Jones was not nearly as impressed with her own accomplishments. Looking back, she writes: '[W]hat was original in fictitious scenes—using what was *not* in the book—for an adaptation of *Daisy Miller*?' (1990: 16, emphasis in original). Jones's reaction suggests that she felt more inspired by and prouder of writing fully original plays. Regardless, her adaptation of James's text reflects a skilful combination of creative and critical work, as her professor pointed out, while also highlighting her continued interest in the experience of the rebellious, sexually liberated female figure.

Interestingly, unlike Sally's 'happy' ending in *The Voice of the Turtle*, Daisy's death symbolizes her punishment for rebellion against social conventions and thus foreshadows the challenges and hardships that Jones herself would face as an independent-minded, rebellious young woman in the late 1950s. Unearthing these three plays from Jones's years as a student not only offers insight into her life as an amateur playwright, but also highlights the intersections between the two defining aspects of her life during the Beat period: that of an aspiring and struggling artist and that of an aspiring artist who also happens to be a woman in a male-dominated countercultural scene.

Jones's graduate school work would mark the end of her formal theatre studies and playwriting, but as this overview suggests, the theatre had provided Jones with some of her first creative experiences. Once a part of the emerging Beat literary scene, Jones's involvement with the theatre would remain relatively inconsistent in her life, although she acted alongside Joyce Johnson in Ursule Molinaro's *The Contest* at the Judson Poets Theatre in 1961. In her memoir, Jones attributes her overall retreat from the theatre to a particular incident that, not insignificantly, symbolizes the general sexism enacted within the larger avant-garde community. 'Having failed to write a line for a week [in 1957],' she recalls, '[I] returned to work in the theater' (1990: 25). She tried to get a job at the Theatre de Lys, but the stage manager instead wanted to sleep with her and 'attempt[ed] to drag [her] to bed' once he got her to his apartment (1900: 25). As she recalls, he 'put [her] out' after she proudly refused to sleep with him (1990: 25). Being denied this job would become an unfortunately memorable experience that 'soured [her] on a life in the theater' (1990: 220). (Incidentally, this man would, seven years later, stage the premieres of Baraka's *Dutchman* and *The Slave*.)

This incident is significant for several reasons: first, it speaks to Jones's withdrawal from what had been a more consistently direct involvement with the theatre and thus reflects her growing ambivalence towards the New York City theatre scene in the late 1950s and 1960s. Second, it illustrates that Jones's conscious rejection of the period's expectations for young women (years prior to living on her own, for example, she deliberately chose a style of hair and dress that would signify a 'sexy, but surefooted woman') would also include exercising control and ownership over her sexual identity (1990: 13). The presumptuous stage manager, for example, could not make her compromise even her 'unconventional' – if not protofeminist – values.[4] Third, this experience demonstrates the fundamental – and largely inescapable – issue of sexism with which Jones would have to contend in the context of the Beat community as well as in the context of her marriage.

Jones and Baraka

Paradoxically, as a wife and mother, even within the countercultural Village scene, Jones found herself struggling with many of the same limitations imposed on the traditional 'suburban matron' – only now these were coupled with her desire to support herself financially, to become a writer, and to foster the work of those around her. Indeed, while the countercultural Beat scene offered Jones the opportunity to live outside the bounds of mainstream society's prescribed path for a young woman in the 1950s and 1960s, she would soon find the ability to pursue her various endeavours thwarted by factors outside of her control, including the practical limitations of motherhood as well as the marginalization she faced while married to Baraka – first as a wife, then as the white wife of a black nationalist.[5]

However inconsequential their racial differences may have been to Jones and Baraka during much of their relationship, Baraka's gradually changing notions about race and what he would come to consider his and Jones's untenable racial differences would come to the fore as he emerged as a playwright in the mid-1960s. Whereas initially the Theatre de Lys stage manager had 'soured' Jones's longstanding affection for the theatre via his sexist proposition, it was now Baraka's playwriting that would further increase Jones's ambivalence towards the theatre via the portrayal of his increasingly polarizing notions about race, often enacted through white female antagonists.

At the time Baraka shifted from poetry to playwriting, around 1962, Jones had been struggling to 'translate' her 'household life' into creative writing of her own (1990: 182). Writing beyond mere observation put 'demands on feeling' and 'require[d] strength' – neither of which the 'holding pattern of call and response' that defined motherhood for her allowed (1990: 183, 182). In addition to being a mother of two young daughters in 1962, Jones continued working with Baraka on the literary magazine *Yugen* where she would help publish plays, such as Kenneth Koch's *Guinevere; or, the Death of the Kangaroo* (in *Yugen* 7 in 1961) and on their Totem Press publications where she edited and typed his various projects. She was also working for Grove Press at this time and recalls that '[t]he books [she] worked on were all by men or about them' (1990: 193). In the meantime, Baraka was transitioning to a focus on drama as he felt that 'action literature ... has to put characters upon a stage and make them living metaphors' (1984: 187). 'Drama proliferates during periods of social upsurge', he continues, 'because it makes real live people the fuel of ideas' (1984: 187). At the eventual cost of their marriage, the need to act upon the Black Nationalist ideas expounded by Malcolm X was becoming more and more urgent for Baraka. Their racial differences – which had once seemed so trivial in the context of their relationship – were now creating an irreparable rift between them. That Baraka's Black Nationalist ideas and beliefs initially took shape via playwriting is all the more ironic in light of Jones's history with the theatre and her involvement in the production of his early plays.

Baraka's play *Dutchman* (1964) is about a manic young white woman, Lula, who seduces and then murders a young black man, Clay, an aspiring poet. *The Slave* (also 1964) is set during a futuristic race war, and depicts the black leader, Walker Vessels, confronting his white ex-wife, Grace, and her new (white) husband, Easley. Both end up dead – the former in a bomb attack on their home, the latter by the protagonist in an act of self-defence. Offstage are the former couple's interracial children, who are either already dead, as Walker claims, or who are left to die at the end of the play. As mentioned earlier, Jones was – and is – assumed by most viewers and critics to be the basis for both Lula and Grace.[6] With bitterness, she recalls, for example, receiving a note from an actress in a production of *The Slave* that read, 'Thank you for Grace' (1990: 220). Such occurrences 'made [her] nuts' (1990: 220). In his own recollection, Baraka notes with remarkable triviality, 'For [Hettie], this period was ... a contradictory thing' (1984: 190). Certainly this statement does not adequately describe the impact that the disparities between their feelings towards their interracial marriage as well as between the status of their respective literary careers had on this pivotal time in her life.

While both plays earned critical acclaim and propelled Baraka into the spotlight (*Dutchman* won an Obie Award for Best New American Play), Jones found herself trying to discern who she was when by his side: 'Lula, the murderer, his white wife, or the former Hettie Cohen?' (1990: 218). She recalls that after the first performance of *Dutchman* at the Playwrights Unit, she was enthusiastically congratulated by a former acting teacher who mistakenly thought she was the playwright. Ironically, Jones was now being confused for the writer of her husband's groundbreaking playwriting achievement for a play in which the white woman needlessly and callously kills the young black poet at a time when her own creative development remained a struggle. Further, Jones would continue to be considered by viewers as the 'inspiration' for Lula and Grace – leading up to and after she actually became Baraka's 'former white wife'. Before they were staged, Jones had also helped Baraka type and revise the plays – she even began to identify as his actual 'secretary' after their production when his career took off (1990: 208). All of this occurred before she learned unequivocally that these two particular plays were prescient of Baraka's ultimate inability to reconcile their interracial marriage with his racial politics.

Indeed, it was not long after the production of both plays, in early 1965 after Malcolm X's assassination, that Baraka cut all ties with the Village, including with his white wife. Andrew Epstein explains that Baraka 'was pressured by the increasingly urgent racial politics of the time to reconsider and rediscover his connection to African-American culture' (2006: 168). When he left Jones and the Village, he relocated to Harlem and then Newark, New Jersey and 'became a spokesman for black cultural nationalism and a militant political organizer and leader' (2006: 168). Although their marriage had been strained for several years, there is no uncertainty that Baraka's racial politics – his desire to authenticate his involvement in the black community – was the primary reason for their divorce (see my discussion of this in Petrich 2012). Certainly, that this 'contradictory' and life-changing event played out via the stage only served to intensify Jones's ambivalence towards the theatre.

Conclusion

In what might perhaps be considered the final irony in this part of Jones's life, not long after the divorce, she began publishing her own writing. No longer in the position to need to clarify – for herself or for others – who she was when she stood beside the 'King of the Lower East Side', Jones would go on to develop her identity as a woman and writer in her own right (Baraka 1984: 188). She hasn't returned to work in the theatre – either on or off stage – but has since made a name for herself as a poet and author of young adult and children's books, among several other genres, and her formative experiences with drama have undoubtedly influenced her subsequent body of work. Specifically, Jones's early theatre studies were shaped by her interrogation of conventional uses of form and language. These same questions have informed her poetics as well – evident, for example, in what Grace describes as Jones's 'experiment[ation] with long prose and tight haiku-like lines as well as alphabetical and anaphoric catalogues' (as cited in Jones 2004: 157). Likewise, Jones's initial focus on the figure of the artist that we see, for example, in her original play *Café au Lait*, has continued throughout her writing, perhaps most frequently in her short fiction, which often centres on various kinds of artists.[7] Perhaps most notable is the progression of Jones's treatment of the rebellious, unconventional female figure, which first appeared in her graduate school plays and evolved into a more overt proto feminism in her Beat poetry and prose. Jones's work as a playwright and with the theatre in general gradually settled into the background of her life and work. As such it is inaccurate – and indeed unnecessary – to consider her a 'primary' figure of the emerging avant-garde theatre scene of the 1950s and 1960s. As this chapter illustrates, her relationship with the theatre might best be described as ambivalent. As a woman in the countercultural Beat scene, Jones was subject to various forms of sexism and misogyny; as the white wife of a black Beat poet turned black nationalist writer and activist, she was subject to what might simply be described as marginalization. These experiences as a woman and as a wife clearly problematized her connection with the theatre as well as her development as an aspiring writer. Thus it is precisely within these contexts that this chapter 'restages' Hettie Jones from her current literary reputation as Beat Generation wife and memoirist, and draws attention to the importance of her involvement with the theatre – beyond her status as Baraka's 'former white wife'. This exploration into Jones's formative experiences deepens our understanding of her development as a Beat writer and as a facilitator of other emerging artists of the avant-garde literary scene. Without her early involvement with the theatre, we might not have the strong female poet we have today; without her tireless work fostering other writers of the counterculture, the Beat Generation legacy itself might look a little bit different. If we continue to recognize Jones only for her marriage or her memoir, we will continue to find only as little as we expect.

Works cited

Baraka, A. (1984), *The Autobiography of LeRoi Jones/Amiri Baraka*, New York: Freundlich.

Baraka, A. (1997), *The Autobiography of LeRoi Jones/Amiri Baraka* (updated edn), Chicago: Lawrence Hill.

Epstein, A. (2006), *Beautiful Enemies: Friendship and Postwar American Poetry*, Oxford and New York: Oxford University.

Grace, N.M. (2002), 'Snapshots, Sand Paintings, and Celluloid: Formal Considerations in the Life Writing of Women Writers from the Beat Generation', in R.C. Johnson and N.M. Grace (eds), *Girls Who Wore Black: Women Writing the Beat Generation*, New Brunswick, NJ: Rutgers University.

Grace, N.M., and R.C. Johnson (2002), 'Visions and Revisions of the Beat Generation', in R.C Johnson and N.M. Grace (eds), *Girls Who Wore Black: Women Writing the Beat Generation*, New Brunswick, NJ: Rutgers University.

Jones, H., Collected Papers, in Boxes 24, 37, and 43, Rare Book and Manuscript Library, Columbia University in the City of New York.

Jones, H. (1952), *Café au Lait*, unpublished undergraduate play, Collected Papers.

Jones, H. (1990), *How I Became Hettie Jones*, New York: Dutton.

Jones, H. (1993), 'Enough of This', *Frontiers: A Journal of Women's Studies* 13.2: 97–100.

Jones, H. (2004), 'Drive', Interview by N.M. Grace in N.M. Grace and R.C. Johnson (eds), *Breaking the Rule of Cool: Interviewing and Reading Women Beat Writers*, Jackson: University Press of Mississippi.

Jones, L. [A. Baraka] (1964), *Dutchman* and *The Slave*, New York: Morrow Quill.

Petrich, T. (2012), *'The Girl Gang': Women Writers of the New York City Beat Community*, (PhD diss.), Philadelphia: Temple University.

Thompson, D. (2002), 'Keeping Up with the Joneses: The Naming of Racial Identities in the Autobiographical Writings of LeRoi Jones/Amiri Baraka, Hettie Jones, and Lisa Jones', *College Literature* 29.1: 83–101.

Van Druten, J. (1971), *The Voice of the Turtle* (1943), New York: Dramatists Play Service.

Watten, B. (2002), 'What I See in *How I Became Hettie Jones*', in R.C. Johnson and N.M. Grace (eds), *Girls Who Wore Black*, New Brunswick, NJ: Rutgers University.

Cowboy in the Rock Garden: Beat Influences in Sam Shepard's Early Plays

Deborah R. Geis

Mention Sam Shepard and most of us immediately see an image of him as a movie star, with his iconic roles in such films as *Days of Heaven*, *The Right Stuff*, and many others from the late 1970s and through the following couple of decades. Beyond that, many of us also think of Shepard as the quintessential American playwright of the late 1970s and early 1980s, when his 'family trilogy' (*True West*, *Curse of the Starving Class*, and *Buried Child*) garnered national attention (and the last of these won the Pulitzer Prize). In these and many other works, Shepard draws upon his California boyhood (though he was in fact an 'army brat' who lived all over the place), mixed with an almost Gothic Midwestern sensibility, as skeletons from the past are (sometimes literally) unearthed.

But little recent attention has been paid to Shepard's earliest plays, which were developed in the off-off Broadway theatres (or sometimes clubs, churches, or people's apartments) of the early 1960s – and which involved many of the creators and supporters of what was by then the later years of the Beat Generation artists and writers. What becomes clear in revisiting these works is that Shepard was drawn to the music and art of this period, as well as specifically to writers like Jack Kerouac, Gregory Corso, and Lawrence Ferlinghetti, whose novels and poems he devoured when he was still a California teenager. Shepard's early drama is also in part the legacy of the hybrid poem-play creations of Diane di Prima, Frank O'Hara, Michael McClure, and others who were working in the New York Poets Theatre just a few years before Shepard began writing his own plays. The energy of these works – and the ground they established for experimental collaborations in New York City in the early 1960s – was crucial in setting the stage for the young Shepard's own earliest pieces. The intention of this chapter, then, is to return to three of Shepard's very first theatre pieces – *The Rock Garden*, *Chicago*, and *Icarus's Mother* – to explore them less in their context as dry runs for his later, more mature full-length plays than as works that are fully informed by Beat aesthetics.

I've written at length about these works in my first book, *Postmodern Theatric(k)s*, which was a study of monologue in contemporary American drama. Shepard's plays, which have so many moments in which all action stops as the characters deliver explosive solo speeches, was the starting point for my interest in what I characterize as a transformational time in the American theatre, during which we see artists as diverse as Shepard, Ntozake Shange, and many others altering our perceptions of narrative time and space by filling their works with monologic discourse. In retrospect, the connection between the solo speeches in Shepard's work and the legacy of the Beat writers is clear. Bonnie Marranca points this out when she spins a thread from Whitman to the Beats to Shepard: 'The rhapsodic solo is the "song of myself" that was sung by the first [B]eat poet, Walt Whitman, then by Kerouac and Ginsberg, and now by Shepard's characters, who carry the [B]eat legacy into dramatic form' (1981: 29).

Stephen Bottoms's study *Playing Underground* (2004) provides a detailed history of the venues such as the Judson Poets Theatre, Theatre Genesis, Caffe Cino, and La Mama, where Shepard and his peers were able to take risks on writing non-commercial plays that often collapsed the boundaries between the actors and the audience, took on sexuality in ways that it had not been talked about on stage before (as in the famous monologue at the end of Shepard's *Rock Garden* that eventually was co-opted for *Oh! Calcutta!*), and emphasized narrative playfulness over plot and character development. The mainstream New York critics, with a few notable exceptions, were confounded over plays like *Chicago* or *Icarus's Mother*, in which the characters seem more interested in telling long, rambling stories and in-jokey role-playing than in following any real kind of through-line or even achieving psychological depth. I would contend, though, that the superficial quality of these early works is deceptive. Like Jack Kerouac's so-called 'spontaneous prose' in *Big Sur* or like Allen Ginsberg's torrent of language in *Howl*, the attention to the everyday (with the emphasis in all of these works on food, bodily functions, sex, garbage, playing records, drinking, and so forth) creates a powerful commentary on American culture in the late 1950s/early 1960s and the cry for dissenting voices from a generation that feared and detested the increasing attempts (through McCarthyism, censorship, etc.) to create 'normative' values. Viewed in this context, re-reading Shepard's earliest works is truly revelatory.

According to biographer Don Shewey (1985), Sam Shepard (then Steve Rogers), as a teenager in California, was a bit of a mixture of all-American boy (he was a Future Farmer of America and belonged to the 4-H Club; he even had a grand champion ram at the county fair) and a tough kid who won a track meet by taking bennies and who claims to have once stolen a car and driven it to Mexico. He began reading work by the aforementioned Beat writers Kerouac, Corso, and Ferlinghetti (Mottram 1984: 7), all of whose voices would influence his later writing. But it was during his brief time as a student at Mt. San Antonio, a junior college in Walnut, California, that he seems to have had a life-altering moment, at least as he tells it, when he was introduced to the work of Samuel Beckett. Shepard says that he was at the home of an older guy, a 'beatnik', and (Chubb 1981: 191):

> we were listening to some jazz or something and he sort of shuffled over to me and threw this book on my lap and said, "Why don't you dig this" ... and it was like nothing I'd ever read before—it was *Waiting for Godot*.

Now, we may take this story with a grain of salt, but the way Shepard and several of his biographers have told it, that moment with the Beatnik and the copy of *Godot* instantly shaped Shepard's love for the theatre. Right after that, he joined a travelling company called the Bishop's Company Repertory Players, which had him performing in churches across the northeast. According to Shepard, 'it really gave you a sense of the makeshift quality of theatre and the possibility of doing it anywhere' (in Shewey 1985: 30).

The next logical step was New York City, where Shepard lived with his high school friend Charles Mingus Jr. (the son of the famous jazz musician) in a condemned apartment building in the East Village. The two of them bussed tables at the Village Gate, the famous jazz club – among other things, Shepard's job was 'bringing Nina Simone ice' (Shewey 1985: 38). Most important, though, was that working there introduced him to to a group of like-minded artists. Ralph Cook, who was the head waiter at the Village Gate, created Theatre Genesis in a space in St. Mark's Church-in-the-Bowery. Shepard's first two plays, *Cowboys* (rewritten three years later as *Cowboys #2*) and *The Rock Garden*, opened there on 10 October 1964 and ran for two weeks. Shepard was just 20 years old.

Initial reviews were less than kind, but audiences began coming in after Michael Smith championed Shepard's work in *The Village Voice*, praising him for work in which 'character transcends psychology, fantasy breaks down literalism, and the patterns of ordinariness have their own lives' (in Shewey 1985: 41). When complaints surfaced about the idea of a church allowing an 'obscene' play to be produced on its premises, its own pastor, Michael Allen, spoke out in defence of the piece, arguing that it was, as Stephen Bottoms puts it, 'more Christian to use offensive language in pursuit of truth than to use decent language in defense of conventionalized lies' (2004: 109). It's not surprising that this echoes some of the arguments used in the famous obscenity trial of Ginsberg's *Howl*, which certainly led to a reconsideration of what countercultural literary and artistic material ought to be considered pornographic.

After that, Shepard began writing play after play. Some of these early pieces never saw the stage, but 18 of them had been produced by the end of the 1960s (Shewey 1985: 41). His career as a playwright was launched precisely because interest in these avant-garde works coming out of New York and San Francisco by the likes of LeRoi Jones, Frank O'Hara, and others were sending audiences into these small, makeshift, low-budget theatres. The Caffe Cino, which began as a storefront space in 1958, evolved from a poetry reading hangout to a place for playwrights to test their work. The choir loft of the Judson Memorial Church was the home for the Judson Poets Theatre, opened in 1961 by the Rev. Al Carmines. Ellen Stewart began La Mama Experimental Theatre Club in 1962 in the basement of a tenement. So Shepard and his contemporaries, at a time when Broadway was becoming increasingly commercial (though, ironically, a portion of *The Rock Garden* would later become part of the Broadway revue *O Calcutta!*), became a community creating risk-taking plays that were less concerned with the niceties of plot, character development, and expensive set designs than with electric, crazy, poetic language; with an unhindered approach to the body and sexuality; and with breaking down barriers between the audience and the actors.

Shepard has spoken in interviews about his writing process during this very prolific time, and he emphasizes that he felt as if he was being taken over by the language of his characters. The connection to his earlier reading of Kerouac becomes explicit when he says (Marranca 1981: 217):

> From time to time I've practiced Jack Kerouac's discovery of jazz-sketching with words. Following the exact same principles as a musician does when he's jamming. After periods of this kind of practice, I begin to get the haunting sense that something in me writes but it's not necessarily me. At least it's not the "me" that takes credit for it.

Attempting to describe the 'plot' of *The Rock Garden* should show exactly why what 'happens' in these early plays is of far less interest than what we see and hear. The piece consists of a series of three tableaux. A teenage boy is the central figure throughout. In the first scene, the father figure reads a magazine at the head of the table while the boy and a teenage girl – who may be his sister or his girlfriend, an ambiguity to which Shepard returns in later works like *Fool for Love* – take turns sipping glasses of milk; eventually the girl drops and spills hers (in a visual moment that foreshadows the ejaculatory imagery of the play's ending). The second scene begins with the boy seated in a rocking chair dressed in his underwear, listening to a woman (presumably his mother) telling rambling stories about the weather and household chores, during which he keeps getting up and coming back into the room with glasses of water, wearing more clothes. In the final scene, the father figure delivers several lengthy speeches about lawn care, during which the boy continually dozes off out of boredom. This culminates in an unexpected torrent of words from the boy himself, who begins, 'When I come it's like a river. It's all over the bed and the sheets and everything' (Shepard 1986d: 43), and goes on to give a very explicit account of the various ways in which he likes to have sex, causing the father to fall off the couch as the lights black out for the ending.

The boy draws upon imagery of the previous scenes, but he has given voice to all of the repressed ideas he has been thinking about while engaging in the banalities of everyday family life. As Mottram puts it, the closing scene 'is an aggressive response to all that is no longer bearable in the boy's home life, especially to the tedium of uncommunicative relationships' (1984: 12). Shepard has acknowledged that this is a play 'about leaving my mom and dad' (Chubb 1981: 193). Despite its abstractions, the piece clearly depicts key generational differences and affirms the young man's need for an escape from the stultifying conventions of domesticity and childhood into the newly discovered realm of creative and sexual freedom.

Bill Hart, who became a friend and important figure in Shepard's development as a playwright, was with *The Village Voice*'s Michael Smith the night that Smith saw and wrote about the double bill of *Cowboys* and *The Rock Garden*. In Hart's recollection of seeing the two works, he explicitly makes a comparison to Beat writing (Oumano 1986: 34):

> I was simply astonished by it [the production] because it was like he was a bop playwright. It was like that spontaneous prosody of Ginsberg, Kerouac—what they were to poetry and the novel . . . I felt elated: he had literally altered my consciousness, which is the greatest thing a piece of theater can do, make you feel a totally different way which you didn't even know. It worked like rhythm and blues, like jazz, like Ginsberg, but he was a whole new thing.

Shepard's play *Chicago* was originally produced alongside Beat playwright Lawrence Ferlinghetti's *The Custom Collector in Baggy Pants*, presented by Theatre Genesis in April of 1965. As Bottoms argues, although Ferlinghetti's play had been published two years earlier, the two pieces worked perfectly together (see Chapter 4 above), as both were 'essentially rhythmically driven monologues' (2004: 117). The production was again praised highly by Michael Smith in the *Village Voice*, who singled out Shepard's lead actor, Kevin O'Connor, for his 'ecstatic plunges into the rich language' (in Bottoms 2004: 118). Shepard won the *Village Voice*'s 1966 Obie award for this play, *Red Cross*, and *Icarus's Mother* (Shewey 1985: 50).

Chicago begins with the central character, Stu, sitting fully clothed in the tub and delivering a series of monologues in which he rather badly impersonates various characters such as an old lady. In the meanwhile, Joy (based on Shepard's then-girlfriend, actress Joyce Aaron) offers him biscuits and makes plans to go out of town, which inspires another storytelling monologue from Stu about an imaginary train trip. Meanwhile, several of their friends join them on stage, carrying fishing poles. At the end, while all of them 'cast their lines into the audience' (Shepard 1986a: 58) – an obvious play on words for what actors actually do – Stu in his closing monologue exhorts them, and eventually the audience, to breathe in and out together: 'Month after month of breathing until you can't stop. Once you get the taste of it. The hang of it. What a gas. In your mouth and out your nose. Ladies and gentlemen, it's fantastic!' (Shepard 1986a: 59). And the play ends as it began, with the traditional theatrical 'trois coups' coming from the club of a Policeman.

The piece's opening visual image was inspired by Shepard's experience of carrying a cast-iron bathtub through the streets of the East Village (Tucker 1992: 37). Like Kerouac and other Beat writers, he was experimenting with the idea of writing whatever came to him and doing very little revision. A he told an interviewer, 'The stuff would just come out, and I wasn't really trying to shape it or make it into any big thing. I would have a picture and just start from there. A picture of a guy in a bathtub, or of two guys on stage with a sign blinking – you know, things like that . . .' (in Oumano 1986: 40). Just as we know that Kerouac actually revised more than he ever claimed, the same is probably true of Shepard. But again, the important point here is that spontaneity and free-form association are what govern not just the composition process, but also the narratives of the pieces themselves. There's also a clear connection here between this associative style and what would eventually become the signature 'transformations' of Joseph Chaikin's Open Theatre, for which Shepard – along with Megan Terry and many other playwrights – eventually wrote: in fact, the 'Joe' with whom the Joy character is speaking on the phone was apparently meant to be Chaikin (Shewey 1985: 53).

Just as Kerouac created narrators who both were and weren't author-surrogates (in *On the Road*, *Dharma Bums*, *Big Sur*, and other novels), like the Boy in *The Rock Garden*, Stu is one of many examples of author-surrogate figures for Shepard. As Mottram puts it, Stu 'is more than a character; he is almost a creator of the play. His function is auctorial, and about him on the stage move the projections of his own imagination' (1984: 15). Of course, author-surrogate figures in fiction are about as old as the genre itself; theatre goers have seen them on stage in the works of Eugene O'Neill and many others. The point is less that this is an 'original' concept than that there was a new kind of transparency and playfulness to what Shepard and Kerouac were doing here – and also some degree of self-criticism and irony. In Kerouac's works like *On the Road*, this often takes the form of a narrator who realizes his own limitations in contrast to a more charismatic and rebellious outsider (as Sal Paradise sees Dean Moriarty). The same is sometimes true of Shepard's narrator figures, as in this play. On the one hand, Stu is the creator and director of the play's stories, since almost all of the 'action' is concentrated within his narratives. On the other hand, he represents the isolation and narcissism of the artist, as he sits alone in his bathtub while the characters around him are actually *doing* things, including preparing to leave him. Michael Bloom describes Stu's existential situation very aptly (1981: 74):

> The disorientation contained in the presence of the bathtub – a real object – on an empty stage rather than in a bathroom setting reflects Stu's condition. He is an inert object stranded between two realities, his fantasies and the world outside himself, trapped by an overwhelming fear of activity.

It's only at the end, when Stu joins the other characters in facing the audience and exhorting everyone to breathe together, that the author-surrogate achieves some kind of momentary connection (the way a playwright does when his or her words come to life on stage). After that, though, one suspects he will return to his bathtub.

Icarus's Mother opened at the Caffe Cino on 16 November 1965, with Michael Smith – who had first championed Shepard's plays in the *Village Voice* – directing. Smith said later that although he loved the play, he felt that his own production didn't do justice to it; he spent too much time working on 'meaning' when he should have realized that the play was 'about a picnic' (1981: 160). The piece was inspired by a visit that Shepard made with Joyce Aaron to Milwaukee, where they attended a Fourth of July fireworks display. He told interviewer Kenneth Chubb (1981: 196):

> One of the weird things about being in America . . . is that you don't have any connection with the past, with what history means; so you can be there celebrating the Fourth of July, but all you know is that things are

exploding in the sky. And then you've got this emotional thing that goes a long way back, which creates a certain kind of chaos, a kind of terror . . .

In the play, five friends are lying on blankets awaiting the fireworks, competing to tell various stories and to outdo each other in their supposed technical knowledge while they watch a pilot buzzing around in a small plane. When Frank gets up to go for a walk for a second time (after he returns once and is unsuccessful in persuading the others to move down to the beach), Howard and Bill attempt to create smoke signals using their blanket and smoke from the barbeque. The two women, Jill and Pat, report later that when they took off their clothes and danced on the beach, the pilot wrote 'E = MC squared' in the sky. At the end – punctuated by tremendous booms and flashes of light – Frank delivers a lengthy monologue about how the pilot, like the Icarus of the title, has crashed his plane into the water, creating a spectacular explosion (Shepard 1986c: 79):

> . . . And the pilot bobbing in the very center of a ring of fire that's closing in. His white helmet bobbing up and bobbing down. His hand reaching for his other hand and the fire moves in and covers him up and the line of two hundred bow their heads and moan together with the light in their faces. Oh, you guys should have come! You guys should have been there!

As I've argued elsewhere, we never know for certain whether the booms and flashes are confirmation of the scenario that Frank describes, or whether they are simply the fireworks and Frank, like the other characters, has blurred the boundaries between reality and fiction (Geis 1993: 52–53).

Commentators on the play have made much of its closing imagery. In the notes quoted earlier by Michael Smith about what he saw as the failures of the original production, he says that the play 'is about fear—specifically, the so-called paranoia of the nuclear present—and its effect on people individually and in community' (1981: 160). Michael Bloom argues that it 'elaborates a gestalt conditioned by the threat of an apocalypse' (1981: 76). Similarly, Martin Tucker writes that 'the plane, foreboding in its power, represents the technology that can rain bombs in the sky' (1992: 42). Ron Mottram provides a different interpretation when he points out that the imagery can be interpreted sexually and artistically, with the plane crash at the end representing a 'colossal orgasmic explosion' (1984: 23). He goes on to claim that since sexuality is a life-giving force and that the artist's role is to challenge conventional perceptions, the disruptiveness of the pilot/plane 'challenges conventional modes of thinking' (1984: 25). Certainly, Shepard returns repeatedly in his slightly later works to culminating images that fuse creation and apocalypticism. In the end of *The Holy Ghostly*, for instance, '*the whole theater is consumed in flames*' (1986b: 196). The final sequence of Michelangelo Antonioni's film *Zabriskie Point*, for which Shepard wrote the screenplay, sees detritus from American consumerism (such as Wonder Bread wrappers) floating in the air after an explosion while lovers copulate on a beach.

It's not at all difficult to see the many connections between Shepard's use of the Fourth of July picnic motif to set up these sexual/apocalyptic themes as a critique of 'normative' American values that we also saw in *The Rock Garden*, and the ways in which his Beat literary heroes did the same. To give only a few short examples, we might consider Ginsberg's *Howl*, in which the 'Moloch' section invokes 'granite cocks! monstrous bombs!' (1986: 88), or his poems 'America' and 'A Supermarket in California'. In Corso's poem 'Marriage', he struggles with the vision of an existence that would bring him 'five noisy running brats in love with Batman' and says, 'when the milkman comes leave him a note in the bottle/Penguin dust, bring me penguin dust, I want penguin dust' (1983: 84, 67). Ferlinghetti's 'The Poet's Eye Obscenely Seeing' laments 'a kissproof world of plastic toiletseats tampax and taxis' (1993b: 17). He even invokes, like Shepard, the Icarus image in his poem 'Autobiography' when he says, 'I flew too near the sun/and my wax wings fell off' (1993a: 107). There are also many such moments in Kerouac, for example, in *On the Road* when Sal Paradise looks into the windows of houses and feels all too keenly aware of his outsider identity.

Eight Plays from Off-Off Broadway, a collection by Nick Orzel and Michael Smith, was published by Bobbs-Merrill in 1966. It was considered a major acknowledgement that the theatrical experiments of Shepard and his peers marked a kind of sea-change, validating the idea that creating innovative plays could be less about money, elaborate design, and star power, and more about bodies, language, and the gathering together of open-minded audience members. The kinship that this moment has with, for example, City Lights' publication of poems by Ginsberg and Corso, is a strong one. Shepard's *Chicago* was included in the volume along with plays by Frank O'Hara, Lanford Wilson, Joel Oppenheimer, Maria Irene Fornes, Megan Terry, and others. In his introductory notes for the piece, Ralph Cook, the artistic director of Theatre Genesis, wrote (1966: 94) that:

> whatever hope we have lies with our artists, for they alone have the ability (if we do not continue to corrupt them) to withstand the onslaught of the mass media and the multitude of false gods. They alone have the ability to show us ourselves.

How oddly resonant and applicable Cook's words still are. How well he understood that Shepard and these other playwrights, like the Beat writers who both preceded and overlapped with them, brought new hope that yes, having the bravery to challenge normative values about what it was acceptable to write and do – on the stage as well as the page – would forever transform the American cultural landscape.

Works cited

Bloom, M. (1981), 'Visions of the End: The Early Plays' in B. Marranca (ed.), *American Dreams: The Imagination of Sam Shepard*, New York: PAJ, 72–78.

Bottoms, S. J. (2004), *Playing Underground: A Critical History of the 1960s Off-Off Broadway Movement*, Ann Arbor: University of Michigan.

Chubb, K., and the Editors of *Theatre Quarterly* (1981), 'Metaphors, Mad Dogs, and Old Time Cowboys: Interview with Sam Shepard' in B. Marranca (ed.), *American Dreams: The Imagination of Sam Shepard*, New York: PAJ, 187–209.

Cook, R. (1966), 'Theatre Genesis' in N. Orzel and M. Smith (eds), *Eight Plays from Off-Off Broadway*, Indianapolis: Bobbs-Merrill, 93–95.

Corso, G. (1983), 'Marriage' in A. W. Allison et al. (eds), *The Norton Anthology of Poetry*, 3rd edition, New York and London: Norton, 1321–1323.

Ferlinghetti, L. (1993a), 'Autobiography' in *These Are My Rivers: New & Selected Poems 1955–1993*, New York: New Directions, 105–112.

Ferlinghetti, L. (1993b), 'The Poet's Eye Obscenely Seeing' in *These Are My Rivers: New & Selected Poems 1955–1993*, New York: New Directions, 1993, 83–84.

Geis, D. R. (1993), *Postmodern Theatric(k)s: Monologue in Contemporary American Drama*, Ann Arbor: University of Michigan.

Ginsberg, A. (1986), *Howl: 50th Anniversary Edition*, New York: Harper Perennial.

Marranca, B. (1981), 'Alphabetical Shepard: The Play of Words', in B. Marranca (ed.), *American Dreams: The Imagination of Sam Shepard*, New York: PAJ, 13–33.

Mottram, R. (1984), *Inner Landscapes: The Theatre of Sam Shepard*, Columbia, MO: University of Missouri.

Oumano, E. (1986), *Sam Shepard: The Life and Work of an American Dreamer*. New York: St. Martin's.

Shepard, S. (1981), 'Language, Visualization, and the Inner Library' in B. Marraca (ed.), *American Dreams: The Imagination of Sam Shepard*, New York: PAJ, 214–19.

Shepard, S. (1986a), 'Chicago' in *The Unseen Hand and Other Plays*, Toronto and New York: Bantam, 45–59.

Shepard, S. (1986b), 'The Holy Ghostly' in *The Unseen Hand and Other Plays*, Toronto and New York: Bantam, 177–196.

Shepard, S. (1986c), 'Icarus's Mother' in *The Unseen Hand and Other Plays*, Toronto and New York: Bantam, 61–80.

Shepard, S. (1986d), 'The Rock Garden' in *The Unseen Hand and Other Plays*, Toronto and New York: Bantam, 33–44.

Shewey, D. (1985), *Sam Shepard: The Life, The Loves, Behind the Legend of a True American Original*, New York, Dell.

Smith, M. (1981), 'Notes: *Icarus's Mother*' in B. Marranca (ed.), *American Dreams: The Imagination of Sam Shepard*, New York: PAJ, 159–161.

Tucker, M. (1992), *Sam Shepard*, New York: Continuum.

Rochelle Owens: Off Beat, Off-Off Broadway

Amy Friedman

The jazzy language is present on the page, there is spoken word powerfully formulated to shake up the status quo, all set against a backdrop of the mid-1960s New York extreme fringe arts scene: the extraordinary drama and poetry of Rochelle Owens. By 1969 her plays had been produced, and she had published poems. *Futz*, her most famous play, had premiered at La Mama Experimental Theatre Club, had caused a sensation, and been made into a film that Timothy O'Leary, writing in the L.A. Free Press, called 'a shocker' (1970: 19). So is her work Beat? If she does belong in the still-evolving, much-discussed canon of transformative Beat Generation writers, then eager scholars would welcome a livewire, cutting-edge voice deserving of both our critical attention and theoretical analysis.

According to David Crespy's comprehensive assessment of the 1960s era which saw the rise of a new fringe theatre scene in New York, when we look at the artistic production of this period we need to consider thoughtfully 'the Beat poets and off-off Broadway playwrights who walked in their footsteps' (2003: 22). The order of that particular parade is significant. There was indeed overlap, and the degree of intersection indicates that it is appropriate to place Beat artists in the context of, and as progenitors of, the dynamic Off-Off Broadway (OOB) phenomenon that evolved to the point of becoming an intrinsic and iconic element of dramatic arts in the US.

This background of Beat-into-Bohemian Theater lays the foundation for this chapter, which examines the work of ground-breaking playwright and poet Rochelle Owens in the context of Beat art. A Beat ethos arguably informs Owens's stance in much of her work, but what may emerge is the argument of equal force which, in the case of Owens, the avant-garde Bohemian vision infuses the Beat to an equal and equally significant degree.

While both Broadway and off-Broadway were well established by the mid-twentieth-century as channels and destinations for artists trained to a high level in performance and theatre craft, OOB emerged from a completely different locus. In 1998 when the journal *Theater* surveyed the cohort of writers who had written for them in the first issues in 1968 when the publication was launched as *yale/theatre*, the responses exploded the extant myth of OOB as a poor stepchild of mainstream theatre.[1] Playwright and producer Maria Irene Fornés emphasized that OOB represented a completely new evolution of performance (Auletta 1998: 32):

> People forget that the real source of energy and inspiration of Off-Off-Broadway had nothing to do with theater. It came from painting, music, dance, from people who were interested in theater but had nothing to do with the theater that existed – not from people already in theater who wanted to do a different kind of theater.

Playwright Robert Auletta's emphasis in the 'Survey' is on the sheer daring of OOB productions at the time: 'Risk was in the air', Auletta asserts (1998: 32). He continues:

> '60s theater took more chances than today's theater does. Big chances, bold, scary chances with acting, production, audiences, and language. The times were breaking boundaries, and the stage, in its traditional role as mirror, was doing what good mirrors were supposed to do: reflecting what passed before it, in all its political, intellectual, social, and spiritual confusion . . . a lot was going on that was truly innovative.

But it is Rochelle Owens who conveys with the most potency and completeness just how emphatically cutting-edge the OOB scene was – that it was categorically not a lesser artistic element adjacent to a more established commercial performance mainstream. This 'fringe' arts realm in the 1960s, Owens asserts (Auletta 1998:32):

> attempted to redefine creativity, art, politics, and sexuality. It was the beginning of radical experimentation. Historians and critics often ignore the avant garde as it shapes its own culture and profoundly challenges conventional perceptions of reality. The poets, playwrights, directors, filmmakers, painters, sculptors, andperforming artists were inventing, finding, gathering, analyzing, and producing the groundwork for those who came later, including the pop culture heroes of the billion-dollar rock music industry.

If we scan for Beat artists who worked in, or had associations with, the OOB movement in New York City from the 1950s, we actually locate in archival listings most of the writers associated with the Beat Generation. We note sponsored OOB poetry readings by Jack Kerouac, Allen Ginsberg, and Gregory Corso; plays by Lawrence Ferlinghetti, Jack Micheline, LeRoi Jones/ Amiri Baraka, Diane di Prima, and Michael McClure.

Critics have tended to credit the founding of Off-Off Broadway to the dynamic Ellen Stewart and her La Mama Theater, '[a]long with Joe Cino of Caffe Cino and Al Carmines of Judson Poets' Theater, giving a home to American playwrights, directors, and performers' (Rosenthal 2006:13). I would, of course, add the Beat-affiliated New York Poets Theatre as a foundational element of the origins of OOB. Most important is to acknowledge that, throughout this early period, much creative cross-pollination, and even messy and undocumented sharing, occurred as actors, directors, writers, painters and dancers sought creative homes. As Erik Mortenson has trenchantly argued in *Capturing the Beat Moment: Cultural Politics and the Poetics of Presence*, 'interest in the theatrical was a hallmark of sixties counterculture. If politics itself was a pageant of unreality foisted on the people, why not fight theater with theater?' (2011: 172).

Rochelle Owens also worked with various artists and companies in intense and mutable downtown settings. The remarkable play *Futz*, written by Owens at age 23 in 1958, was initially set for production with Judith Malina's and Julian Beck's The Living Theatre in 1963. It then shifted to the Judson Poets Theatre, which had previously produced Owens's *Istanboul* and *The String Game*. The play eventually found a home at La Mama, due to Ellen Stewart's overt enthusiasm for the script, and because director Tom O'Horgan was working there. He had previously produced and toured Owens's play *Homos* (Bottoms 2004: 201). (O'Horgan would go on to direct the musical *Hair*.) *Futz* finally premiered at La Mama on 2 March 1967 (Bottoms 2004: 201).

Rochelle Owens apparently navigated all of this with great aplomb. She'd begun reading plays very early and remembers tackling Eugene O'Neill at age 10 (Interview). After she moved from Brooklyn to Manhattan in her teens, she had become aware that OOB was a break from, even an affront to, straight theatre: it was intrinsically non-conventional, and stood in antithesis to the linear, highly staged, conservative, even orthodox, narratives of New York's more established venues and companies. It is incredible and impressive this was where the very young, even precocious, Rochelle Owens, already publishing poems in LeRoi Jones and Hettie Jones's little magazine *Yugen* at age 19, launched her extraordinary theatrical visions: of savage African queens (that is the play *Beclch*), bestial farmyard yahoos confronting the ardent pig-love of a farmer for his sow Amanda (the outrageous *Futz*), and a very salty, in all senses, and extremely hairy female saint in late medieval

LA Free Press, 13 February 1970, p. 20 (Issue #291). Courtesy of the LAFreePress. com. With thanks to Steve Finger, Publisher LA Free Press, and Jesse Friedman.

Constantinople (the comic and delightful *Istanboul*). As Owens later put it, this era of 'radical experimentation' profoundly shaped her as an artist: 'New York of the 60s was a point of origin for my life as a poet and playwright. No matter how far those directions eventually took me, that time and place remain for me, as for so many others, the golden age of beginnings' (Auletta 1998: 32).[2]

The phenomenon of *Futz*

Owens's play *Futz* can arguably be read as an updated version of *The Bacchae* composed for the post-bomb, increasingly drugged-out, politically roiling 1950s and 1960s. A revisiting of ancient Greek drama's incestuous, zoophiliac, murderous depictions, now set as bizarre Americana, populated with genuine country bumpkins. While the focus is on an entirely skewed society, the text does challenge specific ideas about the entrenched, heteronormative possession of females in that society. It's a provocative theatre of violence and lust and, possibly most affronting, rather a lot of hopelessly warped English, spoken by simplistic yahoos with the slatternly sounding family names of Futz, Loop, Satz, and Sluck. The guileless farmer, Cyrus Futz, is furiously enamoured of his sow, Amanda, and offers his own defence early on: 'Isn't no modern sin, old as your Bible, lay down with a calf somebody did and did get no punishment from God' (1968: 9). The play won Obie Awards for Best Play, Best Director, and Best Actor. On tour in Europe with the La Mama Troupe of actors in 1967, *Futz* did very well in an initial run as part of the Edinburgh Fringe Festival. It transferred to London's Mercury Theatre in Notting Hill, then to the venerable West End theatre district's Vaudeville Theatre (Bottoms 2004: 202). The play found widely appreciative audiences, and was embraced by both critics and London punters for its physicality, energy and its ability to shock. The upfront depictions of aberrant sexuality and physicality would have echoed the artistic ripples of the continued Age of Anxiety in Britain at the time: the ventings of Angry Young Men, Beat voices, and an early feminist counterculture. As Stephen J. Bottoms notes (2004: 207), critics revisiting the phenomenon of *Futz* have lauded the play as celebrating a true Dionysian spirit of theatre instead of the mirror of society it wants to see itself as.

Owens was writing these ground-breaking works at same time as fellow OOB playwrights Sam Shepard, John Guare, and Lanford Wilson, who have each gone on to become more familiar names in the landscape of New York theatre. It was the start of OOB casts and companies earning *Village Voice* Obie Awards, drawing audiences to its oddball venues in basements and lofts.[3] Some of Owens's other plays produced in this period include the comedy *Istanboul*, full of charming shysters and saints lurking in fifteenth-century Asian saloons. David Crespy deemed this an extravagant critique of western religiosity and its eastern 'pretentious counterpart' (2003: 108). The epistolary *Chucky's Hunch* is a series of unanswered letters by a man who embodies alienation and frustrated human connection. In *Kontraption*, Owens considers race as a deeply embedded social and emotional construct, while *Three Front* takes on the friction of commerce and sex. Introducing a collection of Owens's plays, Pamela Monk singles out how '[i]n the measured delivery of one person telling another a good joke, [Owens] devises scenarios of outrage, injustice, and absurdity' (2000: 816).

There is a singular niche of Beat writing that, when it appeared, prompted court cases on charges of obscenity in the 1950s and 1960s. The 1957 *Howl* obscenity trial against Lawrence Ferlinghetti and City Lights Bookstore was memorably dramatized in the 2010 film *Howl*. Lenore Kandel's poetry collection *The Love Book* was seized by police on grounds of obscenity from both City Lights Books and The Psychedelic Shop in 1966 in San Francisco. The FBI went after both Diane di Prima and LeRoi Jones after an excerpt of the latter's *The System of Dante's Hell* was published in the little magazine they both produced, *Floating Bear*. We can also place Rochelle Owens's *Futz* in this illustrious Beat company.

A 1969 production of *Futz* in Toronto prompted a criminal prosecution by the Canadian Crown against the producers on charges of 'staging an obscene, immoral, or indecent performance' (Szlawieniec-Haw 2010: 57). Initially found guilty, the producers, two of whom were also lawyers, appealed successfully in 1970. Their effective appeal case included taking the presiding judge, one Judge Lyon, to a performance of the anti-war musical *Hair*, which was then playing in Toronto, to establish their argument that changing standards in theatre productions had created greater acceptance for nudity and depictions of sexuality as an artistic element of a play (Szlawieniec-Haw 2010:57). Judge Lyon's decision eventually agreed that, in legal terms, 'community standards' were no longer unilaterally violated by swearing, nudity, or representations of sexual acts on stage (Szlawieniec-Haw 2010: 58). The case included witness commentary in support of the idea that *Futz*, while referencing sexual taboos, was nonetheless appreciated by audience members as a 'social statement', beyond just acceptance as literal narrative (Szlawieniec-Haw 2010: 57). Overall, the episode fits in with the series of Beat-affiliated and influenced works eventually expanding the legal definition of art in both Anglo and American realms.

What is 'Beat' about Owens's work?

There is much more to Owens's extensive body of work that indicates Beat influences and a Beat ethos. If not overtly identifying as Beat-influenced or Beat-associated, Owens has certainly been grouped with Beat writers. She appeared, for instance, at The Poetry Project at St. Marks Church In-the-Bowery in New York City, reading on the same 2 January 1974 bill as Allen Ginsberg, Gregory Corso, Anne Waldman, Ed Sanders, Jackson Mac Low, Tony Towle. Beat, Owens herself contends, 'was a movement that included those who wanted to change social conventions, and improve what art was about' (Interview). She fits into that cultural moment 'in the sense of being around them at the time and against the social conventions' (Interview). It was Allen Ginsberg who initially directed the young Owens to send her poems to LeRoi Jones; Owens subsequently appears in the volume Jones edited in 1962 called *Four Young Lady Poets*, with Carol Berge, Barbara Moraff, and Diane Wakoski. We would arguably gain critical insight from considering Owens's writing in the context of West Coat Beat poet Joanne Kyger's rewritings of the Greek myth of Odysseus in San Francisco in the 1950s, and di Prima's frequent drawing from classical archetypes. Owens's epic poetic works, *The Joe 82 Creation Poems* (1974) and *The Joe Chronicles Part 2* (1979), would seem to be ideal to consider alongside di Prima's *Loba* (first published 1978) and Anne Waldman's *Iovis* (1992), each a significant book-length poem of mythos, celebration, and drama. The following passages from *The Joe 82 Creation Poems*: XIII 'Wild-Woman Sharply & Triumphantly Watches,' suggest both thematic and stylistic confluences with these other Beat works (Owens 1974):

> woman is a Wild
> scientist   O Lord!   Questioning
> & going forward   like a   raving nightingale (ll 1–3) [...]
> O Woman Innovator!   O Self!   O languid Messiah!
> She plucks out the weeds With
>   a little finger /
>   Proud of her
>   gleaming Mind on the angel's head.   Her
>   dominion/   (ll 25–30)

The central Wild-woman here, in competition with the poem's Wild-man, is strong, imaginative, assured, sexual, and energetic; a 'Woman-Abraham' she names herself, empowered to establish a cult (Owens 1974: 29). Owens's poem-cycle explores power, nature, and the language of origin stories, touching on rites of naming, creativity, creation, the development of knowledge, science and technology, eventual ruinous pollutants, and visions of a better world. Ginsberg, too, drew on Old Testament archetypes and figures and rewrote Jewish liturgy, as does Owens in various works. In *Recollections of My Life as A Woman*, Diane di Prima undertakes briefly something that is extremely rare when writers share an autobiography: she pauses to articulate exactly what she was trying to do as a poet at a specific period in her artistic evolution (late 1950s/early 1960s). Opening a copy of John Wieners's *Hotel Wentley Poems* (1958) in a Sixth Avenue bookshop utterly halts di Prima in her tracks (2001: 272):

> I stood there spellbound, reading the whole thing, recognizing many of the effects I was also at work on: the street language flowing so smoothly it seemed effortless, the almost-cliché shining and made new. A taut nervy lyricism that fooled you – it looked so easy.

For one steeped in Beat works, reading Owens's poetry and poetic theatre pieces immediately brings to mind the unmistakable fire of di Prima, the lyrical lightness of Joanne Kyger, and the shamanism of Anne Waldman. None of which is to imply that Owens's voice is not uniquely her own – instantly a funny, witty, biting, coruscating poetic expression. Consider the confident rewriting of conjectured medieval history in 'Concertina Song' (1968b:17):

> In a hen/house maybe/in 1133 at/ the foot of /it was some/kind of fruit/ fruit-eating/things/in 1133/at the foot/in a whore-/house maybe/in 1133/at the foot/of it was/some narrow/minded bastards/who wanted the/place closed/then shyest/people could/not even look/at the foot/ without think-/ing of pubic/hairs in a hen-/house maybe/in 1133.

Reviewing Owens's *New and Selected Poems 1961–1996*, Sandra Cookson notes with approval the core characteristics of Owens's work: 'the elements of linguistic playfulness, the shock value of graphic imagery, the mixing of texts and vocabularies from many sources, a sensibility that is more European than American, an emphasis on the visual aspects of printed poetry – are all here' (1998: 386). In no small part, Cookson's critical satisfaction derives from being able to assert likewise that Owens's book establishes that 'the reader will find the signal characteristics of avant-gardism alive and well' (1998: 386). Owens today maintains 'a strong identity of being a poet', starting from her late teen years living in the West Village, through establishing connections in New York City with 'a community of playwrights and of visual artists, including Andy Warhol' in the 1960s, and continuing with current poetry and performance projects that locate her solidly in experimental and ethnopoetic practices (Interview).

The end of 'the woman artist' already

Observing Owens's ongoing engagement with questions about feminism in her writing borders some unintentionally humorous terrain. It points to a certain ignored futility in analytic work in returning always to a strictly gender-based assessment of a writer. It is impossible to escape Owens's awareness of a degree of pointlessness when she endures repetitive interviews determined to pin her down as a feminist writer. The undoubtedly extremely well-intentioned Joan Goulianis begins her interview with the following earnest preface (1972: 257):

> By accident, in the spring of 1969, I spent an evening at the La Mama, where they were doing two plays by Rochelle Owens – *Homo* and *The Queen of Greece*. The plays were like nothing I had seen before. They were devastating satires of women as sluts, queens, mothers, and of men as imperialists, consorts, babies. I wrote a review of the plays, and, a few months later, Rochelle Owens called me. She had liked the review, but when I went to interview her, she did not seem to want to talk about her plays in terms of women. Two years later, when her play *Istanbul* [sic] was to be produced, we again did an interview. This time, with women's liberation in her consciousness and mine, she was more willing to talk about her plays as a woman's plays, though *she still insisted upon considering herself as an artist who was involved in broader concerns.* [emphasis added]

The introduction signals irrefutably the slant of the coming conversation, the interviewer relentless in her pursuit of confirmation of feminist interpretation, with Owens parrying sagely with a tested hand (1972: 257):

J[oan Goulianis]　I want to focus on your experiences as a woman playwright, although I understand you want your work to stand for something besides women's liberation.

R[ochelle Owens]　I write about women and men. I have never written a play with only men, and I have never written a play with only women. We both agree that the female mind and the male mind are hopefully equally excitable or functioning in a good way. I don't believe that men are smarter than women. I don't believe that women are smarter than men.

And on it goes.[4] The final published interview also includes two other women theatre artists, actress and director Crystal Field and writer Rosalyn Drexler, who are subject to the same insistent disregard for the artist who chooses to define her work and herself in her own terms. Owens has never gendered her work. Her declarations of artistry are arguably universal, as in 'The Design of the Poem': 'Because I am bored by the traditional, conventionalized and fossilized systems of writing poetry and plays, they are useless, I demolish them', she explains in this collection of writers' manifestos of new poetics (1981: 26). In 1989, Owens once again engages with an interviewer seeking feminist affirmations; one is not convinced Owens's diplomatic evasions are appreciated as the incisive statements they are. Owens does initially concede that her work may be read as feminist 'because it has much to do with my personal and social identity as a woman in a patriarchal culture, and because it resists in both form and idea the absolute power of organized doctrine, principles, and procedures' (Coleman 1989: 20). Owens immediately follows this up with an astute condition that moves her work beyond this initial category: 'One ought', she continues, 'to question the assumptions of the culture which created the social role of women' (1989: 20). To the interviewer's continued examination of her work in terms of anticipating 'much recent thinking about gender and sexual identity', Owens allows the obvious, that she writes with 'a female sensibility' (Coleman 1989: 21):

> But what exactly is it? I really don't believe a female aesthetic can
> be defined, because if it could, where would current knowledge be
> in terms of knowledge of the future? I mean, I really do believe we live
> in an expanding universe, and definitions of art and consciousness
> are not boxed and frozen and rigid. That is why I consider myself
> an innovative artist, an avant-garde writer, and I insist on that word
> ('avant-garde').

In her steadfast assertion of an individual artistic validity and aversion to the relentless imposition of labels that don't seem to widen the audience for artistic work, Owens is curiously in sync with those pioneers of parity in the arts for women, The Guerilla Girls.[5] Alisa Solomon interviewed three of the Girls in 1999, 'AphraBehn', [sic] 'Gertrude Stein', and Claude Cahun, around the time they were plastering the bathrooms of New York, New Jersey, and Connecticut arts venues with stickers reading: 'In this theatre the taking of photographs, the use of recording devices, and the production of plays by women are strictly prohibited.' Solomon and Stein discuss the example of a recent successful stage comedy that received no interest for a commercial transfer (an extended run at a larger venue) because it was perceived solely as a 'feminist comedy' (1999: 51). Stein agrees that the problem can be apprehensions of the 'subject matter' itself, and AphraBehn chimes in (1999: 51).

AphraBehn   [It's] a complex, complex issue. Our focus is just bringing to the public that it exists, and starting some dialogue.

Alisa Solomon   What I find disheartening is that we've been talking about this for more than twenty-five years. The playwrights Maria Irene Fornés, Rosalyn Drexler, Megan Terry, Rochelle Owens, and others established the New York Theater Strategy as early as 1968 to provide what Fornés called "a theater without compromise and sexism." The Women's Project started in the seventies. These numbers have been out there year after year after year. It's great to put them in people's faces, but I'm also so pessimistic.

Gertrude Stein   The [Guerilla] Girls are an absurdist group … We know we're not going to change the world. We have to do something or we'll go nuts. You go on. What can you do? You just go on.

Rochelle Owens has indeed gone on: a book-length work, *Hermaphropoetics*, is currently unfolding online at rochelleowens.org, full of profound images of 'horror and beauty' (Interview). Owens belongs in the critical mosaic of her peers, as a poet and playwright of influence and as a true bohemian visionary. Her work has always embodied that Dionysian jazz of 'theater as risk'.

Works cited

Auletta, R. (1998), '1968–1998 Theater Survey', *Theater*, 28.3: 31–38.

Bottoms, S. J. (2004), *Playing Underground: A Critical History of the 1960s Off-Off-Broadway Movement*, Ann Arbor: Univ of Michigan.

Coleman, C.B. (1989), 'The Androgynous Muse: An Interview with Rochelle Owens', *Theater* 20.2:19–23.

Cookson, S. (1998), 'Review', *New and Selected Poems, 1961–1996 by Rochelle Owens, World Literature Today*, 72.2: 386.

Crespy, D. A. (2003), *Off-Off Broadway Explosion: How Provocative Playwrights of the 1960s Ignited a New American Theater*, New York: Back State.

di Prima, D. (2001), *Recollections of My Life as a Woman: The New York Years*, New York: Viking.

Goulianos, J. (1972), 'Women and the Avant-Garde Theater: Interviews with Rochelle Owens, Crystal Field, Rosalyn Drexler', *Women – An Issue*. *The Massachusetts Review*, 13.1–2: 257–65.

Guerilla Girls (2015), 'Guerilla Girls Interview', Available at: www.guerrillagirls. com/interview/faq.shtml (last accessed 15 January 2015).

Monk, P. (2000), 'Plays by Rochelle Owens' [Review], *World Literature Today*, 74.4: 816.

Mortenson, E. (2011), *Capturing the Beat Moment: Cultural Politics and the Poetics of Presence*, Carbondale: Southern Illinois University.

Murray, T. (1989), 'The Play of Letters: Possession and Writing in *Chucky's Hunch*', in E. Brater (ed.), *Feminine Focus: The New Women Playwrights*, Ann Arbor: University of Michigan, 186–209.

Nash, S. S. (1994), 'An Immense and Continuous Splendor: Thoughts of the Poetry of Rochelle Owens', *Talisman*, 12:129–140.

O'Leary, T. (1970), 'Futz' [review], *L.A. Free Press*, 20 Feb. 1970: 19.

Owens, R. (1962), *Four Young Lady Poets*, LeRoi Jones (ed.), New York: Totem.

Owens, R. (1968), *Futz and What Came After*, New York: Random House.

Owens, R. (1968), *Salt & Core*, Los Angeles: Black Sparrow.

Owens, R. (1969), '*Futz*', *New Short Plays: 2*, London: Methuen.

Owens, R. (1972), *I Am the Babe of Joseph Stalin's Daughter: Poems 1961–1971*, New York: Kulchur Foundation.

Owens, R. (1974), *The Joe 82 Creation Poems*, Los Angeles: Black Sparrow.

Owens, R. (1981), 'The Design of the Poem', *Coherence; a gathering of experiments in writing; towards a new poetics*, 1: 26.

Owens, R. (1991), 'Splendid Examples', *Moody Street Irregulars: A Jack Kerouac Newsletter*, 'The Women's Issue', 24–26: 19–20.

Owens, R. (1997), *New and Selected Poems, 1961–1996*, San Diego: Junction.

Owens, R. (2012), 'Autobiography'. Available at: www.rochelleowens.org/ autobiography.php (last accessed 15 Jan. 2015).

Owens, R. (2013), *Out of Ur: New & Selected Poems 1961–2012*, Bristol, UK: Shearsman.

Owens, R. (2015), Interview with the author, 26 March 2015, Philadelphia, PA.

Rosenthal, C. (2006), 'Ellen Stewart: La Mama to Us All', *The Drama Review*, 50.2:12–51.

Schmidt, K. (2007), 'A Feminist Theater of Transformation: Rochelle Owens's Postmodern Play "in the Process of Becoming"', in C. Henke and M. Middeke (eds), *Drama and/after Postmodernism: Papers given on the occasion of the 15th annual conference of the German Society for Contemporary Theatre and Drama in English*, Trier, Germany: Wissenschaftlicher, 209–222.

Solomon, A. (1999), 'Parody and Parity: An interview with The Guerrilla Girls', *Theater* 29.2: 45–55.

Szlawieniec-Haw, D. I. (2010), '*Futz* Buddies: The Effect of "An Evening with *Futz*" on Buddies in Bad Times', *Canadian Theatre Review*, 142: 55–60.

Rosalyn Drexler:
Savvy, Savage, Sassy Polymath

Dorothy Chansky

'Playfulness, amateurism, irresponsibility, incompetence' is the phrase used by Robert Pasolli to describe a common perception of the Off-Off Broadway scene in which playwright Rosalyn Drexler was a key presence in the seminal 1960s (1968: 152). Writing in 1968, Pasolli believed instead that early Off-Off Broadway work was fresh, original, compelling, and possibly the only important contribution Americans might be making to contemporary theatre writ large. But he was also already mourning a trend towards the pursuit of financial success among the irreverent, anti-commercial playwrights whom he admired for their 'spontaneous, unpremeditated creation' in the early, playwright-focused Off-Off Broadway theatres of the era, contra Broadway, Off-Broadway, and the emerging regional theatres (1968: 151–52). Passolli's disappointment in the professionalization of some of the theatres and individual writers variously called 'downtown', 'underground', or 'alternative' centred on a loss of 'freshness and directness' – qualities he located especially in works by Harry Koutoukas, Soren Agenoux, Maria Irene Fornes, and Rosalyn Drexler (1968: 156). That the latter are women who also worked as visual artists says much about the 'scene' whose putative passing troubled Pasolli. Then and there, as here and now, women claimed fewer places in the ranks of New York playwrights and directors (see Cohen 2008 and Sands 2009). But for iconoclastic polymaths without any class-inflected baggage to shed (or protect), the downtown world was their oyster, albeit one that usually required nutritional supplementation with other, outside, paying work.

Rosalyn Drexler alleged to have had no interest in traditional scripted theatre until she saw Eugene Ionesco's *The Bald Soprano* in her thirties: 'It made me want to write plays because it was so weird and I was, too.' Born Rosalyn Bronznick in 1926, she grew up in the Bronx and Manhattan's Spanish Harlem. Her mother had emigrated as a girl from Russia in 1914, and Drexler spent her youth in a world of 'second-hand possessions and ...

shabby inventions' (1971: 1). Like other kids in her cohort, she had no money for tickets to legitimate theatre, but she had access to vaudeville, as the live performances were free, following screenings of movies, which she could afford. She especially followed the Marx Brothers, as she was related via a blood relative's marriage to Chico Marx; at least one critic invoked the Marx Brothers as an influence on her work (see Gilman 1967: 9). As a child Drexler aspired to sing. She studied voice at New York's High School of Music and Art, from which she was on at least one occasion expelled for cutting too many gym classes (Schapp 1985: n.p.). She would not make her New York singing debut until 1973, performing on radio station WBAI, and shortly thereafter stepping up in a revue called 'The Peaches' ('Briefs' 1973: 12). Acting, on the other hand, held no appeal, despite a scholarship for classes from Erwin Piscator when she was nine or ten. She left after a single lesson: '[I]t may have been because I hated to memorize lines.' She lost her interest in theatre entirely after seeing a Piscator production of *The Brontë Sisters*, which she found, 'depressing ... the language dull, and the story unremittingly tragic' (1971: 1). She did, however, write what she later admitted was her first play when she was a child and transcribed one of her parents' frequent fights. 'Then I gave it to them to read. They threw it in the incinerator. I knew it had not left them indifferent. After that I went on writing' (Lamont 1983: 7). Her habit, carried into adulthood, was to jot down 'dialogues, poems, little paragraphs that sounded like Artaud ...' (Kempton 1968: n.p.)

Drexler's first published work was a novel (*I am the Beautiful Stranger*, 1965, which is about a sexually and intellectually precocious girl who goes to Music and Art), but the road to recognition continued in the style she established early in life: varied, colourful, and fearless. She attended Hunter College for a single semester before dropping out and marrying artist Sherman Drexler in 1946. Their daughter, Rachel, was born the following year; son Danny was born in 1959. Drexler did a brief stint in 1951 as a professional wrestler using the name Rosa Carlo, the Mexican Spitfire, an experience on which she drew for the 1972 novel *To Smithereens* (Solochek 1970: 9). When her 1964 play *Home Movies* was produced at Judson Poets Theatre in 1964, garnering her first Obie award (there would be two more), she had established a respectable career as a visual artist, emerging as a painter on the Pop Art scene (see Feinstein 2007). Both the plastic arts and novels would remain ongoing pursuits for which Drexler received serious attention and critical praise, even as she kept her hand in as a playwright. Art journalist Douglas C. McGill summed up Drexler's creative universe by borrowing from her own description of the zany display she encountered in training for her wrestling gig alongside circus performers: 'Things flying in all directions' (McGill 1986: C28). For *Village Voice* columnist Howard Smith,

Drexler is 'the ultimate Renaissance Woman' (Smith 1973: 40). Critic Rosette Lamont quoted a line from Drexler's 1979 novel *Starburn* to describe the writer herself: 'born without natural defenses against originality' (Lamont 1983: 7).

The genesis and production of Drexler's breakthrough 1964 play *Home Movies* is well described by 1960s theatre scholar Stephen J. Bottoms. Drexler started with 'a collection of whimsical jottings' (Bottoms 2004: 154) that she showed to critic Richard Gilman, who believed the Judson Poets Theatre might provide a home for the work. The Judson was one of the seminal and most important of the Off-Off Broadway theatres, presenting its first play in 1961, but building on a tradition of supporting contemporary art and modern dance. In the hands of director Lawrence Kornfeld and with music by Al Carmines, Drexler's show, whose text is 'largely composed of recycled language' (Bottoms 2004: 156),was staged 'as a kind of homage to burlesque ... [featuring] a booth stage, complete with show curtain ... mimicking the layout of a small burlesque house ... [the] costumes, too, impl[ying] a burlesquing of burlesque conventions, with the female characters being dressed in a variety of bizarre, overtly sexualized outfits' (Bottoms 2004: 157). The central character, Mrs. Verdun, is an upper-bourgeois housewife who 'enjoys herself and others, sexually and conversationally, although pseudo-religiosity is the operational framework' (Drexler 1967: 77). Surrounding her are her controlling husband, 'an exercise nut'; their homely, no-filters, daughter, Vivienne, described as 'a maiden in her thirties [who] longs to be nude in mixed company' (Drexler 1967: 77); and stereotypical, over-the-top renditions of a gay man named Peter Peterouter; an intellectual (man); a 'colored maid', dressed to vaguely suggest Josephine Baker at her least clothed; and a pair of Catholic clerics named Father Shenanagan ('a bit of a lecher') and Sister Thalia ('a refugee from an Eisenstein movie') (Drexler 1967: 78).

Plot is beside the point in this skewering of middle-class propriety and religiosity. ('I've never been strong on plots. I'm more interested in language,' Drexler stated in a 1980 interview [Shewey 1980: 57].) Drexler's work, while verbally dexterous, uses wordplay less because of aspirations to the literary than in the interest of what can be realized in unfettered, embodied stage time. Singing, stripping, punning, and id-driven acting out characterize the characters in performance, the experience of which was summed up by critic Jerry Tallmer in his assessment of Kornfeld's direction: '[It] seizes exactly on the essence – and gives us *theater* (1964: n.p.; emphasis added). Many of the scenes involve seduction, wordplay-driven banter – or even simply chatter – or self-revelation, the latter often in the form of song and dance. Bottoms compares *Home Movies* to Gertrude Stein's oeuvre, noting that 'the primary virtues of both lie in their rhythmic, playful, enigmatic use of language: they are full of strange rhymes, grotesque puns, silly songs, mock dialects and foreign phrases, rat-a-tat word association exchanges, and vaudevillian "bits"' (2004: 155). But it is not only the words as language and the dialogue as interaction that give the play its essence. Home movies – short films typically shot by family members to memorialize family events or activities and not generally of interest beyond an intimate circle – were a phenomenon that gained widespread popularity among Americans after World War II. (The technology to facilitate amateur filmmaking existed earlier, but post-war developments made it less expensive and less cumbersome.) Such films – often silent and usually black and white, as were still photos taken with mass-market cameras until the 1960s – are typically a mix of guile and naivety. Family members put on their best face for the camera ('smile after you blow out the candles!') or are caught unawares in their daily activities, not always to flattering ends. The fact that home movies are shot by and of people who know each other well means that they are often imagined as little more than mementos, leading to combinations of quirky behaviour ('just be yourself') and stylized, culturally predictable self-fashioning (often understood as individuality by the person so fashioning him or herself). Drexler's play both embraces this amateur, *entre nous*, aesthetic and skewers its complacent exuberance.

Parts of the dialogue in Drexler's *Home Movies* today seem almost embarrassingly politically incorrect, such as the hyper-exaggerated 'darky' dialect assigned to the maid, Violet. Repeating the message the 'intellectual', Charles, has whispered in her ear, Violet informs the lustful Vivienne, who has exposed a daisy-covered breast to Charles (asserting her belief that her absent father has arranged for Charles to visit her): 'Mistah Chas. saydat no figit dike goin' tell him whose nooky ta tickle' (Drexler 1967: 94). Yet Violet, who deploys the dialect inconsistently (perhaps strategically), is also revealed to be educated, organized, efficient, and equal to all the other characters as a wily observer of others' motives and a participant in the battle of wits. Consider how, in the above line, she is both outsized stereotype and voice of an outrageous sexual directness unimaginable in a play figured for mainstream consumption. Violet, as a character, is in on Drexler's game – a player rather than a tool. Like a number of the other characters, she is given lines that read like throwaways but do their share of skewering highbrow and middlebrow (white) assumptions of business as usual. When Peter Peterouter arrives, Violet announces him, adding, 'He's wearin' my favorite perfume, "White Shoulders." It never comes true, though' (Drexler 1967: 84). Elsewhere, Drexler embeds observations equivalently trenchant and even more theoretically sophisticated. When Mrs Verdun introduces the intellectual Charles to another character, she says, 'My, my, an author. I've always wanted to write myself, but I've been written already' (Drexler 1967: 94). The double use of 'myself' as both direct object and reflexive modifier may whiz by in performance (or not); the thumbnail deconstructive assessment would, in 1964, for any who caught it, be a gem and not the predictable rhinestone it was destined to become in later decades in the hands of students for whom Barthes and Derrida would be assigned reading.

The fate of *Home Movies* can, in retrospect, be read as a sign of things to come for the 'weird', 'ultimate Renaissance Woman' unafraid to fly in all directions. Orson Bean's interest in moving the production to the Provincetown Playhouse for a commercial run at first blush seems like the next chapter in a success story. But in a 1971 *New York Times* article, Drexler relates how the compromises she was expected to make spelled exactly the kind of obligatory sellout that Pasolli would associate with professionalization in his 1968 article (1971: 1):

> Orson demanded that I take the word 'friggin' out of the play because he said that it would offend the ladies from New Jersey ... I had thought it was a mild expletive used by children ... Barbara Ann Teer, who later won a Vernon Rice Memorial award for her performance [as Violet] ... believed that Orson wanted the word taken out of the play because it was said to a white woman.... At one point during the run of the show, Channel 13 [public television] asked to have some performers do one or two numbers from 'Home Movies.' ... While Sudie [Bond] was rehearsing 'No-one Wants to Pluck My Daisies,' we got word from the executives upstairs that she couldn't sing the song unless the word pluck was either deleted or changed.... But why did I have to change the word pluck, I asked. 'Because you know what pluck rhymes with,' was the answer. All this ridiculous stuff was going on just six years ago!

Drexler, of course, wrote her article with an eye to justifying herself in the eyes of mainstream readers in a paper whose critic, seven years earlier, had reviewed the Provincetown production of *Home Movies* and called it 'a dismal mélange [of] questionable worth and taste', finding it 'difficult to identify the objects that Miss Drexler is jabbing at' (in Bottoms 2004: 162). The word 'friggin' stayed, but the nervous mindset was clear. What in March, at a wholly alternative venue, had been 'freebooting and hilarious' (Tallmer 1964: n.p.), became illegible and offensive in a more professional context. Bottoms points out that *Home Movies* was the 'first off-off-Broadway production to move intact to a "proper" theatre (nine months before the "New Playwrights" triple bill of [Paul] Foster, [Sam] Shepard, and [Lanford]

Wilson plays at the Cherry Lane' (2004: 162). Whether Drexler was ahead of her time; whether she offended particularly for being a woman whose work is 'comic ... [and] whose world is faintly scatological' (Gillespie 1980: 4); or whether she was less interested in the personal facets of working within the system to achieve commercial success than she was in doing her own thing, she would continue to write plays for another two decades but would earn the bulk of her money for her novels and paintings.

Drexler's other plays continued to manifest what Rosette Lamont calls 'a satirical circus approach to our pop culture' (Lamont 1983: 8). *The Line of Least Existence* (published in 1967 and presented at Judson Poets in 1969) depicts the collision of a Hungarian immigrant Pschug (complete with wacky, overblown faux dialect) looking for his lost daughter; the sexually overactive and manipulative daughter; a self-serving, sadistic psychiatrist who has treated the father, slept with the daughter, and misdiagnosed both of them; the psychiatrist's wife; and an anthropomorphized talking dog who may be the savviest character in the play. Pschug calls out genuine corruption in a crazily English-as-a-second language rendition of the language of pop culture: 'Attention competent department! White slavery traders, racketeering, kidnapping, immoral terror gang interest broke. ... I want real U.S. Constitution and law, not a jungle Al Capone law prevail which used even today' (Drexler 1967: 55) The dog is glad of his non-human status but would rather be a machine, as 'machines mean something to people' (Drexler 1967: 55). Both the psychiatrist and his wife spend time wearing microphones and talking into them – an early comment, perhaps, on the embryonic phase of a narcissism some might see in the later explosion and ubiquity of cell phones and social media. In *Softly, and Consider the Nearness* (published in 1967 and produced at the Manhattan Theatre Club in 1973) an unmarried woman named Nona enjoys her closest relationship with her television set, a device with which she flirts, for which she dresses up, and to which she confesses both her loneliness and her love. The discussion of knobs and tubes is, of course, dated, but Drexler's prescience about media-defined identity (recall the 'already written' Mrs. Verdun) remains on target. T.V. (the character's name) reminds Nona that s/he can 'only transmit the messages of others', later replying to Nona's plea for protection that 'I can only protect you from your own thoughts' (Drexler 1967: 194, 203).

The humour in Drexler's plays is parsed by Lamont as 'a mask for tears, tenderness and profound humanity' (1983: 8). Nineteen years after *Home Movies*, critics saw in Drexler's *Starburn* (presented at Theatre for the New City under John Vaccaro's direction and based on Drexler's novel of the same name) 'a wonderful '60s outrageousness' in a play 'as fresh and provocative as a page from *Mad Magazine* [b]ut ... also rooted in the ancient tradition of

Commedia Dell'arte' (Blumenthal 1983: 76; Lamont 1983: 8). In other words, Drexler's work was redolent of a particular era in US culture, but also in sync with longstanding comic traditions of social commentary. *Starburn* features a female punk band whose main character has been accused of murder. Violence, sexuality, and women who are misunderstood, misdiagnosed, or mistreated remained Drexler themes. 'I'm disturbed by violence, lack of love, people who have mental troubles, and I want to show this on stage', she told an interviewer in 1983 (Lamont 1983: 8). She was also disturbed by the lack of opportunities not only for herself, but also for women playwrights overall. In 1980, after a long break from playwriting, she produced three plays; she also said that concentrating on paintings and novels in the 1970s was largely because (Shewey 1980: 57):

> Nobody took me up on anything. Joe Papp was going to do my rock opera *The Line of Least Existence*, and when the Public Theater was being built he took me around and said, 'I want you to make this your home.' Then he changed his mind—I don't know why, although once he told me I reminded him of his sister, maybe that had something to do with it— and I felt so rejected after that I just went into other things.

She had vented her frustration seven years earlier in a mock interview conducted by and with herself in the *New York Times*, where she answered the question (her own) about how one could tell that a play submitted to a producer anonymously had been written by a woman (1973: n.p.).

> A thorough examination of any work will reveal its sex at the moment of heightened excitation. In a female's play the capitals will be shorter, and an excessive use of the letters O and P may be noticed. Thus, POP, POPE, DOPE, and OOPS take on genital overtones. The female play is open and passive. Furtive events crawl right through any play written by any female playwright.

Arch sarcasm aside, Drexler pointed out that rejection in commercial theatre affected both men and women playwrights, although she also underscored how few women playwrights enjoyed productions at all; two were represented on Broadway when her interview was published; she called Off-Broadway equally bleak. She would spend most of the 1970s, however, pursuing other creative outlets. She won an Emmy for writing a Lily Tomlin television special in 1973; she adapted four screenplays as novels under the pseudonym Julia Sorel; and she wrote four original novels. She was also the subject of a 1975 film, *Who Does She Think She is?*, by Patricia Lewis Jaffe and Gaby Rogers, in which her daily world and family life appeared in the context of Drexler talking about herself. When she returned to writing plays, she would win her second Obie in 1979 for *The Writer's Opera* and her third in 1985 for *Transients Welcome*. This group of three one-act plays includes *Room 17C*, a rewriting of *Death of a Salesman* in which Linda, Willy's wife (surnamed 'Normal') has become the family breadwinner, her depressed husband telephoning her in the hotel room where she is on the road garnering sales. Toby Zinman reads in the play a tension between destiny and freedom (Zinman 2014: 105). Linda sees selling as a form of parasitism, its practitioners spending their lives hawking wares for which people have no real need. Clearsighted, perhaps, but Linda perishes in a hotel fire when she returns to answer the phone, knowing Willy is calling, an instance, perhaps of wifely 'destiny'/entrapment trumping the possibility of freedom/escape. The play also includes a talking cockroach (shades of the dog in *The Line of Least Existence*) who represents freedom. Zinman points to the 'emphasis on sexual creepiness as well as an assault on the revered icons of the culture' (2014: 106) in Drexler's plays as well as in her art. Zinman also asserts that the play's 'mash-up seems distinctly contemporary, not least because of its adolescent wish to shock and show off and simultaneously mock the showing off' (2014: 107).

In 2007, Drexler was the subject of a major article in *Art in America*, published on the heels of a retrospective exhibit of her paintings from the 1960s at the Pace Wildenstein gallery in New York (Feinstein 2007: 174). The six paintings reproduced in the magazine are a partial visual correlative to the plays of the 1960s. All of the plastic artworks are collages for which Drexler found 'compelling photographic images in newspapers' (Feinstein 2007: 175) which she then assembled purposefully and painted over, often using very bright colours. Themes are violence, racism, and sexism. The largest of the paintings in the exhibition (four feet by twelve feet) was called *Home Movies*. Its theme was violence; its métier was a kind of storytelling across the canvas that included humour, confrontation, and pathos. Around the same time, Drexler published her ninth novel, *Vulgar Lives*. Writer/art historian Roni Feinstein concluded that Drexler 'is a national treasure and it is high time that her works of the 1960s, which have been resurrected and rediscovered any number of times, receive their due acclaim' (Feinstein 2007: 177). Indeed, Drexler's works had been shown with those of Claes Oldenburg and Jim Dine, and she was represented by the same gallery, Kornblee, as Dan Flavin, Howard Hodgkin, Janet Fish, and Malcolm Morley. As Drexler herself observed in 1986 of the 1960s art world, 'Women were not considered salable at the time' (McGill 1986: C28). Some of her 1960s work was purchased by the Hirshorn collection of the Smithsonian (Washington, DC), the Whitney

Museum (New York), and the Walker Art Center (Minneapolis). She nonetheless hedged her bets and kept writing.

In May 2015, the *New York Times* magazine ran a photo feature called 'Works in Progress', showcasing 11 women headlined as a very small sampling of the 'female artists now in their 70s, 80s and 90s we should have known about decades ago' (Hoban 2015). Drexler, 88 and still painting, looks a bit like a renegade hippie, with her longish hair, bangs, flowered headband, no-nonsense shoes, and black pants and shirt. The six paintings reproduced with the thumbnail biography fairly jump off the screen with their vibrancy and directness. They are erotic, violent, colourful, compelling, sometimes hard to look at and always hard to look away from. They are legible without being glib; they are fun; they are serious; they pull no punches; they take no prisoners; and they offer no apologies. Like the plays of which they are contemporaries.

Works cited

Blumenthal, E. (1983), 'Burning Bright,' *Village Voice*, 8 Mar., 1983, 76.

Bottoms, S.J. (2004), *Playing Underground: A Critical History of the 1960s Off-Off-Broadway Movement*, Ann Arbor: University of Michigan.

'Briefs on the Arts,' *New York Times*, 1 Sept., 1973, Arts: 12.

Cohen, P. (2008), 'Charging Bias by Theaters, Female Playwrights to Hold Meeting,' *New York Times*, 25 October, 2008: C1.

Drexler, R. (1967), The Line of Least Existence *and Other Plays*, New York: Random House.

Drexler, R. (1971), 'Notes on the Occasion of having 'Line of Least Existence & Other Plays' Remaindered at Marboro Book Shops,' *New York Times*, 7 Nov. 1971, Arts: 1.

Drexler, R. (1973), in G. Cryer, 'Where are the Women Playwrights?' *New York Times*, 20 May 1973: 129.

Feinstein, R. (2007), 'Strangers No More,' *Art in America*, June/July 2007: 174–177.

Gillespie, P. (1980), 'American Women Dramatists: 1960–1980,' Paper [typescript] presented at the Annual Meeting of the Southeastern Theater Conference, Nashville, TN, 5–9 Mar., 1980.

Gilman, R. (1967), 'Introduction,' in R. Drexler, The Line of Least Existence *and Other Plays*, New York: Random House.

Hoban, P. (2015), 'Works in Progress,' *New York Times* magazine, 15 May 2015. Available at: www.nytimes.com/interactive/2015/05/15/t-magazine/17older-female-artists-agnes-dene-herrera-rockbourne-farmanfarmaian.html?_r=0> (last accessed 11 August 2015).

Kempton, S. (1968), 'Rosalyn Drexler; Seeking the Life of Most Existence', *Village Voice*, 4 April, 1968: n.p.

Lamont, R. (1983), 'Rosalyn Drexler: The Desire to Astonish Oneself', *Other Stages*, 10 March, 1983: 7.

McGill, D. C. (1986), 'Art People: She Also was a Wrestler', *New York Times*, 15 August, 1986: C28.

Pasolli, R. (1968), 'The New Playwrights' Scene of the Sixties: Jerome Max is Alive and Well and Living in Rome . . .', *The Drama Review: TDR*, 13.1: 150–162.

Sands, E.G. (2009), 'Opening the Curtain on Playwright Gender: An Integrated Economic Analysis of Discrimination in American Theater', Undergraduate Thesis, Princeton University. Available at: http://graphics8.nytimes.com/packages/pdf/theater/Openingthecurtain.pdf. (last accessed 6 August 2015).

Schapp, D. (1985), 'The Author was a Wrestler', *New York Herald Tribune*, 11 January 1985: n.p.

Shewey, D. (1980), 'Playing Around', *Soho Weekly News*, 21 May 1980: 57.

Smith, H. (1973), untitled clipping, *Village Voice*, 7 June 1973: 40.

Solochek, B. (1970), 'At Home with Rosalyn Drexler', *New York Post* magazine, 8 August 1970: 9.

Tallmer, J. (1964), 'The Corpse Sits Up', *New York Post* 23 March 1964, n.p.

Zinman, T. (2014), 'Arthur Miller', in *Replay: Classic Modern Drama Reimagined*, London: Bloomsbury, 99–111.

Part Five

Film and Beat Performance

Kerouac's *The Subterraneans*: When Film Adaptation Becomes Cultural Betrayal

Sara Villa

In July 1960, advertisements for the movie adaptation of Jack Kerouac's novel *The Subterraneans* started being posted in California. The posters said: 'Love among the new Bohemians!' and 'These are the Subterraneans: today's young rebels – who live and love in a world of their own, this is the story told to the hot rhythms of fabulous jazz'. The movie would have its American premiere in New York City soon afterwards; its European distribution happened a year later. From these very first public images of the film, one thing was immediately clear to the audience. The main African-American female protagonist, Mardou, who also has some Cherokee roots stemming from her father's family, had been normalized. Here was, in her place, French actress and ballet dancer Leslie Caron, who had been transported from the 1958 romantic comedy *Gigi* and was now cast as a young French bohemian girl.

It was evident that the betrayal of the feminine role of Mardou had a double connotation: racial and ethnic, related to both her African American and Native American background. Her gender-inflected position in society, in spite of her apparent initial freedom, was still that of an eventually subdued and submissive woman who, at the end of the film, was about to marry, while pregnant with Leo's baby. This finale blatantly negated Kerouac's feminist ending of the novel, where Mardou stresses how her independence is far too important to be sacrificed for the sake of a dysfunctional relationship: 'I want to be independent, like I say' (Kerouac 1958: 126). This chapter will analyze how the reactionary erasure of Kerouac's context related to gender and ethnicity was intertwined with the desire to depict the women of the Beat Generation as rebellious and hysteria-prone and needing to be tamed. This process would have allowed a narrative reconversion of the main female character, in the Hollywood style of the adaptation, to a much more heteronymic and trite idea of femininity. Such a patriarchal perspective implied, first and foremost that, to a woman, marriage, a housewife's role exclusively centred on procreation and *bricolage*, cooking and needlework were their only possible contributions to society and human culture.

If the African American and Cherokee background of the main female character is stripped away from the very beginning of the film, on the other hand, the intellectually engaging, cultivated, and artistic nature of Mardou's identity, which recalled so many female Beat artists of the time, such as Anne Waldman, Hettie Jones, Diane di Prima, ruth weiss and Joanne Kyger, to name but a few (Johnson and Grace 2002: 1–24), is slowly demonstrated to be joined with a psychological instability that only pregnancy and an old-fashioned reparatory wedding would cure. This double layer of betrayal may be the actual reason why the movie, in spite of a renowned cast, stunning jazz music (composed by André Prévin and played by Gerry Mulligan's band, who were some of the best jazz musicians of the time) and Hollywood publicity and distribution, was an utter flop, both in the USA and in Europe. Today, copies of the adaptation are much harder to find than those of its Beat contemporary *Pull My Daisy* (1959), a short movie directed by Robert Frank and Albert Leslie with music by David Amram and adlibbed narration by Jack Kerouac. In the latter case, however, the Beats had no interference from heteronymic culture in any of the production processes of *Pull My Daisy*, with the result that it became one of the most genuine and acclaimed Beat films, as well as a core chapter of the New American Cinema. In the meantime, *The Subterraneans* and its clichéd negative depiction of the Beat Generation – especially Beat female artists – quickly disappeared from the scene.

Why is it important to consider this text which vanished from memory so easily and so fast? One answer is that it mirrors problematic cultural elements that are still, unfortunately, not fully solved today – even beyond the problematic genre of cinematographic adaptation – if we consider that in 2011 alone (to give just one example), according to a report by the Ralph J. Bunche Center for African American Studies at UCLA, 'minorities [were still] underrepresented by a factor of more than 3 to 1 among lead roles in film' (Vv. Aa. 2014: 6).

Obviously, the historical panorama surrounding the production of *The Subterraneans* highly influenced its erasure of one of the most fundamental and discussed topics of Kerouac's novel: the evolution of a mixed-race relationship. The Civil Rights Act of 1964 was passed only four years after the premiere of the movie, several months after the iconic march on Washington of 28 August 1963; the overall climate in many US states was not one of interracial acceptance. The famous *Loving v. Virginia* Supreme Court ruling, which invalidated laws forbidding interracial marriage, would not be passed until 1967. Until that time, 16 American states still had anti-miscegenation laws as part of their legal corpus; talking about a mixed couple on screen would have implied facing state censorship in all of these areas. Moreover, even the internal Motion Picture Production Code, which was still partially applied in mainstream cinema production, included miscegenation in its list of forbidden topics, sadly just after white slavery (Lewis, 2000: 301). In this context it is helpful to understand how brave Kerouac himself had been, with his editor, to publish a novel in which a highly educated African-American and Native American woman shares her life and love with a rebellious white artist. In 1957, just one year before the book was released by Grove Press, Arkansas Governor Orval Faubus ordered that his state's National Guard unit block the admission of nine African American students to Little Rock's Central High School. Clearly, the idea of applying the Federal law and allowing non-segregated educational environments was against his agenda. President Eisenhower responded by sending federal troops to enforce the court order for integration.

This makes one understand, lamentably, the cultural origins of the ridiculous white, French, filmic Mardou who appears in the first scene of the movie. Her agency is here reduced to following the hints of her therapist; her behaviour is an unbalanced shifting from sadness to laughter as in the most stereotypical depiction of hysteria; and we are already warned that her bohemian freedom is nothing but a facade: what she herself may want is a simple marriage. In this initial sequence, Mardou is fighting with an ex-lover to whom she says: 'You cannot reject me, my analyst does not want me to be rejected.' Leo is seeing her for the first time as he hears her former boyfriend say: 'You do not want love, you want marriage.' Thus begins the process of the betrayal of Kerouac's character which will see Mardou's pregnant and soon-to-be wife at the very end of the film (MacDougall 1960: scene 2).

If Mardou's race is erased, her overall gender role in this scene and in the rest of the movie also mirrors the cultural environment of the late 1950s and 1960s, and the overall societal attitude of the time with regard to liberated femininities. Until 1960 it was not uncommon to apply medical treatments as invasive as electroshock therapy on women who were judged to be showing initial symptoms of hysteria, which were extremely broadly conceived (see Waldman 1997: 142–46). Once again, this is another factor that may have not only influenced, but also medically and culturally supported, the depiction of Mardou as psychologically unstable because of her rebellious freedom. Her lack of balance is, in the movie, further stressed by her spiteful attitude towards religious authority. As Mardou is meeting with a priest who distributes free food to young artists, the girl boldly asks him: 'How much spaghetti does it take to save a soul, Reverend?' to which he replies: 'How much bitterness to destroy one?' (MacDougall 1960: scene 3). The Beat defiance towards religious institutions as a site where gender roles were still far from being equal is here trivialized as a reckless and childlike challenging of an authority which is described as charitable and generous above all – once again casting a negative light on the Beat women as immature and spiteful.

Besides Mardou, the only other independent female character in the film, Roxanne, who was invented in the film script, does not seem to be able to escape these same patriarchal parameters and anti-Beat biases. In one of the saddest final scenes of the movie, she leaves San Francisco and says goodbye to Leo, after admitting: 'Today I bought my first skirt. I hadn't bought one since I left home. [. . .] You made me know that I can love and I hate you for that [. . .] I was never lonely before and now I am most lonely' (MacDougall 1960: scene 10). Roxanne seems to move away from San Francisco not to regain her lost freedom, but rather because she knows she cannot have the man she wants. The taming of her bohemian identity, now defeated in front of a love for Leo, is iconized by her buying a skirt and fully abandoning her rebellious black trousers.

Talking about liberated femininity seemed, in mainstream cinema, as hard as representing race, and the phenomenon did not seem to be fully erased towards the end of the 1960s. In 1967, *Guess Who's Coming to Dinner*, the first Hollywood blockbuster to openly discuss interracial relationships, still did so within the context of a soon-to-be married couple, with a stereotypical middle-class female protagonist and in the easy genre of romantic comedy. This movie was produced a good seven years after *The Subterraneans*, six months after inter-racial marriage was fully legalized in the USA, yet its characters were far from being liberated: the African American man played by Sidney Poitier is accepted due to his social position as a doctor, and the middle-class fiancée is the opposite of an independent, artistic Beat poet like Diane di Prima, who describes the New York City years in which she wrote her first two books as a moment in her life in which she 'had come into poverty as into an inheritance' (di Prima 2001: 126).

In 1953, Jack Kerouac first met the woman who would inspire him to create Mardou, the heroine of *The Subterraneans*. Alene Lee, the real Mardou, was rebellious and creative, à la di Prima. Lee was a cultivated and independent African American woman with whom he would have a passionate affair. Unlike her film counterpart, she was an intellectual who worked for a health book company to pay the bills and who openly questioned the capitalistic, submissive young identities of the time: 'In the '50s world it seemed before you could do what you wanted to do, you had to be able to function in the straight business world and a lot of people were having trouble coming to terms with it [. . .] I felt, you know, here we are and what are we doing? And why am I in this office, typing up these bills, answering this correspondence?'

(Alene Lee in Gifford and Lee 1978: 175). This was why the well-read Alene preferred to spend her free time sharing conversations and intellectual stimuli with the Beats, becoming a friend of Allen Ginsberg, who introduced her to Kerouac.

After their breakup, Kerouac would spend three exhausting days typing his first novel written in his unique spontaneous style, as described in his *Essentials of Spontaneous Prose* (1953). Inspired by jazz prosody and improvisation, and completed in a caffeinated 72-hour trance-like method, the novel is far more courageous than the movie in its description of the problems related to mixed couples as well as in the ways in which an undercurrent of primitivistic fascination with the Other can so easily pollute love. This is particularly true when the affective bond ties an independent young woman and a man who, like the narrator of the novel, defines himself as unsettled, fragile and unconfident. Leo Percepied in the book is, in fact, a weak man, clearly showing a mixture of genuine interest in the woman's culture and background, and an evident fetishization of the exotic ethnicity of Mardou – 'Negro mother dead for birth of her unknown Cherokee-halfbreed father' (Kerouac 1958: 25) – mixed with sudden, passionate love, and truthful caring. Some critics, like Jon Panish and Warren French, have strongly argued that the real problem with *The Subterraneans*, an element which would have been impossible to put on screen, is that Leo is blatantly, unforgivably, racist. I do not fully agree with them on this point, just as I do not consider correct Kenneth Rextroth's famous review of the novel where he says that 'Kerouac knew nothing about jazz or Negroes and the story was all about them' (Nicosia, 1983: 568). In the latter comment, the fact that Rexroth had discovered his wife's betrayal with a friend of Kerouac may have just slightly influenced the tone of this review and his subsequent grudge towards him (Nicosia 1983: 569). Regarding the considerations related to Leo's racism, I think, rather, that the character reveals more complex layers in his attitude towards ethnicity in the novel, something which mirrors Kerouac's own internal struggles. What the movie misses is, for instance, the bold description of the white character's contradictory feelings towards Mardou. This, to me, openly aims to denounce how an individual's perception of race and gender can be so highly influenced by the hegemonic discourses surrounding race in the society in which he lives. This may be the reason why many of the critics who label Leo Percepied in the novel as racist always quote one of the most controversial passages in the text, where he thinks things such as (Kerouac 1958: 27):

I wake up from the scream of breeders and see beside me the Negro woman with parted lips sleeping and little bits of white pillow stuffing in her black hair, feel almost revulsion, realize what a beast I am for feeling anything near it, grape little sweet body naked on the restless sheets of the night before excitement [...] I got up and began to dress, apologize, she lay like a little mummy in the sheet and cast the serious brown eyes on me, like eyes of Indian watchfulness in a wood, like with the brown lashes suddenly rising with black lashes to reveal sudden fantastic whites of eye with the brown glittering iris centre, the seriousness of her face accentuated by the slightly Mongoloid as if of a boxer nose and the cheeks puffed a little from sleep, like the face on a beautiful porphyry mask found long ago and Aztechan.

However, these critics also forget to point out that Percepied is meditating after a night of heavy drinking, and he subsequently admits that he has to 'straighten out his hangover'(Keroauc 1958: 27). One may argue that *in vino veritas*, Leo is giving voice to his inherent racism. A more subtle and complex perspective, though, could see this terrifying passage as the voice of the society which is surrounding the narrator, blaming him for loving a black woman, and influencing his subconscious thoughts by making him drunkenly embody the disgusting position of a racist and sexist man, who is also, at the same time, fetishizing the racial otherness of his lover with the final comparison to a beautiful Aztec mask. The possibility of the external world influencing Leo up to this point could stem from his fragile male ego, his being a loser and an outsider as described in the first pages of the novel. Ironically, Leo himself does not seem to fit in the American society of the time, not because of his being black, but due to his 'Canuk' roots, which allow his peers to label him as a masochistic 'other' in the book. Leo's friend Sam in the novel says: 'The trouble with you, Percepied, you've got rotten bags in the bottom of your store, You Canuks are really all alike and I don't believe you'll admit it when you die'(Kerouac 1958: 67). Is this level of internalized alterity one of the additional reasons why Leo has such contradictory views regarding his love for Mardou?

If we consider the intricacy of this context, the revelation of the issue of racism surrounding an interracial relationship – but also showing its fragility from the inside – it is clear that choosing a white female actress to play Mardou and a stereotypical white male lover who is also an American (not a Canadian) to play Leo removes so many of the cardinal and difficult layers of the original text. It waters down the thorough, brutally honest, discussion of gender and racial issues from within a complicated and problematic mixed couple to fit the agenda of Hollywood's white romantic plots. I am not arguing here for a simplistic ethical split where the book stands on the side of the subversive, original, and politically correct, while the movie does not. What I think is sadly lost in the movie is the actual elaboration of Kerouac's treatment of the interracial issue, as well as of the gender role embodied by Mardou, which are two of the most interesting and multi-layered aspects of the novel and of the actual relationship between Kerouac and Alene Lee. With the erasure of Mardou's background on screen, all of the contradictory personal feelings and societal influences that run through Leo Percepied's mind are also irreversibly lost. The film chooses not to show a black, independent Mardou as it also hides a Leo who is an unstable artist and young man, bewildered by the freedom of his black-Native lover, as well as infatuated with her ethnicity in a way that is partially fetishistic but also hints at his own unresolved struggle with racist pressures from his socio-cultural context.

Similarly riddled with contradictions, in fact, was the actual relationship between Alene and Kerouac. The young writer felt the pressure of both the anti-miscegenation culture still lingering in American society, and the internal familiar racism of his mother, Gabrielle, who had once sent him a newspaper clipping about rape in the subway, scrawling on it, 'There's your damned niggers!' (Gabrielle Kerouac in Maher 2004: 277). As Alene Lee recalls in an interview, she and Kerouac truly loved each other: 'he had an openness, a brash quality' and she 'liked Jack, at times like a brother, someone [she] knew well' (Alene Lee in Gifford and Lee 1978: 175–76). But both 'were really play-acting at serious life' and Jack was 'insecure and paranoid to the point where if I went to the hall, he imagined I was sleeping with someone outside the hall' (Alene Lee in Gifford and Lee 1978: 175–76). His possessive love for Alene and her otherness, as well and his drunken paranoia and contradictory feelings mixed with internalized racist pressures, are honestly represented in the book in the fragility of Leo, who is depicted from the very beginning as a complex, haunted, anti-hero.

Considering this multi-layered nature of the literary text, the film adaptation enacts both a racial and gender betrayal of the book and an oversimplification of the characters; this is understandable only according to Hollywood's own internal rules. Such a disastrous film version was, naturally, inconceivable to Kerouac. When the writer saw the preview of the movie, produced by Metro Goldwin Mayer, and was asked to personally sign the posters of the production, he refused: he was traumatized. As Ellis Amburn subtly reminds us in her biography of Kerouac, the writer, speaking to John Clellon Holmes, 'described the film as a "travesty" of his novel' (Kerouac in Amburn 1998: 310), while Barry Gifford and Lawrence Lee, in *Jack's Book*, recall that 'Robert Boles, who was Kerouac's neighbor and friend at Hyannis, remembered harangues of Kerouac against MGM for the scene where Leo slaps Mardou during a quarrel' (Gifford and Lee 1978: 214).

The movie becomes a semi-educational 1960s taming of the French White Shrew. Its epitome is reached at the end, again by a shocking betrayal of Kerouac's intentions. The film, in fact, ends with Leo going back to Mardou, who is pregnant, to guarantee that he will give his surname to the baby, marry her: his final line is a neat 'You'll cook, I'll write'. Ironically, in the book it is Mardou who clearly says how men mistakenly think of women as possessions, and how she will rebel against it and embody a different type of femininity: '[men] consider women as prizes instead of human beings, well I may be in the middle of all this shit, but I certainly don't want any part of it' she says 'in her sweet cultured hip tones of new generation' (Kerouac 1958: 25).

Screenwriter Robert Thom, who was in charge of *The Subterraneans'* script, tried to give some initial room to an almost feminist agenda in the film when he conceived the character of Roxanne, who, as we have already remarked, is an artist, dancer and independent soul, introduced as a strong-willed woman more similar to a true Beat female artist. However, the initial illusion of gender liberation is soon broken by the constant criticism of the rest of the Beat crew, as well as her moving back to a more subdued, in-gown persona who will leave the bohemian noise of San Francisco for the calm of a quiet farm land or island, somewhere (MacDougall 1960: scene 10).

Without any doubt, the Hollywood and societal prescription did not make Thom's adaptation work easy. After this flop, his career would completely shift and he would then become famous for his action-movie *Death Race*. Its plot is summarized on the movie cover as: 'Ex-con Jensen Ames is forced by the warden of a notorious prison to compete in our post-industrial world's most popular sport: a car race in which inmates must brutalize and kill one another on the road to victory.' Was he better suited for action movies than for the film adaptation of highly subversive interracial love stories, or rather, was Hollywood's internal code and the still-unachieved racial integration in the USA forcing him to make narrative choices that he would have much more happily avoided? It is certain that with this adaptation, the movie became a parable of how a Beatnik (in its sense as a derogatory term used by the mainstream to describe the Beats as rebellious Communist types) woman can be handled and reconfigured into the most docile and adorable housewife or, if unmarried, like Roxanne, will be made to wander in desert lands as an outcast. It is more than evident how the most stereotypically patriarchal definition of 1950s and 1960s standard gender roles is constantly reaffirmed throughout the film and finally epitomized in Leo's hinting in the scene that ends the film that Mardou will become nothing but a good mother and housewife. Maybe this very finale was the ultimate trigger which made even a conservative magazine like *Time* write, on 20 June 1960, that 'This picture bears about as much relationship to [Kerouac's] novel as Hollywood does to Endsville' (Maher 2004: 402). The producer of the movie, Arthur Freed, was coming directly from the musical comedy scene of *Singing in the Rain* and *An American in Paris*, and perhaps the tendency of the musical world to prefer a typical happy ending and mostly antifeminist plot may have equally influenced the distorted direction of the adaptation. The critics of the time did not forget to mention that, even through this perspective, *The Subterraneans* looked like a failed musical: Hollis Alpert's unflattering comment in the *Saturday Review* argued that the film was 'like one of Freed's previous musicals, except that both score and lyrics were missing' (Alpert in Amburn 1998: 291). The distortion of Kerouac's ending is, indeed, surreal. In the novel, the troubled affair ends in a betrayal and hurtful breakup separating the lovers, with Mardou reconfirming her need for freedom. Leo then concludes with his iconic line: 'And I go home having lost her love. And write this book' (Kerouac 1958: 126). This reveals the autobiographical nature of the plot, overlapping the fragile and torn protagonist of the novel with the author's own identity. Here, the book works as an attempt to exorcise a failed love story, with Kerouac's new sense of inadequacy following this affective trauma, as well as with the internal and external contradictions and difficulties of inter-racial relationships. The movie turns all of this into an easy-to-forget, utterly anti-Beat romantic drama.

The multiple betrayals of the original text are evident even when we pass from the macro elements of race and gender to subtle connotations of the literary protagonists. In the book, for instance, Mardou is highly independent, but, just like Leo Percepied, she is neither a stereotypical nor a negative image of bohemianism, as the film portrays. She reminds him that 'she never used drugs, she just had some junkies in her life' and the symptoms of 'insanity' in the novel are put into context and linked with forms of abuse she had suffered early in her life (Kerouac 1958: 55). Kerouac does not go so far as to connect hysteria and the pathologizing of feminine anti-hegemonic behaviour, as happens in the film, but he depicts both characters as extremely sensitive and intellectual, interested in psychoanalysis having both faced depression (which Mardou faced using clinical cures, while Leo is incapable of overcoming it and fights with increasing drunkenness). Moreover, Leo is depicted as someone who is torn between what society and his family want him to think and feel (hence his despairing tone) and what he is actually thinking abut and feeling for Mardou. In the film all this disappears. Mardou's nervous breakdown is quickly linked to her hysteria, then pregnancy; the overall solution to the problem is a nice marriage with a former bohemian and future accomplished writer. The constant parallels between Leo's sense of failure and lack of accomplishment and those of Dostoevski's main character in *Notes from the Underground* (which Kerouac identified as a major influence for the novel) are, once again, abandoned in the film's adaptation. What does remain, then, of Kerouac's original book? Racial and gender issues are negated and tamed, and the maze-like nature of the characters' identities is turned into a mere bi-dimensional caricature. Probably the only thing that was faithful to Kerouac's novel was jazz. The marvellous soundtrack was composed by Andre Prévin with some of the top musicians of the West Coast (Carmen McRae, Shelly Manne, Red Mitchell and Art Farmer), including an onscreen role given to Gerry Mulligan, who improvised in a really nice underground café in the movie. This is indeed one of the highlights of the film, as is the depiction of women in the jazz arena, which mirrors how Kerouac describes Mardou in the novel – as someone who could fully understand bebop and even sing it (Kerouac 1958: 80). However, the music was not enough to save the movie from being a flop. Most reviews were critical of the failed adaptation and, overall, its audiences barely paid back the costs of production. *The Subterraneans* was an unfaithful film version of Kerouac's movie, with a stunning jazz soundtrack, which struggles to keep the memory of this movie alive today.

Works cited

Amburn, E. (1998), *Subterranean Kerouac: The Hidden Life of Jack Kerouac*, New York: St. Martin's.

Campbell, J. (1999), 'Kerouac's Blues', *The Antioch Review*, 57.3: 363–70.

Charters, A. (1973), *A Biography of Jack Kerouac*, San Francisco: Straight Arrow.

Charters, A. (ed.), (1999), *Jack Kerouac: Selected Letters 1957–69*, New York: Viking.

Clark, T. (1990), *Jack Kerouac: A Biography*, New York: Paragon House.

Courtney, S. (2004), *Hollywood Fantasies of Miscegenation: Spectacular Narratives of Gender and Race*, Princeton: Princeton University.

di Prima, D. (2001), *Recollections of My Life as a Woman*, New York: Viking.

French, W. (1986), *Jack Kerouac*, Boston: Twayne.

Gifford, B. and Lee, L. (1978), *Jack's Book: An Oral Biography of Jack Kerouac*, New York: Thundermouth.

Grace, N. (2000), 'A White Man in Love: A Study of Race, Gender, Class and Ethnicity in Jack Kerouac's Maggie Cassidy, *The Subterraneans* and *Tristessa*', *College Literature*, 27.1: 39–62.

Johnson, R. and Grace, N. (eds), (2002), *Girls Who Wore Black: Women Writing the Beat Generation*, New Brunswick, NJ: Rutgers University.

Kerouac, J. (1958), *The Subterraneans*, New York: Grove.

Lewis, J. (2000), *Hollywood v. Hard Core: How the Struggle Over Censorship Created the Modern Film Industry*, New York: New York University.

MacDougall, R., dir. (1960), *The Subterraneans*, Los Angeles: Metro Goldwyn Mayer.

Maher, P., Jr. (2004), *Kerouac: His Life and Work*, New York: Taylor.

Menefee, J. (2011), 'Dostoevsky and the Diamond Sutra: Jack Kerouac's Karamazov Religion,' *Texas Studies in Literature and Language*, 53.4: 431–454.

Nicosia, G. (1983), *Memory Babe: A Critical Biography of Jack Kerouac*, New York: Grove.

Nielsen, A. (1993), 'Clark Coolidge and a Jazz Aesthetic', *Pacific Coast Philology*, 28.1: 94–112.

Panish, J. (1994), 'Kerouac's *The Subterraneans*: A Study of "Romantic Primitivism"', *MELUS*, 19.3: 107–23.

Skerl, Jennie (ed.), (2004), *Reconstructing the Beats*, New York: Palgrave-Macmillan.

Sterritt, D. (2004), *Screening the Beats: Media Culture and the Beat Sensibility*, Carbondale: Southern Illinois University.

Theado, M. (2000), *Understanding Jack Kerouac*, Columbia, SC: University of South Carolina.

Vv. Aa. (2014), *Hollywood Diversity Report: Making Sense of the Disconnect*, Los Angeles: Ralph J. Bunche Center for African American Studies at UCLA. Available at: www.bunchecenter.ucla.edu/wp-content/uploads/2014/02/2014-Hollywood-Diversity-Report-2-12-14.pdf (last accessed 15 June 2015).

Waldman, A. (1997), *Iovis Book II*, Minneapolis: Coffee House.

'This Was My Hollywood Career': Jack Kerouac's *On the Road* and 1950s Hollywood

Matt Theado

In September 1957, Jack Kerouac's *On the Road* was more than a bestseller. Identified as the 'testament' of the Beat Generation by Gilbert Millstein in his *New York Times* book review and as the 'Bible of the Beat Generation' on the back cover of the 1958 Signet paperback edition, the book propelled the phrase into the national news press, where it was attached to sordid crimes and juvenile delinquency, and into the slick magazines, where the concept was derided as a fad and the Beat Generation writers were generally belittled. As a controversial cultural bellwether, the phrase also appealed to Hollywood producers. Kerouac had christened the generation of which he was a part, yet despite his movie-star good looks, he was not adequately equipped to manoeuvre within the media and capitalize on his sudden notoriety as its most-recognized figure. Although he relied on his agent, Sterling Lord, to negotiate the proposed movie deals, Kerouac corresponded directly with Jerry Wald, a producer at Twentieth Century-Fox, early in 1958, regarding the conversion of his novel into a movie. Unlike Wald, Hollywood impresario Albert Zugsmith, a producer of sensational B movies, did not pursue the rights to *On the Road*. Instead, he simply appropriated the phrase 'Beat Generation' for his own use in producing an exploitation film of that title.

Kerouac's relationships with Jerry Wald and Albert Zugsmith demonstrate two ways that Kerouac and Hollywood interacted in regard to *On the Road*. Wald represents the Hollywood system; he showed a willingness to share ideas with Kerouac and to justify the transformations necessary to make a successful movie. Zugsmith's interactions with Kerouac are of a different order altogether. The two men never communicated directly; Zugsmith seized the opportunity to capitalize on the Beat Generation phenomenon, trumpeting lurid phrases and printing salacious copy to promote his movie,

The Beat Generation (1959), a process that angered and embittered Kerouac and undoubtedly confounded the public regarding the connotations of the phrase and its connection to *On the Road*. Hollywood did not make a movie version of *On the Road*; it did, however, exploit the Beat Generation in a way that disparaged the novel and denied Kerouac both monetary and intellectual credit.

Kerouac's interaction with Hollywood began long before the novel's publication. In 1950 and 1951, as Kerouac drafted early versions of *On the Road*, he was already working tangentially with the movie business. Kerouac was employed by an office of Twentieth Century-Fox (as the company's name was then written) to provide movie script synopses, earning $25 to $30 per week. Kerouac's letters and journals contain scant details of this job, and he undoubtedly must have considered it hackwork, but it is notable that he was scrutinizing the works of hopeful screenwriters and converting them to summaries. That is, he acted as a go-between for anxious writers, setting them up for their shot at Hollywood success by abbreviating their work to an assessable format. He may have felt this job honed his skills and understanding of the screenwriting craft, for on 27 June 1950 Kerouac submitted his own movie idea to the New York Story Department of Twentieth Century-Fox. Kerouac pitched a western centring on a character named Happy Blanton who returns to his hometown after ten years in prison only to find the town has grown tame. The agent at Twentieth Century-Fox rejected the story but not the writer. In fact, he coached Kerouac on how to submit his movie ideas more successfully in future efforts (Kerouac Papers):

> I always feel that if a writer can't work out a story for pictures with reasonable dispatch, he shouldn't keep hammering away at it. The odds are too much against him, and there are too many other ideas closer to him. When you have time, I'd like you to have another go at a story for us, but this time I suggest you take an idea more in your blood.

At about the same time that he pitched his Western movie treatment, Kerouac also was sketching out ideas for adapting his only published novel, *The Town and the City* (1950) for the screen; apparently he never proceeded with this project beyond a series of notes (Kerouac Papers). Years later, John Clellon Holmes recalled that, although Kerouac loved movies and had an astute sensitivity about them, 'he never understood script-writing as a separate genre'. Holmes concluded that Kerouac had a 'narrative and lyrical gift,' but not an aptitude to develop drama and conflict (Holmes 1989: 3).

Nonetheless, his early Hollywood interactions affected him as a writer and would influence his actions in the coming years.

Given Kerouac's concurrent interaction with Hollywood as well as his life-long love of movies, it is not surprising that he wove numerous movie references into the text of *On the Road*. In the opening pages, the novel's first-person narrator, Sal, describes Dean as a 'young Gene Autry' (Kerouac 1991: 5), conjuring images of the blue-eyed 'Singing Cowboy'. Sal portrays himself a writer who hopes to hit Hollywood to sell his 'shining original' movie manuscript (1991: 63). When Sal finally gets to Hollywood, the Okie families at the tail end of Route 66 fancy they see movie stars on every corner: 'Don Ameche! Don Ameche!' 'No, George Murphy! George Murphy!' (1991: 86) His splendid plan for selling his movie script and relishing the well-stocked bars of Hollywood moguls dissolves instead to a fade-out of Sal, having retrieved his rejected manuscript from Columbia Pictures and down to his last dollar, sitting alone in a parking lot john while above him 'great Klieg lights of a Hollywood première stabbed in the sky'. A bitter incongruence, certainly, and a strained glimpse of a tantalizing future: 'This was my Hollywood career', Sal concludes (1991: 102).

A listing of further movie references in *On the Road* demonstrates the degree to which Kerouac relied on movie tropes to support the novel's descriptions, adding visuality and cultural context. Sal walks to his barracks guard job along 'a road like in *The Mark of Zorro* and a road like all the roads you see in Western B movies' (1991: 64; reference to *Mark of Zorro* starring Tyrone Power, 1940). When Sal confronts the construction workers who are housed in the barracks, he readily admits the scene was 'like a Western movie' (1991: 65). On Sal's bus trip to Los Angeles he meets a young woman who falls asleep in his lap at dawn, 'like the dawn when Joel McCrea met Veronica Lake in a diner, in the picture *Sullivan's Travels*' (1991: 82; *Sullivan's Travels* directed by Preston Sturges, 1941). When Dean gives Sal a whirlwind tour of Bakersfield, Sal's predominant observation of the area is 'the land where everybody somehow looked like broken-down, handsome, decadent movie actors' (1991: 168). When Dean abandons Sal on the sidewalks of San Francisco, Sal perceives that his fellow denizens resemble a 'broken-down movie extra, a withered starlet', or 'disenchanted stunt-men' (1991: 170). Sal spends a night in a Detroit skid row movie theatre through repeated showings of the double feature: 'the strange Gray Myth of the West' – with Singing Cowboy Eddie Dean shooting up rustlers – and 'the weird dark Myth of the East' – where Peter Lorre and Sydney Greenstreet sneer in sinister Istanbul (1991: 244). Before the Mexican trip that concludes their travels, Sal anticipates Dean's arrival in Denver: 'It was like an old-fashioned movie' (1991: 260).

Early interest: Paramount and Warner Brothers

In the ensuing swirl of movie talk in the weeks after *On the Road*'s publication, the first big name to surface was that of Marlon Brando, who had leapt to fame and matinee-idol status in 1951 as Stanley Kowalski in *A Streetcar Named Desire*, followed by his portrayals of Mark Antony in *Julius Caesar*, and Terry Malloy in *On the Waterfront*. No actor in Hollywood brought the man-package of charm, muscle, and suppressed danger to the screen as Mr Brando did in *The Wild One* in 1953. To this day his Johnny Strabler sits astride his motorcycle in his leather jacket and blue jeans in framed posters on the walls of diners and drive-ins as *the* image of the Youthful Rebel, forever answering the question 'What are you rebelling against, Johnny?' with the toss-off reply: 'Whaddya got?' One of Paramount's 1953 movie posters boldly claimed that 'MARLON BRANDO ... IS THE ONLY MAN WHO COULD PLAY ... THE WILD ONE'. Although *The Wild One* today may come across to many viewers as a rather dated, even clichéd, cavalcade of weekend warriors on a lark, the contemporary audience was awed by Brando's edgy vitality, threatening in his next breath to throttle off with their fledgling daughters astraddle his motorcycle seat. It seemed obvious that Marlon Brando was ... the only man who could play ... Dean Moriarty. Kerouac claimed that Brando's father, acting as his agent, called Kerouac within days of the novel's publication to discuss the matter (Kerouac: 1957).

First offers for the movie rights – a reported $110,000 – came not from Brando, but from Warner Brothers, who supported the idea of Kerouac playing Sal (Kerouac 1999: 71). When Kerouac's agent, Sterling Lord, learned that Brando was also interested, he decided to hold out for more money, perhaps to spur a bidding war. According to Kerouac biographer Ann Charters, Lord hoped to sell the rights to *On the Road* for $150,000 (Kerouac 1999: 71 [editor's note]). Meanwhile, Kerouac's stock had shot way up from his lonely night in the Hollywood parking lot john. On the crest of *On the Road*'s success and notoriety, he was being booked for television appearances and newspaper and magazine interviews. At that moment, the sky must have seemed the limit: 'Plays! Productions! Leaping from the author's box to the stage to make flower speeches! Homburgs! Operas! Red linings to black cloaks! Millions!' an exuberant Kerouac wrote to Allen Ginsberg (Kerouac 1999: 80). Kerouac brashly typed a letter to Marlon Brando, opening with a direct appeal: 'I'm praying that you'll buy ON THE ROAD and make a movie of it.' He envisions the two of them together in the movie, with Brando playing Dean and himself playing Sal. Kerouac offers to show Brando just how to play the role of Dean, otherwise he 'couldn't possibly imagine it'. He also tells Brando that he knows how to 'compress and re-arrange' the plot to make it suitable for a movie; he suggests combining the novel's five trips into one (Kerouac, 'Letter to Marlon Brando'). Kerouac understood the novel would need to be altered to suit the new medium; he also wanted to write the screenplay.

Kerouac was not just selling a motion picture treatment. With his characteristic brio and artistic vibrancy, Kerouac lays out for Brando the future of American cinema: his goal is to 're-do the theater and the cinema in America, give it a spontaneous dash, remove pre-conceptions of "situation" and let people rave on as they do in real life'. Despite Kerouac's closing admonition – 'Come on now, Marlon, put up your dukes and write!' – he received no reply. One month later, a dejected Kerouac told Ginsberg that 'Brando is a shit, doesnt [sic] answer a letter from greatest writer in America and he's only a piddling king's clown of the stage' (Kerouac and Ginsberg 2010: 373). Three years later, when the Beat hubbub had subsided to some extent, Kerouac interpreted Brando's silence in an altogether different way. Instead of seeing the snub as a rejection, he observed that Brando was simply behaving as a true artist should, in a manner that Kerouac would hereafter emulate: 'he simply doesn't answer his public type mail, he didn't even answer me about filming ON THE ROAD three years ago, he's smart. He goes about his business, which is making movies, period' (Kerouac 1999: 276).

If making movies was Brando's business, then why didn't he and Paramount acquire the rights in 1957 and begin making the movie, period? Kerouac biographer Gerald Nicosia points out one stumbling block: 'Brando considered *On the Road* too loose to be filmable' (1994: 564). This may certainly have been the case, as the novel recounts multiple trips west, east, and south, and a parade of characters who are spirited in and then out of the narrative. Given the apparent challenges in converting the novel to a movie, it is likely that Paramount was put off by the high asking price for the rights.

Jerry Wald

At least one Hollywood producer was eager to take on the task of transforming Kerouac's novel for the screen, and within three weeks of the publication of *On the Road*, he had already written up a 15-page treatment. Jerry Wald, a Twentieth Century-Fox screenwriter and producer, was a big man with boundless energy who had come out of Brooklyn at a tender age to take Hollywood by storm. Acquaintances repeat the story that Wald was the original Sammy Glick in *What Makes Sammy Run?* If he were not the *de facto* model for the rags-to-riches go-getter in Budd Schulberg's 1941 novel, he certainly ran that path, rising with stunning swiftness from lowly origins to the pinnacle of Hollywood success. *Time* magazine described him as 'moon-faced, jowly, barrel-shaped' (Toth 1981:171) but he knew a thing or two about making movies; in the middle of an immensely fruitful career, he produced two of 1957's big hit movies, *An Affair to Remember* and *Peyton Place*. Screenwriter George Axelrod recalled that Wald was a dynamo: 'He was frantic, but he was a fountain of energy and ideas. He'd say, "George, I've got a wonderful idea. No? Okay, I've got another wonderful idea."' About the fifth idea would be great' (McGilligan 1997: 62). Wald had recently come from a $3,000-a-week job at Columbia Pictures, having risen to a position there from his start at Warner Brothers (where William Faulkner worked for him as a screenwriter) to an even more lucrative deal at Twentieth Century-Fox. Wald had not only arrived, he reigned. He achieved this by tempering fantastic dynamism with intellectual shrewdness. Director Philip Dunne stated flat out that Wald was a one-of-a-kind phenomenon: 'He was an omnivorous reader and he lost none of it. He would get to the office early in the morning and ... he'd copy out pages of Proust and try to introduce it into the dialogue' (Stempl 1988: 127).

On 9 January 1958, Wald introduced himself in a letter to Kerouac, letting him know that he was interested in *On the Road*. 'I think it has a lot to offer,' Wald wrote, 'but it needs dramatization'. Wald noted that although novels and movies are distinctly different forms, he was confident that Kerouac's material would yield an 'exciting film' (Kerouac Papers). Wald pointed out that the biggest task in crafting a successful movie is the focus on a central character who must face and overcome emotional conflict. Ultimately, Wald explained to Kerouac in his letter, the goal is to satisfy the movie critics and attract the paying customers: 'This is the kind of double bull's eye I like to hit.' Wald is certain that Kerouac would like to hit it too, and he asks Kerouac to participate in the process, inviting his suggestions for transforming his book to the screen.

Wald knew that a significant transformation would have to take place before *On the Road*, or just about any novel, could be projected onto the movie screen. In 1954, Wald published an essay that reveals the challenge in satisfying mass audiences with a novel adaptation (reprinted in Phillips 1988: xi):

> *Everyone* who has read the original work has positive and definite ideas and illusions about plot, characterization, background, and motivation which a mere screenwriter, and a mere producer, and a few mere stars, and a couple of mere million dollars, can never equal.

Acknowledging that screenwriters can be as skilful as the best novelists, Wald states the 'two key problems in adaptation are length and changes'

(Phillips 1988: xii). Typically, the adaptation of novel to film requires cutting characters and scenes, visualizing or voicing exposition, reducing subplots, combining scenes, and rearranging (Desmond and Hawkes 2006: 85–99).

The novel Kerouac had written was a picaresque narrative, a rather plotless, rambling chronicle of a string of loosely associated events that would hardly make a coherent movie. Nonetheless, Wald was determined to 'keep the spirit of the original'. By way of sharing his ideas, Wald enclosed in his letter to Kerouac half a dozen pages of notes he put together while 'thinking on the typewriter,' as he put it; his notes reveal how Wald might dramatize the novel for the movie screen. First of all, he sees the events of the movie as taking place immediately after World War II, rather than four years after it, and he would recast the two main characters as former GIs. The movie would open with Dean and Sal in the Army together, overseas: Dean would be a driver who transports various officers. After the war, Dean is arrested in Denver and Sal hitchhikes there to throw his bail. Dean and Sal pick up Marylou. The threesome travels to San Francisco where they dig the Beat gang and the jazz jam sessions, before heading down to Mexico and finally New York. Along the way, Sal sees that Dean is plagued by deep-rooted problems. In New York, Sal marries Laura and establishes a quiet domestic sphere, a turn of events that emotionally crushes Dean. He roars off, pushing his car to top speed, leading to a fiery crash and Dean's martyrdom. The tragic ending provides uplift as Sal assumes his stable position in society, and Dean, who was always lost, conjures up an evocation of similarly named Hollywood icon James Dean, who died in a car crash in 1955.

Wald envisioned the story as one of stark contrasts between two men who share a bond: Sal, the leading character, believes that Dean is a flawed character on a path of self-destruction. The main conflict Dean and Sal face is their adjustment to life after the war; the resolution comes with Dean's death and Sal's recognition of his flaws. Even though he is excited by Dean's energy and insights, Sal is influenced by Laura to settle into domesticity, thus avoiding his fate. Overall, Wald's story would relate the plight of young men after the war, breaking away from the Army's rules, 'unbuttoning', as Wald put it in a memo to a colleague at Twentieth Century-Fox. Wald identifies Kerouac's chief accomplishment in rendering 'the pent up drive of young men trying to avoid being shoved into a mold, trying to avoid being typed and made into conformists' before they are able to discover a life based on their own values' (Kerouac Papers).

It is not clear whether Kerouac knew of Wald's stature in Hollywood, outside of the introduction his letter provided. Several weeks passed and he did not receive a reply from the author. Kerouac did write to his friend Lucien Carr, relating that a movie producer had expressed interest in making a movie that ends with Dean dying in a crash, connecting the movie with the James Dean story (Kerouac 1999: 125). On 20 January 1958, Wald prodded Kerouac with a follow-up. Kerouac wrote a lengthy, thoughtful reply, beginning with these words: 'I think your ideas are very good.'

After accepting Wald's ideas in general, Kerouac suggests that Wald read John Holmes's article in the current *Esquire*, 'The Philosophy of the Beat Generation' to gain a clearer idea of what the phrase connotes. He insists that the Beats are essentially religious and kind. As for utilizing the myth of James Dean to heighten the focus on the Beats, Kerouac accepts it as 'a genuine act of Mythmaking'. There is a stumbling block, though: Kerouac tells Wald that 'in real life Dean can never crash, he's too great and mystical a driver'. However, Kerouac agrees that an intentional crash is possible and that the moviegoers can wonder whether the crash is deliberate or accidental. Despite his understanding that a blazing car crash will imbue the movie's ending with the indispensable mythic element, Kerouac would prefer a different conclusion, one in keeping with the real-life Dean as he knows him. He would rather the movie close with tender scenes of Dean as a working railroad man, coming home in his brakeman's uniform to supper with his family, then putting his kids to bed while saying their prayers with them. So on the one hand, we have Wald's vision of the emotionally unhinged Dean roaring off in his car to destroy himself in an explosive climax, while on the other, we have Kerouac's sympathetic image of an earnest home where Dean is tucking the kids in. By asking Wald to read Holmes's article and to consider the tender ending instead of the fiery one, Kerouac navigates the Hollywood boulevards, doing his diplomatic best to influence the outcome according to his lights.

In Kerouac's version of the movie, tenderness would infuse other scenes as well. Kerouac makes clear to Wald that Dean and Sal never even think of fighting – Wald had suggested a few standoffs between them and others – and unlike their apparent Lost Generation counterparts, the Beats travel to Mexico but not to go to the bullfights. Instead, Sal and Dean are men of peace and empathy, who in the movie, Kerouac suggests, might find their bond in the military when they confess to each other that they are unable to kill. Kerouac had been discharged from the Navy during World War II basically because he reported that he would not kill: 'That's the secret of the Beat Generation', an ethos that he maintained during his Navy training and one that he would promote to Hollywood. Additionally, there is more to Sal's affection than admiration for Dean's exciting ways. Kerouac tells Wald that Sal loves Dean for 'the sincerity of his search, the manliness of his heart'.

Beyond thematic elements for the film, Kerouac also suggests cinematic elements. He envisions a shot that would repeat throughout the movie, one that is likely based on his own view of the road as Neal drove him across the country. Kerouac's words are worth noting in their entirety:

> Put a camera in front seat of car, show the widescreen color road winding into the car like an enormous snake dangerous snake, just show Sal's feet to the right propped up on dashboard, let the dialog roll; let the road of the desert, the mountains, of narrow road, of freeways, roll into the audience, all the way thru the picture; let there be rock and roll on the dashboard radio; let there be occasional hands bongoing on the dashboard. Let that white line in the middle of far west two-lane highways come feeding into the screen steady, get a superlative driver to push the car at 70 and later at 110 for these shots. That's the ROAD.

Kerouac cautions Wald to avoid making a movie about roughnecks and violence, contending that it is a 'sad and tender book'. If Wald were instead to make a picture about 'goodhearted kids in pain of soul doing wild things out of desperation', Kerouac assures him he will have a movie that is far truer to life than Hollywood's typical products that are loaded with 'nerveshattering violence'. Kerouac confesses to Wald one of the key messages he sought to evoke in all his work: 'I have often the sensation that Grace is raining down on our heads so I would like the movie version of On the Road to suggest that basic religious emotion ...'

Despite their correspondence, and for reasons we may never know, Wald did not option the rights to *On the Road*. Kerouac wrote to a friend in July 1958 that Jerry Wald was 'just about to buy it for 20th Century when we sold it' (Kerouac 1999: 156). Apparently, Kerouac and his agent figured that they would have a better deal with little-known Tri-Way Productions, who tendered an offer of $25,000, or else they simply could not come to terms with MGM. Although the Tri-Way price was drastically less than had been hoped for, Lord arranged a deal that would pay 5 per cent of the profits, which Twentieth Century-Fox had not been willing to grant. Kerouac was to receive 10 per cent upfront; he wrote to a friend that he planned to use the movie income to buy a house for him and his mother (Kerouac 1999: 168). Kerouac also claimed that Mort Sahl said he wanted the movie to 'hew very closely to the book', a position not stated by MGM. *On the Road* seemed destined for the silver screen. Yet it was not to be. Tri-Way ran into financial difficulties and tried to rework the contract with a lower price. In the summer of 1958, Kerouac complained, 'the Road movie people have reneged now and offer 5 grand instead of 25, which is mystifying and sounds to me like they must feel that since I'm "beat" I wouldn't know any better' (Kerouac 1999: 145). Kerouac received only $2,500 from Tri-Way before the company went out of business. As late as the spring of 1959, Jerry Wald was still showing interest in producing an *On the Road* movie. In a March 1959 interview, Kerouac claimed that Jerry Wald was writing letters indicating that he was still considering the movie but was unsure how to convert the plot effectively. Kerouac concluded that offers for the movie rights had stopped coming because producers assumed that the rights had already been sold: 'I thought of taking an ad in Billboard: "ON THE ROAD – NOT SOLD!"' (Aronowitz 2005: 152). Major movie producers at that time seemed unwilling to consider heeding Keoruac's suggestions to temper the violence or enact the lyricism that propels his novel. In order to bring *On the Road* effectively to the movie screen, asserts Beat scholar Regina Weinreich, 'film idiom would have to come to its next moment. Can the medium of film be stretched in the manner in which *On the Road* expanded narrative possibilities for literary fiction?' (Weinreich 2009: 195). Although there were numerous independent movie productions in the later 1950s (John Cassavettes' *Shadows* perhaps indicating most strongly a potential course), no such treatment was applied to *On the Road*.

Albert Zugsmith

It must have been especially galling to Kerouac to learn that producer Albert Zugsmith was producing a movie titled *The Beat Generation* for Metro-Goldwyn-Mayer (MGM), scheduled for release in July 1959. Kerouac believed that the title *The Beat Generation* belonged to him because he had, after all, coined the phrase, as credited by John Clellon Holmes in a 1952 *New York Times* magazine essay. If that were not sufficient, he had published a short work in 1955 titled 'Jazz of the Beat Generation'. Nonetheless, both the public use of the phrase and its connotations had been wrested from him in the most ruthless manner imaginable.

In 1952 Zugsmith produced *Invasion USA*, a movie that depicts a devastating atomic bomb attack ('SEE vast U.S. cities vanish before your very eyes!'). It netted $1 million at the box office. Zugsmith was eager to exploit a peril that was displacing atomic warfare as America's greatest menace: beatniks. He started in 1958 with a teen exploitation flick that became the daddy of them all, MGM's *High School Confidential!* a plunge into the teen world of fast cars, marijuana, switchblades, and tight sweaters hopped up on songs by Jerry Lee Lewis. The movie also unspools loads of hip 1950s slang and even stages a Beat poetry reading complete with jazz accompaniment.

High School Confidential! was preceded by another MGM release, *Blackboard Jungle*, based on a novel by Evan Hunter, that promised to reveal 'a new and shattering drama about the new Beat Generation ... a torrid world of temptation, a violent world you never dreamed existed'. Soon after the phrase 'Beat Generation' rose in the popular media, Hollywood yoked it to juvenile delinquency and crime. Kerouac lost control of the phrase he had coined and he was soon to lose the right to use the phrase as the title for a movie as well.

Zugsmith would recast many of *High School Confidential!*'s actors in his next foray into youthful waywardness, shamelessly titled *The Beat Generation*. These included such B-movie luminaries as Mamie Van Doren, John Drew Barrymore, Jackie Coogan (from Charlie Chaplin's *The Kid* who would go on to be Uncle Fester in TV's *Addams Family*), and Charles Chaplin, Jr. For an exotic dash, he cast Vampira as a Beatnik poet; Steve Cochran was cast as the lead. Zugsmith's wacky ensemble alone makes *The Beat Generation* fun to watch, but audiences in 1959 were not so charmed by what we see today as its kitschy cachet. Zugsmith's *The Beat Generation* warns movie-going Americans about the dangers not of atomic bombs nearby, but of the unkempt guys and gals who snap their fingers in coffee houses. In Zugsmith's world, the beatniks are soft-headed followers, shaggy sheep ready to fall in line behind a charismatic hero who foots the bill for their dope-fogged parties. In this case, the scruffy beatniks, unbeknownst even to themselves, harbour a depraved rapist. John Clellon Holmes recalled that Kerouac was 'venomous' about *The Beat Generation* movie though he never saw it (Holmes 1989: 3).

Other Beat Generation-themed movies followed. Walter Paisley, the lead character in 1959's *A Bucket of Blood*, directed by Roger Corman (of *Little Shop of Horrors* fame) is a hapless waiter in a beatnik dive who scores points with the hip crowd when he unveils his startlingly life-like sculptures. Their realistic rendering comes from the fact that they are his murder victims, covered in clay. In 1960 *The Beatniks*, another in the frantic run of Beatsploitation flicks, employed a typically sensationalistic tagline: 'THEIR PASSWORD WAS MUTINY AGAINST SOCIETY! Living By Their Code Of REBELLION And MUTINY!' Late in his life, Kerouac appeared on William F. Buckley's 'The Firing Line' and complained that the popular media had distorted his original ideas with 'Beat Mutiny, Beat Insurrection. Words I never used'.

Kerouac had recently completed a three-act play he titled *The Beat Generation*, and early in January 1959, Kerouac, producer Alfred Leslie, and photographer Robert Frank began making a short, experimental film from the material of the final act, a movie that they intended to call *The Beat Generation*. Apparently, Kerouac, Leslie, and Frank contacted MGM first, claiming that the studio had no right to use the title and that they planned to use it themselves. On behalf of MGM, Benjamin Melniker of Cole, Grimes,

Friedman & Deitz notified them that they were not to use the phrase for the title of *their* movie (Kerouac Papers). He argued that the phrase had been in circulation for years and it would be 'fruitless' to try to identify one person as the source. More significantly, he claimed that 'property rights in a title can be acquired only by actual use of the title in connection with a particular work' and then only if that work achieves popular association with that title. Since the opportunistic Zugsmith already had published *The Beat Generation* as a Bantam paperback tie-in for his movie, Melniker declared, Zugsmith's claim to the phrase overrode Kerouac's. Melniker boldly stated: 'Mr. Zugsmith is the only person who has actually used the title THE BEAT GENERATION in connection with a published work which has achieved widespread circulation.' Apparently he deemed Kerouac's 'Jazz of the Beat Generation' in *New World Writing* (1955) to be insufficiently 'widespread'. Unfortunately, Kerouac had published this short work under the pseudonym Jean-Louis, thus failing to establish a firm connection with his actual name.

In addition to the precedence of Zugsmith's publication, Melniker went on to credit his 'extensive pre-release publicity, advertising and exploitation' of the soon-to-be-released movie that served to establish an association between this particular movie and the phrase. In a parting salvo, Melniker asserted that MGM's lawyers would 'utilize all of the legal remedies available' to prevent Kerouac and his partners from using the phrase 'The Beat Generation' as a title (Kerouac Papers). For his part, Zugsmith seemed uninterested in any connotations of the phrase beyond its mass-media exploitation. Zugsmith categorized his characters in *The Beat Generation* as 'typical beatniks' even though, he confessed, he did not portray them smoking 'tea'. As for the origin of the phrase and Kerouac's claim to it, Zugsmith bluntly retorted, 'Kerouac? What does he have to do with it? I own a copyrighted title on *The Beat Generation* and a copyrighted book . . . We were well launched on this beat thing before I ever heard the name of Jack Kerouac' (Aronowitz 2015).

'They are really crooking me in H'wood,' Kerouac grumbled (Kerouac 1999: 147). MGM's next move barely placated him. The studio paid $15,000 for the rights to make a movie of another Kerouac book, *The Subterraneans*; although the deal provided some much-needed income, he felt the price was low compared to what other writers were being paid. That summer Zugsmith's *The Beat Generation* fulfilled its promise as a B movie while conveying nothing whatsoever of the impetus of the Beat movement, but *The Subterraneans*, released the following summer with Kerouac's novel credited as the basis of the film, was simply embarrassingly bad, depicting the beatniks as imbeciles, converting Kerouac's love story of a white man and a black woman in the early Civil Rights era into a simple-minded, self-absorbed tale of George Peppard and Leslie Caron goofing among graffiti-scrawled cardboard sets.

Neither movie offered tenderness, lyricism, insight, joy, or even the rudiments of sympathy and compassion. A movie poster advertising *The Beat Generation* promised a glimpse 'BEHIND THE WEIRD "WAY-OUT" WORLD OF THE BEATNIKS!' Another poster demanded, 'WHAT IS THE CRIME TOO HOT FOR THE "COOL" WORLD TO HIDE?'

Disillusioned by Hollywood, Kerouac turned to Ginsberg, one of the few people who understood what he had been trying to do: 'What's going on, Allen? It's not money I'm worried about any more, but the perversion of our teaching which began under the Bkyn Bridge long ago' (Kerouac 1999: 203). The film rights to *On the Road* languished. Meanwhile, television broadcast network CBS aired 'Route 66' for four seasons starting in 1960. The show featured two characters who resemble Sal and Dean wandering the country in a Corvette. Film scholar David Sterritt describes this show's derivative portrayals (Sterritt 1998: 167):

> As a peripatetic entertainment devoted to glancing social encounters, speedily resolved adventures, and superficial human relationships, *Route 66* stands in relation to *On the Road* as commercially driven exploitation of the worst sort, substituting easy pleasures of the world for the challenging pleasure of the soul toward which Kerouac's voyagers instinctively gravitate.

When a college student wrote to Kerouac in 1961 asking about the themes of *On the Road*, he replied: 'You'll notice that in ON THE ROAD, unlike the television cheap imitation of it called "Route 66," there are no fist fights, gun fights or horror of that kind at all.' He even seemed relieved that a movie with Marlon Brando had not been made because he felt that the book was too closely associated with The Wild One's 'hoodlum jacket thing' (Kerouac 1999: 330). Later that year, Kerouac made another exasperating attempt to explain his frustration, this time to his agent, Sterling Lord. He pointed out that the Albert Zugsmith movie and the 'Route 66' television show had deprived him of his intellectual property, denying him up to $1 million in profits. He was outraged that Zugsmith himself claimed the copyright to the phrase 'Beat Generation' as a title. He complained to an editor at Viking of the lack of movie offers for *On the Road*, even as television shows such as 'Route 66' were essentially an 'idea-grab' based on his work. He noted that the television show's key representation was the white line of the highway feeding into the car's front fender, an image he had come up with (Kerouac 1999: 344).

In the last year of his life, Kerouac realized that no big check from Hollywood was coming and that his philosophies and characters had been taken from him and used in ways that disparaged and demeaned their original energy. Kerouac died in 1969 without seeing his novel made into a movie. Had he lived until 2012, he may have been gratified to finally see a movie version in cinemas. Realized by the team who had made the award-winning *The Motorcycle Diaries* in 2004, screenwriter Jose Rivera and director Walter Salles, the movie is an interweaving of Kerouac's novel, the novel's original typescript, and biography. It was not commercially successful, however, falling far short of recouping its reported $25 million budget.

Works cited

Aronowitz, A. 'Part 1: The Beat Papers of Al Aronowitz Chapter One: Beat.' *The Blacklisted Journalist.* Available at: www.blacklistedjournalist.com/column21a.html, (last accessed 1 May 2015).

Aronowitz, A. (2005), 'St. Jack', in P. Maher (ed.), *Empty Phantoms: Interviews and Encounters with Jack Kerouac*, New York: Thunder's Mouth, 137–72.

'*The Beat Generation*: Trivia' *Internet Movie Database.* Available at: www.imdb. com (last accessed 29 April 2015).

Desmond, J. M. and P. Hawkes (2006), *Adaptation: Studying Film and Literature*, Boston: McGraw-Hill.

Holmes, J. C., (1989) [untitled letter; 29 March 1983] *Moody Street Irregulars* 22 & 23: 3.

Jack Kerouac Papers, New York Public Library. Berg Collection. Available at: http://archives.nypl.org/brg/19343 (last accessed 20 March, 2012):

1.27   'Motion Picture Treatment – Idea for the Town and the City'.

1.28   'Adaptation from T&C for Screen'.

2.17   Bertram Bloch to Kerouac, 17 July, 1950 (Twentieth Century-Fox Film Corp.)

20.66   Photocopied correspondence between Jack Kerouac and Jerry Wald, concerning a motion picture based on *On the Road*: (1) Typed letter, signed, from Jerry Wald to Jack Kerouac, 2 leaves, 9 January 1958; (2) Typed letter, signed, from Jerry Wald to Jack Kerouac, 1 leaf, 20 January, 1958; (3) Typed letter, signed, from Jack Kerouac to Jerry Wald, 4 leaves, undated; (4) Memorandum from Jerry Wald to Arthur Kramer, 15 leaves, 30 September, 1957.

69.4   Lord to Kerouac, includes typed letter from Benjamin Melniker to Samuel P. Shaw, Jr., 23 April, 1959, regarding use of the title 'The Beat Generation' for a projected motion picture.

75.49   Kerouac to Wald, Jerry, Undated (1 typed letter, signed. photocopy).

Kerouac, J., Letter to Marlon Brando, 'Jack Kerouac/On the Road', *Christie's*. Sale 1600, Lot 293. Available at: www.christies.com/LotFinder/lot_details. aspx?intObjectID=4537761 (last accessed 9 December 2014).

Kerouac, J. (1957), 'The Latest on Jack Kerouac's "The Rambler" Lowell Sun (15 September 1957),' in P. Maher (ed.), *Empty Phantoms: Interviews and Encounters with Jack Kerouac*, New York: Thunder's Mouth, Kindle edition.

Kerouac, J. (1991), *On the Road*, New York: Penguin.

Kerouac, J. (1995), *Selected Letters: 1940–1956*, A. Charters (ed.), New York: Penguin.

Kerouac, J. (1999), *Selected Letters: 1957–1969*, A. Charters (ed.), New York: Penguin.

Kerouac, J. and A. Ginsberg (2010), *Jack Kerouac and Allen Ginsberg: The Letters*, B. Morgan and D. Stanford (eds), New York: Viking.

Matthews, M. E., Jr. (2012), *Duck and Cover: Civil Defense Images in Film and Television from the Cold War to 9/11*, Jefferson, NC: McFarland.

McGilligan, P. (1997), *Backstory 3: Interviews with Screenwriters of the 1960s*, Berkeley: University of California.

Nicosia, G. (1983), *Memory Babe: A Critical Biography of Jack Kerouac*, New York: Grove.

Phillips, G. D. (1988), *Fiction, Film, and Faulkner: The Art of Adaptation*, Knoxville: University of Tennessee.

Staehling, R. (1975), 'From Rock around the Clock to the Trip: The Truth about Teen Movies' in *Kings of the Bs: Working Within the Hollywood System*, T. McCarthy and C. Flynn (eds), New York: E.P. Dutton, 220–51.

Stempl, T. (1988), *Framework: A History of Screenwriting in the American Film*, Syracuse: Syracuse University.

Sterritt, D. (1998), *Mad To Be Saved: The Beats, the '50s, and Film*. Carbondale: Southern Illinois University.

Toth, E. (1981), *Inside Peyton Place: The Life of Grace Metalious*. New York: Doubleday.

Wald, J. (1988), 'Fiction versus Film', *Films in Review* 5.1 (1954): 62–7, reprinted in G. D. Phillips (ed.), *Fiction, Film, and Faulkner: The Art of Adaptation*, Knoxville: University of Tennessee, xi–xv.

Weinreich, R. (2009), 'Can *On the Road* Go on the Screen?' in *What's Your Road, Man? Critical Essays on Jack Kerouac's On the Road*, H. Holiday and R. Holton (eds), Carbondale: Southern Illinois University, 187–201.

Zugsmith, A. (1963), *How To Break into the Movies*, New York: MacFadden.

The Many Movies of Kerouac's *Big Sur*

Terence Diggory

Michael Polish's film adaptation (2013) of Jack Kerouac's *Big Sur* (1962) stakes out a claim to authenticity based on faithfulness to Kerouac's language. 'The nice thing about the adaptation', Polish (n.d.) explains, 'is that I left every word – there might have been twelve words that were my own, but everything else is Jack Kerouac.' Critic Stephen Holden (2013: C6), writing in the *New York Times*, approves this strategy: 'The hot-wired energy and spontaneity of the Beat mystique are embedded in writing that distills its feverish essence better than any hyped-up action.' And no one, Holden implies, could produce such writing better than Kerouac. So 'go to the source and stay there' is the lesson from Polish that Holden would apply more generally to any attempt to adapt Kerouac's work to film.

Of course, Polish exaggerates when he claims that his film captures 'every word' of *Big Sur*. Although the book is moderate in length, 212 pages in the latest paperback edition, it would take eight hours to read aloud. To produce a film of only one hour and forty minutes, Polish had to select from the language of the book. Making that selection required an interpretation that, in turn, informed the filmmaker's choice of image and action to accompany the original language. As most of the original language is in the form of narrative, which Polish presents in voiceover, he has sometimes invented dialogue in keeping with the more standard presentation of language in film drama. The overall result is a film that differs significantly from the book.

To make his movie, Polish chose to concentrate on one of the many movies that make up the novel. I am not referring to the difference between potentiality and actuality, where the novel would be analogous to the block of marble, containing many possible figures (movies), of which the sculptor (filmmaker) chooses one to chisel out. Rather, the *Big Sur* novel, as a completed artwork in its own right, puts many movies into play as part of its actual process. The multiplicity of those movies and even, in some cases, their conflict with each other contributes to the distinctive form of the novel. In contrast, a single story dominates Polish's film, conferring its own distinctive form, but also making it different from the novel. Whereas the conflict between the various movies within the novel composes its form, the conflict of the novel with Polish's movie – an inevitable consequence of his determination to stick close to the text – threatens decomposition. The many movies of *Big Sur* can be identified in terms of medium, genre and mode. In most cases, the difference between a book and a movie might seem clear-cut, but Kerouac's conception of writing as the production of a 'bookmovie' blurs the distinction (Kerouac 1959b: 483). For Kerouac, cinema is a mode of consciousness or awareness that can find expression in a variety of media, though each medium offers particular advantages or disadvantages for achieving that expression. Paradoxically, there is a cinematic dimension in *Big Sur* that is better suited to the book medium.

However, the most obvious differences between Kerouac's and Polish's versions of *Big Sur* involve genre; as such they reflect choices made by the author or director rather than the constraints of medium. Focusing on a particular romantic relationship, Polish composes his film as a romantic drama.[1] It is as if he had reformed *Big Sur* using the mould of *The Subterraneans* (1958). This was, in fact, made into a Hollywood movie (1960) so distorted that it gave extra impetus to Kerouac's flight to the location of *Big Sur* (Gifford and Lee 1978: 268). One of the movies in the *Big Sur* novel can be characterized as a romantic drama, but it comes up against the genre of the western movie to which Kerouac repeatedly makes explicit reference. The interference between these genres is distinctive of Beat drama, as epitomized in *Pull My Daisy* (1959).

As a genre, 'drama', whether romantic or Beat, implies a fictional mode, a presentation of characters and events which suspends the question of their relation to the 'real' world. In Kerouac's case, that question is notoriously difficult. Do the events of *Big Sur* represent what really happened to the man Jack Kerouac or is their relevance limited to a fictional protagonist, whom Kerouac calls Jack Duluoz? To answer that both of these modes are in play is to view the book simultaneously in two movie modes: both drama and documentary. Like many critics and biographers, however, Polish collapses 'The Duluoz Legend' (Kerouac 2011: v), as Kerouac called it, into the life of Kerouac.[2]

Polish strips away the fictional names that Kerouac used in *Big Sur* and presents characters (with one significant exception noted below) using the names of the real people who underwent the experiences on which the book is based. The air of authenticity in the film is enhanced by its 'documentary-like' quality (Rich 2012: 71), but the focus narrows to a diagnosis of Kerouac's problems rather than a broader concern for the full scope of 'The Duluoz Legend', with all that the term 'legend' implies. Ironically, an earlier film, explicitly billed as a documentary, *One Fast Move or I'm Gone:*

Kerouac's Big Sur (2008), manages to acknowledge the fictional dimension of *Big Sur* more clearly than Polish's film. To his credit, however, Polish recognizes fiction as the problem that gives rise to the action of *Big Sur*: Kerouac is terrified to find himself as a fictional character in a story that he did not create.

Visionary cinema

The first image we see in Polish's film is of Kerouac's words, in white lettering set against a black background:

> all over America high school and college kids thinking
> 'Jack Kerouac is 26 years old and on the road all the time hitch hiking'...
> while there I am almost 40 years old, bored and jaded....

These words, taken from the opening pages of the novel (Kerouac 2011:3), pose the problem that sets the plot in motion, at the same time implying that the protagonist, Jack Kerouac (in the book 'Jack Duluoz') may not have the resources needed to solve the problem; he may be too 'bored and jaded.' After the publication of *On the Road* in 1957, Kerouac felt alienated from himself by the image of the 'King of the Beatniks' (Kerouac 2011: 1) projected in the popular media and even by his own publishers on the back cover of *The Subterraneans*. (His image had been kept youthful by the false statement that he was only 25 years old.) In 1960, the date of the events on which *Big Sur* is based, he has come to California to retreat to Lawrence Ferlinghetti's cabin on the Big Sur coast south of Carmel. He 'had to get away to solitude again or die' (Kerouac 2011: 2; VO). The film's opening sequence presents these words by two different means: we see each letter being imprinted on paper by the keys of a typewriter, and we hear the words spoken in voiceover by the actor who plays Kerouac, Jean-Marc Barr. The image of the act of writing reminds us that the book survives the defeat of the man who wrote it, but as the film proceeds the emphasis is increasingly on the defeat.

Kerouac's experience of solitude in the wilderness was highly ambivalent. For instance, the time he spent as a fire spotter on Desolation Peak in Washington State during the summer of 1956 receives two very different treatments. In *Dharma Bums* (1958), the wilderness offers 'the vision of the freedom of eternity' (Kerouac 1976: 243); in *Desolation Angels* (1965), it is rejected in favour of 'hearts not just rocks' (Kerouac 1995: 68). Both of these attitudes eventually emerge in his experience of Big Sur, but in each case he begins with the great Romantic hope that outside the city, with its artificial realm of mass media and publicity, he can reconnect with the natural man inside himself. Understandably, the filmmaker concentrates on the external, and therefore visual, dimension of this quest. Throughout the opening minutes of the film, Polish highlights the nature/city contrast by crosscutting shots of Big Sur's sublime scenery with scenes of San Francisco's Skid Row, where Kerouac's addiction to alcohol almost derailed him. Polish proves the cinematic quality of Kerouac's imagination to be much more profound than David Sterritt found it to be when he compared a quotation from *Big Sur* (Kerouac 2011: 101) with Walt Disney's 1940 film *Fantasia* (Sterritt 1998: 12–13). Nevertheless, Polish fails to give the dark side of the sublime the full weight that Kerouac assigns to it right from the beginning. Neglecting key passages at the start of Kerouac's text, the director also passes up on certain cinematic possibilities, setting this movie *of* a book on a course that diverges from one of the movies *in* the book.

Kerouac devotes considerable detail to a description of Duluoz's arrival at Big Sur, a scene that Polish has cut entirely from his movie. The cut might seem justified on the grounds of narrative economy: the opening montage of the movie shows Kerouac already at Big Sur; there is no need to show him arriving. However, on the level of image rather than narrative, the circumstances of his arrival significantly shape the experience of the landscape. Duluoz arrives at night; only his old railroad lantern lights his way down into the deep canyon where he is in constant fear of stepping off the path into the dark void. With his vision diminished, sounds loom around him monstrously and seem to emanate from dislocated sources; the roar of the ocean seems to come from underground. 'This roaring high horror of darkness' (Kerouac 2011: 8) later persists, even in the light of day, leaving Duluoz incredulous when he later hears people describe Big Sur as beautiful: 'I gulp to wonder why it has the reputation of being beautiful above and beyond its *fearfulness*, its Blakean groaning rough-rock Creation throes' (Kerouac 2011: 12).

The allusion to Blake confirms that Kerouac is well aware that he is presenting an image of nature that belongs to the Romantic tradition, though it stands in tension with the pastoral scenes associated with Wordsworth or with the 'bucolic, all homely woods' that Duluoz had expected to experience at Big Sur (Kerouac 2011: 8; ch. 3). In American Romanticism, the *locus classicus* for 'groaning rough-rock Creation throes' is Thoreau's description of the summit of Mt Ktaadn, 'an undone extremity of the globe; as in lignite, we see coal in the process of formation' (Thoreau 1985: 640). The 'vast, Titanic, inhuman Nature' that presides over this scene rebukes the human intruder in what Thoreau presents as direct address: 'I have never made this soil for thy feet, this air for thy breathing, these rocks for thy neighbors. I cannot pity thee nor fondle thee here, but forever relentlessly drive thee hence to where I *am* kind' (Thoreau 1985: 640–641). In just this way, Duluoz is ultimately rebuked by the sea at Big Sur, after it sends him a whiff of iodine in the breeze (air 'not for thy breathing'): 'The sea seems to yell to me GO TO YOUR DESIRE DONT HANG AROUND HERE' (Kerouac 2011: 33–34; VO). It is a confirmation of the fear Duluoz experienced on the night of his arrival: 'It's been there a million years and it doesn't want me clashing darkness with it' (Kerouac 2011: 9).

This experience of 'clashing darkness' belongs to what Harold Bloom (1969) has called 'the visionary cinema of romantic poetry.' It is intensely dramatic in its 'clashing' but it can seem threateningly 'inhuman' (to use Thoreau's term) in its cosmic scale ('vast, Titanic') – though, of course, such scale is precisely one of the features that make it cinematic. Bloom doubts that this mode could ever be realized in actual cinema, because it awakens the inner eye of imagination (the visionary) by repressing the outer eye of perception (the visible) as Duluoz experiences in his night-time arrival at Big Sur. Negative proof of this axiom is evident in the inadequacy of the imagery produced when Kerouac attempts to make the visionary visible; too often, he falls back on the stock images of the horror movie, as in *Doctor Sax* (1959). Occasionally such images surface in the depiction of landscape in *Big Sur*: 'A slimy green dragon racket in the bush' (Kerouac 2011: 9); 'huge black rocks rising like old ogresome castles dripping wet slime' (Kerouac 2011: 11).

However, the principal channel of perception through which Kerouac tunes in to visionary experience in *Big Sur* is auditory rather than visual. The roar of the ocean that Duluoz finds so disorientating during his arrival eventually becomes a language based on 'the sound of the waves' (Kerouac 2011: 26). This poem was important enough to Kerouac that he had it printed in its entirety as an appendix to *Big Sur*. Polish not only neglects Duluoz's arrival at Big Sur, he entirely omits the text of the sea poem. His Kerouac types out the words 'sound of the sea', but rather than seeing (or hearing) the poem, we then hear a brief clip of actual sea sounds accompanying a view of waves hitting the shoreline. We get the perception, but not the vision.

The text of 'Sea' is much more than a modernist experiment in sound poetry, though even its strongest admirers tend to limit it to that function (e.g. Miles 1998: 268–69). 'Death' is the word that the sea ultimately speaks to Kerouac, as to Whitman in 'Out of the Cradle Endlessly Rocking' (Whitman 1968: 252–53). However, while Whitman experiences union with nature on the shores of Long Island, Kerouac at Big Sur, like Thoreau on Mt Ktaadn, experiences separation, even rejection. While Whitman receives the word 'death' as the beginning of his life as a poet, Kerouac hears the end of his life along with the defeat of his writing: 'The sea'll/only drown me – These words/ are affectations/of sick mortality –' (Kerouac 2011: 204). In desperation, he redirects his words from sea-sounds into prayer addressed to a personal God that he hopes will save him from nature's 'cold' inhumanity: 'Have you [God] sent men/here for this cold clown/& monstrous eater at the world? whose sound/I mock?' He adds, 'God I've got to believe in you/or live in death!' (Kerouac 2011: 204–205).

At the end of *Big Sur*, God will appear in a vision of the Cross that hovers before Duluoz in his darkest hour. At the beginning of the novel, the promise of salvation is manifested much less conventionally, and much more ironically, in a vision of Duluoz as he appears to God in a movie that God has made (i.e. the movie of existence). This appears at the same time that Duluoz hears the sea speak its words of rejection, 'go to your desire', though the sea poem records only the words (Kerouac 2011: 205), not the vision. The latter appears in the prose narrative. Duluoz explains 'this horrible sinister condition (of mortal hopelessness)' into which the sea's rejection has plunged him: 'so I'm left sitting there in the sand after having almost fainted and stare at the waves which suddenly are not waves at all, with I guess what must have been the goopiest downtrodden expression God if He exists must've ever seen in His movie career' (Kerouac 2011: 34).

It might seem here that Duluoz is self-pitying and seeking some consolation in the thought that God might pity him. But an earlier reference to God's 'movie career' rather suggests that Duluoz is purging himself of pity by adopting the distant perspective of the divine spectator, one merely amused by the movie 'which is us': 'all the details of life which now because a million lightyears away have taken on the aspect (as they must've for Proust in his sealed room) of pleasant mental movies brought up at will and projected for further study – And pleasure – As I imagine God to be doing this very minute, watching his own movie, which is us' (Kerouac 2011: 20).

It may be theoretically impossible, as Harold Bloom suggests, to realize this sort of visionary cinema within the medium of film, although David Cronenberg's (1991) adaptation of William Burroughs's *Naked Lunch* (1959) pushes the limits. In any case, no technical limits would have prevented Polish from quoting the passages *about* visionary cinema in *Big Sur* along with the rest of the text that he so proudly presents in voiceover. These passages have been omitted by choice. It may be that Polish, like many readers of Kerouac, finds the religious dimension in the work difficult to digest. However, he does include the vision of the Cross, where it can only be indigestible because it seems to have nothing to do with the story that has come before it. The omissions at the beginning probably reflect Polish's sense of what that story is, and his impatience to get on with telling it.

The film's opening quotation tells us that Kerouac suffers from a boredom that makes him unequal to the task of resisting the pressures of fame. Escaping to Big Sur relieves him of some of those pressures but does not relieve him from boredom. 'On the fourth day I began to get bored and noted it in my diary with amazement', Duluoz confesses (Kerouac 2011: 25; VO). As soon as Kerouac speaks these words in the film, he begins to speed up his narration and the sequence of images keeps pace with it. Effectively, in this account, Kerouac is already preparing to depart Big Sur, although, in fact, he stayed for another two-and-a-half weeks, with 'only 3 or 4 days of boredom' (Kerouac 2011: 37; VO). In rushing through Kerouac's first three weeks at Big Sur in 12 minutes of film, Polish proves himself to be more bored than Kerouac. The director cannot wait to involve his character in the interpersonal dynamics of the city, as opposed to the impersonal play of natural forces at Big Sur. The drama of the *Big Sur* movie is overwhelmingly a human drama, concerned with 'hearts not just rocks' (Kerouac 1995:68).

Romantic drama and western movies

The contrast of 'natural versus human' provides a very schematic structure for the action in *Big Sur*, which has been praised by critics as Kerouac's most tightly constructed novel (Wiegand 1962: 42; French 1986: 106; Theado 2000: 162). Propelled from the solitude of Big Sur during his first visit, Duluoz flees to the city to gather companions, who serve as reinforcements (this military metaphor is actually used [Kerouac 2011: 82; VO]) during a second visit to Big Sur, which occurs in the middle of the novel. The second half of the book leads back to the city but concentrates on one companion, a woman named Billie, whose relationship with Duluoz ends, disastrously, on a third visit to Big Sur at the book's conclusion.

Among Kerouac's companions are many writers who, as portrayed in the film, add a lot of colour, each with an identifying idiosyncrasy: Lawrence Ferlinghetti (Anthony Edwards) is soberly but sympathetically paternal; Philip Whalen (Henry Thomas) coolly philosophical; Lew Welch (Patrick Fischler) frenetically intense; Michael McClure (Balthazar Getty) sexy and competitive; Lenore Kandel (Stana Katic) just plain sexy. However, relationships with writers are not what drives Kerouac's story, even though the misfortune of his success as a writer drove him to Big Sur in the first place. As Polish interprets it, what really drives Kerouac is a desire to be loved, but to be loved for who he really is, rather than what the publicists and the public want him to be. This quest for love revolves around a smaller circle of characters at the centre of the film: Neal Cassady (Josh Lucas), his wife Carolyn (Radha Mitchell), and his mistress Billie (Kate Bosworth). Concentrating on this circle situates the film squarely (Beat connotation intended) in the genre of romantic (with a small 'r') drama. 'A little drama going on', Duluoz observes sardonically after one of his most intense clashes with Billie during his third visit to Big Sur (Kerouac 2011: 165).

The larger-than-life proportions of the character of Neal Cassady ensure that 'The Duluoz Legend' overall is more than 'a little drama'. Cassady is, of course, the charismatic hero of *On the Road*, where he is called Dean Moriarty. In *Big Sur* he is called Cody Pomeray. A reunion with his hero at Cassady's suburban home in Los Gatos prompts Kerouac to remark on how much freedom both men have lost since they lived on the road, before that life became a famous book. Kerouac narrates in the film: 'I can see in Neal's eyes that he can see in my own eyes the regret we both feel that recently we haven't had chances to talk, like we used to do driving across America.' In the book, this passage continues: 'too many people now want to talk to us and tell us *their* stories, we've been hemmed in and surrounded and outnumbered – The circle's closed in on the old heroes of the night' (Kerouac 2011: 56; VO). Unlike Kerouac, however, Cassady seems to have adjusted to his situation. Even though he has just spent two years in prison for dealing in marijuana with two undercover policemen, he is not bitter. He is married with three children and he 'actually loves his home' (Kerouac 2011: 56; VO). Of particular importance, Cassady controls his drinking and disapproves of the lack of control that fuels Kerouac's self-destructive course. Cassady 'really loves me like a brother', Kerouac narrates, 'and more than that, he gets annoyed at me sometimes especially when I fumble and bumble like with a bottle' (Kerouac 2011: 115; VO).

If Kerouac wants to be loved, Cassady's love for him 'like a brother' could supply that need. In fact, the alcoholic binge on which Kerouac launches immediately after his return to San Francisco from Big Sur has been sparked by the news from home that his cat has died; this reawakens the childhood trauma of the death of Kerouac's brother Gerard (Kerouac 2011: 43; VO). The many deaths of animals to which Kerouac seems unusually sensitive throughout *Big Sur* – an otter (Kerouac 2011: 91; VO), a mouse (Kerouac 2011: 94–95; DL), some goldfish (Kerouac 2011: 144–45), a sea trout (Kerouac 2011: 174; VO) – are repetitions of that death, from which he seeks salvation in his appeal to God in his 'Sea' poem. While Kerouac doubts his own belief in a personal God, he cannot doubt Neal Cassady's existence as a person, a lover of life (Kerouac 2011:121), and potentially a lover of Kerouac if he will accept Cassady as a brother.

Still, this relationship depends on an 'angelic' ideal that Kerouac secretly doubts as much as he doubts the existence of God: it supposes 'some kind of new thing in the world actually where men can really be angelic friends and not be homosexual and not fight over girls' (Kerouac 2011: 116). Kerouac's relation to Cassady arouses, on the one hand, homosexual panic – clearly in evidence on a later visit to a hot springs bath house on the Big Sur coast (Kerouac 2011: 91–92) – and on the other hand, the panic of betrayal. Kerouac is in love with Cassady's wife, Carolyn; she returns his feelings, as Polish dramatizes in two scenes of intimate dialogue largely invented for the film. But Kerouac does not want to end up fighting over Carolyn with Cassady, whom he also 'always loved' (Kerouac 2011: 58; VO).

The book and the film agree in their presentation of this basic situation, but the film diverges significantly in assigning Billie, Cassady's mistress, a role at least equal to if not, in fact, greater than the role played by Carolyn. In real life Billie was Jacky Gibson, a woman who featured only briefly in Cassady's love life and even less in Kerouac's. It is not clear why she is the one character whose real name is not used in the film, but the retention of her fictional name has the ironic and no doubt unintentional effect of underscoring the fictional nature of her role as assigned by Polish and originally by Kerouac, each for a different purpose.

Kerouac, or Duluoz in the book, projects onto Billie the images of people in his life who mean more to him. When Duluoz first meets her, he calls her Julien, the fictional name for Kerouac's New York friend Lucien Carr, 'who hates Cody's guts and Cody hates him' (Kerouac 2011: 148; VO). In Billie's case, Duluoz fears, the antagonism is really directed at Cody's [Neal's] wife: Billie 'is the great enemy of Evelyn' (Kerouac 2011: 126). Nevertheless, to deflect his anxiety about taking Evelyn from Cody, Duluoz takes Billie, with Cody's cooperation, as a substitute Evelyn. Toward the end of their relationship, he finds himself calling Billie 'Evelyn' (Kerouac 2011: 164), and as he watches Billie wading in the surf at Big Sur, he elevates her as 'ST. CAROLYN [Evelyn's real name] BY THE SEA' (Kerouac 2011: 159). The film retains Kerouac's identification of Billie with Lucien; it is just further evidence of Kerouac's Beat craziness or perhaps the clinical madness into which he is descending. However, the identification of Billie with Carolyn gets cut from the film. Polish has a different role in mind for Billie – one which seems to coincide with the role that Billie wants to play in Kerouac's life.

If Kerouac wants love, Billie is willing and able to give it; she demonstrates this implausibly in the film by jumping onto Kerouac and rolling with him onto a couch, immediately after Cassady has introduced them. (In the book they reach this stage only after considerable talk 'about Cody and eternity' [Kerouac 2011: 125].) The guilt already entailed in Kerouac's much-less-demonstrative relationship with Carolyn is removed, in Billie's case, by the fact that Cassady has made it clear to Kerouac that she is just on loan (though her eagerness seems to raise doubts in Cassady about whether he will ever get her back).[3] Rather than threatening both a marriage and a friendship, Kerouac's relationship with Billie holds out the additional promise of further cementing his relationship with both Carolyn and Neal. 'I can see it now, a great big four way marriage with Cody and Evelyn', Duluoz fantasizes (Kerouac 2011: 126; VO), evidently assuming that Billie's enmity toward Evelyn will vanish once another husband is in view. While this statement about a four-way marriage appears in the book only after Duluoz has met Billie, we hear it twice in the film's voiceover: we hear it first in the earlier scene of Kerouac's initial visit to the Cassadys' home. It provides the keynote against which Kerouac's failure to achieve harmony in his life tragically resounds.

To dispel any doubt about the cause of Kerouac's failure, Billie provides the diagnosis as well as offering the cure. During supper with Billie and her four-year-old son, Elliott, Duluoz disturbs what the book describes as 'a little family home scene' (Kerouac 2011: 145–46; VO) by reporting that he does not want to marry Billie as they had previously planned. Sensing the disturbance, he asks, 'What have I done wrong?' In the film, Billie asks this question about herself, and then turns on Kerouac: 'I'll tell you what you've done wrong.' Her answer, in both the book (Kerouac 2011: 146) and the film, is that Kerouac is wrong to 'withhold your love from a woman like me and previous women and future women like me'. As Billie delivers this line in the film, she seems to bare her face to the camera; as viewers, we are to detect no pretence in what we see. In contrast, when the camera turns to Kerouac for his reaction, he seems to shrink from the force of its gaze, which has become identified with Billie's gaze and the truth that Polish identifies with her point of view.

The book and the film approach this scene from different perpsectives. In the book, which maintains Duluoz's point of view even when he reflects on how someone else sees him, we have already been told repeatedly that he is 'utterly bored' by Billie's ideas (Kerouac 2011: 126–27), a judgement that prepares us to dismiss what Billie says in the supper scene. Given the significance that the film assigns to Kerouac's boredom, this view of Billie clues us in that she does not hold the answer to his problems. However, the film does not see Billie from Kerouac's point of view. While Kerouac finds her boring, Polish is fascinated by her. He told an interviewer that he had determined her role to be 'very pivotal'. When he began writing the adaptation (Polish and Bosworth n.d.), he cut any references to Billie as boring. By casting Kate Bosworth in the role, he identified his point of view with hers to retain independence from the two powerful egos invested in the male leads. 'I needed somebody to be in front of the camera that could navigate these two guys' Polish explained. 'It's tough because Josh was very focused on being

Neal, Marc was very focused on being Jack, and I didn't have an ally. So she became my ally in between this.' Eventually, Bosworth became more than an ally. She and Polish were married shortly after filming completed.

To say that Polish had special motives for adopting Billie's point of view is not to invalidate it. Late in the book, Duluoz himself wonders if she is right about his withholding love (Kerouac 2011: 159; VO). At least one biographer has extended this judgement into a general condemnation of Kerouac's 'utter lack of comprehension of what it meant to have a relationship with another person, man or woman' (Miles 1998: 271). However, if Polish's task is to adapt Kerouac's book into a movie, the main question to ask is not 'Who was Kerouac?' but rather 'What story is Kerouac trying to tell in this book?' To answer that question, Kerouac's (Duluoz's) point of view must be taken into account. From his perspective, Billie's claim that he is withholding his love would seem not only boring but false. He has been giving her plenty of love, though even that has come to seem boring (Kerouac 2011: 129). What Billie is asking him to give, it must seem to him, is not only his love, but his freedom. She wants him to conform to the roles and rules of 'a little family home scene' (Kerouac 2011: 145–46; VO). Far from offering a path to salvation – for which Duluoz continues to look to Evelyn (Kerouac 2011: 117) –Billie is one of those who have 'hemmed in and surrounded and outnumbered . . . the old heroes of the night' (Kerouac 2011: 56; VO).

What kind of story is Kerouac trying to tell? When Duluoz speaks of the constricting circle drawn around 'the old heroes of the night', it is easy to imagine 'Don't Fence Me In' playing faintly in the background. In fact, references to the Old West, and to western movies, punctuate the adventures of Duluoz and Cody in the novel. During the second visit to Big Sur, Cody critiques Duluoz's imitation of Wallace Beery in the 1940 film *Twenty Mule Team* (Kerouac 2011: 111). The prelude to their rendezvous with Billie is a bust-up visit to a frontier town theme park, the venue for a 'hiss-the-villain play' that Evelyn has been working on. The 'sheriff' proprietor, 'in a menacing voice like T.V. western movies', bawls out Duluoz for playing real piano in the fake saloon (Kerouac 2011: 119). Perhaps most significant is the prelude to a scene where Duluoz stages a 'face to face' meeting between Evelyn and Billie (Kerouac 2011: 154; VO), stopping off at the Pomerays' home on the way to his third stay at Big Sur. During the drive, while Billie watches over the sleeping Elliott in the back seat, Duluoz, Dave Wain (Lew Welch in real life) and Romana Swartz (Lenore Kandel) have a drunken song-fest up front, belting out old favourites like 'Home on the Range' and 'Red River Valley'. They are literally supplying the soundtrack for what Duluoz imagines as 'the next adventure something that's been going on in America ever since the covered wagons clocked the deserts in three months flat' (Kerouac 2011: 153).

To neglect this western theme, as Polish does, is to miss an important undercurrent in the ensuing scene at the Pomeray/Cassady homes. In fact, it is what makes this scene quintessentially Beat. As it happens, the Cassady home is the site of events that inspired Kerouac's play *Beat Generation* and subsequently the script for *Pull My Daisy* (Allan 1998: 187). This is the most authentic Beat movie insofar as original Beat writers (Corso, Ginsberg, and Orlovsky as well as Kerouac) played a direct role in creating it. The strategy is to start with 'a little family home scene' (Kerouac 2011: 145–46; VO), as Duluoz refers to his supper with Billie and Elliott, then explode its conventions by dropping a western into the middle of it. The Cassadys are the family and the cowboys are the poets: Corso, Ginsberg, and Orlovsky in *Daisy*; Kerouac, Welch and Kandel in *Big Sur*. (Kandel is supposed to be present, though she never shows up on camera during this scene in the film.)

In *Daisy*, the cowboy identity emerges toward the end when 'the poets parody a western movie' (Sterritt 1998: 97). In *Big Sur*, the poets' song-fest on the way to the Pomerays has already conjured up the spirit of western adventure, which continues at their home in the spirit of sexual adventure, a common association in Kerouac's work. With his eye on the wide open spaces, Duluoz introduces Billie into the Pomerays' 'little family home scene' (Kerouac 2011: 145–46; VO) in order to expand it to 'Home on the Range' – the 'great big four way marriage' (Kerouac 2011: 126) that Duluoz envisions outside the confines of accepted social conventions. As it turns out, 'Evelyn is not perturbed at all' by her introduction to Billie (Kerouac 2011: 154). He is surprised, however, to see 'the look of absolute fright on Cody's face'. Unlike Milo – Cassady's character in *Pull My Daisy* – Cody seems reluctant to rejoin the cowboys, 'to resume down that road singing bawdier and darker songs', that Duluoz anticipates (Kerouac 2011: 155). It is a measure of Cody's acceptance of the circle that has closed around him and of his betrayal of his namesake, Buffalo Bill Cody.

If Polish has noticed Kerouac's western theme at all, he dismisses it as childish. In the earlier supper scene at Billie's apartment, four-year-old Elliott wears a cowboy hat. What grown-ups do in serious drama, which is clearly what Polish wants his film to be, is to commit to stable relationships, as Billie instructs Kerouac at the supper table, and to defend such relationships by civilized means, as Carolyn does when confronted by Billie, under Polish's direction. From the moment Carolyn lays eyes on Billie in the film, the expression on her face leaves no doubt that she is 'perturbed' by the presence of her rival, but she conceals this so as not to betray weakness. Her suggestion that Kerouac should invite Billie into the house is not a gesture of inclusion but an acceptance of a challenge. The source of the challenge, however, appears to be Kerouac rather than Billie, who plays the role of a more-or-less innocent pawn in a game of which she does not approve.

Billie shows no sign of the enmity toward Carolyn that Duluoz earlier attributed to her. Her tone is friendly when she attempts to engage Carolyn in small talk (invented for the film): 'I just love the color of these walls, Carolyn. What do you call that color?' 'Yellow', is Carolyn's contemptuous reply. It is telling that this exchange narrows the conflict to the two women alone, decorously waging their battle on the ground of home décor. In the book, the small talk is interrupted by Duluoz, who appeals to Dave Wain as he attempts to shift Billie's attention to the 'Home on the Range' awaiting them at Big Sur: 'And small talk at that, like Billie saying, "I always wanted a nice fireplace" and I'm yelling "Don't worry we got one at the cabin hey Dave?"' (Kerouac 2011: 155).

In recollections of the incident that formed the basis for this scene, both Carolyn Cassady and Jacky Gibson explain that the men with whom they were involved saw their lives in terms of movies. Carolyn resented the expectation 'that instantly a rival woman would make you jealous. I mean, these are such square, conventional ideas, and here are all these people who are so far-out. They assumed that obviously, just like the movies, we were going to tear each other up' (Gifford and Lee 1978: 285). While this does appear to be the assumption of Polish's movie, Kerouac's book preserves the unconventional stance of the Beats ironically by setting one movie convention against another, each strongly gendered.

Carolyn Cassady's recollection may accurately reflect how the men expected the women to behave according to the conventions of romantic drama, but that does not mean that they approved of such behaviour, and certainly not that they would expect men to behave that way (hence Duluoz's surprise at Cody). Jacky Gibson's recollection explains the men's expectations in terms that more closely fit the conventions of western movies: 'Remember the old M-G-M films? Jack and Neal were just acting out what they considered to be a reasonable relationship, based on their movie experiences. The buddies. The good guys. The crafty Americans who figure everything out' (Gifford and Lee 1978: 284). The complication that Gibson overlooks is that the buddy film could turn tragic if one buddy betrays another.

During the final visit to Big Sur, after a climactic blow-up with Jacky, Duluoz spends a sleepless night that reminds him of such a buddy film, *The Treasure of the Sierra Madre* (1948): 'turning over rigidly my eyes wide open staring full fright into the dark like the time in the movie Humphrey Bogart who's just killed his partner trying to sleep by the fire and you see his eyes staring into the fire rigid and insane' (Kerouac 2011: 177). This is what becomes of the fire to which Duluoz pointed so enthusiastically back at the Pomerays' home. The fear in Duluoz's eyes now reflects the fear he saw in Cody's eyes. The reflection of that fear through the lens of a movie, a kind of contemporary western, suggests that what haunts Duluoz at the end of his story is the failure of his relationship with Cody, not Billie.

The movie of what everything is

As Kerouac's relationship with Billie completely unravels in the story's final episode, that of a disastrous weekend that Billie and Kerouac spent at Big Sur with Lew Welch and Lenore Kandel, Polish keeps his eyes on Billie. We view the experience through Duluoz's/Kerouac's eyes, to the point that image and sound occasionally blur to convey his drunkenness. Quick glimpses of human figures with vulture heads suggest he has actually gone insane. Billie provides the explanation for what is wrong with Kerouac: 'you're always groaning about how sick you are, you really don't think about others enough' (Kerouac 2011: 162; DL). Finally, after Kerouac freaks out over a garbage pit that Billie has dug, and which he views as a grave intended for Elliott, Billie sums up her diagnosis: 'you're so fucking neurotic' (Kerouac 2011: 187; DL).

But the film, struggling to be true to the book, does not end there. Billie walks away with Elliott, leaving Kerouac to shovel dirt to fill in the garbage pit. Breathing heavily from the exertion, he suddenly experiences release from his madness and guilt: 'Just a golden wash of goodness has spread over all and over all my body and mind' (Kerouac 2011: 188; VO). This line opens a long monologue in which Kerouac foresees a happy ending for himself and his companions, including Billie and Elliott: 'Billie will go on being golden one way or the other. The little boy will grow up and be a great man.' By moving these lines to the beginning of the monologue, Polish maintains his emphasis on the relationship with Billie; in fact he has inserted her name in place of the more ambiguous identity 'St. Carolyn by the Sea', which appears in the text of the novel (Kerouac 2011: 188). For the most part, however, the monologue spoken by Kerouac in the film accurately follows the text. It concludes: 'Something good will come out of all things yet – And it will be golden and eternal just like that – There's no need to say another word.'

It is hard to accept a shift of mood that comes so suddenly, both in the film and in the novel, though the latter provides some space for transition by having Duluoz actually enjoy a few minutes of sleep – something he has sorely lacked over the preceding days – before he senses 'blessed relief' upon awakening (Kerouac 2011: 187). When Stephen Holden (2013: C6), in his otherwise admiring review, writes that 'the major flaw of "Big Sur" is a rushed quasi-happy ending', he seems to be faulting the book more than the film. The ending 'is really an admission of defeat', Holden asserts, presumably because the hope it holds out seems unrealistic. Thus, Holden can commend the film for its realism because it allows us to recognize a defeat that Kerouac himself cannot admit. The sudden shift of mood reveals a flaw in Kerouac's character, as yet another instance of his penchant for self-delusion, but the mood of the film is consistent overall in portraying the path to defeat as inevitable, given his character. 'Filmed without a trace of sentimentality', Holden concludes (2013: C6), '"Big Sur" is an achingly sad last hurrah.' For Holden, as for Polish, the focus is on who Kerouac was, rather than the story he was trying to tell, using Duluoz as a character in a 'legend'.

If the ending of *Big Sur* fits with the rest of the story, it is certainly not the part of the story that concerns the relationship with Billie, at least not as Polish has interpreted it. Polish appears to agree with Billie's judgement that Kerouac is withholding his love, but there is no indication that the euphoria of the ending involves the giving of love. The relationship with Billie in particular has completely ended, as the ending of the novel makes explicit in words dropped from the film: 'she'll forget me, her life'll go on' (Kerouac 2011: 188).[4] Beyond omitting words, the film omits an entire dimension of the novel with which the ending, despite all of its suddenness, fits coherently. Essentially, this is the Beat dimension. Apart from his appreciation of the rhythms of Kerouac's language, Polish's understanding of beatness is largely superficial: being sexy, jazzy and crazy makes his characters Beat. I have already suggested that he misses the Beat function of the intrusion of western movies into romantic drama. He also misses what Duluoz identifies as 'a lesson in beatness' (Kerouac 2011: 98) in the middle of his second visit to Big Sur. The lesson applies directly to the sudden shift from despair to euphoria at the end of the novel.

In context, Duluoz's 'lesson in beatness' is intended for Ron Blake, one of the young wanna-be-Beats whom Duluoz had been hoping to escape by retreating to Big Sur. Ron had attached himself to Dave Wain, and Duluoz did not have the heart to cut him out when the entire pack of poets descended on Big Sur for a weekend party, the occasion of his second visit to the scene. When the partying leaves Duluoz with a bad case of the DT's, Ron Blake is the only one still around to witness his agony. At least, Duluoz hopes, the kid has now seen the dark side of Beat life, the 'down and out' condition to which the term 'Beat' originally applied (Kerouac 1959a: 570).

That is Part One of the 'lesson in beatness' and it is as far as we get in the film (where Ron Blake is called by his real name, Paul Smith, played by John Robinson). The film omits Part Two of the lesson, which begins when Ron leaves Duluoz alone in the canyon and 'soon as the sun goes down I swear on

my arm I'm as well as I ever was: just like that suddenly' (Kerouac 2011: 99) –
just as suddenly, in fact, as his emergence from despair into bliss at the
end of the novel: 'suddenly hopelessly and completely finished I sit there in
the hot sun and close my eyes and there's the swarming peace of Heaven
in my eyelids' (Kerouac 2011: 187). The suddenness conveys the essential
Beat paradox of simultaneously being beat (defeated) and feeling 'beatific'
(Kerouac 1959a: 571).

As at the end of the novel, Duluoz's ascent from despair during his second
stay at Big Sur is more than a restoration of health. It is an elevation into a
sense of holiness, which may explain why Polish eliminates this scene from
his film, if I was right in my earlier conjecture that he is allergic to Kerouac's
religious dimension. But at the end of the film, despite Polish's attempt to
naturalize the experience by running images of Big Sur's crashing surf and
giant trees against Kerouac's monologue, the terms of the monologue remain
religious, in a sense more specific to Kerouac than the image of the Cross that
he envisions earlier at the height of his madness. The terms of the monologue
look beyond suffering: 'Something good will come out of all things yet—And
it will be golden and eternal just like that' (Kerouac 2011: 188; VO).

'Golden eternity' was Kerouac's name for the beatific vision, of heaven or
of God, which he once experienced during a moment of unconsciousness,
recalled as 'that fainting vision of the Golden Eternity' (Kerouac 2011: 100)
after Ron Blake leaves Duluoz alone at Big Sur. Kerouac's expanded meditation
on that vision, entitled *The Scripture of the Golden Eternity*, illuminates 'the
swarming peace of Heaven in my eyelids' that Duluoz describes at the end
(Kerouac 2011: 187). The term 'golden', he explains in *The Scripture*, 'came
from the sun in my eyelids' during his fainting spell, whereas the term
'eternity' came 'from my sudden instant realization as I woke up that I had
just been where it all came from and where it was all returning, the everlasting
So' (Kerouac 1960: 597).

Kerouac describes here an experience of transport, of having been in a
different place, which suggests a way of understanding the sudden shift of
mood at the end of *Big Sur* in terms that are more secular without being any
less religious, at least according to Kerouac's understanding. The mood shifts
because Duluoz has experienced a radical shift in point of view. It is identical
to the shift that he describes during his first visit to Big Sur, when he views 'all
the details of life' from 'a million light years away', as if in a movie made and
viewed by God (Kerouac 2011: 20).

For Kerouac, the beatific vision is not merely a vision of God, but an
identification with God's vision, and point of view. In *The Scripture of the
Golden Eternity* he calls this identification 'Human Godhood' (Kerouac 1960:
592). Moreover, he employs the movie metaphor both to convey the vision in

human terms and to expose its fictionality, a more humane take on the concept of nothingness that Kerouac derived from his study of Buddhism: 'This world is the movie of what everything is, it is one movie, made of the same stuff throughout, belonging to nobody, which is what everything is' (Kerouac 1960: 592). Kerouac's understanding of 'what everything is' provides a different standard of realism than the one Stephen Holden applies to Polish's movie. Polish gives us a movie that pretends we are really watching a life. Kerouac gives us a book that assumes we are really living a movie.

Works cited

Allan, B. (1998), 'The Making (and Unmaking) of *Pull My Daisy*', *Film History*, 2: 185–205.

Big Sur (2013), M. Polish (dir), Big Sur Productions, Ketchup Entertainment DVD.

Bloom, H. (1969), 'The Visionary Cinema of Romantic Poetry', in A.H. Rosenfield (ed.), *William Blake: Essays in Honor of S. Foster Damon*, Providence: Brown University, 1969, 18–35.

Case, C. (1996), *The Ultimate Movie Thesaurus*, New York: Henry Holt.

Dowd, J. J., and N. R. Pallotta (2000), 'The End of Romance: The Demystification of Love in the Postmodern Age', *Sociological Perspectives* 43.4: 549–80.

French, W. (1986), *Jack Kerouac*, Boston: Twayne.

Gifford, B., and L. Lee (1978), *Jack's Book: An Oral Biography of Jack Kerouac*, New York: St. Martin's.

Holden, S. (2013), 'A Writer Who's Beat in Search of a Refuge', rev *Big Sur* (2013), *New York Times* 1 November: C6.

Jacobs, L. (2008), *The Decline of Sentiment: American Film in the 1920s*, Berkeley: University of California.

Kerouac, J. (1959a), '*Beatific*: The Origins of the Beat Generation', in Kerouac (1996), 565–73.

Kerouac, J. (1959b), 'Belief & Technique for Modern Prose', in Kerouac (1996), 483–84

Kerouac, J. (1960), *The Scripture of the Golden Eternity* (selections), in Kerouac (1996), 590–97

Kerouac, J. (1976), *The Dharma Bums*, New York: Penguin.

Kerouac, J. (1995), *Desolation Angels*. New York: Riverhead.

Kerouac, J. (1996), *The Portable Jack Kerouac*, (ed.), Ann Charters, New York: Penguin.

Kerouac, J. (2011), *Big Sur*, New York: Penguin.

Miles, B. (1998), *Jack Kerouac, King of the Beats: JA Portrait*. New York: Henry Holt.

Moore, Dave (n.d.), 'Character Key to Kerouac's Duluoz Legend'. Available at: www.beatbookcovers.com/kercomp/index.htm (last accessed 6 December 2014).

Naked Lunch (1991), D. Cronenberg (dir), Naked Lunch Productions.

One Fast Move or I'm Gone: Kerouac's Big Sur (2008), Curt Worden (dir), Kerouac Films.

Polish, M. (n.d.), 'Director Michael Polish on Bringing Kerouac Back to "Big Sur,"' H. Weston (int), *BlackBook*. Available at: www.bbook.com/director-michael-polish-bringing-kerouac-back-big-sur/ (last accessed 6 December 2014).

Polish, M., and K. Bosworth (n.d.), 'Michael Polish and Kate Bosworth, Director and Muse', E. Brown (int), *Interview*. Available at: www.interviewmagazine.com/film/kate-bosworth-michael-polish-big-sur (last accessed 6 December 2014).

Pull My Daisy (1959), R. Frank and A. Leslie (dirs), G-String Enterprises.

Rich, B. R. (2012), 'Sundance', *Film Quarterly*, 66.2: 66–72.

'Romantic Drama Movies' (n.d.), IMDb. Available at: www.imdb.com/list/ls057668863/ (last accessed 6 December 2014).

Sterritt, D. (1998), *Mad to Be Saved: The Beats, the '50s, and Film*, Carbondale: Southern Illinois University.

Subterraneans, The (1960), Ranald MacDougall (dir), Metro-Goldwyn-Mayer.

Theado, M. (2000), *Understanding Jack Kerouac*, Columbia: University of South Carolina.

Thoreau, H.D. (1985), *The Maine Woods* (with *A Week on the Concord and Merrimack Rivers*, etc.), New York: Library of America.

Whitman, W. (1968), 'Out of the Cradle Endlessly Rocking', in *Leaves of Grass*, H.W. Blodgett and S. Bradley (eds), New York: Norton, 246–53.

Wiegand, W. (1962), 'A Turn in the Road for the King of the Beats', rev Kerouac, *Big Sur* (2011), *New York Times Book Review* 16 September: 4, 42.

Angel Tendencies and Gratuitous Acts: *Kill Your Darlings* and the Legacy of Lucien Carr

Fiona Paton

When Lucien Carr died in 2005, his *New York Times* obituary described him as 'a literary lion who never roared' (Hampton 2005), a strange accolade for a man who worked quietly for fifty years as a news editor for United Press. Nonetheless, it captures the complexity of Carr's position as a key member of the nascent Beat Generation as it developed around Columbia University in the mid-1940s. Although he never published any literature himself, Carr was a galvanizing force in the artistic development of Allen Ginsberg and Jack Kerouac, leading the search for a 'New Vision' as these young men sought to define themselves and their generation in the immediate aftermath of World War II. In a 1952 letter to Kerouac, Ginsberg announced that the collection of poems he was working on would be dedicated to 'Jack Kerouac, Lucien Carr, and Neal Cassady: "VAST GENIUSES OF AMERICA WHO HAVE GIVEN ME METHOD AND FACT"' (Ginsberg 2008: 76). Several years later, Ginsberg dedicated the groundbreaking poem 'Howl' to Lucien Carr, an honor that Carr declined, asking that his name be removed (Campbell 1999: 190). Kerouac also paid tribute to Carr in 1956 by titling his long, surrealistic poem 'Lucien Midnight' but again Carr protested, and the poem became 'Old Angel Midnight' (Maher 2004: 326). Lucien Carr provided the link between Burroughs and Ginsberg, and between Ginsberg and Kerouac, and seems to have been as important as Burroughs in broadening their literary horizons. Hence the author of Carr's *New York Times* obituary, United Press colleague Wilborn Hampton, has some justification when calling him the 'inspirational muse' (Hampton 2005) to the leading Beat figures, even though Carr himself sought to efface his legacy within their group.

While he may never have given a literary roar, Carr did literally roar – and howl – on many occasions. His exploits were widely chronicled by his Beat peers and their biographers, such as the time he wrecked Burroughs' car in the East St. Louis red light district when he was was 14 years old (Gifford and Lee 1999: 44). Or when he dressed up as the Phantom of the Opera and gate crashed the *Swan Lake* cast party at the Metropolitan Opera House (Kerouac-Parker 2007: 125). Or the time he rolled Kerouac down the street in a barrel (Kerouac 1982: 221). How about the time he crunched a beer glass between his teeth? (Morgan 2006: 41). Oh, and the time he killed a man. Hampton's obituary (2005) understandably downplays this incident, noting its centrality in the Carr legend but offering a simplified account: 'In repulsing the homosexual advances of a hanger-on of the Beat crowd, Mr. Carr stabbed his pursuer with a Boy Scout knife and killed him. Mr. Carr served a brief time in prison for manslaughter, but was later pardoned.'

This 'hanger-on' was David Kammerer, also from St Louis, who was already friends with William Burroughs prior to meeting Carr. Carr met Kammerer as a youngster in his hometown of St Louis, and a close friendship developed between the two, of which Carr's mother seemed initially to approve. Kammerer took Carr on a trip to Mexico in 1939, thereafter following him to various private schools and colleges, the last being Columbia University in 1943. In the early hours of 14 August 1944, Carr stabbed Kammerer multiple times in the heart with his Boy Scout knife and dumped the body in the Hudson River (Griffin 2014).

Although, as far as we know, Carr never wrote about the experience himself, his relationship with Kammerer has generated multiple representations in both literature and film. The most important of the print works is the short novel co-written by Kerouac and Burroughs in 1945 called *And the Hippos Were Boiled in Their Tanks*, which was only finally released in 2008 after Carr's death (he had suppressed its publication during his lifetime). Ginsberg began drafting a novel called *The Bloodsong* immediately after the murder, but discontinued it after negative reactions from both the Dean and his advisor at Columbia (Ginsberg 2006: 115). Kerouac made the murder the culminating event in his first novel, *The Town and the City*, and related it in detail in one of his last books, *Vanity of Duluoz*. Aaron Latham, who at one point was drafting a biography of Kerouac, published an article titled 'The Columbia Murder that Gave Birth to the Beats' in *New York* magazine in 1976, subsequently composing a play about the incident called *Birth of Beats: Murder and the Beat Generation* which debuted in New York City in 2012. More recently, the 2000 movie *Beat*, directed by Gary Walkow, brought together Burroughs' accidental shooting of Joan Vollmer and the Kammerer murder by dramatizing Ginsberg and Carr's 1951 trip to Mexico, using flashbacks to reveal Carr's memories of the 1944 killing. Finally, we have the subject of this chapter, *Kill Your Darlings*, written by Austin Bunn and directed by John Krokidas, ten years in the making, which came out in 2013. First screened at the Sundance Film Festival and then given limited release in North America, the film received mixed reviews, with the lead performances by Dane Dehaan and Daniel Radcliffe generating most of the praise and the perceived overuse of Beat clichés most of the criticism.

Why does it matter now, 70 years later, that Lucien Carr killed David Kammerer in Riverside Park on 14 August 1944? The murder has repeatedly been cited as the catalyst for the birth of the Beat generation. The Beats themselves wrote about it and talked about it extensively. But it also matters because the portrayal of the two main characters continues to raise difficult issues about sexual identity that are far from being resolved. In both literary and cultural terms, *Kill Your Darlings* is an important film. In recreating the formation of lasting alliances that were instrumental in the emergence of postmodernism, it is obviously of interest to Beat scholars. But the story it tells is larger than this: the film also examines the ethics of desire and complicity in a culture built on the normative oversimplification of sexuality.

Screenwriter Austin Bunn and director John Krokidas were well aware of these complexities when they undertook the project in 2003. As college roommates at Yale, Krokidas and Bunn shared a love for the Beat writers, especially Allen Ginsberg. In an interview with the Writers Guild Foundation, Bunn recalls that 'as a young gay closeted creative writer from New Jersey, Allen Ginsberg just meant the world to me' (Bunn and Krokidas: 2013). He also recalled 'feeling angry that at a certain point in American history you could get away with killing a gay man if you portrayed him as a predator'. Krokidas agrees, saying that it was the inequity of the situation that continued to 'reignite the creative force inside of me' as he struggled with the project over ten years: 'You could literally get away with murder by portraying your victim as a gay man' (Bunn and Krokidas: 2013). Despite such a forthright acknowledgement of their agenda, Bunn and Krokidas have crafted a nuanced portrayal of Lucien Carr and David Kammerer based on their careful synthesis of primary Beat texts. Their refusal to oversimplify the dynamic between the two is one of the film's greatest strengths, in terms of both narrative action and historical accuracy. However, such nuance has also triggered the harshest attacks against it.

Mark Judge, a journalist for *The Daily Caller*, offers one example of the rising conservative anxiety about sexual identity in his untidily titled article 'Son of famous Beat murderer Lucien Carr disputes "Kill Your Darlings" film's version of events'. The opening lines, 'Hollywood is defending another pedophile. This time he's also a stalker', could themselves have been written in the 1950s, when Hollywood was the supposed stronghold of homosexual and communist subversion. He describes *Kill Your Darlings* as 'a completely false and agenda-driven piece of Hollywood propaganda' (Judge: 2014). Judge's paranoid vision of the liberal conspiracy within Hollywood would not be worth remarking on except that his article includes a complete letter from Lucien Carr's son Caleb, who takes an equally reactionary view of the film, although his enemy is not so much Hollywood in general but Allen Ginsberg specifically.

One would be hard pressed to challenge the general perception of Kammerer as a sexual predator; *Kill Your Darlings* does not sidestep this issue. But to excoriate Ginsberg, and by extension the film maker, as endorsing child sexual abuse indicates a deeper anxiety about homosexuality. To claim that the film presents Lucien Carr as the 'Judas of the Beats' and that John Krokidas and Daniel Radcliffe represent 'the very extremist wing of the gay movement' (Judge: 2014) is blatant misrepresentation. Caleb Carr's position should, of course, be taken in context – as the recipient of violent abuse from his father Lucien, Caleb understandably would resist any positive depiction of David Kammerer. However, his attack on the film and its creators highlights the issue of historical accuracy, especially since writer Austin Bunn has stated, 'I'm really proud of how much is in the script that is actually direct from historical experience' (Bunn and Krokidas: 2013). Reviewers and critics have repeatedly presented Kammerer's murder as the formative moment of the Beat Generation. In his biography of Ginsberg, Morgan states: 'It was a catalyst for a complete change in their way of seeing and reacting to the world. No could understand exactly what had gone wrong with their "New Vision" theories, which should have made everyone more tolerant of people like Kammerer' (2006: 52).

But focusing solely on the stabbing diminishes the much more important story of how these young intellectuals came to formulate their 'New Vision', a philosophy that shaped their behaviour and attitudes prior to the stabbing and, one might even say, enabled it. The New Vision had more to do with Andre Gide's *act gratuit* than with tolerance. It was also significantly informed by a shared valorization of madness within the group, an attitude that Carr transmitted in part through his championing of Rimbaud. Kerouac, however, shared this willingness to embrace the 'systematic derangement of the senses', having been diagnosed with *dementia praecox* during his initial training in the United States Navy in 1943. According to Ellis Amburn, who had access to the Lowell archives when writing his biography: 'His diagnosis was changed from dementia praecox to "schizoid personality" with "angel tendencies." By "angel tendencies," the doctors meant delusional self-aggrandizement, but Kerouac and Ginsberg would later give the word "angel" a new meaning for their generation' (1998: 73). This semantic turn is one of the most recognizable elements in the Beat vocabulary, thanks largely to Ginsberg's famous phrase 'angelheaded hipsters' in 'Howl'. Kerouac, too, uses it in *Vanity of Duluoz*, in a telling description of Carr as the group's 'falling star Lucifer angel boy demon genius' (Kerouac 1982: 226). This paradoxical phrase may be taken as a compressed description of Dane Dehaan's portrayal of Lucien Carr in *Kill Your Darlings*, and it is to his credit that, in conjunction with screenwriter Bunn and director Krokidas, he is able to capture both aspects of the young man whose New Vision fused together the markedly different personalities that became the Beat Generation.

Kill Your Darlings begins with its ending: Lucien Carr awkwardly cradling David Kammerer in his arms as the dark waters of the Hudson swirl around them. This unsettling opening shot gains intensity through the physical difference between the two men; David, played by Michael C. Hall, is much taller than the slight Lucien, played by Dane Dehaan. The physical weight of Kammerer makes concrete the emotional burden of his love, as well as his dependency on the younger man. The soundtrack here is 'Lili Marlene', one of the most famously sentimental songs of World War II, but any maudlin effect is undercut by the reverse cinematography, so that the dead Kammerer rises out of the water into Carr's arms, and seems to come back to life. His shocked, dying gaze locks onto the gasping Carr, whose horror and grief are made all the more dramatic by his naked, blood-spattered torso. We then hear a voice-over from Daniel Radcliffe's Ginsberg saying, 'Some things, once you've loved them, become yours forever. And if you try to let them go, they only circle back and return to you. They become part of who you are ...' The camera then cuts to Lucien Carr behind bars, with the script cleverly synchronized so that Lucien completes Allen's lines with '... or they destroy you'. This suggests two important and controversial things about the Carr/Kammerer relationship: that Carr at one point felt love for Kammerer and that, in refusing to acknowledge that love, and hence his own sexuality, he came close to self-destruction. Carr is then visited by Ginsberg, whom Carr has asked (we learn later), to write his deposition. The document is not what Carr needs or wants: he angrily confronts Ginsberg: 'You weren't even there. It's your truth. It's fiction.' As Ginsberg wrestles the deposition back, Carr's panic escalates and the frame freezes, with his final guttural plea – 'Allen! No! Don't ...' – inter-cut with the title in stark capital letters. These opening scenes contain everything that Caleb Carr finds objectionable about the film: Lucien is portrayed as sexually conflicted, manipulative and morally unrepentant. The fact that the title is followed by the words 'BASED ON A TRUE STORY' makes the opening sequence especially controversial.

We might begin by noting that Krokidas and Bunn's depiction of Carr is a lot more positive than it could have been. If we go back to the first literary treatments of the 'Kammerer affair' by the Beats themselves, the Carr who emerges is not only sexually conflicted but also brash and narcissistic. Ginsberg's short narrative *The Bloodsong*, which alternates between invented and real names, introduces Carr presiding over a group of male students in his room, 'naked and waving a towel around his head', having just taken a shower (Ginsberg 2006: 94). Having confided that Kammerer is a 'fruit' who has followed him across the country (Ginsberg 2006: 96), Carr takes Ginsberg to the West End Bar, where he leaps into the centre of the room yelling his favourite lines from Baudelaire. Carr's love for decadent excess is more graphically illustrated when he appears in Ginsberg's room the next night, filthy and covered with blood, his signature red shirt ripped. Telling Ginsberg that he has been in a brawl with a gay artist who tried to 'paw' him, Lucien confesses, 'When I get drunk I become pathological. I kicked Rubenstein over and jumped on him, and then I began biting him' (Ginsberg 2006: 103). It turns out, however, that the blood is David's; Lucien has left bite wounds all over his back and injured his fingers (Ginsberg 2006: 109).

In *And the Hippos Were Boiled in Their Tanks*, Burroughs and Kerouac narrate alternate chapters, with Burroughs adopting the Chandler-esque persona of Will Dennison and Kerouac the Hemmingway-esque persona of Mike Ryko. Dennison introduces us to the Lucien Carr figure, Phillip Tourian, on the second page of the novel, when he enters Dennison's flat with three other people: 'This Phillip is the kind of boy literary fags write sonnets to, which start out, "O raven-haired Grecian lad …"' He was wearing a pair of very dirty slacks and a khaki shirt with the sleeves rolled up showing hard muscular forearms' (Burroughs 2008: 4). While Ramsay Allen, the David Kammerer figure, is mocked for his slavish devotion to young Tourian, he is treated quite sympathetically by Burroughs and Kerouac. For instance, Dennison learns that Tourian has actually come on to Allen, kissing him 'passionately' on a rooftop before pushing him away, and then inviting Allen to commit suicide with him by jumping because, as Phil says, 'After this we have to … it's the only thing left. Either that or go away' (Burroughs 2008: 27). The difference between this Kammerer and Kerouac's much later version in *Vanity of Duluoz* is striking. In the 1967 work, Kammerer becomes Franz Mueller', the Marquis de Sade scoutmaster …' (Kerouac 1967: 251) who relentlessly pursues Claude de Maubris, with Kerouac's Duluoz persona assuring the reader, 'Now I'm not a queer, and neither is Claude, but I've got to expand this queer tale' (Kerouac 1967: 221). There are surely some grounds for attributing this change to pressure from Carr himself, who consistently expressed his anxiety about his former notoriety (Kerouac 2010: 162). As we know, *Hippos* would not be published until after Carr's death, but *Vanity of Duluoz*, with its glib treatment of the murder and its insistence that Claude 'was no fairy'(Kerouac 1982: 221) was presumably given the go ahead.

Vanity of Duluoz does, however, mention Carr/de Maubris' fascination with Gide: 'Claude was a great one for what Gide called the *act gratuite* [sic] ("the gratuitous act") the doing of an act just for the hell of it. Seeing his veal Parmesan didnt [sic] taste too hot in one of the restaurants he simply picked up the plate, said "This is crap," and threw it back over his shoulder with just a flick of the wrist, no expression, suavely picking up his glass of wine to sip . . .' (Kerouac 1982: 241). Indeed, Carr might well have created his own persona from Gide's anti-hero Lafcadio, who in *Les Caves de Vatican*, pushes a man out of a train simply because he can (Fowlie 1965). The gratuitous act is the motiveless act, free will exercised without constraint or concern for the consequences. Gide, Rimbaud, and Yeats are constantly evoked, quoted, and referenced by the group as the keystones of their New Vision, the gist of which is voiced by Tourian in *Hippos*: 'The ultimate society has to be the completely artistic society. Each of these artist citizens must, during the course of his lifetime, complete his own spiritual circle' (Burroughs 2008: 39).

This sentiment finds similar expression in the work of Rimbaud. Krokidas and Bunn acknowledge his importance several times in the script. Lucien quotes Rimbaud: 'In the dawn, armed with a burning patience, we shall enter the splendid city!' Later, Burroughs quotes Rimbaud when he mocks Ginsberg's manifesto for the New Vision, advocating 'the derangement of the senses' in place of words. Rimbaud's love affair with the older Verlaine bears an uncomfortable resemblance to the relationship between Carr and Kammerer, as Kerouac noted in *Vanity of Duluoz* ('exactly like Rimbaud and Verlaine' [Kerouac 1982: 238]). Both couples lived lives of excess that included alcohol (especially absinthe), drugs (especially hashish), periodic violence, and a passionate commitment to poetry and the new forms it might assume. It is almost as though Carr and Kammerer deliberately acted out those roles in their own ways. Carr was 19 when he killed Kammerer; Rimbaud was 18 when he broke with Verlaine and wrote *A Season in Hell*. It was one of the two books Carr took with him to the Tombs (Schumacher 1992: 45).

The other book was *A Vision* by W.B. Yeats. This is still an obscure text today, but it was even more so in 1944. To describe this work as esoteric is an understatement; it is a surprising text for a 19-year-old to be absorbed by, to the extent that he not only studied it himself but encouraged others to study it. *Kill Your Darlings* uses the 1925 edition, which begins with a diagram of the Great Wheel and a poem describing the phases of the moon. What is most important to our understanding of Carr and the New Vision is the necessity of completing all phases and cycles to begin again at a more advanced spiritual level. Neal Mann describes Yeats' system in terms of 'amoral humanism' (2012: 13). It is not difficult to see how such a system, embraced by a young man both brilliant and unstable, could authorize extremes of behaviour as necessary to individuation. Kerouac seems especially perceptive in the following description of Carr, when he writes to Ginsberg in September

1944: 'I prefer the new vision in terms of art', which implies a distinction between life practice and aesthetic practice (Kerouac 1995: 82). Kerouac seems concerned that Carr's life practice of the gratuitous act is vindicated though the abstruse philosophy of Yeats.

Unlike Yeats and Rimbaud, Gide is not referenced in *Kill Your Darlings*. One significant improvement to Carr's character in the film is the replacement of the more callow gratuitous acts recorded by his fellow Beats (e.g. throwing restaurant food over his shoulder, urinating out of hotel windows, making lewd pronouncements in theatre foyers) with acts of more meaningful rebellion, such as the spontaneous reciting of Henry Miller during a tour of Columbia's Butler Library and the elaborate midnight 'library heist' episode, in which Carr, Ginsberg, Burroughs, and Kerouac replace the venerable tomes of Western literature displayed in glass cases with banned works from the restricted section. Both of these incidents are invented, but as Krokidas explained, he needed a way to actualize on screen the kinds of literary conversations the Beats were having at the time (Stein: 2013). The sequence may evoke the mania of a *Scooby Doo* chase scene, but it allows Carr to emerge as the truly committed iconoclast, who refuses to leave the library until his mission is complete, despite the thick-headed, burly cops bearing down on him. Leaving behind a row of cut out letters that spell 'The New Vision', Carr makes his escape with Ginsberg's help, and the four renegades disappear into the night. In the next scene, the library guide leads his tour group past glass cases filled with copies of *Ulysses*, *Tropic of Cancer*, *Lady Chatterly's Lover*, *Billy Budd*, and various works of pornography opened to images of seduction, copulation, and flagellation.

The assault on tradition is, unsurprisingly, one of the key themes of the film. It is present right at the start in the tension between Allen and his father Louis Ginsberg, also a poet (as he was in real life) but one who is very traditional. It is foregrounded in Allen's interactions with Professor Steeves, who worships the sonnet, disparages Whitman, and scathingly tells Allen 'This university exists because of tradition and form ...'. It is brilliantly displayed during Ginsberg's first guided tour of the Butler Library, described by the guide as a 'church' containing the 'sacraments' of Western civilization (such as the first folio of *Hamlet*). This is interrupted by Lucien Carr leaping onto a table and reciting from Henry Miller. Ginsberg, delighted by this performance, senses a kindred spirit in Lucien, who likewise is drawn to Allen's challenging of Professor Steeves in class. When they meet in his dorm room, Carr toasts Whitman, salaciously murmuring, 'you dirty bastard' as he stares appraisingly at Ginsberg. In their first excursion together to 'the edge of the world' (i.e. the Village), Ginsberg recognizes Ogden Nash in a bar. Having been treated to a recital of one of Nash's poems by Burroughs and

Kammerer, Carr identifies him as an example of the Enemy, a home-grown fascist in fact, who, along with metre and rhyme (and Professor Steeves, as Allen enthusiastically interjects) functions as a prison guard in the service of tradition. Ogden Nash is a bit of a straw man in terms of representing the literary establishment, but he gives Lucien the chance to say: 'They're all guards in some prison. Let's make the prisoners come out and play. Let's come up with new words, new rhythms.' However gauche these lines may sound to our post-post-modern ears, they are entirely fitting for young writers receiving their humanities education at Columbia, one of the bastions of the literary establishment. The inspired energy imparted by Dehaan at moments like this is one of the most authentic elements in the film.

Lucien Carr *was* a brilliant non-conformist. Throughout his education, from elementary through high school and into college, Carr had issues with authority and at various times received disciplinary action, was put on probation, and expelled. However, according to tests done at Taylor School, where he completed high school, his IQ was 138–140 (Griffin 2014). While his physical beauty and magnetism were noted by virtually everyone he encountered, his intelligence was emphasized as much, if not more. Ginsberg wrote to Neal Cassady in 1949, 'As long as I have thought of us as artists, it has been Claude [Carr] who I thought of as central to any active inter-inspiring school or community of creation, and him to whom I have looked for the strength to assume responsibility for the truest aesthetic knowledge' (Ginsberg 2008: 31). Dehaan comes admirably close to capturing this Lucien Carr, playing him with a compelling mix of bravado and vulnerability. When Carr unleashes Henry Miller's *Tropic of Cancer* before the shocked audience in Butler Library, the words are enunciated with such relish that we really believe that he has committed passages to memory. When Ginsberg follows the strains of Brahms' Third Symphony down the hall and discovers Carr in his room, we really feel the depths of the reverie that it has taken him to. When Carr proffers Yeats's *A Vision* to Ginsberg and says 'It's completely brilliant and impossible', Dehaan communicates genuine excitement rather than superficial name dropping. Yet he also shows us the pain of the boy whose father left him, who has attempted suicide, who is so afraid of failure he cannot complete anything. Dehaan's Carr is certainly not the Carr recalled by another Columbia student, Alan Temko, who described him as 'loathsome' and said, 'I had no common ground with this spoiled and destructive boy' (Gifford and Lee 1999: 74). Instead, Dehaan gives us Kerouac's 'falling star Lucifer angel boy demon genius' (Kerouac 1982: 226). It is Carr who emerges as the instigator of the movement that they call the New Vision, although Ginsberg is given credit for naming it; such is Dehaan's performance that we believe in it. The irony, of course, is that Carr was unable to write anything himself.

This point brings us to what is thematically the most complicated and controversial aspect of Carr's portrayal in the film: the compromised relationship between his creativity and his sexuality. Ginsberg's own journal entries about Carr from 1944 are quite incisive in this respect. Ginsberg notes that 'His plea is that art can't satisfy him. His plea may be true. He does not finish by saying that the reason he is not satisfied is that he has no artistic fire, that he cannot make new forms of art. He takes refuge in life, in exhibitionism' (Ginsberg 2006: 49). In his notes for his unfinished novel *The Bloodsong*, Ginsberg gives his character analysis of Carr more specificity (see Ginsberg 2006: 114). The film builds on these observations much more explicitly. Lucien's radical self-doubt requires him to depend on David Kammerer for his college papers, a responsibility transferred to Allen when Lucien breaks with David. Historically, this intellectual dependency is accurate – in *Vanity of Duluoz*, Kerouac cheerfully confesses to writing papers for Carr. But *Kill Your Darlings* makes a much more direct connection between Lucien's creative block and his repressed homosexuality, or ambivalent bisexuality, through intensive cross-cutting in the murder sequence; this symbolically interweaves the actions of Lucien, Allen, Jack, and William.

At this point in the story, we have seen Lucien attempt to end his relationship with David twice: once in the West End Bar after the library heist, then when David climbs in the window of Jack's apartment in the night to ask for Lucien's forgiveness. Lucien's solution to David's obsessive pursuit is to ship out with Jack as a merchant seaman. Allen, however, hurt after Lucien's brusque rejection, tells David where he is; Lucien is then forced to confront him a third time in the National Maritime Union Hall. By this time his emotional exhaustion is evident in his face, and when the final rejection fails ('I'm leaving because of you'), Lucien tells David, 'We're taking a walk'. We now follow four different plot lines: Jack returning to his girlfriend Edie and listening to the last phonograph recording from his wounded war friend Sebastian; Allen having sex with a stranger he meets in a bar; William taking his first shot of heroin, and Lucien in a heated altercation with David in Riverside Park. The words of the dying Sebastian, with a melancholy piano accompaniment, provide the soundtrack as we witness those moments of loss, desire, ecstasy, and violence. The visual cross-cutting of moments of penetration – needle, knife, and penis – explicitly contrasts the actions of those who deny their sexual identities – William and Lucien – with those who embrace them, presumably Jack, reunited with Edie, but particularly Allen, whose decisive commitment to his own homosexuality allows him to find his voice at a writer. His story concludes with two very positive scenes. The first shows him at home with his father, both writing in companionable silence as the end of the war is announced on the radio. His confiscated final paper about the New Vision and the murder is returned in the mail with the inscription 'Walt Jnr.: Keep this. Keep going. Professor Steeves'.

The final scene depicts Allen writing at a table in the West End Bar and declaring (in a close approximation of Ginsberg's own words), 'Like all [lovers and] sad people, I am a poet' (Ginsberg 2006: 62). For Allen, then, the film ends on a note of affirmation: in claiming his homosexual identity, he also claims his identity as a poet.

Much of *Kill Your Darlings* is historically accurate, from the large arc of the formation and demise of the first Beat 'libertine circle' to the small details such as the words 'Lu – Dave' carved into the plaster above David Kammerer's bed (Kerouac 2010: 3). But several key aspects of the story have been changed or omitted to create what might be called an 'agenda' (to use Caleb Carr's words). Barry Miles is the only biographer who implies in any way that Ginsberg had a hand in writing Carr's deposition. Even then, he only asserts that Carr was required by the District Attorney to write an autobiographical statement as part of his defence, and that Ginsberg 'helped Carr with his interview with the DA' (Miles 1989: 53). It is a very different matter to present Allen as being asked by the desperate Lucien to actually write his deposition, and instructing him to present the murder as an 'honor slaying'. Allen does so, but wrestles with the moral implications, because he wants Lucien to 'tell the truth'. Allen takes the statement he has written to the DA's office but leaves before he can deliver it, thus saving his friend but also perpetrating Lucien's version of events. It's a somewhat odd sequence that doesn't quite work. All Lucien has to do is deny authorship of the document (it is typewritten, after all). Why, then, would Allen even think that his version of the murder would be admissible in court? And why would the DA consider it appropriate to receive it from Allen, rather than directly from Lucien himself?

It could be argued that this aspect of the plot is aesthetically necessary, in terms of continuity, because the story is ultimately about Allen Ginsberg. John Krokidas described the film as 'a birth of an artist's story' and also 'a certain kind of love story' (Bunn and Krokidas: 2013). Allen's moral quandary generates dramatic tension, which makes the film more compelling for a general audience beyond Beat devotees. It remains true that Carr's defence depended almost entirely on establishing his heterosexuality. Newspaper reports show that this is exactly how Carr's defence was conducted: the legal definition of 'honour slaying' at the time allowed a heterosexual man to be convicted of manslaughter rather than murder if his assailant was homosexual.

However, some more serious issues with the screenplay remain, such as the complete omission of Carr's girlfriend at the time, Celine Young. One might argue that this, too, is necessary to strengthen the focus on Allen's development and his unrequited love for Lucien, but nonetheless it does oversimplify Carr's sexual identity, creating a much stronger impression of repressed homosexuality. The portrayal of Kammerer's death is even more problematic. As noted previously, the film opens with a tableau of Lucien in the dark river holding the dying David in his arms. Near the film's conclusion, William Burroughs, as he packs to leave town, tells Allen, 'David was alive, Allen, until Lucien made him drown'. Clearly, we are meant to understand that Carr knew Kammerer was still alive as he methodically tore up his own shirt, bound Kammerer's hands and feet, and filled his pockets with rocks. This is a serious distortion, since Kammerer's death certificate clearly states that the cause of death was 'stab wound left chest, pericardium and heart' (Berube: 2011). Bunn and Krokidas seem to have derived their version from James Grauerholz's 'Afterword' to *Hippos*, in which he states that after stabbing Kammerer twice, 'Lucien assumed he was dead and he rolled Dave's limp body into the Hudson River – unconscious and bleeding out, arms tied together with shoelaces, pants pockets weighted with rocks – to drown' (Grauerholz 2008: 187). Their script goes further, giving us a Lucien Carr whose intention is not self-defence but murder.

Of course, there is a degree of metafictional irony in the jail scene confrontation between Lucien and Allen over the deposition. When Lucien yells, 'You weren't even there. It's your truth. It's fiction', Bunn and Krokidas tacitly acknowledge the fiction of their own story, which focalizes events via Allen's point of view. The final moments between Lucien and David are strongly based on Ginsberg's recreation in *The Bloodsong*, to the extent that David actually walks into Lucien's knife. In Ginsberg's 1944 version of the 'Death Scene', Kammerer begins to weep as he sees 'Lucien's eyes maddened in conflicting ecstasies of fear and desire, revulsion and attraction, hatred and love . . .' (Ginsberg 2006: 114). Language like this was obviously very troubling to Caleb Carr, who views *Kill Your Darlings* in its entirety as a projection of Allen Ginsberg's sick extremism. Mark Judge, who quotes Caleb Carr's entire letter in his article, asserts that 'Lucien Carr was not gay, and had no desire to be gay, and it drove David Kammerer insane. Kammerer tried to rape Carr – perhaps not for the first time – and Carr, after years and years of abuse, exploded' (Judge: 2014). What is at stake for both Judge and Caleb Carr, apparently, is the imminent collapse of American culture due to the pernicious influence of decadent Hollywood homophiles. At the end of his letter, Caleb Carr argues that the real truth of the Carr–Kammerer story would have been more interesting, but 'it would not have served the sexual agenda of John Krokidas, of Daniel Radcliffe, or of the very extremist wing of the gay movement' that they represent. This, he says, is a pity, 'but that is the disease of our times – the subordination of truth to agenda.' He concludes that 'It may just be the end of the nation . . .' (Judge: 2014).

While both Judge and Caleb Carr purport to be objecting only to paedophiles, their inflammatory generalizations suggest a deeper concern with the slow but steady acceptance of gay identity in the twenty-first century. What makes their reactions especially troubling is their readiness to ignore much of the laudable complexity of both script and performance in *Kill Your Darlings*. The film deftly sets up the homophobic social context for the action right at the start, when Allen's roommate Luke warns him against going to the Village: 'Land of the fairies. Go there and you'll never come back.' Other moments reinforce the considerable risks of homosexuality, such as the arrest of two gay men during the group's visit to a jazz club, when the phrase 'fucking perverts' is muttered offstage. Within this homophobic culture, there is no safe space for the expression of same-sex love. Nor is there a safe space to even talk about homosexuality as possible or desirable in a social discourse that is replete with the words 'fag'; 'fairy'; 'fruit'. Leaving aside the question of his own inclinations, Lucien Carr's sexual identity was compromised by such attentions in a society that routinely depicted homosexuality as monstrous.

James Grauerholz has claimed that 'there is much more to be said ... about Lucien Carr's early life and youthful bisexuality than has ever been published in even the fullest, most reliable biographies of the major Beat figures' (Grauerholz 2008: 188). But he is incorrect when he cites *The Book of Martyrdom and Artifice* as evidence that 'Lucien did, for example, share a number of sexual encounters with Ginsberg in 1944'. Ginsberg actually records his coming out to Carr two years later, in 1946 (Ginsberg 2006: 162). So, how problematic is it that *Kill Your Darlings* portrays Carr as at least sexually adventurous, by having Lucien and Allen kiss for a few passionate moments on screen? According to Morgan, Carr did finally go to bed with Ginsberg in 1948 – just once (Morgan 2006: 106). More important, surely, is the sincere attempt to humanize the three key players. Dehaan channels real anguish when Lucien is forced to acknowledge the nature of his relationship with David ('He is a goddamn fruit who won't let me go'), and when he turns on David at the end: 'I was just a kid, you dragged me into your perverted mess!' Michael C. Hall inhabits his role as David with admirable restraint, poised and in control much of the time, but obviously jealous and possessive of his 'precious Lu-Lu' when Allen comes on the scene. While the script allows him to emerge, by the end, as the stage manager behind Lucien's brilliance, neither are the sinister details of his obsession omitted. One such episode is the attempted gassing of Jack and Edie's cat, which in reality was Kammerer's attempt to hang the cat, prevented only by the timely intervention of Burroughs (Nicosia 1983: 127). The final confrontation between Lucien and David is a threatening one, with David grabbing Lucien in a head lock from behind – certainly not the innocent victim of 'gay panic'. Radcliffe, meanwhile, imparts just the right combination of courage and naivety to the part of Allen Ginsberg, combining pathos with some fine comic moments. We might feel disappointed by Ben Foster's overly neurotic and passive rendition of Burroughs, and by Jack Huston's overly chipper Kerouac. We are certainly justified in wishing for a better presentation of the women in the group; not only is Celine Young completely omitted from the story, but Edie Parker is reduced to a wistful stay-at-home rather than the carousing, cursing, long-shore worker who actually introduced Lucien Carr to Kerouac in the first place. Overall, though, *Kill Your Darlings* merits watching on its own terms, whether one is 'into' the Beats or not, as a film that engages both the historical past and the present through characters that bring nuanced performances to difficult roles.

Technically, we might say the film enacts Rimbaud's 'derangement of the senses' through use of flashback and flash-forward, and fast and slow motion (Allen's breakthrough writing session while under the influence of Pervitin is especially entertaining). However, it is not really an example of Beat cinema in the same way as John Cassavetes or Jonas Mekas. This is not experimental cinema, but nonetheless, it does have an eclecticism that captures the Beat disregard for formal rules. For instance, the 1940s soundtrack is completely ruptured during the library heist sequence, when 'Wolf Like Me' by TV on the Radio erupts into the aesthetic space. Like many other aspects of the film, the choice of 'Wolf Like Me' resonates on multiple levels. With a droll nod in the direction of Ginsberg's 'Howl', the lyrics capture marginality and evoke the excess and ecstasy of the 'restricted' material being placed in the glass cases. By being overlaid onto a period film, they also function as a commentary on homosexuality during a time when the red scare was accompanied by the homophobic lavender scare.

What, then, of Lucien Carr? Was he ever to escape that 'hideous thing inside', what Kerouac called his self-hatred (1995: 81), or did he make his peace with it? Beat letters and journals make frequent reference to Carr throughout the following decades, usually describing his continued hard drinking, often accompanied by assorted gratuitous acts. Although Ginsberg reported in 1949 that Carr was in psychoanalysis and writing short stories (Ginsberg 2008: 31), he would never publish them. Instead, he worked his way up through the ranks of United Press International, proving to be immensely popular with his colleagues and an able mentor to young journalists (Hampton 2005). He was, in fact, by the end of his life, quite respectable. Lucien Carr's legacy as the Beat Generation's 'falling star Lucifer angel boy demon genius' (Kerouac 1982: 226) is obviously complex. Carr's 'angel tendencies', a kind of inspired hubris, combined with his decisive break with conventional morality, seem, at least initially, to have endured even after his conviction of manslaughter. This is not to say that the murder of Kammerer was itself a gratuitous act; one might find motive enough given the preceding years of romantic pursuit. But Carr's precocious consumption of Gide, Yeats, and Rimbaud surely added momentum to a lifestyle that actively flirted with violence. What Carr seems to have imparted to the group most strongly is an unflinching defiance of convention, combined with an iconoclastic faith in the power of art and literature.

This legacy is well represented by *Kill Your Darlings*, even if the film does not allow him to fully own the intellectual prowess that others so often celebrated in him. Beyond the Beat Generation, *Kill Your Darlings* might bestow another legacy on Lucien Carr, making him posthumously a means whereby western society can continue to grow beyond its fear of difference and its need to standardize identity. Daniel Radcliffe, in an interview with *British* GQ, commented on the disproportionate attention paid to his sex scene compared to other aspects of the film: 'And particularly in this country, everybody has been making a joke about it . . . Like they're afraid to ask. It's sort of the acceptable face of homophobia, in that you can still highlight that as being not normal, as being something weird' (Franklin-Wallis: 2013). To 'kill your darlings' is to excise from your writing that which you love most, the implication being that is where you are weakest. To challenge the logic of that phrase should also be part of the legacy of Lucien Carr.

Works cited

Amburn, E. (1998), *Subterranean Kerouac: The Hidden Life of Jack Kerouac*, New York: St Martin's Griffin.

Berube, J. (2011), 'The Truth behind David Kammerer's Murder'. Available at: www.jenniferberube.com/the-truth-behind-david-kammerers-murder/ (last accessed 12 March 2015).

Brown, M. (2009), 'The Battle for Kerouac's Estate', *The Telegraph*, 28 October, Available at: www.telegraph.co.uk/culture/books/booknews/6396321/ The-battle-for-Jack-Kerouacs-estate.html (last accessed 2 July 2015).

Bunn, A. and J. Krokidas (2013), Interview with Writers Guild Foundation, 8 October, Available at: www.wgfoundation.org/exclusive-interview-writers-kill-darlings (last accessed 12 March 2015).

Burroughs, W. S. and J. Kerouac (2008), *And the Hippos Were Boiled in Their Tanks*, Afterword by J.W. Grauerholz, New York: Grove.

Campbell, J. (1999), *This Is the Beat Generation*, Berkeley: University of California.

Collins, R. and D. Skover (2013), *Mania: the Story of the Outraged and Outrageous Lives That Launched a Cultural Revolution*, Top Five Books, Kindle edition.

Davidson, M. (2004), *Guys Like Us: Citing Masculinity in Cold War Poetics*, Chicago: University of Chicago.

Fowlie, W. (1965), *Andre Gide: His Life and Art*, New York: MacMillan, *Center for Gidean Studies*. Available at: www.andregide.org/studies/vatfow.html (last accessed 2 July 2015).

Franklin-Wallis, O. (2013), 'GQ&A: Dane Dehaan and Daniel Radcliffe', *British GQ*, Available at: www.gq-magazine.co.uk/entertainment/ articles/2013-12/06/daniel radcliffe dane-dehaan-interview (accessed 23 July 2015).

Gifford, B. and L. Lee (1999), *Jack's Book: An Oral Biography of Jack Kerouac*. Edinburgh, Scotland: Rebel.

Ginsberg, A. (2006), *The Book of Martyrdom and Artifice: First Journals and Poems, 1937–1952*, B. Morgan (ed.), Cambridge, MA: Di Capo.

Ginsberg, A. (2008), *The Letters of Allen Ginsberg*, B. Morgan (ed.), Philadelphia: Di Capo.

Grauerholz, J. (2008), Afterword to *And the Hippos Were Boiled in Their Tanks* by W.S. Burroughs and J. Kerouac, 185–214, New York: Grove.

Griffin, D. (2014), 'The St. Louis Clique: Burroughs, Kammerer, and Carr', *Journal of Beat Studies* 3.1, *Gale Literature Resource Center*. Available at: https:// libdatabase.newpaltz.edu/login?url=http://go.galegroup.com.libdatabase. newpaltz.edu/ps/i.do?id=GALE%7CA384779888&v=2.1&u=newpaltz&it= r&p=LitRC&sw=w&asid=224f9ab4d2dcb9035763c420637487c2 (last accessed 10 March 2015).

Hampton, W. (2005),'Lucien Carr, a Founder and Muse of the Beat Generation, Dies at 79', *New York Times* 30 January. Available at: www.nytimes. com/2005/01/30/obituaries/lucien-carr-a-founder-and-a-muse-of-the-beat-generation-dies-at-79.html?_r=0> (last accessed 12 February 2015).

Judge, M. (2014), 'Son of famous Beat murderer Lucien Carr disputes "Kill Your Darlings" film's version of events', *The Daily Caller*, 24 February. Available at: http://dailycaller.com/2014/02/24/son-of-famous-beat-murderer-lucien-carr-disputes-kill-your-darlings-films-version-of-events/ (last accessed 2 March 2015).

Kerouac, J. (1982), *Vanity of Duluoz* (1967), Herts, England: Granada.

Kerouac, J. and A. Ginsberg (2010), *Jack Kerouac and Allen Ginsberg: The Letters*, B. Morgan and D, Stanford (eds), New York: Viking Penguin.

Kerouac-Parker, E. (2007), *You'll Be Okay: My Life with Jack Kerouac*, T. Moran and B. Morgan (eds), San Francisco: City Lights.

Kill Your Darlings (2013), Dir. J. Krokidas, KYD Film LLC, Sony Pictures Classics, DVD.

Maher, P. (2004), *Kerouac: The Definitive Biography*, Lanham, MD: Taylor.

Mann, N. (2012), 'The Foundations of *A Vision*', in N. Mann, M. Gibson, and C.V. Nally (eds), *W.B. Yeats's A Vision: Explications and Contexts*, 1–21, Clemson, SC: Clemson University Digital. Available at: www.clemson.edu/ cedp/press/pubs/vision/vision_book.pdf (last accessed 10 July 2015).

Miles, B. (1989), *Ginsberg: A Biography*. New York: Simon and Schuster.

Morgan, B. (2006), *I Celebrate Myself: The Somewhat Private Life of Allen Ginsberg*, New York: Viking Penguin.

Nicosia, G. (1983), *Memory Babe: A Critical Biography of Jack Kerouac*, Middlesex, England: Penguin.

Rimbaud, A. (1986), *A Season in Hell* (1793), P. Schmidt (trans.), R. Mapplethorpe (photos), Boston: Bulfinch.

Schumacher, M. (1992), *Dharma Lion: A Critical Biography of Allen Ginsberg*, New York: St. Martin's.

Stein, S. (2013), 'Kill Your Darlings: A Conversation with John Krokidas', *Cultural Weekly*, 17 October. Available at: www.culturalweekly.com/kill-darlings-conversation-director-john-krokidas/ (last accessed 20 June 2015).

Tankard, F. (2008), 'Birth of the Beats Is Born, 64 Years Later', *Lawrence.com*. 17 November. Available at: www.lawrence.com/news/2008/nov/17/birth_beats_born_68_years_later/ (last accessed 2 March 2015).

TV on the Radio (2006), 'Wolf Like Me', From the album *Return to Cookie Mountain*, Interscope Records. Available at: http://lyrics.wikia.com/wiki/TV_On_The_Radio:Wolf_Like_Me (last accessed 15 July 2015).

Notes

Chapter 1

1 See Hunt (2014), 'A Book Always Has a Voice,' in particular Chapter 2, p. 37, for a discussion of this quotation.

2 A 14 October, 2012 National Public Radio story, both text and sound file archived at www.npr.org/2012/10/14/162877038/kerouacs-lost-beat-generation-finally-hits-stage, reported that the play was to receive a staged reading by the Merrimack Repertory Theater at the Jack Kerouac Literary Festival to be held that month in Lowell, MA.

3 'BOPCAP' is plausibly a typo for 'BOPCAT', presumably occurring in Kerouac's typescript, the play's only text.

4 In his elegiac essay on his friend Jack Kerouac, 'The Great Remember', John Clellon Holmes evokes and assesses the impact of *On the Road's* publication on Kerouac. See Holmes 1967, especially 83–86.

5 The figure of 'the mysterious outside reader' threads throughout the 18 pages of Kerouac's 28 December 1950 letter to Cassady. How this figure and its presence complicated Kerouac's attempt to write *On the Road* is considered in Chapter 2 of Hunt (2014). For a consideration of Kerouac's attempts to develop a mode of writing in which the writer would engage the reader as if an actual 'you', see Hunt (2014), Chapters 4 and 5, which analyze the series of experiments that became *Visions of Cody*.

6 David Amram's chapter, 'Spontaneous Commotion: The Making of *Pull My Daisy*', in his memoir of his creative partnership with Kerouac (Amram 2002) offers an account of the making of the movie and Kerouac performing the narration; see in particular pp. 72–78.

Chapter 2

1 It is a conundrum of Engaged Buddhism: politics is the organization of hatred, and Buddhism turns its back on Buddhism. So the engaged Buddhist activist fumbles forward, tacking between radical commitments. My comment, surely correct only some of the time, is the enshrinement of a memory of seeing Ginsberg on television, not hating. For a more responsible description of Ginsberg as a political hater, see Ide (2006).

Chapter 3

1   See Shaw (2006): This study offers insightful models for identifying and
    analyzing coterie writing and writers by its focus on New York School
    poets.

2   See Podhoretz (1958): The infamous 'No-Nothing Bohemians' unfairly and
    inaccurately attributed violent behaviour and intention to Beat writers,
    especially Kerouac and Ginsberg.

3   Some critical sources citing Corso claim *In This Hung-Up Age* was performed
    in 1954 (Andre 1981: 128; Skau 1999: 200); Corso also states its debut
    performance at Harvard was in 1955 (Corso 1962b: 90).

4   See Stephenson: 'Corso's screenplay, "That Little Black Door on the Left", was
    commissioned by Bob Booker and George Foster as a self-contained
    sequence for their motion picture comedy "Pardon Me Sir But Is My Eye
    Hurting Your Elbow?" The film, as far as I am aware, was never made, but the
    film manuscript was issued in book form' (1989: 95).

5   Killian and Brazil wonder 'what . . . makes something a "poets' theater" play?
    Is it any play written by a poet? Must it be tied to a "scene"?[We looked] for
    plays written by writers with an independent reputation as poets . . .
    selections veered mainly toward writers whose theater works were important
    though non-identical to the work upon which their reputation was built'
    (2010: xii). The latter category describes the Corso play in their anthology;
    his plays are 'non-identical' to the poetry upon which his standing as
    mid-century American poet is built.

6   Lineaments of the legend of the life of Gregory Corso are repeated, almost
    without deviation, by biographers, critics, and Corso himself in letters. See
    Andre (1973); Schwartz (1983); Skau (1999); Morgan (2003); Killian and
    Brazil (2010); Selerie (1982); Gaiser (1961). Of the many letters Corso wrote
    recounting his life story – apparently an obligatory recital – the most crucial
    include a 1956 letter to Randall Jarrell (Morgan 2003: 19); a 1958 letter to
    Isabella Gardner, (Morgan 2003: 130–31); and a 1958 letter to Jack Kerouac,
    (Morgan 2003: 117–26) which contains an extensive heartfelt narration of
    Corso's life history.

7   Peter Sourian was born in Boston in 1933. He is the author of three novels,
    and was a young Harvard novelist at the time of Corso's sojourn in
    Cambridge. Sourian is of Armenian American descent, a critic and Emeritus
    Professor at Bard College. He has a venerable reputation as a leader of
    second generation American Armenian writers, and was a colleague of
    William Saroyan.

8   The 1978 recording of *Sarpedon* by Corso at the Naropa Institute (now
    University): 'Socratic Poetry Rap, 7/20/1978', published by the Allen Ginsberg
    Library and Naropa University Archives. My comments are taken from my
    transcription of parts of this reading and have been assisted by an informal
    transcription of the whole made by Rick Schober. I am indebted to Schober

for locating this recording and sharing it and his transcription of *Sarpedon* with me.

9 Corso's 25 October 1978 account to James Loughlin of *Sarpedon*: the play was 'an attempt to replicate Euripides, though the whole shot be an original. Like the great Greek masters, I took off where Homer left an opening (like Euripides did with the fate of Agamemnon). My opening was found in the *Iliad*. Sarpedon, son of Zeus and Europa, died on the fields of Troy, and Homer had him sent up to Olympus with no complaint from Hades, who got all the others what died there. Thus I have Hades complain, demanding from his brother Zeus, all the dead, from said fields. It being only equitable, since Poseidon, another brother, sided with the Trojans, and Zeus with the Argives, via his daughter Athena' (Morgan 2003: 405–406).

10 See note 8. A manuscript of this play is held in the Pierpont Morgan Library (e-mail from Rick Schober to author, 31 July 2015). Dick Brukenfeld, who was at Harvard when Corso was there and published *The Vestal Lady on Brattle* in 1955, says this about *Sarpedon*: 'I have no recollection of the play, and Gregory's explanation is convincing at first sight. BUT my guess is he didn't write it when he first hit Harvard . . . It makes sense that after he was established there and known as an avid-for-knowledge poet, one of Finley's assistants would give him the challenge of writing a Greek play to stay. Of course . . . the challenge makes a good story and could be Corso's reinvention.' (E-mail from Brukenfeld to Rick Schober, ca., 23 May 2015). Schober kindly passed Brukenfeld's memories and speculations on to me as I was writing about *Sarpedon* for this chapter.

11 In a 1957 letter to Don Allen, Corso notes: 'Lived in Village until 1954 when beautiful now dead Violet Lang saved me and brought me to Harvard where I wrote and wrote and met beautiful people for the first time in my life. Had *Vestal Lady* published there by contributions from fifty or more students from Radcliffe and Harvard, *Harvard Advocate* first to publish me, then many times *ie., The Cambridge Review* . . .' (Morgan 2003: 55). Students, mainly Peter Sourian, Bobby Sedgwick, and Paul Grand, underwrote the printing expenses of Corso's first book, *The Vestal Lady on Brattle*. A subscription was taken up by Dick Brukenfeld in 1955.

12 See, instead, Leroi Jones's *Dutchman* (1964) for the use of the subway train as a dramatic setting.

13 'In *Power* I destroy the meaning you [Ferlinghetti] attribute me, and gave it a new one' that 'had nothing to do with NeoPound fascism; believe me. . . .' (ca. Oct. 1958; Morgan 2003: 159).

14 The play *Streetcorner* is almost explicitly signified in the following lines of 'Power', which offer the most obvious connection between the poem and its antecedent play: 'Power/What is Power/The world is Power/ Being afraid is Power/What is poetry when there is no Power/Poetry is powerless when there is no Power/*Standing on a street corner waiting for no one is Power* . . .' (Corso 1968: 89; emphasis added).

15 The family fall-out shelter depicted in the play did not come into vogue until the mid-1950s; photographs of the ideal shelter (readily available online) are dated 1957. This suggests that Corso may have added the fall-out shelter passages later, before the play's 1962 publication; so far, no evidence to support this supposition has surfaced.

Chapter 5

1 For a relatively current (2002) and comprehensive study, see James Grauerholz's *The Death of Joan Vollmer Burroughs: What Really Happened?* This does an excellent job detailing and sifting through the various eyewitness accounts and media representations of both the event and its aftermath. There are other sources of information about the shooting including, most recently in 2014, in *Call Me Burroughs: A Life* by Barry Miles, which narrates a succinct account. Ted Morgan's 2012 *Literary Outlaw: The Life and Times of William S. Burroughs* also contains good summary and multiple perspectives on the event.

2 Even in death it seems he still cannot escape Joan's death. His involvement in her death became a consistent theme in the various notices of his own death. He will forever be known and reduced to the guy that wrote all those weird books, did all that heroin and shot his wife.

3 Earlier in his journal, he (Burroughs 2000: 213) writes, 'grace for me came in the form of a cat, Ruski, and then other cats – all cats and lemurs and weasels'.

Chapter 7

1 See, in particular, Chapters 1 and 2 in Werner Sollors, *Amiri Baraka/LeRoi Jones: The Quest for a 'Populist Modernism'* (New York: Columbia University Press, 1978), pp. 11–63, along with Kimberly Benston's *Baraka: The Renegade and the Mask* (New Haven, CT: Yale University Press, 1976). Sollors's book is groundbreaking in its attempt to offer a systematic approach to Baraka's writing.

2 Jerry Gafio Watts refers rather dismissively to such an experience as 'ethnic catharsis'. He goes on to suggest: '[T]he centrality that Jones grants to ethnic catharsis and other emotive responses might, in practice, obscure the difference between this so-called revolutionary theatre and black group therapy.' See Watts, *Amiri Baraka: The Politics and Art of a Black Intellectual* (New York: New York University Press, 2001), p. 172.

3 His remark has a lot in common with what A. Robert Lee will later say about Baraka, Joans, and Kaufman and how they manifest 'a Beat articulation ... of the "black" senses'. See Lee, 'Black Beats: The Signifying Poetry of LeRoi

Jones/Amiri Baraka, Ted Joans and Bob Kaufman' in *The Beat Generation Writers*, ed. Lee (London: Pluto, 1996), p. 162.

4 See Immanuel Wallerstein, *World-Systems Analysis: An Introduction* (Durham, NC: Duke University Press, 2004).

5 For an account of these developments, see Robeson Taj Frazier, 'The Congress of African People: Baraka, Brother Mao, and the Year of '74,' in *The New Black History: Revisiting the Second Reconstruction*, ed. Manning Marable and Elizabeth Kai Hinton (New York: Palgrave, 2011), pp. 135–53.

Chapter 8

1 References to the graffiti as part of a larger performance – *Bird Lives!* – will appear in italics. References to 'Bird Lives!' as words will appear in quotation marks.

2 On the original typescript in the Ted Joans papers at the University of California-Berkeley's Bancroft Library, just above the typed title, 'For Cricket Magazine' is written in Joans' handwriting.

3 Thanks to Sonya Seifert and Deborah Geis for their very helpful comments on this chapter and for different, but no less valuable, kinds of patience. Thanks also to the staff at the UC-Berkeley's Bancroft Library for their assistance with the Ted Joans Papers. Finally, thanks are due to the Faculty Research and Development Program, College of Liberal Arts and Social Sciences at DePaul University for assisting this project with a Faculty Summer Research Grant.

Chapter 11

1 This conference had no official ties to the Poets' Theatre. In a 1958 interview, Phelps and Howe claim that *The Hidden King*, by British playwright Jonathan Griffin, which was presented as an exemplary verse drama, didn't represent the kind of work that the Poets' Theatre was trying to do (Discussion 1958: 27).

2 A revival of the Poets' Theatre took place in 1986 and continued until 2004. It was recently revived once again, in 2014, premiering with a commemorative and star-studded staged reading of Dylan Thomas's *Under Milk Wood*; that incarnation continues to produce today.

Chapter 12

1 *The Kenning Anthology* incorrectly identifies February 1964 as the New York premiere of *Murder Cake*.

2 See University of Texas Ransom archives and *Recollections* (di Prima 2001).

3 See The Poetry Center Digital Archive, a project of The Poetry Centre at San Francisco State University, for an audio recording of di Prima and John Braden performing 'The Seasons' section of Poet's Vaudeville on 24 April 1968, at San Francisco State University. Also see Reva Wolf's discussion of Andy Warhol's parody of *Poet's Vaudeville* (1997: 43–45).

4 One exception may be LeRoi Jones/Amiri Baraka, who is widely recognized as both a poet and a playwright.

5 See Anthony Libby's essay 'Nothing is Lost; It Shines In Our Eyes' (2002) for a discussion of di Prima's poetry and letters.

6 Some individuals from that period did call it a movement. For example, see Wassily Kandinsky's essay 'The Problem of Form' published in the Blaue Reiter Almanace (1912) and excerpted in Kolocotroni *et al.* (1998: 275).

7 I am using the definition of Modernism espoused by Vassiliki Kolocotroni, Jane Goldman, and Olga Taxidou, editors of *Modernism: An Anthology of Sources and Documents* (1998).

8 Ezra Pound, 'A Retrospect,' from Preface to Remy de Gourmont's *The Natural Philosophy of Love*, 1926.

9 Di Prima has said regarding the art of poetics, 'Well I think I learned early on that, aside from what I learned early on, going through trying to read everything in the *ABC of Reading* [by Ezra Pound], everything I learned through Pound, the place where I learned the most about poetics, was actually typing those poems for the *Floating Bear*, onto those green stencils.' See Hadbawnik (2002).

10 Perhaps the most famous example is Marcel Duchamp's transformation into the female Rrose [sic] Selavy, famously photographed and filmed by Man Ray.

11 Killian and Brazil state that *Rain Fur* was written in 1961, based on their e-mail correspondence with di Prima, but di Prima's typescript in the Louisville archives states 1959, the date clearly typed at that time. Unfortunately, Killian and Brazil provide no bibliographic information about the e-mail; they merely state that it exists.

12 A prime number can be divided only by itself or by 1; it must be larger than one. Three, for instance, is a prime number, but four is not. A sub-prime number is the prime number minus 1.

13 David Hadbawnik, in his blog entry on di Prima's *Rain Fur* (2010), points out the pun in the name reversal but provides no further analysis of its possible significance.

14 Habdawnik (2010) claims that the repetition of 'di' by A[1] is a clue to the audience that the A's represent *di* Prima. However, that clue, if it is such, functions only for a reader, not someone viewing a live performance, since 'di' when pronounced can be interpreted as 'die' or 'dye'. The di Prima clue works only as a visual clue on the printed page.

15 See a YouTube video of a production of *Murder Cake* performed on 27 October 2012 at WNYBAC for Big Night in Buffalo, New York,

for a representation of how the characters remain nameless (di Prima 2012). Costuming provides no clues either: for example, the actor who played Dante, Alison Fraser, appears in the uniform of a contemporary female police officer.

Chapter 15

1   Wieners was, however, affected by Ginsberg's treatment of sexual themes. In Wieners' poem 'Memories of You' (1988: 58–59), he discusses homosexuality and directly references Ginsberg's famous line 'get fucked in the ass by saintly motorcyclists' from *Howl*.

2   The group was repeatedly harassed by the police. Alan S. Marlowe, president of the American Theatre for Poets, Inc., received a suspended sentence after being convicted of 'showing an unlicensed motion picture in a public space of amusement' and had been into trouble earlier in the year when showing Jack Smith's allegedly obscene film *Flaming Creatures* (New York Poets Theatre 1964). Such harassment was not confined to the group, however. As Stephanie Gervis Harrington reported (1964: 1), 'The current zeal of the City's Department of Licenses for the strict enforcement of licensing regulations against small avant-garde creative ventures has so far resulted in the temporary closing of three off-Broadway theatres, the suspension of poetry readings at Le Metro, and a general malaise among culturally minded New Yorkers.' See also Diane di Prima's 'Futz's Progress' (1964: 463–65) in *The Nation*, where she rails against such 'harassment of the arts'.

3   Pepperman (2015) claims that the space was not really conceived of as 'Beat', since it occurred after the Beat heyday and before the term 'Hippie' became popular. Yvonne Rainer, who played the character of 'Girl in Patchwork Green' and would go on to a very successful career in dance, agrees. Though she was present at the famous Six Gallery reading where Ginsberg performed *Howl*, she did not consider herself 'Beat' (Rainer 2015).

4   The bound copy of the New York Poets Theatre's plays at the Harry Ransom Center gives the opening date as 23 November 1961, while a handwritten copy says 23 February 1962 (Box 1, File 4, Harry Ransom Centre). A 4 December 1961 press release, however, claims that the play will open on 10 December 1961. Di Prima, in her memoir *Recollections of My Life as a Woman*, claims that the plays opened in December (2001: 279). Unfortunately, as Di Prima relates, 'There is no visual record of our doings at that time' (2001: 348).

5   Pepperman (2015) relates that he was given no directions or guidance on how to perform; each actor was left to decide for themselves how to play their parts.

6   David Buuck, in 'Some Remarks on Poets Theater', lists several proscriptions for the genre, including 'For every performer at least one friend in audience'

(in Killian and Brazil 2010: xiii–xiv). Such an intimate audience must have led to a highly dense set of personal allusions.

Chapter 16

1 Descriptions of Living Theatre performances of *A Day in the Life* come from the author's first-hand viewing of these performances in Greencastle, Indiana; Rock Island, Illinois; Macomb, Illinois; and Boston, Massachusetts; and from discussions about the play and workshop with Jerry Goralnick and Lois Kagan Mingus from 2004 to 2012.

Chapter 17

1 This traces the life and work of the young, not-yet-published Hettie Cohen through her marriage and subsequent married and published name, Hettie Jones. LeRoi Jones did not change his name/identity to Amiri Baraka until after their marriage. However, in order to refer consistently to subject of the this chapter (Hettie Cohen/Jones) and to prevent confusion between her and her husband during the course of their marriage, I refer to the former as Jones and to the latter as Baraka. My intention is not to collapse the very distinct stages of LeRoi Jones/Amiri Baraka's life into one, or to in any way unduly emphasize the underlying racial politics that existed during their marriage but did not come to a head until their split in 1965.

2 See N.M. Grace, 'Snapshots, Sand Paintings, and Celluloid' and B. Watten, 'What I See in *How I Became Hettie Jones*'.

3 In a review of this production of *Arms and the Man*, George St. Julian lauds Jones's performance, claiming that she 'virtually "stole" the first act with a one-minute walk-on' and 'drew the evening's biggest applause and laughter' (as cited in Jones, *Collected Papers*).

4 R.C. Johnson and N.M. Grace argue that to characterize women Beat writers as feminist would be anachronistic; in fact, the scholars clarify that the protofeminism of the women Beats was 'fostered unintentionally' (2002: 9). Nevertheless, as Johnson and Grace explain: 'Members of the group display a persistent understanding of the importance of asserting themselves as women in the alternative communities in which they lived, and which denied them, during the fifties, and even to some extent today, value as artists specifically because of their gender. Their recognition of this condition exemplifies their protofeminist impulses' (2002: 13–14). See also my discussion of this elsewhere (Petrich 2012).

5 In the updated version of his autobiography, Baraka lambasts what he calls Jones's 'lie mongering': 'She said . . . that she was a writer, but she had sacrificed her writing, even hidden it from me, because of the crushing

weight of my male chauvinism and her selfless desire to forward my career' (1997: xxii). This is one among many of Baraka's denials of 'her cottage-industry martyrdom' (1997: xxii).

6 In his autobiography, Baraka recalls trying to explain *Dutchman*, including its origins: 'A confrontation between two people, between two symbols? I improvised from my deepest feelings. It is about how difficult it is to become a man in the US. That, I knew, was true and honest. But a naïve black youth, a soi-disant intellectual murdered by a mad white woman he had hoped to seduce? Shit, and it was only that crazy Dolly I'd dressed up and set in motion and some symbols from out of my own life' (1984: 188).

7 For example, see 'Enough of This,' published in *Frontiers* (Jones 1993: 97–100).

Chapter 19

1 Writers in the survey (in order of appearance): Jonathan Price, Kenneth Brown, Arnold Weinstein, Irving Wardle, Robert Auletta, Rochelle Owens, Maria Irene Fornés.

2 Owens recalls taking a draft of *Futz* to Leroi Jones's apartment, and his quick enthusiasm for her work. A deeper bond grew with Hettie Jones: 'I loved her!' Owens remembers, and that they shared 'terrific long conversations' in the apartment that always seemed to have young writers and artists dropping by (Interview).

3 Owens attended classes at Yale Drama School with Maria Irene Fornés and Lanford Wilson, eating breakfast together on the early train from New York. The unabashed privilege of Yale both horrified and enraged her; the return trip to Manhattan was always a relief [Interview].)

4 The interviewer continues, inexorable in her determination to wring from Owens an overt declaration of feminist identification. Owens fakes concession by merely echoing Goulianis, only to have the interviewer gain momentum from the feint, and continue triumphantly:

J. You and I agree about that, but the world doesn't. Women artists have been suppressed, neglected.

R. Yes. Ignored. Hidden away.

J. This means that the woman artist functions in the world in a different way than the man artist . . . (1972: 257)

5 The Guerrilla Girls are 'a bunch of anonymous females who take the names of dead women artists as pseudonyms and appear in public wearing gorilla masks. We have produced posters, stickers, books, printed projects, and actions that expose sexism and racism in politics, the art world, film and the culture at large' (Guerilla Girls: n.d.).

Chapter 23

1 Except for the silent film era (Jacobs 2008), the concept of romantic drama has received little attention in film genre theory. However, it is a logical complement to the more recognized genre of romantic comedy (Dowd and Pallotta 2000) and, as such, has served the purpose of compiling film lists (Case 1996; 'Romantic Drama Movies' n.d.).

2 Citations of *Big Sur* give page number in the 2011 Penguin paperback edition (Kerouac 2011). 'VO' or 'DL' indicates that the cited passage is heard either in voiceover or dialogue in the film.

3 In Jacky Gibson's view, Cassady intended to end their relationship by handing her over to Kerouac (Gifford and Lee 1978: 284).

4 Jacky Gibson married jazz musician Arnett Mercer in 1961 (Moore n.d.). She died in 1997, long after the deaths of Neal Cassady (1968) and Jack Kerouac (1969), but before the death of Carolyn Cassady (2013).

Index

Amram, David 23, 282, 345 n.6
Artaud, Antonin 6–7, 56, 58, 190,
    193–4, 198–9, 270
    in Baraka 85–6, 66–91
    in The Living Theatre 221–31
    Theatre of Cruelty 6, 56, 89–91,
        193–4
Auden, W.H. 41, 141

Baraka, Amiri (LeRoi Jones) 1–2, 4, 6,
    8, 71–2, 102, 125–6, 155–8,
    173, 208, 213, 248, 259, 262–3
    avant-garde and politics 83–95
    relationship with Hettie Jones
        233–43
Beck, Julian 7, 208–9, 259
    development of The Living
        Theatre 221–31
Beckett, Samuel 50, 141, 152, 247
Black Mountain School 7, 83, 205–6,
    209, 225
Blake, William 26, 29, 109–10, 197, 312
Bottoms, Stephen J. 3, 56, 144–5, 187,
    213, 215, 246, 249, 261, 271
Brando, Marlon 296–7
Brecht, Bertolt 141, 223
Breton, Andre (see also Surrealism)
    34, 56–8, 121, 128–9, 167, 170
    in Baraka 84–6, 88, 91
Buddhism
    in di Prima 173
    in Ginsberg 28, 30, 345 n.1
    in Kaufman 118–19
    in Kerouac 325
    in Waldman 79
Burroughs, Joan Vollmer 6, 63–70,
    125, 348 n. 1
Burroughs, William 2, 5,6, 33, 37, 173,
    189, 196, 206, 208, 314
    in Adrienne Kennedy 125, 128–33

Lucien Carr and Kill Your
    Darlings 327–41
    relationship with Joan Vollmer
        Burroughs 63–70
Butler, Judith 72, 77

Caffe Cino 3, 246, 248, 251, 259
Cage, John 162, 206, 209, 213
Cambridge Poets' Theatre 6, 187, 206
    Corso 36–7, 39–40
    development by Bunny Lang and
        others 139–53
Carr, Lucien 8, 125, 213, 299–300, 317
    Kill Your Darlings 327–43
Cassady, Carolyn 4, 233, 315–18,
    320–1
Cassady, Neal 4, 14, 19, 315–21, 327,
    335
Cayce, Edgar 14, 16
City Lights 55, 253, 262
Cocteau, Jean 89, 141, 162
Corso, Gregory 2, 3, 5, 15, 23, 142,
    206, 245–7, 253, 259, 263, 320
    Beat plays of Cambridge era
        33–53
Cowen, Elise 112
Creeley, Robert 109

Dadaism (see under Surrealism)
di Prima, Diane 2–3, 4, 6–7, 83,
    177–8, 190, 198, 206, 208–10,
    213–15, 245, 259, 262–4, 282–4
    New York Poets Theatre plays
        155–75
Doolittle, Hilda (H.D.) 26, 160
Drexler, Rosalyn 2, 8, 266–7
    artistic career 269–78
Duncan, Robert 25–6, 83, 157, 160,
    208, 210, 215
Dylan, Bob 191

Eliot, T.S. 25, 31, 141, 152, 223
Ellison, Ralph 98, 105
Esslin, Martin 35, 41, 45, 50, 162

Ferlinghetti, Lawrence 2, 5, 27, 133,
    191–2, 200, 245, 247, 249–50,
    253, 259, 262, 311, 315
    one-act plays 55–61
Fornes, Maria Irene 2, 4, 8, 253, 256,
    267, 269
Frank, Robert 2, 4, 15, 23, 282, 303
Frazer, Brenda 233
Futurism 88–9, 161

Gardner, Isabella 35, 39
Garin, Leo 4, 19
Gelber, Jack 8, 209, 213, 221, 225–9
Ginsberg, Allen 1, 8, 15, 23, 33, 36–7,
    58, 79, 110, 125–6, 133, 189,
    191, 197, 206, 208, 246, 248,
    253, 259, 262–4, 285, 296–7,
    305, 320
    and Burroughs 63–7
    and Carr 327–41
    and *Howl* 2–3, 5, 25–31

Greek drama 38–9, 261
    at Living Theatre 224
    Orpheus and Eurydice 145–7
Guest, Barbara 157
Gysin, Byron 5

Herko, Fred 6, 155, 157, 187, 208
Holmes, John Clellon 1, 37, 133, 287,
    294, 302–3
Huncke, Herbert 1

James, Henry 14, 19
Joans, Ted 2, 6, 84–5, 125–6
    and Charlie Parker graffiti 97–107
Johnson, Joyce 112, 233, 238
Jones, Hettie 2, 4, 8, 92, 259, 282
    connections to theatre 233–43
Jones, LeRoi (*see under* Baraka,
    Amiri)

Judson Poets Theatre 3, 162, 21, 238,
    246, 248, 259, 271

Kammerer, David
    and Lucien Carr 327–41
Kandel, Lenore 262, 315, 320, 322
Kaufman, Bob 2, 6, 58, 85, 98
    prophetic poetry 109–24
Kennedy, Adrienne 6
    and Beat influences 125–35
Kerouac, Jack 1–5, 8, 27, 33–8, 41, 79,
    98, 125–6, 133, 162, 191, 198,
    206, 213, 259
    Beat Generation (play) 13–24, 303,
        320
    Big Sur (novel and film) 309–26
    Gabrielle Kerouac (mother) 287
    and Lucien Carr 327–41
    On the Road (in Hollywood)
        293–307
    and Sam Shepard 245–8, 250–1
    The Subterraneans (film
        adaptation) 281–91, 304–5, 310
Kesey, Ken 195
Koch, Kenneth 157, 234
Kyger, Joanne 28, 133, 263–4, 282

Lamantia, Philip 3, 27
Lang, Violet 'Bunny' 2, 6, 37–8, 158
    and Cambridge Poets' Theatre
        139–53
Leslie, Alfred 4, 15, 23, 282, 303
Living Theatre, The 3, 7–8, 20, 56, 78,
    152, 172, 208–9, 215, 259
    and 1950s artistic forms 221–31
Lorca, Federico Garcia 141, 152, 223,
    235
Lumumba, Patrice 91, 129–30

MacDowell, John Herbert 6, 155, 208,
    215
MacLeish, Archibald 141, 148, 151
McClure, Michael 2–3, 7, 27, 83, 156,
    158, 206, 208, 210, 245, 259, 315
    The Beard 189–204

Mailer, Norman 36, 41, 44, 189–90, 196

Malina, Judith 7, 78, 208–9, 259
  development of Living Theatre
    221–31

Marcuse, Herbert 190, 192–3, 196,
  201

Marlowe, Alan 6, 83, 155, 157, 187,
  208, 351 n. 2

Miller, Henry 334–5

Molinaro, Ursule 238

New York Poets Theatre 3, 6, 7, 83, 93,
  245, 259
  and di Prima 155–75
  and O'Hara 177–88
  and Wieners 205–17

Noh drama 143–4, 209

O'Hara, Frank 3–4, 7, 83, 142–3, 147,
  152, 157, 245, 248, 253
  Loves Labor, an eclogue 177–88

Olson, Charles 7, 109, 196, 198,
  205–8, 210

Oppenheimer, Joel 4, 253

Orlovsky, Peter 15, 23, 33, 36, 320

Orzel, Nick 4, 253

Owens, Rochelle 2, 8, 221, 229–30
  and off-off Broadway 257–68

Parker, Charlie ('Bird') 86, 212
  and Ted Joans 97–107

Pinter, Harold 59, 189

Pound, Ezra 41, 44, 209
  and di Prima 158–9, 161–2,
    167–8, 172, 174

Rexroth, Kenneth 3, 26, 55, 58, 111,
  121–2, 126, 221, 223–4, 285

Rosenberg, Julius and Ethel 44, 48, 49

Sartre, Jean-Paul 190, 200–1

Shelley, Percy Bysshe 7, 37

Shepard, Sam 2–3, 8, 56, 261, 273
  early plays 245–55

Smith, Michael 3–4, 247, 249–53

Snyder, Gary 3, 18, 27–8, 133, 208

Spicer, Jack 197–8, 210

Stein, Gertrude 4, 157–8, 167, 215,
  221–3, 271–2

Stevens, Wallace 157–8, 177, 208, 214

Surrealism (*see also* Breton, Andre) 6,
  34, 50
  and Baraka 83–95
  and Dadaism 45–8, 177, 181–2
  and di Prima 160–2, 164, 167, 170
  and Ferlinghetti 55–6
  and Kaufman 113, 119–21
  and Kennedy 128–9

Tallmer, Jerry 3, 215

Terry, Megan 250, 253, 267

Theatre of Cruelty (*see under* Artaud,
  Antonin)

Theatre Genesis 3, 56, 246–7, 253

Thompson, Hunter S. 195–6

Vega, Janine Pommy 133

Waits, Tom 5

Waldman, Anne 6, 133, 263–4, 282
  The Stoop 71–80

Warhol, Andy 48–9, 189, 208, 215,
  265

Waring, Jimmy 6, 7, 83, 155, 157, 162,
  166, 208–9

weiss, ruth 158, 282

Welch, Lew 27, 315, 320, 322

Whalen, Philip 3, 27, 28, 133, 208, 315

Whitman, Walt 27, 110, 118, 246, 313,
  334

Wieners, John 2, 7, 83, 157, 264
  Still Life 205–17

Williams, William Carlos 26, 29, 221,
  223–5

Wilson, Lanford 4, 253, 261, 273–4

X, Malcolm 92, 240–1

Yeats, William Butler 34, 109–10, 334,
  341